The Decline of Substance Use in Young Adulthood

Changes in Social Activities, Roles, and Beliefs

Research Monographs in Adolescence
Nancy L. Galambos/Nancy A. Busch-Rossnagel, Editors

Coté • Adolescent Storm and Stress: An Evaluation of the Mead–Freeman Controversy

Cohen/Cohen • Life Values and Adolescent Mental Health

Seiffge-Krenke • Stress, Coping, and Relationships in Adolescence

East/Felice • Adolescent Pregnancy and Parenting: Findings From a Racially Diverse Sample

Bachman/Wadsworth/O'Malley/Johnston/Schulenberg • Smoking, Drinking, and Drug Use in Young Adulthood: The Impacts of New Freedoms and New Responsibilities

Alsaker/Flammer • The Adolescent Experience: European and American Adolescents in the 1990s

Leadbeater/Way • Growing Up Fast: Transitions to Early Adulthood of Inner-City Adolescent Mothers

Call/Mortimer • Arenas of Comfort in Adolescence: A Study of Adjustment in Comfort

Whitman/Borkowski/Keogh/Weed • Interwoven Lives: Adolescent Mothers and Their Children

The Decline of Substance Use in Young Adulthood

Changes in Social Activities, Roles, and Beliefs

Jerald G. Bachman
Patrick M. O'Malley
John E. Schulenberg
Lloyd D. Johnston
Alison L. Bryant
Alicia C. Merline
Institute for Social Research
University of Michigan

LAWRENCE ERLBAUM ASSOCIATES, PUBLISHERS
2002   Mahwah, New Jersey   London

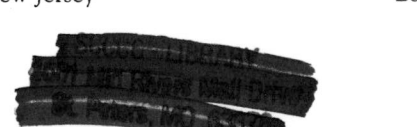

Lawrence Erlbaum Associates, Inc., Publishers
10 Industrial Avenue
Mahwah, NJ 07430

Cover design by Kathryn Houghtaling Lacey

Library of Congress Cataloging-in-Publication Data

The decline of substance use in young adulthood : changes in social
    activities, roles, and beliefs / Jerald G. Bachman ... [et al.].
        p. cm.
    Includes bibliographical references and index.
ISBN 0-8058-3964-X (cloth : alk. paper)
1. Young adults—Substance use—United States. 2. Young adults—
    United States—Attitudes. 3. Young adults—United States—
    Social life and customs—20th century.   I. Bachman, Jerald G.
HV49999.Y68 D46   2001
362.29´120835 —dc21   2001033278
                                                                    CIP

Books published by Lawrence Erlbaum Associates are printed on acid-
free paper, and their bindings are chosen for strength and durability.

Printed in the United States of America
10   9   8   7   6   5   4   3   2   1

Contents

Series Editors' Foreword ix

Preface xi
   This Book and the Earlier Book: Distinctions
     and Overlaps xii
   Guidelines for Using this Book xiii
   Acknowledgments xiv

1   **Introduction and Overview** 1
   Observations on Data Quality and Breadth
     of Generalization 4
   Studying Complex Causal Relationships in Natural
     Settings 6

2   **Literature Review: Conceptual and Empirical Overview** 8
   of Issues
   Young Adulthood 8
   Social Roles 11
   Values, Attitudes, and Behaviors 17
   Conclusions 22

3 Examining Mediating Variables—Sample Characteristics 24
   and Analysis Strategies
      Sample Characteristics and Representativeness 25
      A Four-Step Analysis Strategy 27
      Additional Panel Analysis Issues and Strategies 32

4 Religious Attendance and Importance 40
      Patterns of Age-Related Change in Religiosity 40
      How Changes in Religiosity Relate to Changes
         in Substance Use 45
      Analyses Linking Religiosity With Post-High-School
         Experiences 59
      Summary 70

5 Time Spent on Various Social and Recreational Activities 71
      Patterns of Age-Related Change in Evenings Out
         and Related Behaviors 72
      How Changes in Evenings Out Are Linked With Changes
         in Substance Use 77
      How Changes in Other Social-Recreational Behaviors
         Are Linked With Changes in Substance Use 91
      Analyses Linking Recreational Lifestyle With
         Post-High-School Experiences 97
      Summary 116

6 Perceived Risks and Disapproval of Smoking, Heavy 121
   Drinking, and Illicit Drug Use
      Focusing on Views About Specific Substances Rather
         than Substance Use in General 122
      Patterns of Age-Related Change in Perceived Risks
         and Disapproval 123
      How Perceived Risks and Disapproval Are Correlated
         With Substance Use 133
      Analyses Linking Perceived Risks and Disapproval
         With Post-High-School Experiences 146
      Summary 154

7   Friends' Use of Substances, and Perceived Availability   156
    of Illicit Drugs
        Patterns of Age-Related Change in (Perceived) Friends'
            Use of Substances and in Perceived Availability
            of Illicit Drugs   158
        How Perceptions of Friends' Use Are Correlated With
            Substance Use   167
        How Perceptions of Availability Are Correlated With
            Substance Use   169
        Analyses Linking Friends' Use of Substances With
            Post-High-School Experiences   172
        Analyses Linking Perceptions of Availability With
            Post-High-School Experiences   178
        Summary   179

8   Putting the Pieces Together—Structural Equation Models   181
        Decisions About Variables, Samples, and Models   182
        Analytic Approach   189
        Findings From the Structural Equation Modeling   190
        Summary   200

9   Summary, Conclusions, and Implications   202
        Conceptual Overview Revisited: Fitting Together
            All of the Pieces   202
        Impacts of the New Freedoms and New Responsibilities
            in Young Adulthood   209
        Conclusions and Implications   216
        Concluding Comments on Declining Substance Use
            in Young Adulthood: Impacts of Social Activities,
            Roles, and Beliefs   218

    Appendix   221
        Sampling and Data-Collection Procedures   221
        Patterns of Post-High-School Experiences   224
        Multiple Classification Analyses Predicting Changes
            in Mediating Variables   236

References   287

Author Index   295

Subject Index   299

Series Editors' Foreword

Nancy L. Galambos
University of Victoria

Nancy A. Busch-Rossnagel
Fordham University

The Monitoring the Future project, which has followed large, nationally representative, and successive cohorts of high school seniors in the United States into their adulthood, is the data source for the results presented in this volume. Beginning with the high school class of 1976, Monitoring the Future has assessed trends in and psychosocial predictors of the use of tobacco, alcohol, and other drugs by young adults. In their earlier works, including a volume published in this series in 1997 (*Smoking, Drinking, and Drug Use in Young Adulthood: The Impacts of New Freedoms and New Responsibilities*), the investigators examined how the major transitions that typically take place in young adulthood–engagement, marriage, pregnancy, and parenthood–can be linked to significant declines in the use of tobacco, alcohol, marijuana, and cocaine. Something about making commitments to and being responsible for significant others, whether an intended lifelong partner, a spouse, or a child, seemed to steer young adults away from earlier levels of drug use. Interestingly, a break in such commitment–evidenced in divorce–heralded increases in drug use.

In this monograph, the authors explore *why* the role transitions of adulthood precipitate changes in drug use patterns. What is it about marriage or parenthood that leads to changes in smoking, drinking, and the use of marijuana and cocaine? Are declines attributable in part to religious views and behaviors? Do changes in recreational activities such as going out in the evening explain shifts in the use of alcohol and other drugs? Are attitudes toward drug use and drug use by friends a part of this picture? Through the careful and systematic analysis of data, which is based on the experiences of individuals who were followed for up to fourteen years after high school, the authors are able to draw some conclusions about the facilitators of stability and change in substance use. We congratulate the authors on seeking the answers to these questions and on their significant contribution to understanding the intricacies involved in the complex links between the transitions of adulthood and the use of drugs. We also commend the authors for their commitment to and leadership in demonstrating how rigorous scientific work can be used to chart and explain trajectories of change across long periods of time in the lives of individuals.

Preface

This book is in some respects a sequel to an earlier volume in this series in which we demonstrated that the new freedoms and responsibilities associated with young adulthood have important impacts on drug use. Those earlier findings, summarized in chapter 2 of this book, give rise to a new set of questions to be answered concerning how changing freedoms and responsibilities relate to changes in drug use during young adulthood. What are the underlying mechanisms? To what extent are the mechanisms—the mediating variables—involved with marijuana use similar to those for cocaine use, or for alcohol use and abuse, or for cigarette use? Similarly, do the different freedoms and responsibilities operate via different or similar mechanisms as they influence smoking, alcohol use, and illicit drug use?

In order to address these new questions, we again employ data from the Monitoring the Future project, which provides a representative sampling of high school graduates who entered young adulthood in the United States during the past two decades. Our data set includes all the measures and respondents used in our previous book, plus a number of additional measures and additional respondents from recent high school classes. Specifically, our samples include members of the high school classes of 1976 through 1997 who participated in follow-up surveys extending (for the older cohorts) throughout their twenties and into their thirties. More than 38,000 of them contributed data for this volume (up from more than 33,000 for the previous volume).

THIS BOOK AND THE EARLIER BOOK:
DISTINCTIONS AND OVERLAPS

There are at least three key distinctions between this book and the earlier one. The most important of these is that we now address a new set of questions, adding a new set of variables to those previously covered. Many of the new variables involve attitudes and perceptions—dimensions that can be much more difficult to measure and report accurately, in contrast to more factual dimensions of drug use and post-high-school roles and experiences. The second key distinction is that this volume employs an expanded set of analysis techniques, as outlined in chapter 3 and detailed in chapters 4 through 8. The additional analysis approaches address the measurement difficulties already noted, and some deal also with the problems of estimating more complex relationships among "independent," "mediating," and "dependent" variables. (The quotations marks recognize some arbitrariness of such distinctions with survey data, even longitudinal panel data—a point to which we return from time to time throughout this book.) The third distinction is that we have expanded the sample to include several years of additional data available from the Monitoring the Future project. The contribution of these additional data is incremental; they provide additional cases for analysis and expand the breadth of time sampled, but the new data do not substantially alter fundamental patterns reported earlier.

Specifying the overlaps between this and the previous book is perhaps less straightforward than noting the distinctions. We have already mentioned that the samples and variables included in the first book represent a large proportion of those included in the second. Also, the findings presented in the first book are a starting point for this book, and those earlier findings are revisited from time to time as needed. The analysis strategies and specific methods employed in this book include virtually all of those used in the first book. We are using the earlier strategies and methods again because we think they served us well in the previous book and because we confront many of the same issues in this book. Thus, unavoidably, readers of the earlier book will find some of the same observations, interpretations, and conclusions stated again here.

In sum, the authors' approaches and viewpoints—and their biases, if you will—have not changed greatly during the several years between the two books. What has changed are the range of questions and variables we address and, to some extent, the range of analysis methods we employ. The findings are more complex this time around and sometimes less definitive, but in our view they are certainly no less interesting.

GUIDELINES FOR USING THIS BOOK[1]

Users of research monographs are often selective, sometimes wanting only the "big picture," sometimes wanting full technical details, and sometimes wanting only one particular part of the picture. This book, like the preceding one, has been organized so as to be responsive to all of those needs.

Readers wanting an overall summary of our findings will find that in chapter 9; it has been designed to stand alone, but of course it will have more meaning if read following the other chapters. Readers wanting more background will find an overview in chapter 1 and a review of relevant literature in chapter 2. An orientation to data sources and analysis techniques is found in chapter 3, with further information in the appendix. Readers wishing full details of our analyses involving religiosity, social and recreational activities, views about drugs, or friends' use of drugs (along with perceptions of availability of illicit drugs) will find these in chapters 4 through 7, respectively. Results explaining how we integrated many of the findings using structural equation models are in chapter 8.

Readers vary in their need for technical detail. A great deal of analysis work was carried out in the months and years leading up to the completion of this monograph—far more than would be possible to include in this book and far more than most readers would wish to confront. Our task was to develop ways of presenting our main findings in a format that would be clear and straightforward, but also to include the more complex multivariate findings, which are an essential part of our overall analysis strategy. Acknowledging the trade-off between clarity and complexity, we concluded that we could not do justice to both in a single reporting format. Instead, we chose to present our findings at two distinct levels within the book—text and appendix. For those few readers desiring even more detail, there is also a supplementary technical report available from the authors (Bachman et al., 2001).

In the text we rely primarily on graphs rather than tables of numbers; we find them much easier to use and we believe the same is true for most of our readers. These graphs provide a wealth of valuable descriptive detail, although they are not intended to capture overlapping relationships that can be revealed by multivariate analyses. Such multivariate analyses are a key ingredient of this monograph and underlie all of our conclusions, and thus we refer to such results frequently in the text. Some readers may be content with our summaries of such findings in the text; others will wish to see for themselves, and the appendix is intended to meet their needs.

The findings from our regression analyses are not inherently difficult; indeed, we have selected a format (described in the appendix) designed to

---

[1] Portions of this section were adapted from our earlier book.

make the results more readily interpretable than is often the case. Nevertheless, large numbers of variables were included in our regression analyses, and that necessarily produced large and somewhat imposing tables of regression coefficients. We therefore opted to present these tables, along with guidelines for their interpretation, in the appendix. (The appendix also includes details of sampling and data collection procedures, which will be of greater interest to some readers than to others.) Thus for readers interested in the regression details and willing to invest a few minutes to review the guidelines for interpreting our tabular format, the information is all in the appendix.

ACKNOWLEDGMENTS

Throughout the life of the Monitoring the Future project, the sponsor has been the National Institute on Drug Abuse (NIDA). We are indebted to the various NIDA directors, division directors, and project officers who provided their support and assistance during the past 26 years. The data collections and analyses reported here were carried out under NIDA Research Grant No. R01 DA 01411.

Our project has benefitted from the efforts of many individuals in the Survey Research Center at the University of Michigan's Institute for Social Research. These include members of the sampling, field, telephone, and computing facilities, as well as field interviewers throughout the nation. In addition, of course, past and present members of the Monitoring the Future staff have been essential to the success of the project.

Three staff members in particular made many direct and valuable contributions to this book. Nicole Ridenour provided extensive analysis support, especially during the early stages of development of the book. Peter Freedman-Doan provided further analysis support, manuscript review, and oversight during the later stages of development. Tanya Hart provided extensive editorial support and coordination.

We appreciate the contributions of our series editor, Nancy Galambos, whose early encouragement, prompt reading, and constructive suggestions helped the authors and improved the book. We also appreciate the thoughtful comments and suggestions of our colleague, John Wallace.

Finally, we wish to extend a special thanks to the thousands of school principals and teachers who cooperated with us in attaining nationally representative samples of students each year, and to tens of thousands of those students who stayed with us over the years as participants in the panel studies being reported here. We are very much in their debt.

1

Introduction and Overview

First come the new freedoms, then the new responsibilities. It is hardly that simple, of course; there are a great many exceptions. Nevertheless, the sequence experienced by most young adults is an opening up of new freedoms soon after completing high school, followed in most cases by the gradual assumption of an increasing number of new responsibilities ...

What do we conclude ... about whether changes in drug use during young adulthood can be attributed to new freedoms and responsibilities? In the case of cigarettes, we think that the increases during the first several years after graduation are attributable fairly directly to the fact that young smokers escape the close constraints on smoking imposed by high-school attendance. Turning to the declines observed from the early twenties onward in consumption of alcohol, marijuana, cocaine, and even (among women) cigarettes, we think they are caused in considerable measure by the shifting balance between freedoms and responsibilities—the fact that increasing proportions of young adults assume new obligations, especially to spouses and children, as they move through their twenties and into their thirties.

—Bachman, Wadsworth, O'Malley, Johnston,
and Schulenberg, 1997, pp. 183, 185

We quote these conclusions from our previous book because they represent the starting point for this book. These earlier findings left us convinced that a variety of changes in drug use during young adulthood can be traced—directly or indirectly—to changes in role constraints and responsibilities that occur during the years following high school. The task now is to discover *why* new freedoms and responsibilities cause drug use to change.

1

In this book we ask two broad questions: What characteristics of some post-high-school environments and experiences often lead to increased drug use? What characteristics of other environments and experiences often lead to reduced use? The specific questions addressed in this book include the following: As young adults experience new freedoms and new responsibilities, do their attitudes about drugs change? Do their religious views and behaviors shift? Do their friends or their friends' use of drugs change? Do the new freedoms lead to more time spent in recreation, including going to parties and bars, and do the new responsibilities lead to less time in such activities?

These questions are interesting in their own right, but they are intriguing also because earlier research (see chap. 2) showed that each of the dimensions mentioned is related to drug use during young adulthood (Arnett, 1998; Bachman, 1994; Bachman, Johnston, & O'Malley, 1990, 1998; Bahr, Maughan, Marcos, & Li, 1998; Donahue, 1995; Hawkins, Catalano, & Miller, 1992; Hundelby, 1987; Johnston, 1982; Osgood, Wilson, O'Malley, Bachman, & Johnston, 1996; Resnicow, Smith, Harrison, & Drucker, 1999; Rose, Chassin, Presson, & Sherman, 1999; Schulenburg, Bachman, O'Malley, & Johnston, 1994; Urberg, Degirmencioglu, & Pilgrim, 1997; Wallace & Bachman, 1991). It therefore seems likely that any or all of these factors are *mediating variables*. That is, they may help to explain why the new freedoms and responsibilities of young adulthood contribute to changes in smoking, drinking, and drug use. Indeed, as we note in chapter 2, this approach can help address some longstanding issues in the literature.

Figure 1.1 provides a schematic overview of the variables and relationships explored in this book. Arrow *a*, linking the new freedoms and responsibilities directly to drug use, represents the primary focus in the previous book. In this book our focus turns primarily to the extent to which certain values, attitudes, and lifestyle behaviors function as mediating variables. For example, do married people spend fewer evenings out for fun and recreation, and is this why marriage on average leads to reduced marijuana use and reduced instances of heavy drinking? Or does marriage change individuals' attitudes about drug use? Or do both of these processes contribute to changes in drug use associated with marriage?

Given that this book focuses on values, attitudes, and lifestyle behaviors as potential mediating variables, we are especially interested in the connections represented by arrows *b* and *c* in Fig. 1.1. Obviously, both kinds of connection would need to be present if any value, attitude, or lifestyle behavior is to "explain" or "account for" any portion of a causal effect of the new freedoms and responsibilities on drug-using behaviors. That is, connections *b* and *c* are two necessary links in a possible causal chain.

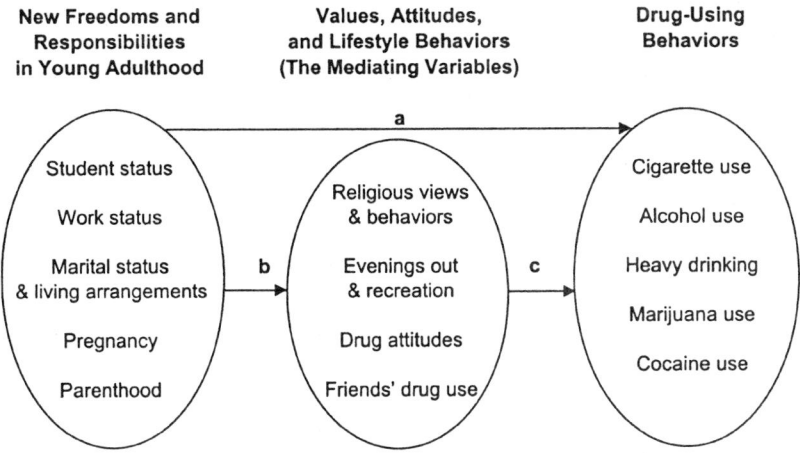

FIG. 1.1.   Overview of variables and linkages.

Our primary analysis strategy, described in chapter 3, involves looking one at a time at each of the four categories of mediating variables shown in Fig. 1.1 (devoting one chapter to each) and focusing attention on the individual links in the possible causal chain. We have chosen to work backward in the causal chain, because an important early question is whether a given value, attitude, or lifestyle behavior dimension actually is connected to drug use. Accordingly, the first step in our approach is to examine, both cross-sectionally and longitudinally, the ways in which a potential mediating variable is correlated with each of the drug-using behaviors—arrow c. The next step, again using both cross-sectional and longitudinal data, is to examine how the potential mediating variable may be influenced by the new freedoms and responsibilities in young adulthood—arrow b.

Each of these two steps is complicated, and in each of four chapters (chaps. 4–7) the steps are repeated for a number of measures involving interrelations among values, attitudes, and behaviors. The reader should not expect that, at the conclusion, we will be able to consolidate the findings into one "grand model." In earlier publications we stressed the need to examine the different sets of drug-using behaviors separately, rather than using a composite measure of "drug use" (e.g., Bachman, Johnston, & O'Malley, 1990, 1998; Bachman et al., 1997), and we continue to examine the drugs separately in this book. However, even focusing on just one dimension of drug-using behavior poses difficulty in taking simultaneous account of all potential patterns of connection implied in Fig. 1.1. Fortunately, we do not need to do so. Instead, we focus on some of the clearest and most important findings from the first two steps in order to examine a sort of "reduced form" of the linkages outlined in Fig. 1.1. That final stage of analyses is presented in chapter 8.

Chapter 8 focuses on transitions into marriage occurring during the early twenties (between modal ages 19–20 and modal ages 23–24) and the finding that, on average, marriage is associated with reductions in most forms of substance use (Bachman et al., 1997). Using structural equation modeling, the chapter explores to what extent any "marriage effects" on substance use may be mediated by religiosity, frequency of evenings out for recreation, and perceived risks or disapproval associated with that substance. We do not view these structural modeling exercises as substitutes for the more detailed analyses in chapters 4–7; rather, we view the models as an alternative method for summarizing *a limited portion* of the relationships treated in greater detail in the earlier chapters.

OBSERVATIONS ON DATA QUALITY AND BREADTH OF GENERALIZATION

Our data come from the Monitoring the Future project, which for more than a quarter of a century has been studying drug use and related attitudes and behaviors among youth and young adults. The samples used in this book include more than 38,000 young people, first surveyed in the high school senior classes of 1976–1997, who also completed follow-up questionnaires from 1977 through 1998. The young adults from the earliest classes provided up to seven follow-up surveys (at 2-year intervals) extending to 14 years beyond high school; the younger adults from later classes provided (at the point when these analyses were conducted) proportionately fewer follow-up surveys. The total number of questionnaires included in these analyses exceeds 171,000.

These samples are quite large, but not extravagantly so. As we saw in the previous book and see again here, some subgroups have fewer cases than we would prefer because only small proportions of the total population of young adults are involved at any one time in some post-high-school experiences (e.g., military service, pregnancy, living in a dormitory). Moreover, many of the measures treated as mediating variables in this book appear in only one of the six questionnaire forms used in each of the Monitoring the Future surveys of high school seniors and young adults (five forms were used prior to 1989). This use of multiple forms permits a much broader range of topic coverage than would otherwise be possible, but it means that for items that appear on only one form ("single form" items), the samples consist of random subsets of about 16% to 20% of all respondents.[1]

Our samples are nationally representative, in addition to being large and extending across more than two decades. This breadth in coverage of both time and geography makes our findings more descriptively useful and more broadly generalizable than is typically the case for panel studies of drug use. Our findings do not, however, represent the entire age cohort. Our analysis samples omit nearly all of the approximately 15% of young people who did not graduate from high school, and the samples also underrepresent frequent absentees (Johnston, O'Malley, & Bachman, 2000a). Further, the samples omit individuals who failed to participate in follow-up surveys and a small proportion of other respondents for reasons noted in chapter 3— those who at the end of high school had already married, or had become parents, or had moved out of the home of their parents or guardians. (The samples and survey methods are described in greater detail in the appendix. See also Bachman, O'Malley, et al., 1996.)

A fundamental question for any research involving survey data regards survey response accuracy, which depends in large measure on the ability and willingness of those surveyed to provide accurate responses. When it comes to questions about whether one is married, virtually all respondents know the correct answer and are willing to provide that answer. Matters are more difficult when it comes to self-reports about drug use, partly due to social desirability and partly simply because of difficulty of accurate recall. Most smokers know their daily rate of consumption well enough, but most who use illicit drugs do so infrequently enough so that they do not always know their actual amount of use (see Johnston et al., 2000a, pp. 54–56, for a discussion of the evidence supporting the validity of self-reports of substance use). The problem of accuracy in survey data can be even more complicated when the responses are judgments using a qualitative scale; whether to check "Disapprove" or "Strongly disapprove" in response to a question about smoking marijuana occasionally may be a judgment call for some respondents, and the answer could differ from day to day for largely random reasons.

Because of these difficulties in accuracy and consistency, some of our analyses have incorporated adjustments for estimated measurement reliability. We have addressed accuracy in self-reports of drug use elsewhere

---

[1]Of course, the use of multiple forms also restricts us from examining direct correlations between items that appear only on separate questionnaire forms. This problem was mitigated, in part, through the combination of key items from the forms into a new Form 6 added in 1989 and through other changes in questionnaire forms made about the same time. These changes permit the use of a small but growing segment of the Monitoring the Future panel respondents to examine correlations among previously "single form" items. We used this capability at key points to check our findings and conclusions.

(Bachman et al., 1997; Johnston et al., 2000a; Johnston & O'Malley, 1985; Wallace & Bachman, 1993). For now, we point out that we have attempted to take account of reporting problems throughout our analyses and in our interpretation of findings, and we remain confident that reporting problems have not invalidated our findings. Finally, to the extent that biases remain in the self-reports of drug use, we suspect that the more frequent direction of error is underreporting; that is, we think actual drug use levels among young high school graduates are at least as high as our estimates and might be somewhat higher.

STUDYING COMPLEX CAUSAL RELATIONSHIPS IN NATURAL SETTINGS

Imagine two young women who graduate from high school at the same time. Imagine that they are identical, except that one enters college and lives in a dormitory, whereas the other takes a job, marries, and soon becomes pregnant. This premise that two otherwise identical people would choose such vastly different life paths is nonsensical, of course. Two women headed in such different trajectories are likely to differ in many other fundamental ways—backgrounds, past accomplishments, and established patterns of behavior. This, in a nutshell, illustrates the problem of studying real people making real choices about what kinds of environments they will experience during young adulthood—what kinds of new freedoms and responsibilities will be theirs.

Young adulthood is especially interesting to researchers because of the great diversity of choices and resulting experiences available during this portion of the life span. Experiences during the high-school years seem almost uniform and lockstep in comparison with the wider range of opportunities that opens on graduation. In addition to being interesting, the young adult period is especially challenging to researchers; the challenges arise not only because of the new diversity of options, but also because the choices among the options are not made entirely—or even mostly—at random.

—Bachman et al., 1997, p. 180

The fact that individuals are not "randomly assigned" to social contexts, as they might be in laboratory experiments, creates a fundamental problem for surveys that study individuals in natural settings. The problem is that one cannot be certain about the causal processes underlying an observed pattern of connections between variables—because the possibilities always remain that a reverse causal process operates in addition to or instead of the one hypothesized, or that other more fundamental (and perhaps unexamined) factors are the real causes.

Panel survey data, collected from the same individuals followed across time (usually a number of years), can provide some leverage in dealing with competing causal interpretations and in sorting out temporal sequences. We have tried to make good use of these advantages of panel data in the analyses presented here. Nevertheless, we stress that panel data alone cannot establish causation with certainty. To be sure, panel data are sometimes proclaimed to be the solution for such problems of drawing causal conclusions, but it generally turns out that those doing the proclaiming have only been admiring panel data from afar. Our own experiences in working closely with a number of panel data sets have left us much more cautious.

In our previous book we found that certain important differences in drug use are *correlated* with certain post-high-school experiences, and we were willing to make informed judgments about whether the changes in drug use are *caused* by those particular post-high-school experiences. For example, having found that becoming married is linked with declining marijuana use and with decreased instances of heavy drinking, we weighed the evidence and reached the conclusion that marriage contributes to declines in these kinds of substance use. Nevertheless, we were at pains to be clear that our panel data did not *prove* that direction of causation.

This book takes us into areas that are complex and often murky. For example, we confront the question of whether we can sort out the causal connections between changes in frequency of evenings out, on the one hand, and changes in frequency of marijuana use or frequency of heavy drinking, on the other hand. Panel data alone, especially when obtained in 2-year intervals, simply cannot provide the leverage to solve the riddle of which variable is in the causal driver's seat. We can, of course, construct causal models that allow us to place "causal arrows" pointing in whatever direction we choose, and then unleash elegant mathematics to "confirm" our assumptions (or sometimes not). In fact, we do make use of those techniques at several points in this book, but always with a great deal of caution. Indeed, in one instance we run a model with causal arrows going in one direction and then repeat the exercise with the direction reversed, just to demonstrate whether it really makes any difference in the numbers. In the end, we are still left with the need to make judgments about causation.

One type of evidence that is relevant to concluding that causation exists, however, is the specification and demonstration of intervening (or mediating) processes that can explain how A influences B. Insofar as we can demonstrate that such processes are associated with particular new freedoms and responsibilities in young adulthood, we have considerably strengthened the case for a causal interpretation. That is the task we have undertaken in this book.

2

Literature Review: Conceptual and Empirical Overview of Issues

By what mechanisms do the new freedoms and responsibilities associated with young adulthood contribute to changes in substance use? This issue arose in our earlier book, and it is the driving question in our current effort. Specifically, we want to understand how some values, attitudes, and lifestyle behaviors change with the roles and responsibilities of young adulthood. We also want to understand how these values, attitudes, and behaviors might explain the effects of roles and responsibilities on substance use.

This chapter reviews the literature concerning the ways in which roles and responsibilities during young adulthood relate to substance use. We look at what is currently known regarding the associations between substance use and student status, employment status, marital status, living arrangements, pregnancy, and parenthood. In addition, we examine available evidence regarding how the roles and responsibilities of young adulthood relate to behavioral and lifestyle mediators and how those mediators relate to substance use.

YOUNG ADULTHOOD

The transition to young adulthood is a time of changing roles, responsibilities, and lifestyles. It is the period in which most individuals move from their parents' homes, complete their educations, enter the workforce, find partners, get married, and perhaps start families. Each of these roles moves them further from the experimentation and "youthful excess" of adolescence and closer to the realm of adulthood. However, between adolescence and adulthood is a period that for most young people in our present-day society is marked by an increase in freedoms with relatively little increase in responsibilities. During this period, risk taking—especially in terms of health risk behaviors—tends to increase. This increase in risk taking is manifested in behaviors such as abusing substances and having unprotected sex. Research is beginning to show that these types of behaviors tend to co-occur (Galambos & Leadbeater, 2000; McGee, Williams, Poulton, & Moffitt, 2000).

According to Arnett (2000) and others (e.g., Aseltine & Gore, 1993; Schulenberg & Maggs, in press), a primary reason that many individuals exhibit more risk-taking behaviors during this period is that they are exploring their identity and are not restrained by social roles such as spouse and parent. This requisite exploration can be viewed as a prelude to successful entry into adulthood roles. The assumption of adult social roles is likely to make many of these behaviors appear to be more risky for young adults (if only because they have more to lose by engaging in such risks). Assuming adult roles can also mean that young adults have more of a stake in society and a commitment to normative values (Hawkins et al., 1992). For these reasons, substance use becomes incompatible with the new social roles, and so it decreases (Yamaguchi & Kandel, 1985b). Attachment to mainstream society, as exhibited in investment in normative roles and a commitment to normative values, is often related to low or decreased substance use. For example, individuals who used illegal drugs as adolescents are more likely to stop as young adults if they had positive relations with their parents and good school performance during high school (Maggs, Frome, Eccles, & Barber, 1997).

The time following graduation from high school is a period when life paths begin to diverge. Young adults must make a myriad of choices, including whether to further their educations, which type of job they will take, and whether or when to start families. Most of these choices take them away from roles that are familiar and into new arenas of life in which roles may be unclear. These changes may provide more opportunities for growth and for occasional missteps. Thus, the new freedoms of this period, combined with the uncertainties that may come with unfamiliar roles, make this a time of experimentation and stress. Some young adults turn to substance use to cope with the stressors encountered during this time (Johnson et al., 2000; Johnson & Pandina, 2000).

As we describe in more detail later, the roles and responsibilities that typically follow high school (living at or away from home, or becoming a student, employee, spouse, or parent) all relate to substance use. In addition, these roles may relate to other factors also associated with substance use, such as number of evenings spent away from home. Patterns of decreased substance use by the end of young adulthood have led us and many others to suggest that there is a normative "maturing out" of substance use that occurs during this period (Arnett, 1998; Bachman et al., 1997).

Linking Transitions to Changes in Substance Use

As discussed in chapter 1, the purpose of this book is to examine factors that may explain why the new roles and responsibilities that follow high school are associated with changes in substance use. The extent of religiosity, types of recreational behaviors engaged in, attitudes regarding substance use, numbers of friends who use drugs, and perceived drug availability all can be related to the roles filled in the years after high school. Each of these factors is also linked to substance use. The analyses in this volume show how the roles and responsibilities of young adulthood are associated with these factors and how strongly these factors, in turn, are related to substance use. Many connections between the roles and responsibilities and the mediators are logical and expected. For example, students probably spend more evenings out and attend more parties and bars than young adults who are not students. However, the relation between the roles and responsibilities and most of these mediating factors has not been documented. Whether students are more religious than nonstudents, and whether those who are employed perceive drug use as riskier than those who are not employed, to take just two examples, have not yet been investigated.

This book examines factors that may mediate the association between social roles and substance abuse. For example, we know that substance use decreases when young adults get married and then increases again following divorce (Bachman et al., 1997; Leonard & Rothbard, 1999). If getting married were related to higher religiosity or an increase in religiosity, this relation could help explain the association between marriage and lower substance use. Similarly, if young adults entering into marriage decrease the number of evenings they go out for fun and recreation, this could explain why marriage is associated with patterns of decreasing substance use. Divorce could undo this effect of marriage by returning the types of recreational activities associated with substance use back to premarriage levels. Perhaps when young adults get married they associate with a different group of people; they might then have fewer friends who use drugs, and they might begin to see drugs as more difficult to acquire. One could imagine that entering the military could affect substance use in similar ways. Young adults in the military may befriend other military personnel, thereby reducing the proportion of their friends who use illegal drugs and thus their own access to such drugs.

SOCIAL ROLES

Student Status

Education beyond high school is a pivotal factor in many aspects of an individual's life. The lives of those who attend college or other post-high-school institutions differ from those who begin work immediately after graduation. Whether or not young adults enter college following high school has implications for their patterns of substance use. Although patterns of substance use vary considerably between those who attend college and those who do not, the differences between these groups are too complex to allow us to characterize one group as more likely to abuse substances than the other. Rather, the differences in substance use between these two groups are particular to each substance under consideration and represent both selection effects (i.e., preexisting differences) and socialization effects (e.g., college students spend time in environments—colleges, universities—having relatively few smokers). In general, during high school the college-bound students use less of all classes of substances compared to their noncollege-bound peers (Bachman et al., 1997). During the years immediately following high school, however, college students tend to experience relatively greater increases in alcohol and marijuana use, whereas cigarette use rates remain low.

As other analyses of Monitoring the Future data have shown, alcohol use increases between ages 18 and 22 among college students living either at home or away, more than for those who are employed and living at home or those who are married (Schulenberg, O'Malley, Bachman, & Johnston, 2000). Problem alcohol use—particularly binge drinking or heavy party drinking—tends to be higher among college students (Johnston et al., 2000a; Wechsler, Dowdall, Davenport, & Castillo, 1995). Although those who drink heavily during high school are less likely to attend college, college students experience a more rapid increase in alcohol use than nonstudents do, and their alcohol use eventually surpasses that of their nonstudent peers (Bachman et al., 1997).

Differences in marijuana use between students and nonstudents are similar to differences in alcohol use. For example, between ages 18 and 22 marijuana use increases more rapidly among college students than among other groups the same age (Schulenberg et al., 2000). Noncollege-bound seniors use marijuana more during high school, but by 3 or 4 years out of high school, use is equal for the two groups (Bachman et al., 1997). Cocaine use is different from either alcohol or marijuana. Use of this drug is higher among noncollege-bound seniors and remains higher in the years following high school (Bachman et al., 1997).

Although alcohol use is higher among college students, and college students exhibit an increase in marijuana use, use of cigarettes is higher among those who do not enter into post-high-school education. Among those who enter college, there are fewer smokers and their consumption of cigarettes is less likely to increase compared to those who do not enter college (Bachman et al., 1997). Cigarette use increases two to three times as much among nonstudents as among full-time students during the 4 years after high school. The difference in smoking rates may reflect a combination of selection effects and socialization effects. Those who smoke cigarettes are less likely to be in college, primarily due to selection effects related to social class and college aspirations (Chassin, Presson, Sherman, & Edwards, 1992). College plans and college attendance are also negatively related to post-high-school cigarette use (Schulenberg et al., 1994).

Employment Status

Previous research documents differences in substance use between young adults who work part-time or full-time, are enlisted in the military, or are homemakers (e.g., Bachman et al., 1997). Young adults who work full-time after high school have average levels of alcohol, marijuana, and cocaine use during high school. After high school, their cigarette use, alcohol use, and marijuana use increase only slightly. Part-time employees, on the other hand, show patterns of substance use nearly identical to college students. This is likely because most young adults who hold part-time jobs are, in fact, also college students. Young adults who are neither employed nor enrolled in college after high school are more likely than average to have smoked during high school and to increase their smoking following high school (Bachman et al., 1997; Schulenberg et al., 2000). They drink less than other young adults and show virtually no increase in alcohol use following high school. Young adults with a history of marijuana use also have an increased risk of becoming unemployed (Brook, Richter, Whiteman, & Cohen, 1999).

Entering the workforce indicates assuming an adult role. Commitment to this role may reduce a young adult's tendency to abuse substances. Evidence shows that young adults who work full-time reduce their use of some drugs and show a below-average increase in their use of others. Young adults who begin full-time employment after high school tend to increase their daily smoking more than those who are unemployed or in the military (Bachman et al., 1997). This group shows very little change in 30-day alcohol use following high school, but an above-average decrease in heavy drinking. Marijuana use typically declines for young adults who become full-time workers, but not as much as it does for those who become military employees or women who become homemakers. Individuals who work full-time after high school tend to use marijuana relatively frequently during their senior year of high school; their use of marijuana is second only to that of high school seniors who become unemployed nonstudents. Finally, other studies have shown that leaving college to begin full-time employment is related to decreased alcohol consumption (Gotham, Sher, & Wood, 1997). The decrease in alcohol use with employment may be more likely for men than for women (Gotham et al., 1997; Wilsnack & Wilsnack, 1992).

The employment classification with the most distinctive patterns of substance use is military service. There are striking differences between those employed by the military and those in all other employment categories (i.e., full-time, part-time, nonemployment, homemaking). Studies conducted in the 1970s suggested that illicit drug use was higher among those in the military than among the civilian population (Johnston, 1973; Robins, 1974; Segal, 1977). More recent studies have shown great declines in use of illicit substances among those in the military. The most recent surveys showed steady declines in cigarette, alcohol, and other drug use among military personnel from 1980 to 1992. However, military personnel were still found to be more likely than their civilian counterparts to use alcohol and smoke cigarettes, although less likely to use illicit drugs (Bray, Marsden, & Peterson, 1991; Kroutil, Bray, & Marsden, 1994). Our earlier work showed that young adults in the military are more likely to smoke during high school and show further increases in smoking after enlistment (Bachman et al., 1997). They consume more alcohol than average young adults. They use an average amount of marijuana during high school, but show dramatic declines in both marijuana and cocaine use once they enlist. The decrease in cocaine use is more dramatic for military personnel than for any other employment group. These patterns of change are most likely related to the military policy of preenlistment drug testing and random drug testing after enlistment (Bachman, Freedman-Doan, O'Malley, Johnston, & Segal, 1999).

Homemakers are less likely than other young adults to increase their smoking. They also show some decrease in alcohol use following high school. During high school their marijuana use and cocaine use are average, and use of both drugs declines after high school. Because homemakers are usually married and many are current or expectant parents, most of these effects are likely related to their marital and parental status, rather than to the nature of their employment status (Bachman et al., 1997).

Living Arrangements and Marital Status

As we found earlier, living arrangements and marital status are related to substance use (Bachman et al., 1997). Indeed, much of what is found in regard to differences between college students and their unenrolled peers relates to living arrangements. For college students, living in a dormitory is more conducive to increased substance use than is living at home. During high school, alcohol use and marijuana use are low among those young adults who go on to live in dorms, but use of both substances increases dramatically after the transition to dorm life (Bachman et al., 1997). Use of cocaine, on the other hand, is lower than average among college-bound high school students and remains low throughout young adulthood. Moreover, dorm residents have a history of low smoking during high school and show virtually no increase in smoking with the move to a dorm. Other analyses of Monitoring the Future data also indicate that overall alcohol use as well as occasional heavy drinking (five or more drinks in a row) are higher among college students living outside of their parents' homes than among college students living with their parents (Schulenberg et al., 2000). Social aspects of dormitory living and fraternity or sorority living in particular have been cited as promoting frequent and intense use of alcohol (Brennan, Walfish, & AuBuchon, 1986; Wechsler et al., 1995).

Newcomb and Bentler (1985) found significant covariation between substance use during adolescence and living arrangements during young adulthood, although their work emphasized the selection interpretation of these results. Those living with their parents as young adults reported the lowest levels of alcohol and marijuana use of any group as adolescents. Those living with roommates, alone, or in arrangements not categorized by this schema did not show patterns of substance use different from their age-mates.

Whether young adults are married and live with a spouse relates consistently to their substance use. Both cross-sectional and prospective studies suggest that marriage is negatively related to alcohol use and illicit drug use (Arnett, 1998; Brook et al., 1999; Brown, Glaser, Waxer, & Geis, 1974; Burton, Johnson, Ritter, & Clayton, 1996; Donovan, Jessor, & Jessor, 1983; Gotham et al., 1997; Kandel & Davies, 1991; Leonard & Rothbard, 1999; Miller-Tutzauer, Leonard, & Windle, 1991; Robbins, 1991). Recent research also indicates that alcohol use decreases when young adults enter into marriage (see Leonard & Rothbard, 1999). However, other studies have shown marriage effects for women, but not for men (Brunswick, Messeri, & Titus, 1992; Horwitz & White, 1991; Newcomb & Bentler, 1987; Yamaguchi & Kandel, 1985b).

We learned earlier that both engagement and marriage are related to reductions over time in alcohol, marijuana, cocaine, and cigarette use (Bachman et al., 1997), although the effects of engagement are often not as strong. Married individuals are less likely to start smoking after high school than single individuals, and among those who started smoking in high school, there is some decrease in smoking with marriage, particularly for women. Alcohol use decreases with marriage for women but does not change substantially for men. Heavy drinking and marijuana use decrease with marriage for both sexes. Additional analyses of Monitoring the Future data show that single persons exhibit more of an increase in substance use from age 18 to 22 than do married persons (Schulenberg et al., 2000). In sum, there is evidence for an influence of marital status on drug and alcohol use for both men and women, but the evidence is perhaps stronger in the case of women.

For most substances, the patterns of change that occur with divorce are the reverse of the changes that accompany marriage (Bachman et al., 1997). Following divorce, cigarette use increases; moreover, even prior to the event, those headed for divorce were more likely to smoke than those who would remain married. Both men and women increase their alcohol use following divorce, and the same is true for marijuana use. The increase in cocaine use following divorce is substantial enough to equal or exceed the decrease in cocaine use associated with marriage. The increases in substance use with divorce suggest that young adults going through a divorce are at risk for increased problem behaviors more generally and may be an important target group for prevention efforts.

Cohabitation is similar to marriage in that it involves living with a romantic partner. Accordingly, one might expect substance use among young adults who cohabit to be similar to that of married young adults. In fact, however, the two groups show distinctly different patterns of substance use, and these differences indicate selection effects and also socialization effects.

Previous analyses of Monitoring the Future data provided ample evidence for selection effects. Before leaving high school, young people who would later become cohabitants were much more likely than average to smoke, drink, occasionally drink heavily, use marijuana, and use cocaine (Bachman, O'Malley, & Johnston, 1984; Bachman et al., 1997). This may reflect lower traditionalism and higher deviance among young people who later choose to cohabit outside of marriage (Newcomb, 1987; Thornton, Axinn, & Hill, 1992; Yamaguchi & Kandel, 1985a).

Previous Monitoring the Future analyses also showed that, unlike marriage, cohabitation does not have socialization effects of consistently lowering substance use; instead, among most cohabitants substance use tends to remain above average (Bachman et al., 1984). On the other hand, among *engaged* cohabitants, there are declines in substance use that appear to be weaker versions of the "marriage effects" (Bachman et al., 1997).

Previous analyses compared the substance use by young adults living alone to the use by those living with their parents. Those who live alone are more likely to increase their smoking and to show a higher than average increase in alcohol use (Bachman et al., 1997). Patterns of change in marijuana use and cocaine use, however, are not different from average for young adults who live alone. Those who live with their parents as young adults usually had low substance use during high school and are not likely to increase their substance use after high school. Their alcohol use does increase during young adulthood, but this increase is lower than what is expected for members of this age group. Both the amount of cocaine use during high school and the change in cocaine use afterward are average for these young adults.

Pregnancy and Parenthood

Becoming pregnant and becoming a parent are regarded among the most dramatic changes that occur during adult life, and the impacts on other aspects of life are far-reaching. Pregnancy is related to changes in substance use that are sometimes dramatic for women, although there are few effects for men. For women, decreased smoking is related to becoming pregnant more than to any other factor studied, including race, student status, employment, and marital status (Bachman et al., 1997). There is no impact of having a pregnant spouse on men's smoking, however. Pregnant women also show large decreases in alcohol consumption, marijuana use, and cocaine use. Men show some declines in use of these substances when their wives are pregnant, but these effects can be explained almost entirely by marital status alone.

Parenthood shows effects similar to pregnancy. For example, individuals entering into parenthood are significantly less likely to initiate or continue marijuana use (Kandel & Raveis, 1989; Yamaguchi & Kandel, 1985b). Becoming a parent also relates to decreased use of cocaine (Kandel & Raveis, 1989). However, because most parents are also married, substance use effects of parenthood are confounded with marital status. In fact, some research has shown that many "effects" of parenting are better attributed to the influence of marital status (Bachman et al., 1997; Burton et al., 1996; Gotham et al., 1997). There are, however, some interesting differences between single parents and married parents. Married mothers decrease their smoking, but there is no change for married fathers (Bachman et al., 1997). Unmarried parents of both sexes are likely to increase their level of smoking. Unmarried mothers decrease their alcohol consumption, but there is no effect of parenthood on alcohol use among unmarried men.

Arnett (1998) presented findings indicating that decreased substance use among young adult parents is part of a pattern of reduced risk-taking behavior that occurs with getting married and starting a family. This study shows decreased binge drinking and drunk driving among parents, but no effect of parenthood on marijuana use. Decreased drunk driving is the only consequence of becoming a parent that remains after the effects of marriage are considered.

One reason for the variations among the findings cited here is the differential effect of parenthood on women and men. For both married and single parents, women are more likely to decrease alcohol use between ages 18 and 22 than are men (Schulenberg et al., 2000). Marijuana use also decreases with parenthood among women only (Kandel & Raveis, 1989).

VALUES, ATTITUDES, AND BEHAVIORS

Clearly, as recent literature shows, changes in social roles and experiences during the transition to young adulthood relate to changes in substance use. As to how social role changes and experiences link to substance use changes, our view is that certain values, attitudes, and behaviors serve as mediating influences. That is, changes in social roles (e.g., marriage) relate to lifestyle changes (e.g., decreased time with friends), and these changes, in turn, contribute to changes in substance use. As we mentioned earlier, such associations are logical and expected, but little empirical literature documents this process. This section summarizes the literature concerning how various values, attitudes, and behaviors relate to substance use during adolescence and young adulthood. Where possible, we consider how the given lifestyle characteristic might serve as a mediator between changes in social roles and changes in substance use.

Religious Views and Behaviors

Research relating young adults' religious beliefs and practices to their substance use presents a very consistent picture: adolescents who are religious are less likely to use alcohol, marijuana, and other substances (Bahr et al., 1998; Donahue, 1995; Hawkins, Catalano, & Miller, 1992). They also tend to have friends who do not use these substances (Bahr et al., 1998). Evidence from adolescent respondents suggests that those who are religious are more likely to have rejecting attitudes toward substance use (Francis, 1997). High school students who consider religion to be important are less likely to drink. Previous analyses of Monitoring the Future high school senior data have shown that frequency of attending religious services and importance of religion are related to lower use of cigarettes, alcohol, and illicit drugs (Bachman, Johnston, & O'Malley, 1981; Brown, Schulenberg, Bachman, O'Malley, & Johnston, 2001; Schulenberg et al., 1994). Other analyses of the senior data have shown that historical trends in marijuana use tend not to affect individuals who are strongly religious (Bachman, Johnston et al., 1990; Wallace & Forman, 1998). Young adults who are more religious drink and drive less, binge drink less, and use marijuana less frequently than those who are less religious (Arnett, 1998). Religiosity may also be a protective factor that can reduce the impact of other factors on substance use (Newcomb & Felix-Oritz, 1992).

Religious belief and activity decline beginning in the teenage years, and religiosity reaches its lowest point around the end of adolescence or during young adulthood (Cornwall, 1989; Stolzenberg, Blair-Loy, & Waite, 1995). Those in their twenties participate in fewer religious services than do those in any other decade of life (Roof, 1993; Stolzenberg et al., 1995). Belief and activity increase starting in the late twenties and early thirties (Cornwall, 1989). Although religious activity decreases during young adulthood, there is some evidence that religious importance does not change with age during this time (Wallace & Forman, 1998).

There are several potential explanations for the association between substance use and religiosity. Most religions discourage use of illicit drugs, either through direct teachings or through philosophical doctrine.[1] For example, the Christian tradition teaches that the body is a temple and should therefore be respected. In this tradition, substance use is considered a way of abusing one's body and is thus considered immoral. Religions such as Seventh Day Adventism and the Church of Jesus Christ of Latter-Day Saints (Mormonism) specifically proscribe the use of all mind-altering substances including caffeine, alcohol, and cigarettes. Both being religious and abstaining from substance use may be related to conformity. Individuals who are very religious may socialize primarily with other members of their religious group; this could mean fewer opportunities for substance use. It could also be that if using illicit substances is incongruous with the tenets of a religion, then individuals who try a drug may feel dissonance between their actions and their beliefs. This dissonance could be enough to change their beliefs, if not their actions. Faith in a higher power is also an important component in some addiction and recovery programs, most notably 12-step programs like Alcoholics Anonymous and Narcotics Anonymous. Moreover, individuals with high religiosity may use religion to cope with various problems, whereas those with low religiosity may be more likely to use substances to cope.

---

[1]Although most major religions do not promote substance use, some religions incorporate substance use into their rituals. This use ranges from the wine shared at some Christian services to the marijuana (ganja) shared during Rastafarian rituals or the use of peyote during Native American Church rituals. Adults who practice these religions may be more likely to use these substances, and the implications could carry over to children raised in these religious traditions.

Religious views and behaviors have important links with various social roles during young adulthood. In particular, most religions emphasize the importance of the family as an institution and the maintenance of family relations; they also tend to discourage premarital sexual activity. Perhaps because of this, religiosity is related to both living arrangements and marital status, with those who are religious being more likely to be married (Arnett, 1998), and those who cohabit tending to be less religious (Stolzenberg et al., 1995). Furthermore, religious young adults are also less likely to divorce, and those who divorce tend to show decreases in religiosity (Stolzenberg et al., 1995). With regard to parenthood and religiosity, young adults who are very religious are more likely to be parents (Arnett, 1998). Young adults with children are more likely to participate in religious activities than are those without children (Stolzenberg et al., 1995). Similarly, if young adults do not have children, they are not likely to experience the normative increase in religiosity that tends to occur during the twenties and thirties (Stolzenberg et al., 1995). Thus, it is likely that one reason that marriage, pregnancy, and parenthood relate to decreased substance use is that they tend to be associated with increased religiosity.

Recreational Behaviors

The increasing freedoms with relatively few personal responsibilities that characterize young adulthood leave ample time and opportunity for frequent participation in recreational behaviors. Compared to adolescents and adults in general, young adults go on more dates, attend more parties, and spend more time in bars. Each of these activities provides situations conducive to substance use. The association between recreational activities and substance use has been investigated more thoroughly among adolescents than among young adults. One general finding in the adolescence literature is that socializing with friends is a strong correlate of substance use (e.g., Hundelby, 1987; Oetting & Donnermeyer, 1998). Likewise, other Monitoring the Future analyses found that socializing with peers away from home is related to substance use among adolescents (e.g., Bachman, Johnston et al., 1981; Osgood et al., 1996; Schulenberg et al., 1994). Osgood and colleagues (1996) showed that among recreational behaviors, some activities provide more opportunities for substance use than do others. The behaviors most likely to involve substance use are social activities that are unstructured and do not involve authority figures.

In previous Monitoring the Future analyses of young adults, a similar relation was found between substance use and social and recreational time. For adolescents and young adults, evenings out are related to use of alcohol and illicit drugs and, to a lesser extent, cigarette use (Schulenberg et al.,

1994). How frequently young adults spend evenings out for fun and recreation is a stronger predictor of substance use than are a number of demographic and attitude variables (Wallace & Bachman, 1991). One could argue that young adults who wish to use substances choose recreational behaviors that will make these behaviors more likely or acceptable. Another possibility is that some third factor, such as gregariousness, sensation seeking, or low conventionality, determines both substance use and recreational behaviors.

Recreational behavior is likely to change as young adults assume new social roles. Clearly, assuming the joys and responsibilities of family life contributes to a decrease in time available for the various recreational activities common during adolescence and emerging adulthood. Becoming a parent, for example, is associated with reported restrictions on leisure activities, at least among men (Crawford & Huston, 1993). Indeed, couples with children probably engage in more family-oriented leisure activities than couples without children. Married couples also report that they engage in leisure activities less frequently after they have their first child (Belsky & Pensky, 1988). Similarly, the limitations on leisure time that come with marriage and employment are likely to allow few opportunities to engage in the recreational activities common among older adolescents. Thus, a decrease in recreational activities is likely to serve as an important mediator between assumption of adulthood roles and decreases in substance use.

Drug Attitudes

How risky one views the use of a given substance and how much one disapproves of its use are likely to be related to the amount one uses. If use of a substance is viewed as risky, one might avoid it. Likewise, if one thinks that it is wrong to use a certain substance, one will be less likely to use it. Evidence for the association between perceived risk and use has been found for cigarettes, marijuana, and cocaine. Heavy users of cigarettes or marijuana perceive less risk of regular use of these substances than do those who use them occasionally (Resnicow et al., 1999). Analyses of Monitoring the Future data showed that perceived risks and disapproval affect use of both marijuana (Bachman et al., 1998; Johnston, 1982) and cocaine (Bachman, Johnston et al., 1990). The argument could also be made that if one uses a substance and does not suffer any negative consequences, one may perceive the substance as less risky. Although it is conceivable that use of a substance leads to a perception of low risk and to increased approval of its use, evidence from Monitoring the Future suggests the opposite causal path: that perceiving a substance as risky and disapproving of its use cause lower use of that substance (Bachman, 1994).

It should be noted that the effects of perceived risk and disapproval are specific to each substance. In other words, perceiving a substance to be risky or disapproving of its use relates primarily to low use of that particular substance, and the association between perceived risk of one substance and use of another is relatively weak (Bachman, Johnston et al., 1990).

As one assumes the various roles of adulthood, it is likely that attitudes toward drug use become more conservative. This happens for a variety of reasons including increased conventionality (Donovan, Jessor, & Costa, 1991), gaining a longer term perspective on lifestyle choices, and acquiring more of a stake in avoiding risky and illegal activities. Thus, as young adults fill new adult roles, we would expect them to disapprove of substance use and perceive substance use as more risky.

Friends' Drug Use

Social factors like associating with friends who use drugs or approve of their use, and seeing drugs as easily attainable, are linked with higher amounts of use. Rates of substance use are higher among those who perceive their friends' use as frequent. For adolescents, peer use of alcohol is one of the strongest predictors of alcohol use (Hawkins et al., 1992). In particular, adolescents who have a close friend who uses alcohol are more likely to start using alcohol, and adolescents whose friends use alcohol are more likely to begin drinking to intoxication (Urberg et al., 1997). Peer use is also a strong predictor of adolescent smoking, even after accounting for the effects of other variables (Rose et al., 1999). Adolescents with close friends who smoke are more likely to try cigarettes, and those whose friends smoke are more likely to begin smoking (Rose et al., 1999; Urberg et al., 1997).

Although the association between friends' use and an individual's use is well established, ascertaining the causal direction underlying this association is complicated. The typical assumption is that peers influence substance use. However, there is some evidence that adolescents choose friends who are similar to them in a number of ways, including substance use (Ennett & Bauman, 1994). A study of 6th, 8th, and 10th graders found that adolescents were similar to their friends in cigarette and alcohol use and that these similarities were present even before the friendships began (Urberg, Degirmencioglu, & Tolson, 1998). Another longitudinal study of adolescents concluded that selection of friends also plays an important role in alcohol abuse (Schulenberg et al., 1999). It seems likely that similarities in substance use among young adults and their friends reflect both selection of similar friends and mutual socialization among friends.

In addition to having friends who use a given substance, perceiving that the substance is easy to get can also relate to use. We might expect young adults to use substances that are easily available and not seek out those that are difficult to obtain. Although this idea makes intuitive sense, evidence so far has not supported it. Perhaps because perceived availability is generally fairly high, it is not related strongly to use. Particularly when compared to such factors as disapproval or perception of a drug as risky, availability shows only modest relationships to use (Bachman, 1994).

Changes in friends' substance use—via either a reduction in substance use among existing friends or changes in friendships or both—are likely to occur as one assumes the pivotal adulthood roles of employment, marriage, and parenthood. Thus, young adults who occupy more adult roles will likely have fewer substance-using friends, be more likely to perceive illegal substances as difficult to acquire, and therefore use less. In contrast, young adults who are still relatively free from adult responsibilities will likely have friends who abuse substances, see illegal substances as fairly accessible, and use more.

CONCLUSIONS

Clearly, as we and others have shown in previous research, the changes in roles and responsibilities that characterize the transition to young adulthood are related to changes in substance use. Our current focus is on the ways in which these roles and responsibilities may also relate to individual and social behaviors and attitudes that are associated with changes in substance use. Factors such as how religious one is; how often one goes out to parties or bars; and whether one thinks of substance use as risky, disapproves of substance use, or has friends who use substances may provide the links that explain why changes in roles during young adulthood are associated with changes in substance use.

Although there are good reasons to believe that social roles during young adulthood relate to the proposed mediating factors, most of these associations are not well documented. One purpose of the analyses in this book is to show that roles and responsibilities in young adulthood are related to the behaviors and attitudes that we believe act as mediators. Many of these behaviors and attitudes are related to substance use, and these associations have been documented. The purpose of this book is to establish the extent to which the roles and responsibilities of young adulthood exert their influence on substance use through their association with behaviors and attitudes.

In addition to their association with substance use and role changes, some of the mediating factors are also likely to be related to each other. For example, individuals who are religious may disapprove more of substance use and may be less likely to have friends who use illicit drugs. Similarly, individuals who frequently spend evenings out at bars may have more substance-using friends and may see drugs as more readily available. Accordingly, the analyses in this book also investigate the associations between these mediating factors, roles, and substance use.

Ideally, the developmental process of moving from adolescence to adulthood is one of replacing behaviors that are no longer perceived as beneficial or functional (e.g., because they become perceived as more risky) with ones that are beneficial and functional (e.g., perceived as consistent with emerging identities and social roles of adulthood). To the extent that this idealized process occurs, our analyses should show that changes in social roles relate to changes in individual and social behaviors, which in turn relate to changes in substance use.

3

Examining Mediating Variables—Sample Characteristics and Analysis Strategies

As stated in chapter 1 and illustrated in Fig. 1.1, our task in this book is to explore *why* the new freedoms and responsibilities of young adulthood may cause changes in substance use. We focus on four categories of mediating variables: importance of religion and frequency of attendance at services (chap. 4); recreational behaviors including evenings out in general, and parties and going to bars in particular (chap. 5); perceived risks and disapproval associated with use of cigarettes, alcohol, marijuana, and cocaine (chap. 6); and perceptions of friends' use of these substances, as well as perceived availability of marijuana and cocaine (chap. 7).

In earlier research, each of these categories of potential mediating variables showed substantial correlations with substance use, particularly among adolescents. What is not so well established is how these factors change with age during young adulthood, and to what extent shifts in these variables are linked with shifts in drug use. Thus, for example, it is well known that adolescents for whom religion is very important are unlikely to be involved in substance use, but it is less well known whether changes in religiosity during young adulthood are accompanied by changes in substance use. Does a decline in religious attendance or importance, or both, lead to an increase in drug use? Conversely, does "getting religion" cause a drop or cessation in use? These questions are among those indicated in Fig. 1.1, arrow *c*. Answers to such questions are central to establishing the value of religiosity as a mediating variable.

Showing how changes in religiosity may be linked with changes in substance use is only one of our central analysis tasks; another task involves showing how the new freedoms and responsibilities of young adulthood are linked with any changes in religiosity. Thus, we consider whether going to college or becoming married or other important changes in roles lead to shifts in religious attendance or importance. These are examples of the issues indicated in Fig. 1.1, arrow *b*.

SAMPLE CHARACTERISTICS
AND REPRESENTATIVENESS[1]

Most analyses in this book make use of Monitoring the Future panel data from the high school classes of 1976–1997 and follow-up surveys conducted from 1977 through 1998; some analyses use only subsets of these data. (The appendix includes descriptions of sampling and survey methods.) Our decision to use all of the available panels in most analyses means that we have complete (i.e., 13–14 year) follow-up data on only the early cohorts, whereas the later cohorts have aged less and thus contribute data for only the earlier follow-ups. This can be seen in Fig. 3.1, which summarizes the panel data used in these analyses. Note that follow-up surveys were conducted during even years for one random half of each cohort and during odd years for the other half.

Some relatively minor limitations of our samples and design should be mentioned here. Age and cohort are somewhat confounded in these analyses; data from the oldest age brackets (modal ages 31–32) are necessarily limited to those who graduated in the classes of 1976 through 1984, whereas the youngest age bracket (modal ages 19–20) includes data from 22 graduating classes from 1976 through 1997. This presents a few complications in the analyses; however, our techniques are able to manage such problems to a large extent. In any case, because the cohorts differ in some important respects, any analysis that seeks to reach general conclusions applicable across cohorts must take such differences into account.

---

[1]This section is an updated version of the corresponding section in our earlier book (Bachman et al., 1997, pp. 26–29), taking account of the expanded sample coverage (i.e., the addition of panel data from the high school classes of 1995–1997).

FIG. 3.1. Observations available for analyses. Full sample analyses were based on observations collected from all the survey administrations represented in this figure. Restricted analyses were based on subgroups shown.

Our obtained samples are limited in a few other respects. Most notably, our panels of respondents begin with high school seniors, thus omitting those who dropped out before reaching the end of 12th grade. Additionally, panel attrition further reduces representativeness (e.g., men and non-Whites showed lower than average rates of follow-up participation).[2] Finally, in order to give everyone much the same starting point in terms of primary role responsibilities, our present analyses exclude the small propor-tion of respondents who at the end of 12th grade were married, had chil-dren, did not live with parents, or were any combination thereof.

These limitations notwithstanding, our general conclusion is that the obtained samples are quite similar to the target samples, and thus reason-ably representative of the large majority of young adults in the United States during the last quarter of the 20th century. Moreover, it should be kept in mind that our primary purpose here is to examine a complex set of linkages among variables, rather than to provide precise estimates of the proportions of young adults who fall into each of our analysis categories. Our obtained samples are very well suited to that purpose.

A FOUR-STEP ANALYSIS STRATEGY

"You buy the premise, you buy the sketch!"

—Johnny Carson, the *Tonight Show*

During the many years that Johnny Carson hosted the *Tonight Show*, a fre-quent occurrence was a sketch performed by the "Mighty Carson Art Players." The sketch was usually based on a very far-fetched premise, which was then followed to its bizarre conclusion. More often than not, when the drama reached a particularly outlandish point, the audience would groan loudly. That was Carson's cue to step out of character for a moment in order to look offended and address the audience thus: "Hey, look folks, you buy the premise, you buy the sketch!"

Carson's dictum often comes to mind (well, to the mind of at least one of the authors) when considering structural equation modeling. Guided by some theory, or at least some theorizing, the structural equation modeler connects a set of variables by drawing arrows showing the hypothesized di-

---

[2]See Bachman, O'Malley, et al., 1996, Table 2.1 for details. In other analyses and publications, we carefully adjust for panel attrition in order to provide more accurate estimates of trends in drug use during young adulthood (e.g., Johnston et al., 2000a; O'Malley, Bachman, & Johnston, 1984, 1988a, 1988b). Such adjustments provide small but useful corrections to our data on overall trends. However, a similar attempt at adjustment would be complex and cumbersome if applied throughout the present analyses and would not have any appreciable impact on our main findings.

rections of causation. Then some very complicated equation solving takes place in order for the modeler to be able to attach numbers to the arrows and to assess the degree of fit—that is, how consistent the data are with the hypothesized structure. What the model's numbers do not tell us, however, is whether the arrows really do run in only one direction, whether the direction specified is the "true" direction, or indeed whether there are variables left out that should be included. Rather, the reader is often left to decide whether to "buy the premise …" We should add that Carson's dictum is by no means limited to structural equation modeling. Rather, it seems applicable to a great deal of social science analyses carried out using real data from real people in real (i.e., nonexperimental) circumstances.

We mention Carson's dictum at the start of this section on analysis strategy not to suggest that we have solved the problem of deriving causal conclusions from correlational data, but rather to acknowledge (once again) that we have not. At points during our analyses, we impose assumptions that we ourselves recognize are not entirely plausible, because such oversimplifying assumptions are sometimes necessary to advance the analyses. We try at such points to acknowledge our assumptions, sometimes by referring again to Carson's dictum.

With these cautions in mind, let us review four broad analysis steps used in this book. Throughout chapters 4–7 we focus on one mediating variable at a time, each time proceeding through the first three analysis steps outlined next. Only in chapter 8 do we reach the fourth step.

Step 1: Describing the Mediating Variables and Age-Related Changes

In dealing with each potential mediating variable, our first step is to describe the variable, showing any changes linked to increasing age (ages 18 through 32). We considered several ways of examining and displaying age-related shifts. One way would simply show data based on all of the cases represented in Fig. 3.1; that is, we would combine all of the base-year data (modal age 18), all of the first follow-up data (modal ages 19–20), all of the second follow-up data (modal ages 21–22), and so on up to the seventh follow-up data (modal ages 31–32). Although this approach has the advantage of using all available data (an approach used in many of our analyses), it has the disadvantage that it does not represent the "early life histories" of any particular set of individuals, because individuals from the later cohorts have not (yet) been able to participate in more than a few follow-ups. Thus, for example, the age 18 data would be based on the classes of 1976 through 1997, whereas the ages 31–32 data would be based only on the classes of 1976 through 1984.

We chose an alternative approach that solves that problem while raising another. Our approach for describing age-related changes in mediating variables focuses on only the classes of 1976 through 1984, because these nine high school classes have been in the study long enough to be able to provide complete follow-up through ages 31 or 32, as can be seen in the shaded portion of Fig. 3.1. Moreover, in order to avoid any apparent changes due to panel attrition, we limit these particular analyses to those who continued their participation through the sixth or seventh follow-up.

However, this approach, although it accurately reflects the overall experience of those in the classes of 1976–1984, leaves some uncertainty about how to interpret any observed shifts. For example, if religious attendance decreased for individuals in these classes as they moved though their twenties, does that indicate age-related changes that are likely to hold true for other cohorts, or could it simply reflect a general downward trend in religious attendance during the last quarter of the century? There are several ways of dealing with this problem, and we illustrate them beginning in chapter 4. The point to be noted here is that tracking one cohort (or a combined set of cohorts) across time cannot, by itself, demonstrate whether an observed change is (a) a function of things having to do with changing age (and related role changes), (b) a reflection of broad historical shifts or "secular trends" during the period under study, or, less likely, (c) "cohort" effects, reflecting some processes peculiar to this particular cohort (or set of cohorts).

Step 2: Linking the Mediating Variables to Substance Use

The next two analysis steps correspond to arrows *c* and *b* in Fig. 1.1. These represent the two links in the causal chain connecting post-high-school experiences (the new freedoms and responsibilities) to drug use via a mediating variable. We found it clearer and more interesting to work backward in the causal chain. Thus, we first establish (in Step 2) whether and how strongly the mediating variable relates to each dimension of substance use, and only then do we examine (in Step 3) how the mediating variable seems to be affected by various post-high-school experiences.

Analysis Step 2 reports how the mediating variable relates to substance use, not just at modal age 18 (the end of high school), but also during the follow-ups extending through modal ages 19–32. We examine the strength and patterning of relationships at multiple time points, looking to see whether cross-sectional correlations evident at the end of high school remain about the same size, increase, or decrease during young adulthood.

As a part of this analysis step, we sometimes present very simple structural equation models, incorporating adjustments for measurement reliability. These models enable us to explore the extent to which stability of relationships across time reflect stability of both factors, versus continuing (i.e., constantly renewed or "refreshed") impacts of the mediating variables on substance use. A number of distinctions emerge at this level of analysis—distinctions among drugs and distinctions among mediating variables. For example, cigarette use is noticeably more stable across time than are the other kinds of substance use; accordingly, relationships with smoking evident at age 18 tend to persist across time even if there is relatively little additional input from the mediating variable. Another set of differences involves the mediating variables, some of which (e.g., the importance of religion) are much more stable across time than others (e.g., frequency of evenings out for fun and recreation).

At the conclusion of this analysis step, we will have estimated the strength and patterning of linkage between the mediating variable and each of a number of substance use dimensions, the linkage shown by arrow c in Fig. 1.1.

Step 3: Linking the Mediating Variables to New Freedoms and Responsibilities in Young Adulthood

Step 3 focuses on the other link in our causal chain, shown by arrow b in Fig. 1.1. In this phase of analysis, our purpose is to show how the mediating variables differ according to post-high-school experiences, and we continue to focus on one mediating variable at a time. We report our findings using two quite different types of analysis; one is descriptive and the other is multivariate, and both make use of "before" (i.e., senior year of high school) and "after" (i.e., post-high-school) scores for each mediating variable.[3] These two analysis approaches are nicely complementary; although there is some degree of overlap, each approach reveals some aspects of the picture that the other cannot.

The first type of analysis is a straightforward descriptive presentation of "before" and "after" scores for each mediating variable linked to various sets of post-high-school experiences. For example, we see (in chap. 4) that during the first 4 years after high school, those who were full-time (college) students reported slightly higher levels of attendance at religious services than did those who were not students; but the 12th-grade data show similar and equally large differences between those who would go on to college and those who would not. By this simple expedient of showing subgroup scores both before and after the individuals sort themselves (and are sorted) into various post-high-school experiences, we often are able to draw important

---

[3]The "before" measure is relatively uncomplicated; it consists of the "base-year" survey taken late in the 12th grade of high school (modal age 18). The "after" measure, on the other hand, could consist of any of up to seven follow-up surveys (modal ages 19–32). For most analyses, all follow-up surveys are used and pooled, as discussed later in this chapter and in the appendix.

conclusions about likely patterns of causation. Actually, this type of analysis is particularly useful in helping to rule out some causal interpretations; taking the last example, the "before" and "after" data lead us to conclude that the higher levels of religious attendance by college students are *not* primarily a result of their post-high-school educational experiences.

The second type of analysis is a multivariate "prediction" of changes in each mediating variable (still taken one at a time) linked to the full range of post-high-school experiences.[4] There are two approaches to the prediction of change in such analyses, and in this book we use both. The first approach involves computing a change score by subtracting the "before" measure from the "after" measure, and then using that change score as the "dependent variable." The second approach uses the "after" measure as the "dependent variable" and includes the "before" measure as one of the "predictors" (i.e., a covariate). In either case one could say that the earlier score is being "controlled," but the means of controlling differ and the results of the analysis also can differ—sometimes in important ways. By using both of these multivariate analysis approaches, we provide some additional evidence for use in reaching our own conclusions, and we also make an effort to accommodate those readers with a strong preference for (either) one over the other.

The multivariate analyses are particularly helpful in dealing with the fact that the post-high-school experiences studied here do not occur independently from one another. Thus, for example, high school graduates who go on to become full-time college students are, not surprisingly, less likely than their age-mates to be employed full-time; they are also less likely to marry, but more likely to leave their parents' homes, and thus more likely to live in housing with other people their own age (dormitories and student rentals). In previous multivariate analyses, we were able to take account of these overlaps and demonstrate, for example, that the larger-than-average increases in alcohol use among college students could be attributed primarily to their living arrangements and marital status (Bachman et al., 1997, especially pp. 105–107). We note similar overlaps and their implications when they occur in this book.

Step 4: Exploring the Full Causal Sequence through Complex Structural Equation Models

Steps 1, 2, and 3, discussed previously, are carried out separately for each of a number of potential mediating variables studied in the next four chapters

---

[4]We use quotation marks here and in some other places as a way of acknowledging that one cannot prove causation with correlational data, and that our causal interpretations are simply that—*interpretations*.

(chaps. 4–7). For each such mediating variable, we examine, separately, the two possible causal links depicted by arrows *b* and *c* in Fig. 1.1. In chapter 8 we "put the pieces together" by looking simultaneously at arrows *a*, *b*, and *c* in Fig. 1.1; we explore how several important mediating variables may be interrelated and how they jointly may help to explain how post-high-school roles and experiences have impacts on substance abuse. Our approach in this stage of the analysis is necessarily selective, focusing on only the most important variables that have emerged in the earlier analyses. The analyses in chapter 8 illustrate that what has been learned in the previous analysis steps can be combined meaningfully; they also illustrate the great complexities involved. During this analysis step, as well as the previous ones, we try to remain cautious about our causal assumptions, keeping Carson's dictum firmly in mind.

ADDITIONAL PANEL ANALYSIS ISSUES AND STRATEGIES

"Panel analysis is a black hole."

—J. Bachman, office chalk board, 1979–1993

A black hole is a "…region from which it is not possible to escape … Anything or anyone who falls into the black hole … will come to an end of time."

—S. Hawking (1993, p. 18)

Previous analyses of Monitoring the Future panel data employed a wide variety of methods. Some analyses decomposed the cross-time correlations for self-reported drug use into estimates of stability and reliability (Bachman, Johnston, et al., 1981; O'Malley, Bachman, & Johnston, 1983). Other analyses distinguished among age, period, and cohort effects (O'Malley et al., 1984, 1988a, 1988b). Annual descriptive reports of drug use among college students and other young adults used panel analyses to correct for the effects of differential sample attrition on drug use estimates (e.g., Johnston et al., 2000a). One early analysis reported "before" and "after" percentages of drug users for subgroups defined in terms of various post-high-school experiences and also reported regression analyses in which the "before" (i.e., senior year) measure of drug use was included among the predictors of the "after" (i.e., post-high-school) measure of drug use (Bachman, O'Malley, & Johnston, 1981; Bachman et al., 1984). Other analyses used LISREL to estimate more complex structural equation causal models (Bachman, Schulenberg, O'Malley, & Johnston, 1990; Osgood, Johnston, O'Malley, & Bachman, 1988; Schulenberg et al., 1994); and some recent analyses have taken a pattern-centered approach to examining change over time (Schulenberg, O'Malley, Bachman, Wadsworth, & Johnston, 1996; Schulenberg, Wadsworth, O'Malley, Bachman, & Johnston, 1996). A number of these techniques were used also in our previous book (Bachman et al., 1997). We have used these multiple methods in part because our purposes have varied from one analysis to another. But another motivation for using multiple analysis methods is precisely because we do not consider any single approach to be free of risks and potential blind spots; we have greater confidence in findings that replicate across analysis methods. The findings reported here have met that criterion.

The Complexity of Panel Data and the Need to Simplify

A perennial problem in analyzing Monitoring the Future panel data is how to analyze tens of thousands of individual data records—or "case studies"—and discover those underlying patterns that can be considered generally applicable. It is necessary to simplify along either or both of two dimensions. One approach is to restrict drastically the range of current role experiences examined; another approach is to limit the number and complexity of time points examined. Both approaches are worth illustrating.

As one example, on several occasions we focused on just one role dimension—marital status—and analyzed various "trajectories" from single to married. In analyses originally reported in 1987 (Bachman, 1987) and later updated showing the same results with much more extensive data (Bachman, Johnston, O'Malley, & Schulenberg, 1996), we covered five points in time, and thus four time intervals (from the senior year of high school up to 8 years later). Specifically, we distinguished five different groups—those who remained single throughout and those who made a transition from single to married in the first interval, the second, the third, or the fourth. These analyses showed clearly that marriage was associated with a decline in proportion of marijuana users and that the decline was much the same whether the marriage occurred in the late teens, early twenties, or mid-twenties. In order to keep things manageable across five time points, we needed to omit those who followed less typical trajectories, such as moving from single to married to divorced to married again, etc. Additionally, we did not control statistically for a variety of other potentially relevant factors such as pregnancy and parenthood (because other analyses had led us to conclude that the impacts of marriage were of primary importance). Given the increased numbers of cases now available, we have extended that analysis to cover the full range of seven follow-ups; the results are presented in Fig. 3.2. Once again the analysis shows a "marriage effect"—a drop in proportion of marijuana users in the 2-year interval during which marriage occurred, and it is now clear that the pattern extends through the late twenties and into the early thirties.

Another example comes from our previous book and shows a different trade-off between the number of time points and the complexity of material considered at any one point. In this approach we wished to examine more complex transitions into and also out of marriage, so we considered many—but not all—of the possible transition patterns involving four categories of marital status—single, engaged, married, or divorced. This time, importantly, the transition patterns were based on just two points in time. Eight different transition patterns were shown, illustrating consistently that the

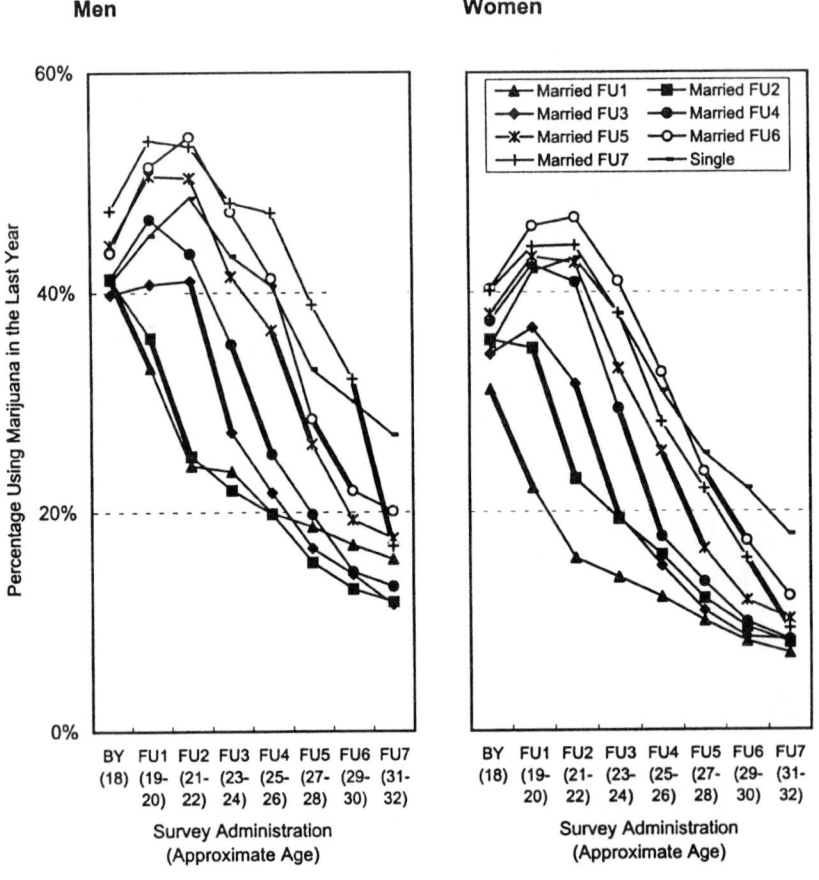

FIG. 3.2.   Annual marijuana use related to marital status for the classes of 1976–1984 across eight points in time. No missing data were allowed. Respondents who were engaged were considered single. Bold line indicates the time interval during which marriage occurred.

transition *into* marriage was linked to a decline in likelihood of heavy drinking, whereas the transition *out of* marriage was linked to an increase of roughly comparable size. The findings also illustrate the complexity of discriminating among eight distinct trajectories—even when the main patterns of results are relatively strong and clear (Bachman et al., 1997).

Distinctions in terms of marital status are relatively simple, however, compared to the more complex dimension of living arrangements, in which one could be living with parents, a spouse, a cohabitant, dormitory mates, other nonrelatives, or alone. Those six categories of living arrangements, considered at multiple points in time, immediately generate an unmanageably large set of possible transition patterns. If one considered just three follow-up points, the number of possible patterns is six to the third power, or 216. Even if most of these patterns were excluded, the remainder would overwhelm the unfortunate analyst!

Studying Change Across Just Two Points in Time

Our solution to this problem required a great deal of preliminary work, followed by some careful streamlining for the final analyses. Our first major streamlining decision was to restrict many, but not all, of our panel analyses to just two time points—an initial "before" measure, plus one follow-up "after" measure.

Treating Senior Year as the Starting Point

The second major streamlining decision was that the "before" measure for most analyses would be the base-year survey, which occurred when our respondents were seniors in high school. This had the effect of giving everyone much the same starting point in terms of primary role responsibilities. The primary occupation of each high-school senior was considered to be student. Additionally, nearly all seniors surveyed were single, living with their parents, and did not have children of their own; the fewer than 7% who did not meet those three criteria as seniors were excluded from the present analyses. By thus streamlining the "before" point in our before–after analyses, we are able to deal with a complex set of post-high-school experiences examined at the "after" point. This is so because each of the "after" conditions reflects not only the situation at that point in time, but also a change (or nonchange) from the "before" conditions. For example, an individual living in a dormitory at the time of follow-up also has made a major transition in living arrangements, whereas someone (still) living with parents has not.

Pooling Data Across Multiple Follow-Ups

Most of our panel respondents have participated in several follow-up surveys, and many have participated in seven. Of course, our respondents often change circumstances from one follow-up to another. Although some transitions (e.g., from single to married) typically occur only once in young adulthood, there are many exceptions; moreover, other transitions (e.g., changes in living arrangements or student status) tend to occur several times and thus are less permanent. Accordingly, we found it useful to consider each new follow-up survey completed by a panel respondent as providing a new set of findings, both in terms of mediating variables (as well as drug use measures) and also in terms of then-current post-high-school role experiences and responsibilities. Each of these follow-up surveys, when coupled with the senior-year surveys (i.e., the "before" measures), provided a different set of change scores, as well as a different set of "predictor" measures.

In exploratory analyses conducted some years earlier, we compared findings across four base-year to follow-up intervals: spans of 1 or 2 years, 3 or 4 years, 5 or 6 years, and 7 or 8 years. These analyses yielded two important lessons. First, conducting analyses separately for each of four follow-up intervals generated a nearly overwhelming amount of detail. Second, such detail proved to be unnecessary, because the general patterns of findings for those relationships were quite similar no matter which of the four intervals was considered.

Based on these preliminary findings, plus additional confirming analyses, we decided to combine findings across all base-year (before) to follow-up (after) intervals. Thus, a hypothetical "Jane Jones" who participated in seven follow-ups would generate seven different "cases" for inclusion in these analyses; each "case" would correspond to her circumstances and behaviors at one of the seven follow-ups, and in each instance her senior-year (or before) behaviors would provide a comparison point.[5]

One exception to that generalization is worth noting. When examining the correlates of college attendance, it is most useful to concentrate on the first 4 years after high school in order to compare students with their

---

[5]In effect, this approach takes account of the fact that Jane Jones is not exactly the same person at each follow-up point, and it does so by treating her as seven different cases. It may be useful to think of these cases as "Jane Jones #1" (corresponding to the first follow-up), "Jane Jones #2" (corresponding to the second follow-up), and so on up to "Jane Jones #7." The seven cases generated by Jane Jones would not, of course, be strictly independent of each other because they share a common "before" measure. Accordingly, it might be inappropriate for us to base tests of statistical significance on the total numbers of "cases" or observations, as shown in the appendix. Instead, we have taken the very conservative approach of basing such tests on only the numbers of individuals involved. In effect, Jane Jones would add only 1.0, rather than 7.0, to the total N used in tests of statistical significance.

age-mates who did not go on to college. If later follow-ups are included, the result is to compare college students not only with their age-mates who did not go to college, but also with older adults who may have attended college years earlier. Accordingly, we repeated many of our multivariate analyses with only the first and second follow-ups included. The contrast between the full set of panel data and the first two follow-ups can be seen in Fig. 3.1; the first two follow-ups are outlined and form a diagonal area from the left of the figure to the lower right.

Pooling Data Across Multiple Cohorts

Just as it would have been overwhelming to sort through detailed analysis data for seven different follow-up intervals, it also would have been unwieldy to examine and interpret analyses separately for each of the different cohorts of high school seniors. Instead, we generally combined results across all of the cohorts. One exception is that when we describe overall patterns of change over time in a mediating variable, we focus on the earliest cohorts (graduates of the classes of 1976–1984), represented by the nine shaded rows in Fig. 3.1. This approach allows us to give a complete "natural history" of age-related changes in the mediating variables from the late teens through the early thirties.

Multivariate Analyses Predicting to Mediating Variables

We make use of several descriptive analysis approaches in this monograph, especially in showing how various post-high-school experiences are related to each of the mediating variables. However, underlying all of these relatively simple bivariate analyses is a series of multiple regression analyses; in these analyses a variety of post-high-school roles and environments are examined simultaneously, with several key background factors also taken into account, and with all of these factors treated as "predictors" of *changes* in each dependent variable between senior year and follow-up.[6] This approach enables us to take account of a considerable number of factors simultaneously; further, by looking at various subsets of these factors separately, we are able to sort out some of the ways in which post-high-school experiences may have overlapping effects. The appendix provides considerable detail on our multiple regression analysis approach, including tables of regression coefficients and guidelines for interpreting the tables. In this chapter we discuss our regression analysis strategy at a more general conceptual level.

---

[6]The "dependent variables" in these regression analyses consist of what we have labeled *mediating variables* in Fig. 1.1. The analyses very closely parallel those analyses in our earlier book in which the dependent variables were various dimensions of drug use.

An important feature of these regression analyses is the use of change scores, calculated in a straightforward manner; specifically, the "before" measure for the dependent variable (derived from the senior-year survey) is subtracted from the "after" measure of that variable (from the follow-up survey). Positive change scores thus indicate an increase in the dependent variable over time, whereas negative change scores indicate a decrease. There has been much discussion of the advantages and disadvantages of change scores in panel analyses. Our own views, along with a good deal of supporting argument, have been spelled out by Rodgers and Bachman (1988).[7] For additional discussions see Cronbach and Furby (1969), Kessler and Greenberg (1981), Liker, Augustyniak, and Duncan (1985), and Rodgers (1989). In brief, we judged the advantages to far outweigh the disadvantages for our present purposes. Nevertheless, an alternative approach (predicting to the after score of the dependent variable, while including the before measure among the predictors as a control variable) can sometimes provide additional insights; for that reason we added this form of analysis to the data presented in the appendix.

Comparison Among Overlapping Predictor Sets

For each dependent variable (i.e., each of the mediating variables treated in chaps. 4–7), we conducted four multivariate regression analyses predicting to change scores. The first used only background and control variables as predictors. The second treated work and student status (along with the background and control variables) as predictors. The third used living arrangements, engagement, pregnancy, and parenthood (again, along with the background and control variables) as predictors. The fourth included all of those predictors. (Only the first and fourth analyses are reported in the appendix; the others are available in Bachman et al., 2001.)

This sequence of regression analyses reflects our view that for most high school seniors, a key decision is whether or not to attend college, and then other decisions—at least as to the timing of other role experiences—flow from that decision. College and work often compete for the finite number of hours young adults have to use, and these roles overlap in complex ways; thus, we included student status and work status in a single predictor group so as not to assign priority to one over another. We are also especially interested

---

[7]Rodgers and Bachman argued as follows: Change scores provide a single meaningful measure of the dependent variable. Although conventional wisdom suggests that the use of change scores should be avoided because the standard errors of estimates based on change scores are greater than those based on static scores, such is not always the case. For reasonably large sample sizes, such as those used here, the ratio of sampling errors for estimates based on change scores to those based on static scores is not excessively large. (See Rodgers & Bachman, 1988, for further discussion.)

in patterns of prediction when this second group is considered jointly with the third group (living arrangements, engagement, pregnancy, and parenthood). By entering these predictors in separate blocks, we are able to assess shared (i.e., overlapping) and unique (i.e., nonoverlapping) contributions of each.

It should be stressed that our analysis strategy does not commit us or our readers to one interpretation of the causal orderings among work status, student status, and living arrangements. On the contrary, the strategy is neutral as to which is causally prior, while dealing with the obvious interrelationships between the sets of predictors.

Separate Analyses for Men and Women

Although basic findings are largely parallel for men and women, there are also some important differences. Accordingly, we report most results separately for males and females. This is particularly important for those analyses involving drug use, because there are substantial differences between males and females along some of these dimensions—for example, higher proportions of men than women reporting heavy drinking, or marijuana use, or cocaine use (see Bachman et al., 1997). There also are overall male–female differences along a number of the mediating variable dimensions, as shown in chapters 4–7. The decision to present male and female findings separately side-by-side rather than combined makes it easy to see both the parallels and the overall differences, as well as the occasional patterns that are not strictly parallel.

4

Religious Attendance and Importance

The large majority of high school students and young adults attend religious services at least occasionally and say that religion has some importance in their life. There is, however, considerable variation along these dimensions, with far fewer than half of young people attending on a weekly basis or rating religion as "very important" in their lives. These variations in religious involvement are linked to variations in substance use, and they are also linked to some extent with role changes that occur in young adulthood. All of these factors are examined in this chapter.

High school students who consider religion to be very important in their lives and who attend services frequently are much less likely to smoke, drink, and use illicit drugs. There are a variety of possible explanations for these relationships, as discussed in chapter 2. In this chapter we focus on the less often studied topics of change (and stability) in religious attendance and importance during young adulthood. We first report overall change and stability along these dimensions; then we examine how religiosity is related to substance use and also to the new freedoms and responsibilities that come with adulthood.

PATTERNS OF AGE-RELATED CHANGE IN RELIGIOSITY

We use the term *religiosity* at times as a shorthand for two quite distinct, though strongly correlated, dimensions: frequency of attendance at reli-

40

gious services and self-ratings of the importance of religion in one's life. (The product–moment correlations between these two dimensions range from .62 at age 18 to .67 at ages 25–32, based on 1990–1998 data shown in Appendix Table A.2.) In many analyses, including those in chapter 8, we found it useful to combine our measures of these two dimensions into a single two-item index; however, in this chapter it seems better to preserve the distinctions. We considered it possible, for example, that changes in lifestyle during young adulthood might influence patterns of attendance without necessarily influencing overall importance of religion. As we shall see, the two dimensions show many similarities in their patterns of relationship with drug use and with post-high-school experiences, but there are also some differences, especially in terms of overall change.

Frequency of Attendance at Religious Services

Figure 4.1 tracks frequency of religious attendance for those from the high school classes of 1976–1984 who participated in most or all follow-up surveys. The proportions of men and women who attended once a week or more dropped about 10 percentage points in the first year or two after high school and another 6 points two years later, before settling at about 22% for the men and about 29% for the women. Weekly attendance rose very slightly (3–4 percentage points) by ages 31–32. The proportions who reported never attending services increased from 10% to 15% among the males and from 7% to 10% among the females.

We believe that these changes accurately reflect the actual experiences of the majority of young people who graduated from high school in the classes of 1976–1984 (although the levels of attendance shown here are slightly higher than would have been the case had there been no losses from the sample due to panel attrition). However, it would not necessarily be accurate to conclude that the changes shown in Fig. 4.1 reflect simply the effects of aging and that the same age-related patterns would be evident for those from different high school classes. The data in Fig. 4.1 capture not only changes related to age (the shift from modal age 18 to modal ages 31–32), but also changes related to recent history (from the years 1976–1984 to the years 1989–1998). In other words, respondents from each cohort shown in the figure aged by 13–14 years, and at the same time each cohort passed through 13–14 years of history. Thus, any historical changes (also termed *period effects*) that occurred during that period may have contributed to the changes shown, so we should not jump to the conclusion that age and its correlates are solely responsible for the observed decline in religious attendance.

There was, in fact, a modest gradual decline in frequency of attendance at religious services by high school seniors during the period covered by Fig.

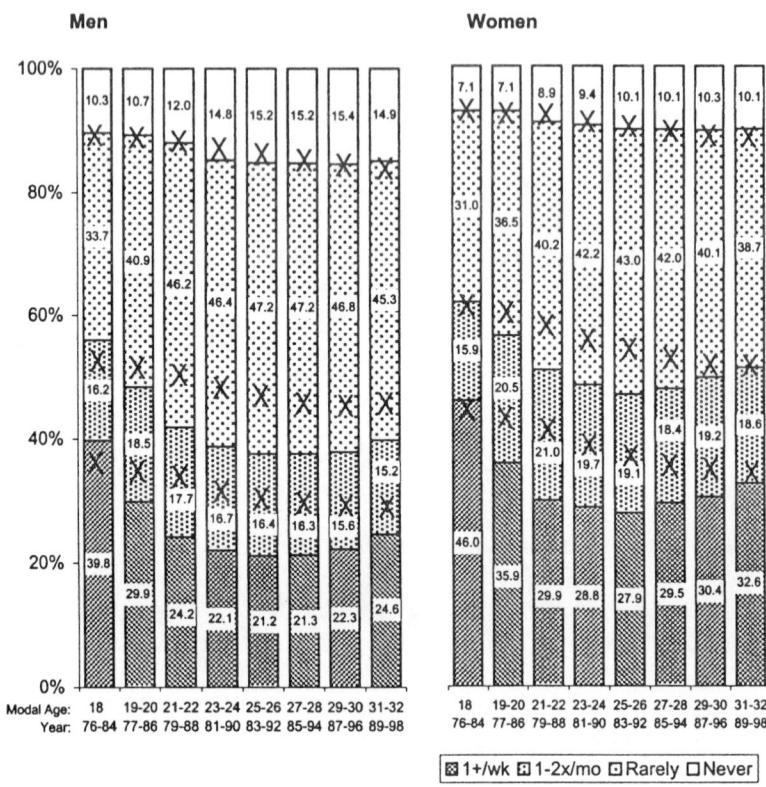

FIG. 4.1.   Attendance at religious services for panel respondents followed from age 18 to ages 31–32. Bar percentages are based on high school senior data, plus follow-ups 1–7, from class years 1976–1984; one person could contribute up to seven follow-up observations (see Additional Panel Analysis Issues and Strategies section in chap. 3). The sample is restricted to those respondents who answered this question at follow-up 6 and/or follow-up 7. Approximate numbers of observations per age group for men: 4,400; for women: 5,400. X notations demarcate the boundaries between the frequency of attendance categories for the senior year data within the given year ranges. Senior samples include approximately 69,000 men and 72,000 women in each year grouping.

4.1. We showed these changes in the figure by using X notations showing the scores for *all high school seniors* (as estimated by our full cross-sectional surveys) at each reporting period shown in the figure. For example, the graduating classes of 1976–1984 reached modal ages 31–32 in the years 1989–1998; therefore, the X notations shown on the right-hand bars for men and women in Fig. 4.1 are based on the responses for high school seniors averaged across the graduating classes of 1989–1998. Looking at the top of Fig. 4.1, we see that the age-related gradual increases in percentages of young men and women reporting that they never attended religious services is matched almost perfectly by the increase in percentages of high school seniors reporting never attending. Thus, it would be difficult to attribute this shift solely to aging, when it seems that it may be part of a broader societal change (albeit a modest one). On the other hand, when we look at the percentages attending weekly or more often, shown at the bottom of Fig. 4.1, we see that the sharp drop just after leaving high school (i.e., from modal age 18 to ages 19–20) is not matched by any sharp change among high school seniors during that period; accordingly, we are inclined to view this as largely an age-related phenomenon.[1]

When the panel data from the classes of 1976–1984 are compared closely with the cross-sectional data from high school seniors at matched times, the patterns suggest the following curvilinear relationship with age: religious attendance does drop somewhat during the first few years after high school, but after about the mid-twenties attendance increases slightly compared with what we suspect are overall societal trends. Confirmation of that conclusion is provided by another set of tabulations, reported in Bachman et al. (2001); when we examined data from all base-year and follow-up surveys collected in the years 1990–1998 (thus holding period effects constant while examining age differences), we found that 33% of the seniors (modal age 18) attended weekly or more often, compared with 25% of those aged 19–20, 21% of those 21–24, 23% of those 25–28, and 28% of those 29–32. Again, the relationship with age is clearly curvilinear.

Importance of Religion

Figure 4.2 shows age-related changes in the importance of religion that are quite different from the curvilinear pattern of changes in attendance just described. Ratings of importance showed a slow but steady rise during young adulthood, with the "very important" category rising from 24% to 29% among men and from 33% to 41% among women. At the other end of the scale, about 14% of men and 8% of women rated religion "not important" in their lives; those percentages remained essentially unchanged from age 18 through age 32.

---

[1]It is worth noting in Fig. 4.1 the small discrepancies, especially for males, between the age-18 panel data and the cross-sectional data shown by the X notations. The slightly higher levels of religious attendance shown for the panel data reflects panel attrition; those who dropped out of participation in the follow-up surveys were somewhat lower in religious attendance than the overall average, and their absence resulted in a slight upward bias for the panel sample in terms of religious attendance.

We noted in the previous section a modest gradual decline in frequency of religious attendance by high school seniors during the period of the study. There was not, however, any clear trend in religious importance ratings of high school seniors over time (and thus no X notations are included in Fig. 4.2). Accordingly, we view the gradual rise in religious importance shown in Fig. 4.2 as reflecting typical changes occurring during young adulthood, unconfounded with any substantial period effects.

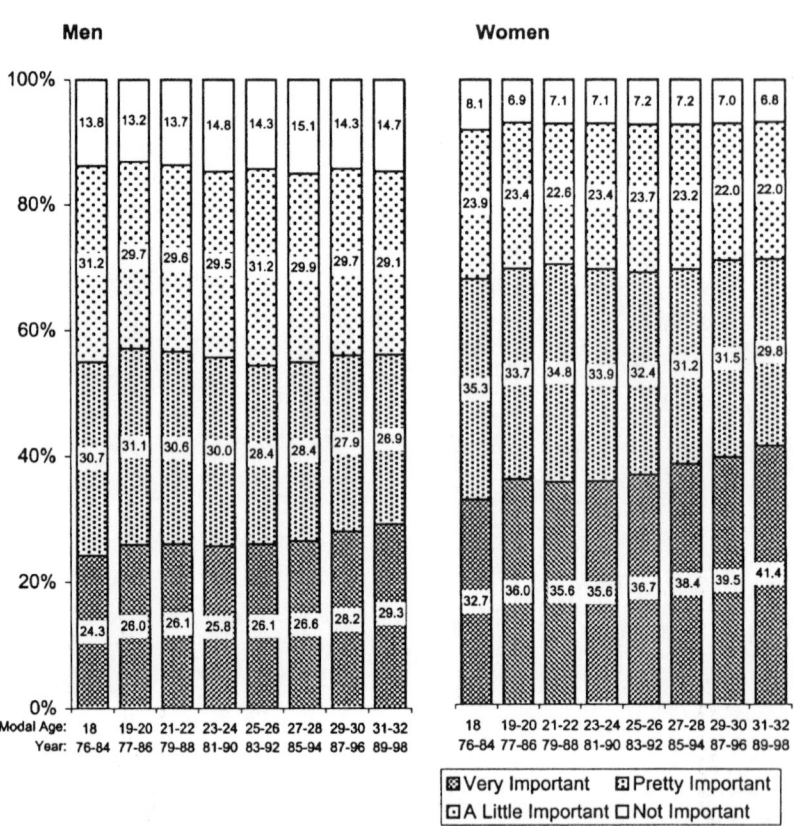

FIG. 4.2. Importance of religion for panel respondents followed from age 18 to ages 31–32. Bar percentages are based on high school senior data, plus follow-ups 1–7, from class years 1976–1984; one person could contribute up to seven follow-up observations (see Additional Panel Analysis Issues and Strategies section in chap. 3). The sample is restricted to those respondents who answered this question at follow-up 6 and/or follow-up 7. Approximate numbers of observations per age group for men: 4,400; for women: 5,400. Inasmuch as there were no major secular trends in 12th grade data, importance of religion is not compared to the average high school senior class data for each year range.

HOW CHANGES IN RELIGIOSITY RELATE TO CHANGES
IN SUBSTANCE USE

We now examine one of the causal arrows shown in Fig. 1.1 in chapter 1. Working backward from substance use, we begin with arrow c in the figure, showing how religiosity is related to substance use.

Change and Stability in Religiosity

We described earlier the overall trends in religious attendance and importance among young adults ranging from modal ages 18 to 32; we saw that attendance first dropped and then rose slightly, whereas importance rose gradually throughout that portion of young adulthood. Those were aggregate changes, based on some individuals who shifted in one direction and some who shifted in the opposite direction; however, most individuals did not shift at all from one survey to the next in their answers about religion. In other words, both of the religiosity measures showed very high levels of stability across time.

Some very simple structural equation models, presented in the next portions of this chapter, provide estimates of the stability of the religiosity measures across time. These models, which incorporate adjustments for measurement reliability, yield stability estimates for the 1- or 2-year interval between the senior-year survey and the first follow-up, as well as the 2-year intervals between the first and second follow-ups, the second and third follow-ups, and the third and fourth follow-ups. These stability estimates are path coefficients that can be interpreted as the estimated "true" (i.e., error-free) correlation between a characteristic at one point in time and that same characteristic at a later point in time. (All this is subject to a number of assumptions, of course, and we say more about that later.)

The estimated stability for religious attendance between the senior year of high school (modal age 18) and the first follow-up 1 or 2 years later is .86; the coefficients for the following 2-year intervals are .87, .89, and .92. The corresponding values for religious importance are even higher: .90, .90, .93, and .96. Clearly, in spite of the overall shifts noted earlier, there is a great deal of year-to-year consistency. Some individuals undergo dramatic religious conversions of one type or another during young adulthood, to be sure, but it seems clear from these data that the great majority do not.

As noted earlier, religiosity is negatively correlated with substance use. The linkages, which are clear by the end of high school, remain undiminished during young adulthood. However, a key question remains: Do those fairly stable patterns of correlations reflect ongoing "impacts" of religiosity on substance use (assuming that is the dominant direction of causation), or do they reflect relationships that arise before the end of high school and then continue simply because of the stability of the variables involved? The answer differs from one drug to another, as we will see.

Cigarette Use Linked to Religiosity

Given what is currently known about the health consequences of cigarette smoking, any notion of "treating one's body as a temple," as is taught by many religions, is entirely incompatible with smoking. Indeed, as discussed in chapter 2, some religious groups specifically proscribe the use of tobacco, whereas in other groups the incompatibility is less explicit. Broadly speaking, therefore, it is reasonable to expect that individuals highest in religious commitment would be least likely to smoke cigarettes.

Figure 4.3 shows, in some detail, how cigarette use (percentages of respondents who reported any smoking during the past 30 days) varies across the four categories of religious attendance. The data shown are for panel participants from the high school classes of 1976–1984 at base year when they were seniors, at each of the first three follow-ups, and then at follow-ups 4 and 5 combined and follow-ups 6 and 7 combined. The linkages are a bit stronger and clearer from the second follow-up onward, but the overall relationship is basically the same at all time points: The pattern is curvilinear with smoking rates highest among those who never or rarely attended religious services (nearly 40% smoked in the early follow-ups), slightly lower among those who attended once or twice a month, and sharply lower (just under 20% at the first follow-up and gradually lower thereafter) among those who attended services weekly or more often.

The importance of religion also shows a curvilinear relationship with smoking, very consistent across time but slightly weaker than that for religious attendance. (The data are displayed in Bachman et al., 2001.) Smoking rates were distinctly lower (roughly 20% smoked) among those who rated religion as "very important" in their lives; smoking rates were higher and nearly equal (at roughly 35%) among those who rated religion as "pretty important" or "a little important" or "not important" in their lives.

In sum, the overall connection between religiosity and smoking seems to change rather little between ages 18 and 32. So now we can return to the question raised earlier: Does this stable pattern of relationships reflect an ongoing "impact" of religiosity on substance use (assuming that is the dominant direction of causation), or does it reflect a relationship that arises before the end of high school and then continues simply because of the stability of the variables involved? We addressed this question using the

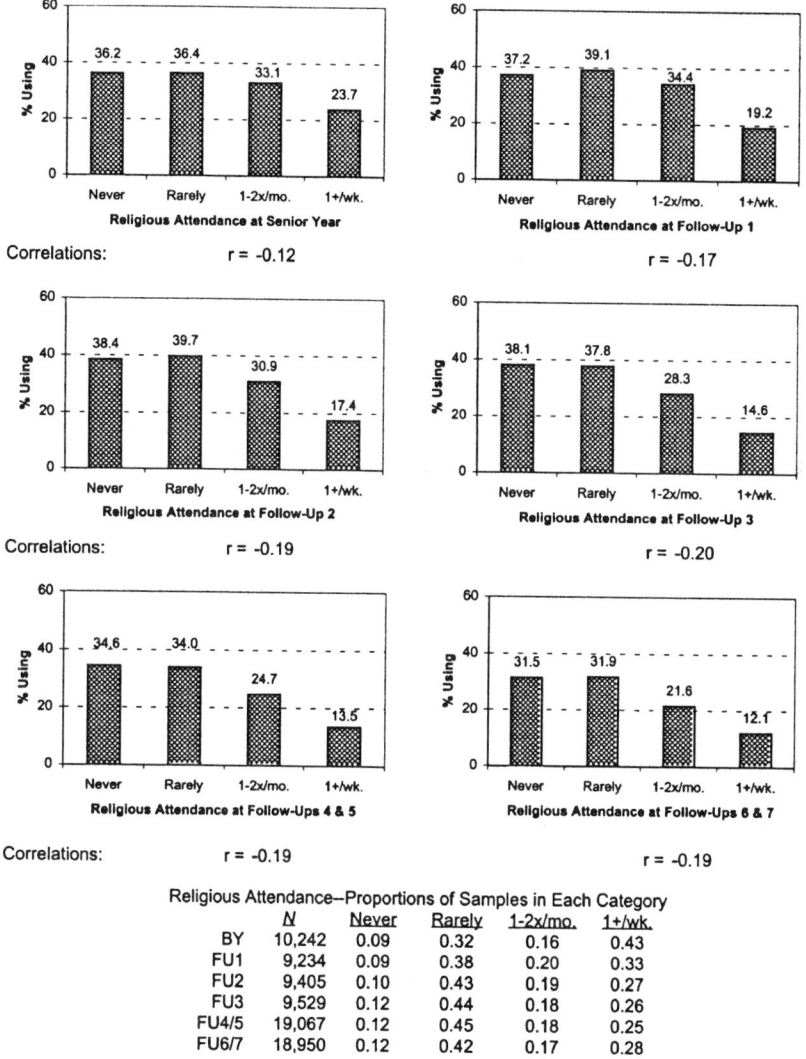

FIG. 4.3. Thirty-day prevalence of cigarette smoking related to frequency of attendance at religious services. Percentages are based on the classes of 1976–1984 followed from age 18 to ages 29–32 (follow-ups 6 and 7, combined). The sample is restricted to those respondents who answered the questions on both 30-day cigarette use and religious attendance at follow-up 6 and/or follow-up 7. Correlations are based on the drug use measure recoded as a dichotomy.

very simple structural equation model shown in Fig. 4.4.[2] The same type of model is used to examine many other linkages in this book, so we describe this first application in some detail. Recalling Carson's dictum ("You buy the premise, you buy the sketch"), let us specify the assumptions contained in this model.

First, it is assumed that the only measured "cause" of religious attendance at one (measurement) point in time is the level of religious attendance at the immediately prior (measurement) point in time (which occurred 2 years earlier, except for the first follow-up, which was either 1 or 2 years earlier). Further, it is assumed that any impacts of still earlier patterns of religious attendance occur only *indirectly*, via the immediately prior point in time (i.e., 1 or 2 years earlier). Of course, as is true in much of causal modeling, we do not take these assumptions literally. What we really believe is that a whole array of unobserved factors (such as an individual's own religious views, as well as the religious views and behaviors of friends and family) underlie religious attendance at one point in time, and these same factors are likely to be largely unchanged at the next point in time.

The other major assumption is that at any one point in time religious attendance is a cause of cigarette smoking rather than the other way around. (This is signified by the direction of the vertical arrows in Fig. 4.4.) This also is not taken entirely literally. We do not really think that attending religious services causes individuals not to smoke (except, perhaps, during the time

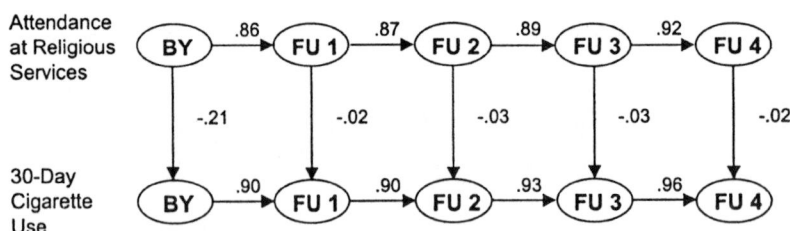

Note: This simplified model shows only the structural portion of the model; the measurement portion is not shown.

FIG. 4.4. Impacts of attendance at religious services on 30-day cigarette use, shown at five points in time: senior year of high school (BY, for base year) and the first four follow-ups (FU1–FU4).

---

[2]Only the "structural" portion of the structural equation model is shown in this figure and in subsequent figures of this type.

they are actually attending). Rather, we think that there are things about the content of most religious teachings that discourage smoking (and other forms of substance use), that those attending religious services frequently are exposed to such teachings and to other people who subscribe to those teachings, and that this leads in turn to greater resistance to smoking.

Another assumption made in Fig. 4.4 is that the hypothesized causal path from religious attendance to smoking behavior is contemporaneous—that is, there are no cross-lagged paths relating religious attendance at one time to smoking behavior at a later time. We consider this assumption to be quite plausible. Whatever effects there are from religious attendance should be evident in current smoking behavior, as opposed to smoking 2 years hence.

One assumption that is *not* made is that cigarette use is a determinant of religious attendance. This reflects our view that religiosity is somewhat more fundamental, for most youth and young adults, than is smoking behavior, but this, too, is surely something of an oversimplification. For example, it is probably the case that young people who smoke a lot would find themselves somewhat unwelcome in certain religious groups (unless they showed some willingness to try to quit). But we have not tried to take account of such "reciprocal causation" in this simple model.

Finally, the model does not take account of common prior causes—factors that may affect both religious attendance and smoking. For example, young people who are rebellious may, as a consequence, be less likely to attend services and also more likely to smoke. Conversely, those who get along well with their parents may be more likely to go along to church or synagogue and less likely to take up smoking.

Why bother with such a model when we know it includes so many oversimplifications? Why should we ask anyone to "... buy the premise"? One answer is that this little model, simple as it is, is more informative than just a table of correlations. It gives us estimates of stability over time, of course; more important, it provides some perspective on how to interpret the fact that relationships between aspects of religiosity and cigarette smoking remain fairly consistent as young adults increase in age.

The perspective provided by Fig. 4.4 is that religious attendance and cigarette use are negatively related by the end of high school (a path coefficient of −.21) and that the relationship is maintained over time primarily by the high stabilities of both dimensions, but also by a small additional negative contribution (−.02 or −.03) at each point in time. The results for religious importance (reported in Bachman et al., 2001) are fairly similar to those for attendance, with the following exceptions: the stabilities for importance are slightly higher than those for attendance (as discussed earlier), the initial senior-year coefficient is a bit smaller (−.16), and the additional contributions also are smaller (−.01 or −.02).

The findings for cigarette use reflect, to a considerable extent, the fact that smoking behavior is generally very stable across time (because most regular smokers have become quite nicotine dependent). We see somewhat different patterns of results for other kinds of substance use behaviors, which are less stable over time than cigarette use (and among most young people are less likely to involve dependency).

Alcohol Use Linked to Religiosity

The United States has a long history of religious opposition to "demon rum." The evils of alcohol were much clearer to religious leaders a century ago than were the dangers of cigarette use. By the end of the 20th century, the story has changed in several ways. On one hand, the health dangers of cigarette use are now well documented. On the other hand, carefully managed moderate use of alcohol by adults has been found to have medical benefits that outweigh many of the risks (Thun et al., 1997). So "treating one's body as a temple" might not necessarily require total abstention from alcohol use. Nevertheless, some religious groups continue to view *any* alcohol use as sinful (particularly by those under legal age for purchases), and among most religious groups the heavy use or abuse of alcohol would be contrary to norms and teachings. So there is good reason to expect religiosity to be inversely related to alcohol use in general, and especially to heavy alcohol use.

Substantial majorities of young adults in our samples used alcohol at least occasionally (i.e., once or more per month). Even among the most strongly religious, as we see next, half or more were using alcohol monthly by the time they reached ages 21 or 22. Alcohol use was thus normative, at least in the statistical sense, among young adults in late 20th-century America. But having five or more drinks in a row is not moderate use; that type of alcohol consumption is widely considered to be abuse, even if done only occasionally. In this section we examine two measures of alcohol use—reports of any use during the 30 days preceding the survey and reports of consumption of five or more drinks in a row at any time in the 2 weeks preceding the survey.

Figure 4.5 shows, for those from the classes of 1976–1984, how alcohol use (any use during the past 30 days) varied by religious attendance. The curvilinear pattern noted earlier for cigarette use is evident again here; during their late teens and early twenties, roughly 60% of those who attended services weekly or more often used alcohol, whereas at the other three levels of attendance (once or twice a month, rarely, or never) the proportions were all about the same at roughly 80%. The figure also shows that among these young adults who graduated in the late 1970s and early 1980s, proportions who used alcohol rose only slightly from the senior year of high school to the second follow-up (modal ages 21–22) and thereafter declined slightly.

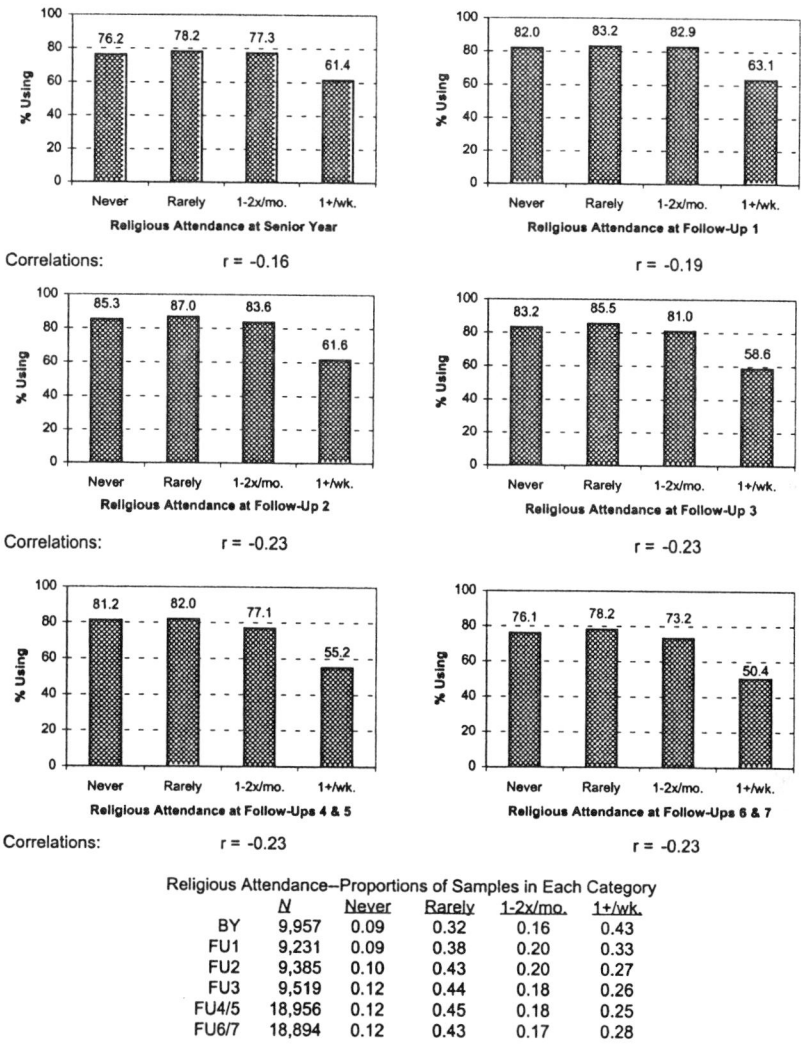

| Religious Attendance—Proportions of Samples in Each Category |||||
	N	Never	Rarely	1-2x/mo.	1+/wk.
BY	9,957	0.09	0.32	0.16	0.43
FU1	9,231	0.09	0.38	0.20	0.33
FU2	9,385	0.10	0.43	0.20	0.27
FU3	9,519	0.12	0.44	0.18	0.26
FU4/5	18,956	0.12	0.45	0.18	0.25
FU6/7	18,894	0.12	0.43	0.17	0.28

FIG. 4.5.   Thirty-day prevalence of drinking alcohol related to frequency of attendance at religious services. Percentages are based on the classes of 1976–1984 followed from age 18 to ages 29–32 (follow-ups 6 and 7, combined). The sample is restricted to those respondents who answered the questions on both 30-day alcohol use and religious attendance at follow-up 6 and/or follow-up 7. Correlations are based on the drug use measure recoded as a dichotomy.

We also examined the linkages between religious attendance and drinking using base-year and follow-up survey data averaged across years 1990–1998 (thereby revealing age-related differences during the 1990s while removing any period effects). We found curvilinear patterns of relationship with religious attendance that are very similar to those in Fig. 4.5; however, the age-related differences were more pronounced. High school seniors and recent graduates in the 1990s were less likely to drink than seniors and young adults 15 years earlier, when the minimum drinking ages in many states had been lower (data available in Bachman et al., 2001).

Analyses parallel to those for religious attendance were carried out focusing on the importance of religion, with fairly similar results. Among those in the classes of 1976–1984 who rated religion of little importance in their lives or of no importance, 80% or more had used alcohol during the past month. The percentages were nearly as high for those who rated religion as pretty important in their lives, but alcohol use was distinctly lower among those who rated religion as very important (ranging from about 53% to 63%, depending on age). Here again, when the analyses were repeated using data from the 1990–1998 surveys, relationships with importance of religion remained essentially the same, but age-related differences were more pronounced (data available in Bachman et al., 2001).

All of the analyses of the 30-day alcohol use measure were repeated using the measure of instances of heavy drinking (defined as having five or more drinks in a row at least once during the 2 weeks preceding the survey). The results of these analyses, provided in Bachman et al. (2001), are very closely consistent with the results for monthly alcohol use, except that overall frequencies were lower (although still distressingly high). Among those who attended services rarely or never and among those for whom religion was of little or no importance, rates of occasional heavy drinking reached 50% when they were in their early twenties. Among those in their early twenties for whom religion was very important and who attended services weekly or more often, rates reached 25% to 30%. So even among the most strongly religious, a surprisingly high proportion of respondents reported occasional heavy drinking; but among the least religious, rates were even higher.

Earlier in this chapter we examined the relatively stable negative relationship between religiosity and cigarette use; we concluded that it reflected primarily a pattern in place before the end of high school, plus a small additional negative contribution over time. When we carried out similar analyses linking religiosity and each dimension of alcohol use, we again found patterns clearly in place by the end of high school, but this time we also found a larger continuing contribution over time. Figure 4.6 shows the structural equation model linking religious attendance and 30-day alcohol use. Very similar results were obtained for religious attendance and instances of heavy drinking, although coefficients averaged smaller by about .02.

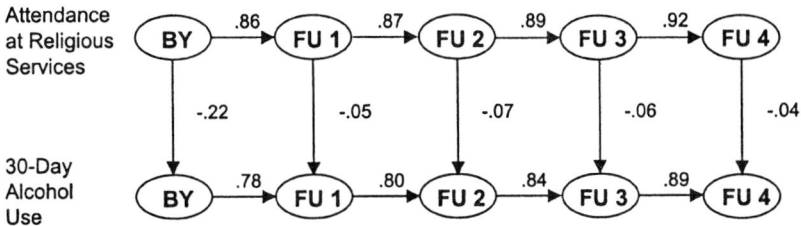

Note: This simplified model shows only the structural portion of the model; the measurement portion is not shown.

FIG. 4.6. Impacts of attendance at religious services on 30-day alcohol use, shown at five points in time: senior year of high school (BY, for base year) and the first four follow-ups (FU1–FU4).

The findings for religious importance showed much the same pattern as for religious attendance, although the coefficients this time were stronger. The structural equation model linking religious importance and 30-day alcohol use is shown in Fig. 4.7. The coefficients for importance and heavy drinking were again very similar but smaller by about .02.

We interpret the results highlighted in Figs. 4.6 and 4.7 as indicating that religiosity during young adulthood does tend to constrain alcohol use. Why should religiosity show substantially larger continuing impacts on alcohol use than on cigarette use? We think it is because by the time young adults leave high school, cigarette use patterns are essentially established and are much more stable than alcohol use. We think it is quite possible that many young adults who experience an increase in religiosity would like to be able to stop all substance use, but many of those habituated to cigarette use feel unable to do so. Of course, some young adults habituated to alcohol may similarly feel unable to quit; however, most young adult users of alcohol (or, for that matter, marijuana or cocaine) have not reached the point of dependency, whereas a high proportion of young adult cigarette smokers have (see Johnston, O'Malley, & Bachman, 2000b, p. 99).

Marijuana Use Linked to Religiosity

Religious strictures against defiling one's body (e.g., with carcinogens such as tobacco smoke) and against intoxication (e.g., heavy drinking) would certainly apply also to marijuana use, which involves both kinds of risks. Additionally, most religious traditions teach obedience to law, and throughout the period of this study marijuana use has been illegal in the United

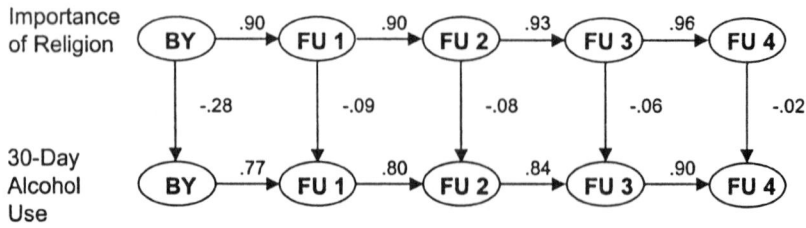

Note: This simplified model shows only the structural portion of the model;
the measurement portion is not shown.

FIG. 4.7.   Impacts of importance of religion on 30-day alcohol use, shown at five points in time: senior year of high school (BY, for base year) and the first four follow-ups (FU1–FU4).

States. So there are multiple reasons to expect marijuana use to be negatively related to religiosity.

Marijuana is used by high school seniors and young adults much less frequently than alcohol; nevertheless, substantial minorities reported some use during the past 30 days. Figure 4.8 shows, for panel respondents from the classes of 1976–1984, that marijuana use was consistently most likely among those who never attended religious services and least likely among those who attended weekly or more often. The figure also shows that as these individuals grew older, their likelihood of marijuana use decreased but the relationship with religious attendance remained consistently strong. The relationships between marijuana use and the importance of religion were much the same (as reported in Bachman et al., 2001).

Our earlier research led us to conclude that the declines in marijuana use among young adults who had been high school seniors in the late 1970s and early 1980s "reflect the joint effects of two distinctly different phenomena—(a) the overall historical decline in marijuana use (across various age groups) during much of the period; and (b) a separate set of age-related shifts (common to various class cohorts) ..." (Bachman et al., 1997, p. 112). When we reexamined the relationships between religious attendance and marijuana use across the same ages as shown in Fig. 4.8, this time using survey data from years 1990–1998 (so as to focus on age-related differences while removing any period effects), we found very similar negative correlations between religiosity and marijuana use; however, the age-related differences were smaller (data available in Bachman et al., 2001).

It is interesting to note that controlling for secular trends in the manner described here led to distinctions for alcohol use and marijuana use that

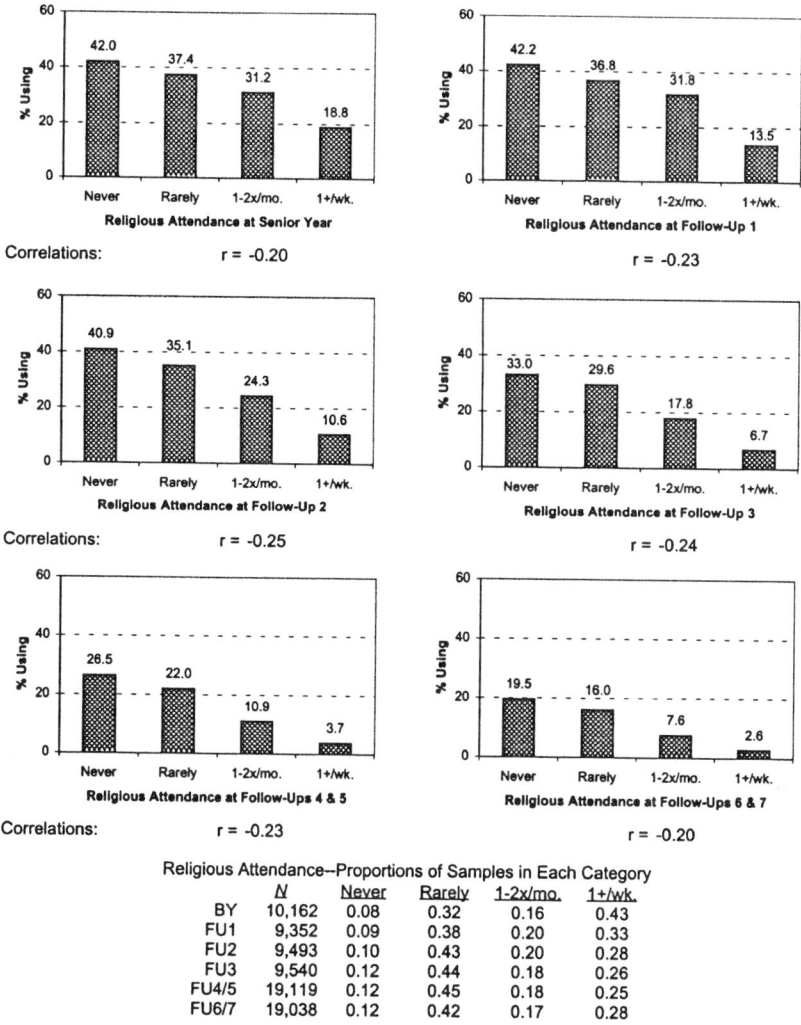

FIG. 4.8.   Thirty-day prevalence of marijuana use related to frequency of attendance at religious services. Percentages are based on the classes of 1976–1984 followed from age 18 to ages 29–32 (follow-ups 6 and 7, combined). The sample is restricted to those respondents who answered the questions on both 30-day marijuana use and religious attendance at follow-up 6 and/or follow-up 7. Correlations are based on the drug use measure recoded as a dichotomy.

were opposite in one respect and the same in another. When we focused on the same years (1990–1998) rather than the same cohorts (classes of 1976–1984), we found that the age-related differences were increased for alcohol use, whereas they were decreased for marijuana use. For both types of substance use, however, the focus on recent years showed lower rates of use among high school seniors and those in their early twenties. In other words, high school seniors in the 1990s were less likely to drink or to use marijuana than those who were seniors in the late 1970s and early 1980s. Could those declines over time in substance use reflect an overall trend of increasing religiosity? Not according to our measures; religious attendance actually declined over the same period, as noted early in this chapter. In other analyses, we demonstrated in some detail that overall declines in marijuana use during the early 1980s were not at all matched with secular trends in religiosity (Bachman, Johnston, O'Malley, & Humphrey, 1988), and recently we again demonstrated that lack of relationship across a much longer period of time (Bachman et al., 1998).

Figure 4.9 presents the structural equation model linking religious attendance and 30-day marijuana use. The pattern here is very similar to the pattern for alcohol use, with a strong link evident by the time of the senior year of high school and modest continuing contributions (negative path coefficients) from religious attendance to marijuana use. The model linking religious importance and marijuana use showed nearly identical results. We thus conclude for marijuana use, as we did regarding alcohol use, that among most young adults this form of substance use is fairly susceptible to change, and among the factors contributing to such changes in substance use are changes in religious attendance or the importance of religion or both.

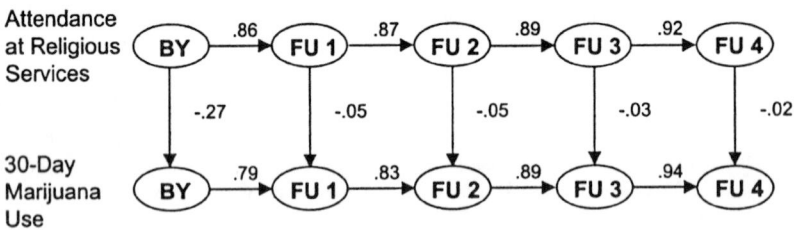

Note: This simplified model shows only the structural portion of the model; the measurement portion is not shown.

FIG. 4.9. Impacts of attendance at religious services on 30-day marijuana use, shown at five points in time: senior year of high school (BY, for base year), and the first four follow-ups (FU1–FU4).

Cocaine Use Linked to Religiosity

Just as for marijuana use, there are multiple reasons to expect cocaine use to be negatively related to religiosity. Indeed, cocaine can carry much more serious risks to health than marijuana. Cocaine use is also a more deviant behavior, at least in the statistical sense; even among those least involved in religion, only very small proportions used cocaine, as shown in Fig. 4.10. The figure shows the same sort of negative relationships as found for the other forms of substance use; it also shows that for those from the high school classes of 1976–1984 there was some increase in likelihood of cocaine use between senior year and the early twenties, after which there was a marked decline. This rise and fall in cocaine use took place largely among those who rarely or never attended religious services (or, when we focus on the other dimension of religiosity, among those who did not rate religion as very important in their lives—data available in Bachman et al., 2001).

The structural equation model linking religious attendance and 30-day cocaine use is shown in Fig. 4.11. The pattern shows that religiosity makes important additional contributions to cocaine use or nonuse during late teens and early twenties, above and beyond patterns established during high school. In other words, because cocaine use increases during early adulthood, the "protective" functions of religion also become increasingly evident during early adulthood.

Here, as was true for marijuana use, the changes in cocaine use experienced by graduates of the high school classes of 1976–1984 reflect secular trends as well as age-related factors. By 1990 cocaine use levels were distinctly lower, less differentiated by age, but still correlated with religiosity (see Bachman et al., 2001).

We conclude that religiosity is negatively linked with cocaine use and that the associations are somewhat similar to those involving marijuana use except that (a) the less frequently used cocaine (with its lesser amounts of variance to be explained) shows weaker relationships overall, and (b) the relationships grow somewhat stronger in early adulthood as usage levels increase.

Substance Use Linked to Religiosity: Summary

These findings are consistent with much other research (see citations in chap. 2) in showing that individuals high in religiosity—those who attend services most frequently and who rate religion as very important in their lives—are least likely to smoke cigarettes, use alcohol, drink heavily, or use the illicit drugs marijuana and cocaine. However, our special focus in this volume is on change and stability in young adulthood, particularly factors

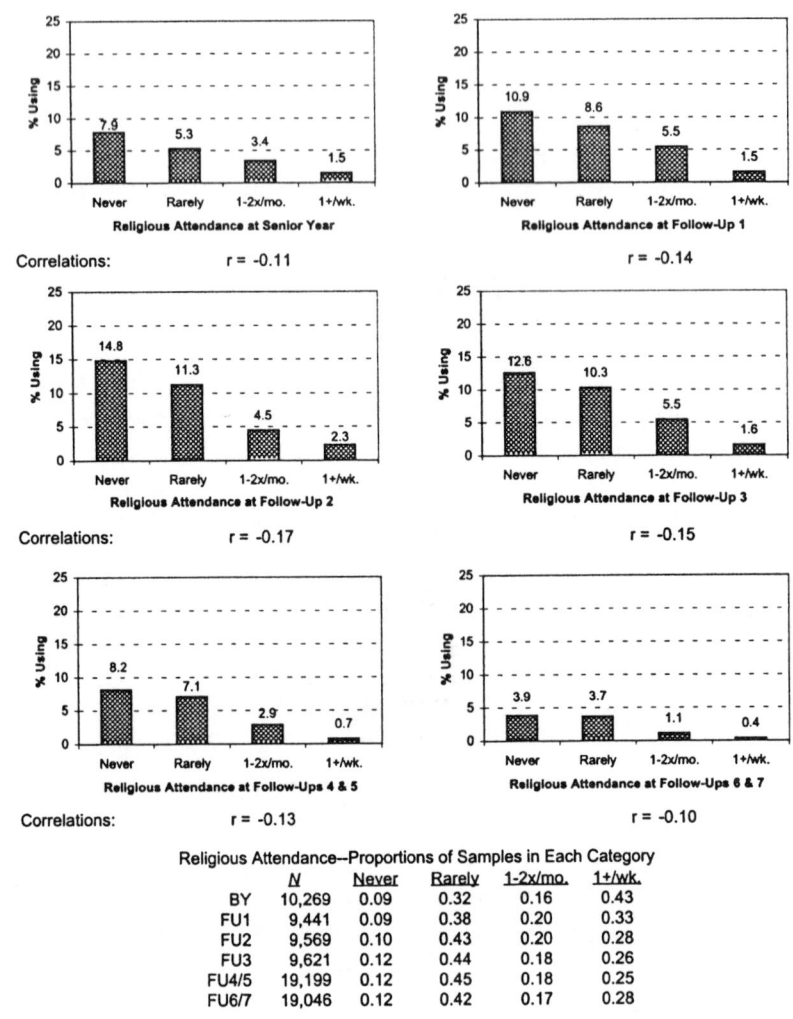

Religious Attendance--Proportions of Samples in Each Category

	N	Never	Rarely	1-2x/mo.	1+/wk.
BY	10,269	0.09	0.32	0.16	0.43
FU1	9,441	0.09	0.38	0.20	0.33
FU2	9,569	0.10	0.43	0.20	0.28
FU3	9,621	0.12	0.44	0.18	0.26
FU4/5	19,199	0.12	0.45	0.18	0.25
FU6/7	19,046	0.12	0.42	0.17	0.28

FIG. 4.10.   Thirty-day prevalence of cocaine use related to frequency of attendance at religious services. Percentages are based on the classes of 1976–1984 followed from age 18 to ages 29–32 (follow-ups 6 and 7, combined). The sample is restricted to those respondents who answered the questions on both 30-day cocaine use and religious attendance at follow-up 6 and/or follow-up 7. Correlations are based on the drug use measure recoded as a dichotomy.

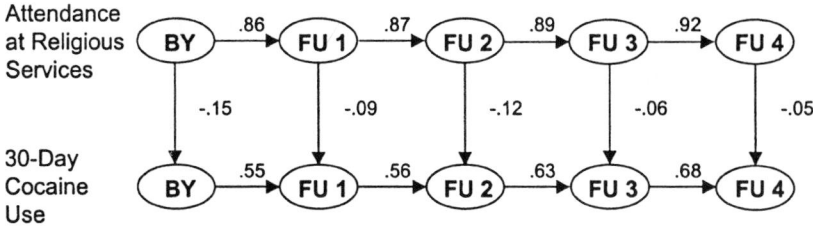

Note: This simplified model shows only the structural portion of the model; the measurement portion is not shown.

FIG. 4.11. Impacts of attendance at religious services on 30-day cocaine use, shown at five points in time: senior year of high school (BY, for base year) and the first four follow-ups (FU1–FU4).

that may contribute to changes in substance use. What we have found thus far is that both aspects of religiosity studied here, attendance and importance, are highly stable during the years of young adulthood. This stability, of course, limits the extent to which changes in substance use are likely to be attributable to changes in religiosity. Nevertheless, we found that for alcohol use, marijuana use, and cocaine use there are ongoing contributions from religiosity as shown in the structural equation models (see Figs. 4.6, 4.7, 4.9, and 4.11). For cigarette use, however, we found very little change attributable to changes in religiosity (see Fig. 4.4), and we attribute that lack of change to the overall difficulty of changing smoking habits that are largely in place before the end of high school.

The stability of religiosity sets boundaries also on the extent to which it is likely to be changed by post-high-school experiences. The next section explores whether the new freedoms and new responsibilities of young adulthood affect religious attendance and importance. But we begin our search with the knowledge that religiosity is well-ingrained by the time most young people leave high school and thus not likely to shift around much in response to other changes in lifestyle.

ANALYSES LINKING RELIGIOSITY WITH POST-HIGH-SCHOOL EXPERIENCES

Now, having examined how religiosity relates to substance use (arrow c in Fig. 1.1), we are ready to explore how a variety of post-high-school experiences are related to religiosity (arrow b). The different dimensions of post-high-school experiences and the proportions of respondents in each category at each follow-up are documented in Tables A.1.1–A.1.5. It should be noted that some of these proportions differ between males and females; in particular, women tend to become married and become parents somewhat earlier, on average, than men. Accordingly, the analyses in this section are reported separately for males and females.

As discussed in chapter 3, our analyses linking post-high-school experiences to mediating variables such as religious attendance and importance employ two types of analysis. One is a descriptive presentation of "before" and "after" scores for the mediating variable linked to various sets of post-high-school experiences (Fig. 4.12 is an example). This form of analysis shows whether there are any subgroup differences, and it also shows whether and to what extent any such differences already were present during the senior year of high school (i.e., in the "before" scores). However, the "before–after" descriptive analyses do not reveal possible overlapping effects of several different sets of post-high-school experiences. The second type of analysis overcomes this limitation; it involves multivariate "prediction" of the mediating variables. The results of these multivariate analyses are cited in the text and reported in the appendix (Tables A.4.1 for religious attendance and A.4.2 for importance). The appendix also provides a description of the analysis procedures and guidelines for interpreting the tables.

The two dimensions of religiosity showed different patterns of change, as described at the start of this chapter, with attendance declining somewhat by age and with importance showing a very slight age-related increase. Those differences notwithstanding, the two dimensions showed very similar patterns of relationship with post-high-school experiences. Because the distinctions involving attendance were generally slightly larger than those involving importance, we focus attention here on the attendance dimension. However, we have examined the importance dimension closely and report full details for both dimensions in Bachman et al. (2001).

Student Status Related to Religiosity

Figure 4.12 shows that full-time college students at follow-up were slightly above average in religious attendance, nonstudents were slightly below average, and part-time students were just about average. However, the figure also shows exactly the same pattern of differences at senior year, before the college-bound and noncollege-bound left high school. The figure further shows that after high school all groups declined slightly in levels of attendance. Finally, this figure and those that follow show that women report higher religious attendance than men on average; women also average higher in their ratings of the importance of religion in their lives.

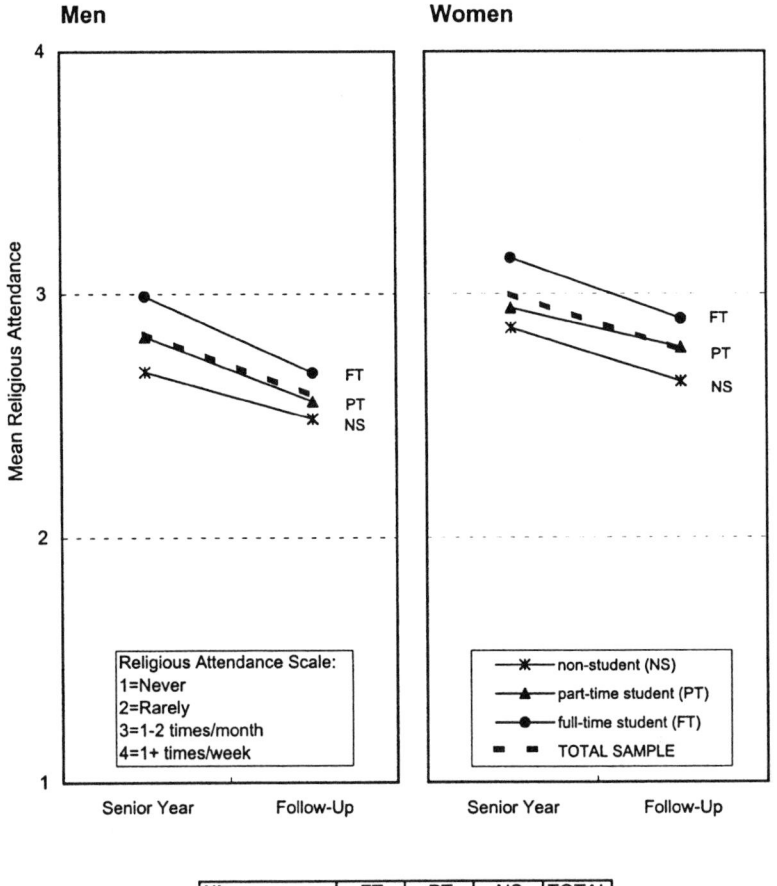

FIG. 4.12. Change in mean attendance at religious services related to student status at the time of follow-up. High school seniors from the classes of 1976–1984 were followed up twice between modal ages 19 and 22. In this figure, one person could contribute up to two follow-up observations (see Additional Panel Analysis Issues and Strategies section in chap. 3). The approximate standard deviations for religious attendance at senior year were 0.93 for males and 0.93 for females.

The figure provides no evidence that post-high-school student status contributes to religious attendance, because the differences were clearly in evidence before the end of high school. However, it is worth noting that high school grades and college plans show modest positive correlations with senior-year religiosity (see next to last column in Tables A.4.1–A.4.2). In sum, although going to college does not seem to make individuals more religious, it does appear that highly religious individuals are somewhat more likely than average to do well in high school and also more likely to attend college. This is the first example, in this book, of a pattern that appears often: panel data showing that differences observed during young adulthood were well established before the end of high school. Obviously, if we were limited to the young adult data only, we would not be able to identify such preexisting differences.

Employment Status Related to Religiosity

We distinguished five categories of employment in these analyses: full-time employment, part-time employment, nonemployment (and not a student), full-time homemaking, and military service. Religious attendance differed only modestly among these categories; the importance of religion varied even less; and only two patterns of change departed from the overall averages. First, among women who identified their occupation as homemaker, the importance of religion increased to above average between base-year and follow-up, and religious attendance declined scarcely at all (which was much less than the average decline). The multivariate analyses (see Tables A.4.1–A.4.2) indicate that these departures from average overlap to some extent, but not entirely, with other predictors—especially parenthood and marriage. It should be noted that among males, only 0.3% of follow-up responses listed homemaker as occupation; nevertheless, these men showed the same sort of relative increase in religiosity as did the female homemakers.

A second departure from average involved the 0.6% of female follow-up responses indicating military service as the occupation. These women in the armed forces showed greater than average declines in religious attendance as well as a very slight relative decline in religious importance. Neither finding appeared among men in military service.

Living Arrangements and Marital Status Related to Religiosity

Our analyses combined marital status with five other categories of living arrangements. We did this because we were interested primarily in the interpersonal aspects of living arrangements. Among all the living arrangements, being married (and thus living with a spouse) is likely to be the most permanent and also the most important in terms of interpersonal relationships.

Figure 4.13 displays base-year and follow-up means for each of the six living arrangements categories. A quick overview reveals that all categories show an overall decline in attendance, that there is a modest amount of *differential* change, and that there are larger ongoing differences among groups—that is, differences that were evident during high school and thus preceded selection into different living arrangements.

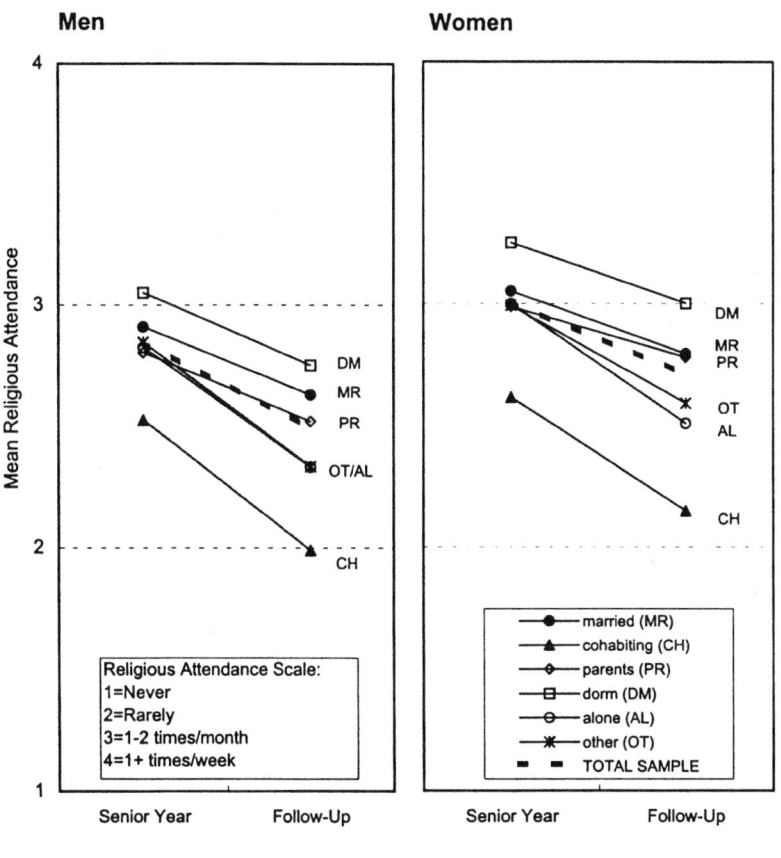

N's	M	CH	PR	DM	AL	OT	TOTAL
Men	15,796	3,167	11,816	2,257	4,569	7,816	45,421
Women	23,558	4,377	11,873	2,543	3,782	7,462	53,595

FIG. 4.13.   Change in mean attendance at religious services related to living arrangement at the time of follow-up. High school seniors from the classes of 1976–1984 were followed up as many as seven times between modal ages 19 and 32. In this figure, one person could contribute up to seven follow-up observations (see Additional Panel Analysis Issues and Strategies section in chap. 3). The approximate standard deviations for religious attendance at senior year were 0.93 for males and 0.93 for females.

Being Married. Figure 4.13 shows that those married at follow-up were a bit above average in their attendance at religious services, but they also were slightly above average in high school. The multivariate analyses showed a small positive contribution of marriage to the religious attendance of men, but not women (shown in Table A.4.1). The findings for religious importance (shown in Table A.4.2) were much the same.

Cohabiting. Those living unmarried with a partner of the opposite sex were lower than average along both dimensions of religiosity, but as can be seen in Fig. 4.13, the same was true when they were seniors in high school (and not cohabiting). So, not surprisingly, these data show that young people with a history of low religious involvement and commitment are more likely than average to spend some of their early adulthood in unmarried cohabitation. It appears also that when cohabiting occurs, it may contribute further to low religiosity; specifically, cohabitants showed greater than average declines in religious attendance (Fig. 4.13 and Table A.4.1) and in religious importance (Table A.4.2).

Living With Parents. Those living with their parents at the time of follow-up showed just about average rates of attendance at that time and also when they were high school seniors. The same is true for importance of religion (Table A.4.2).

Living in a Dormitory. As expected, given the findings for full-time students, those living in dormitories were above average in religiosity—both attendance (shown in Fig. 4.13) and importance (Table A.4.2). Here again, equally large distinctions were present by the senior year of high school, so there is no evidence to suggest that dormitory life—or student life in general—leads to any further increase in religiosity.

Living Alone and in Other Living Arrangements. Among those not included in any of the previously listed four living arrangements, we distinguished between those living alone and those in all remaining living arrangements (which typically includes living in apartments or houses with several others, but which also includes military barracks or shared off-base housing). As is shown in Fig. 4.13, religious attendance for both living alone and other living arrangements were very similar; attendance had been average when these individuals were seniors in high school (and living in their parents' or guardians' homes), but was slightly below average at the time of follow-up. The same is true for importance of religion (Table A.4.2).

Pregnancy and Parenthood Related to Religiosity

Pregnancy. Women who are pregnant, and men with pregnant spouses, may be more likely than average to feel new responsibilities as they anticipate the impending birth. As we reported in Bachman et al. (1997), pregnant women were more likely than average to decrease smoking tobacco and also marijuana and were much more likely than average to reduce or stop their use of alcohol. These reductions in substance use could be the direct result of health warnings and the desire to avoid damage to fetuses. Perhaps also involved is some broader commitment to religious activities and teachings; if so, pregnancy might be expected to be associated with greater than average religious attendance and importance.

The present analyses revealed that pregnant women, as well as men with pregnant spouses, were slightly above average along both dimensions of religiosity. To a considerable degree those differences were evident at the end of high school, however, and thus could not be attributable to pregnancy. Additionally, the changes overlap the broader effects of marriage, such that for men the changes associated with having a *pregnant* spouse are little different from the changes simply associated with having *any* spouse (documented in Tables A.4.1 and A.4.2). So it seems likely that any declines in drug use resulting from pregnancy are due more to specific health concerns than to fundamental shifts in religiosity.

Parenthood. Most religious traditions stress the responsibilities of parents to raise their children "in the faith." We thus might expect parenthood to increase religiosity—both importance and attendance. Of course, most parents are married; thus, differences associated with parenthood might really be due at least in part to marriage. Significant numbers of parents in our samples were not married, however, so it was useful to examine data for nonmarried (i.e., single) parents as well. Our earlier research showed that drug use data were often different for these two groups of parents; thus, we continued in the present analyses to treat single and married parenthood separately.

As is shown in Fig. 4.14, those who were married parents at the time of follow-up were above average in levels of attendance at religious services. Although these individuals had also been slightly above average while they were high school seniors, the shift associated with married parenthood (actually, a partial "resistance" to the overall decline in attendance among young adults) was greater than that associated with marriage or with pregnancy (shown in Table A.4.1). Ratings of religious importance increased among married parents, and here again the changes were slightly larger than those associated with marriage or with pregnancy (Table A.4.2).

Single parents, in contrast, were below average in attendance; however, they were equally below average in attendance while they were in high school long before they became parents (see Fig. 4.14 and Table A.4.1). It thus appears that less frequent attendance at religious services is (slightly) predictive of becoming a single parent. Interestingly, the single parents were

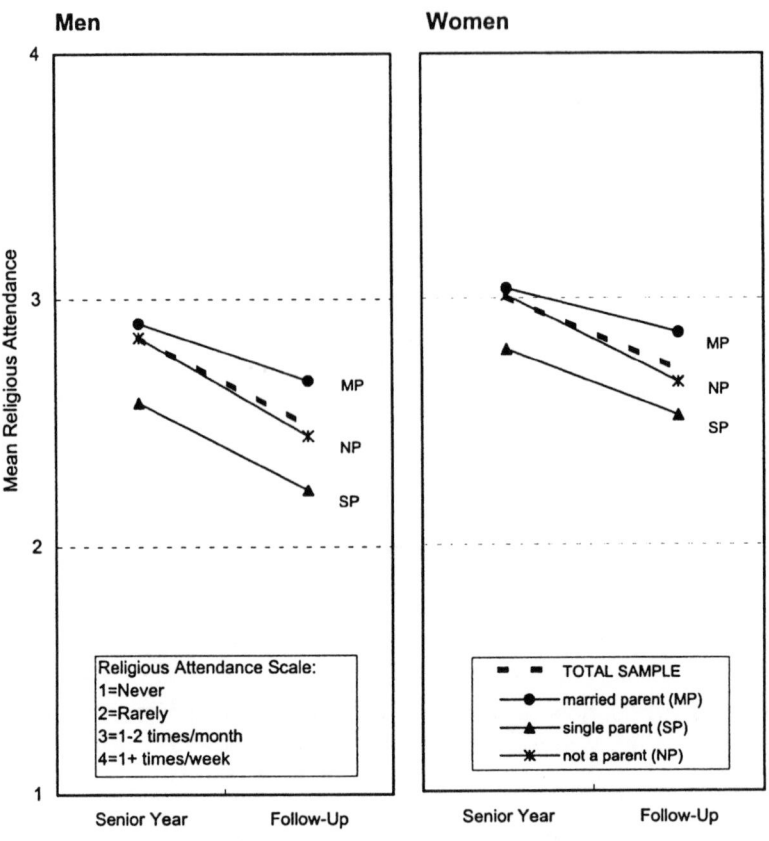

N's	MP	SP	NP	TOTAL
Men	9,554	2,006	33,861	45,421
Women	14,582	3,607	35,406	53,595

FIG. 4.14.   Change in mean attendance at religious services related to parenthood status at the time of follow-up. High school seniors from the classes of 1976–1984 were followed up as many as seven times between modal ages 19 and 32. In this figure, one person could contribute up to seven follow-up observations (see Additional Panel Analysis Issues and Strategies section in chap. 3). The approximate standard deviations for religious attendance at senior year were 0.93 for males and 0.93 for females.

not substantially different from nonparents in their professions of the importance of religion in their lives (see Table A.4.2)—they were simply less likely to attend.

Further Findings on Marital Status and Religiosity

Engagement. We already noted that religiosity was slightly above average among those who married and distinctly below average among those cohabiting but not married. Another important distinction is whether respondents were engaged to be married. Earlier research showed "engagement effects" on drug use similar to the "marriage effects." Figure 4.15 illustrates that religious attendance differed between those who were engaged at follow-up and those who were not; some of these distinctions reflect relatively stable differences, but some reflect differential change (see also Tables A.4.1 and A.4.2). Among cohabitants, engagement was associated with slightly higher religiosity at both base-year and follow-up. Similarly, religiosity was slightly higher among those who were engaged but not cohabiting, compared with other singles who were not cohabiting.

Divorce. We also examined differences in religiosity linked to divorce, using data from all 2-year follow-up intervals. During the 2-year intervals, some married individuals continued to be married whereas others became divorced, some who had been divorced remained divorced and others remarried, and some who were single remained single whereas others married or became engaged. On the whole, our analyses revealed very little in the way of differential change in religiosity linked to these marital transitions. However, we did find slightly lower than average levels of religiosity among those who became or remained divorced; we also found slight increases in religiosity among those who made the transition from divorced to remarried—consistent with the more general positive link between marriage and religiosity (data available in Bachman et al., 2001).

Conclusions Based on Multivariate Analyses

Our multivariate analysis approach was outlined in chapter 3 and is detailed in the appendix. Tables in the appendix provide multivariate analyses linking post-high-school experiences with religious attendance (Table A.4.1) and religious importance (Table A.4.2).

We begin with several general observations. First, the multivariate results for the two dimensions of religiosity are quite similar; accordingly, we continue our practice of focusing on attendance. Second, religiosity at the end of high school (base year) is by far the most powerful predictor of fol-

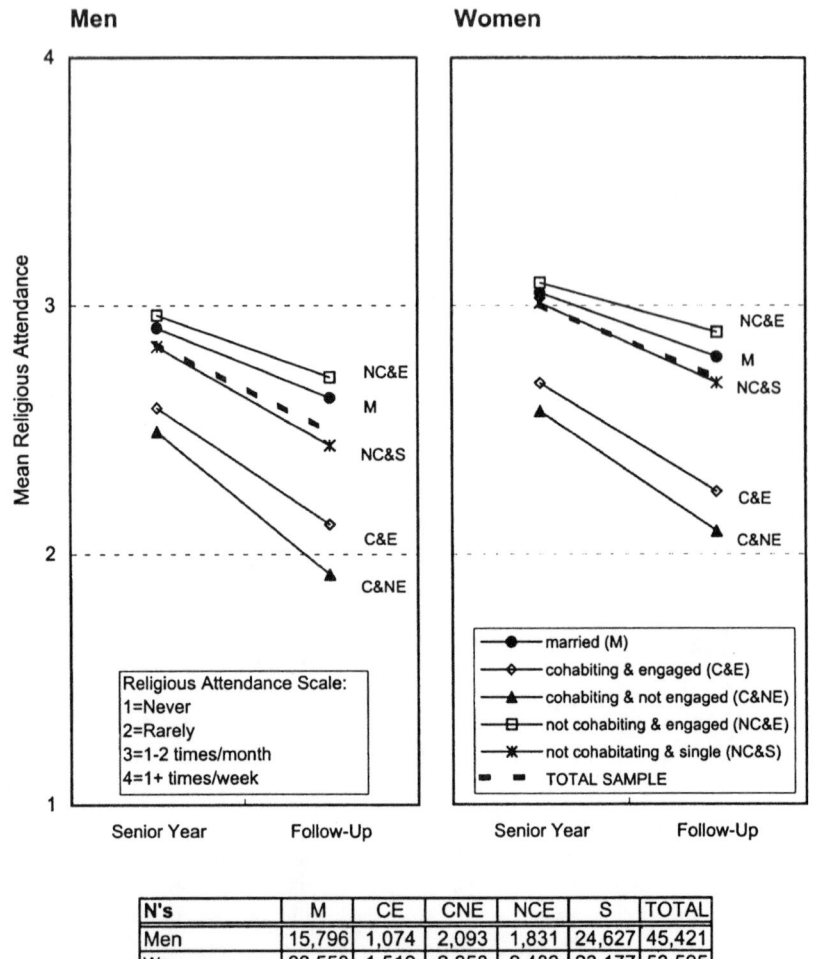

FIG. 4.15. Change in mean attendance at religious services related to engagement, cohabitation, and marriage at the time of follow-up. High school seniors from the classes of 1976–1984 were followed up as many as seven times between modal ages 19 and 32. In this figure, one person could contribute up to seven follow-up observations (see Additional Panel Analysis Issues and Strategies section in chap. 3). The approximate standard deviations for religious attendance at senior year were 0.93 for males and 0.93 for females.

low-up religiosity (as shown near the bottom of the last column of Table A.4.1 and also Table A.4.2); this matches the finding reported earlier in this chapter that religiosity shows very high stability over time. Third, consistent with this high stability, the overall amounts of variance explained in the religiosity *change scores* are quite low; in other words, if religiosity does not change very much during young adulthood, then it is understandable that there are not strong effects attributable to post-high-school experiences. Fourth, comparisons among the several columns in Tables A.4.1 and A.4.2 can nevertheless provide further insights about the ways in which the several categories of predictors overlap.

Our examination of the tables reveals that what we have called *background variables* can account for 1.1% of variance in religious attendance change scores among females and 1.6% among males. Adding measures of student and work status along with the living arrangements measures explains an additional 1.1% among females and 1.3% among males above and beyond the variance explained by the background variables. More detailed multivariate analyses (Bachman et al., 2001) reveal that most of the small contribution of student and work status overlaps with living arrangements (the unique contribution to explained variance made by student and work status is only 0.1%).

Background Factors.   Table A.4.1 shows that two of the background variables account for most of the explained variance. The first of these variables is race, with African American respondents showing smaller than average declines in attendance (the coefficients actually are positive, but not nearly as large as the overall negative constant). The table also shows that African Americans were above average in religious attendance at base year (senior year of high school). Table A.4.2 shows that African Americans had far higher ratings of the importance of religion while they were in high school, and their importance ratings increased a bit more than average at follow-up. We must add a note of caution about the panel data on African Americans: Sample attrition was greater than average for this subgroup, thus placing some limits on representativeness. That said, it is worth adding that these patterns observed in the retained panel samples appear also in cross-sectional reports based on the total senior-year samples (e.g., Johnston, Bachman, & O'Malley, 1997).

The other "background" factor that relates to religious attendance is follow-up number, which is really a proxy for age. We noted earlier the age-related decline in attendance, which we suggested may reflect, at least in part, a downward historical trend or "period effect." Table A.4.1 shows some "unmasking" or enhancement of this age-related or historical trend when other factors are controlled; specifically, the pattern becomes a bit stronger and more linear after controlling for other factors that may contribute to age-related differences (e.g., increasing proportions who were married and were parents). Also consistent with our earlier observations about little or no historical trend in religious *importance*, Table A.4.2 shows little relationship between importance and follow-up number.

Living Arrangements, Including Marital Status and Parenthood.
Tables A.4.1 and A.4.2 confirm several observations made earlier in this
chapter. Religiosity appeared to be negatively affected by unmarried cohabitation, but positively affected by being engaged and by being a married parent. Interestingly, several of these relationships involving attendance
actually were larger in the multivariate analyses (third column of Table
A.4.1) than in the bivariate analysis (first column). As noted, older respondents showed more of the downward historical trend in religious attendance, but the older individuals were also more likely to be married and
have children (producing modest positive effects on attendance); therefore, these opposite effects tended to cancel each other until "unmasked" in
the multivariate analysis.

SUMMARY

Two aspects of religiosity, frequency of attendance and importance, were
found to be highly correlated among high school students and young adults;
however, they showed some differences in patterns of change and thus were
analyzed separately in this chapter. Religious attendance dropped among
the young adults followed in our samples; some of that decline appears attributable to certain post-high-school experiences (e.g., leaving parents'
homes), but some also may have been a reflection of a broader downward
secular trend in attendance during that period.

Overall, the most impressive aspect of the religiosity measures in these
panel analyses is not change but stability. To a very considerable extent, patterns of religiosity seem to be firmly in place by the end of high school.
Changes occur, to be sure, and new family responsibilities tend to increase
religiosity. Nevertheless, it remains true that by far the most important predictor of religiosity in young adulthood is religiosity during high school.

Religiosity shows strong negative relationships with substance use. In the
case of cigarette use, the most stable of the substance-using behaviors studied here, the links with religiosity are strong at the end of high school and
change little thereafter. The usage patterns for the other substances—alcohol, marijuana, and cocaine—are less firmly fixed by the end of high school.
Accordingly, religiosity during young adulthood appears to make some continuing (negative) contribution to the use of each of these substances.

Do the new freedoms and responsibilities show their impacts on substance use primarily via changes in religiosity? The answer is complicated.
On one hand, the links between religiosity and substance use are substantial. On the other hand, religiosity is well established by the end of high
school and is only modestly affected by post-high-school experiences. So although religiosity seems to play some part as a mediating variable, it is surely
not the only one.

5

Time Spent on Various Social and Recreational Activities

Nearly all high school seniors report that typically they "go out for fun and recreation" at least one evening per week, most report doing so two or three evenings, and nearly a quarter go out more often. Going out provides the opportunity to do things with friends, often away from the supervision of parents. For some young people these evenings away from home provide the chance to initiate (and continue) cigarette use. For many more young people, evenings away from home sometimes include consumption of alcohol. And for some individuals, the evenings out provide opportunities for using marijuana, cocaine, or other illicit drugs.

Given that evenings out provide such opportunities for substance use, it is not surprising to find that high school students who spend the most evenings out for fun and recreation are also the most likely to smoke, drink, and use illicit drugs. Indeed, evenings out and substance use are so closely related as to make causal interpretation quite complicated. On one hand, for most high school students being out of the home is a necessary, or at least highly facilitating, condition for substance use. On the other hand, the desire to smoke, drink, or do drugs may be an important reason why some young people choose to spend frequent evenings out "for fun and recreation."

In this chapter we explore evenings out for fun and recreation, as well as a number of related activities such as going out on dates, attending parties or other social affairs, visiting bars (or taverns or nightclubs), and getting together with friends informally. Our reporting of analysis results follows the general approach used in the previous chapter. We focus first on how these recreational behaviors change during young adulthood. Then we examine how these behaviors are related to substance use. Finally, we explore how evenings out and related behaviors seem to be influenced by the new freedoms and responsibilities of young adulthood.

PATTERNS OF AGE-RELATED CHANGE IN EVENINGS OUT AND RELATED BEHAVIORS

Obviously, there is a great deal of overlap in the social and recreational behaviors that are the topic of this chapter. Consider just one example: a young man or woman could spend an evening out for fun and recreation, with a date, attending a party, held in a nightclub. Indeed, except for occasions hosted in one's own home, nearly all dates, parties, and informal get-togethers also involve evenings out for fun and recreation. Accordingly, our primary focus in this chapter is on the evenings-out measure, which is a key survey item included in all of the Monitoring the Future senior year and follow-up questionnaires. Data on the other behaviors listed are introduced more briefly (although each dimension has been analyzed extensively, and backup tables and figures are reported in Bachman et al., 2001).

Evenings Out for Fun and Recreation

Figure 5.1 shows how the frequency of evenings out for fun and recreation declined steadily and substantially for young men after age 20 and for young women after age 18. Combining the top two categories in the figure, we can see that whereas at age 18 (end of the senior year of high school) only 18% (i.e., 6.2% and 11.8%) of young men and 23% of young women reported going out one or fewer days per week, by ages 31–32 the proportions were 59% and 69% (respectively). And whereas at age 18 about half (52% of men, 48% of women) reported going out three or more times per week, by ages 31–32 only 15% of men and 11% of women did so.

There were no important secular trends in this dimension; that is, the patterns of evenings out were much the same across senior classes from 1976 through 1998. We are thus confident in concluding that the changes shown in Fig. 5.1 represent age-related shifts with no confounding historical changes during the period under study. (Incidentally, the same is true for all social and recreational behaviors studied in this chapter, with one interesting exception noted later.)

The age-related declines in evenings out are not, of course, a simple function of aging. Rather, they appear to be largely, but not entirely, explainable in

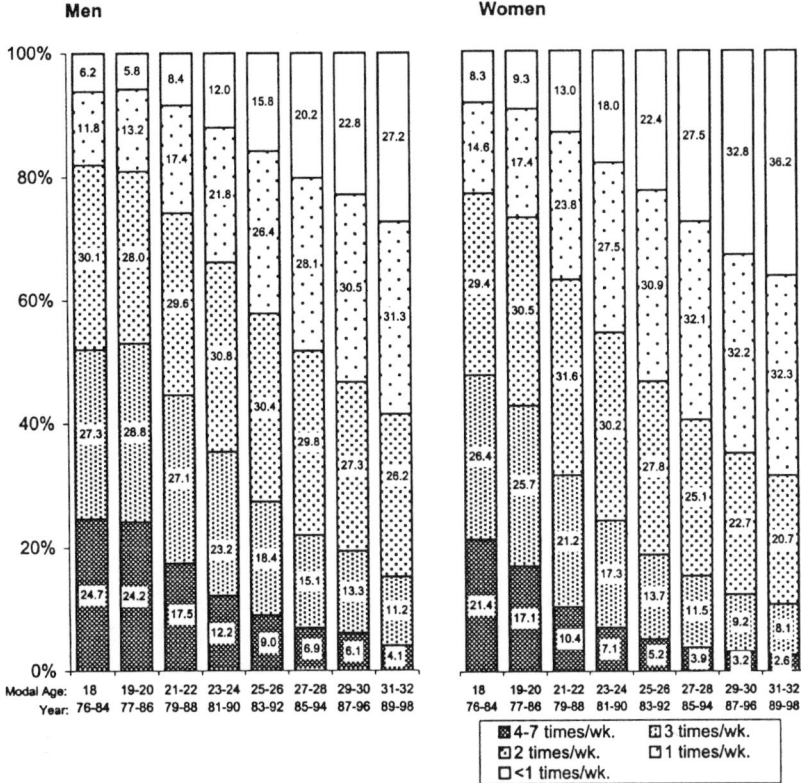

FIG. 5.1. Number of evenings out for fun and recreation per week for panel respondents followed from age 18 to ages 31–32. Bar percentages are based on high school senior data, plus follow-ups 1–7, from class years 1976–1984; one person could contribute up to seven follow-up observations (see Additional Panel Analysis Issues and Strategies section in chap. 3). The sample is restricted to those respondents who answered this question at follow-up 6 and/or follow-up 7. Approximate numbers of observations per age group for men: 4,400; for women: 5,400. Inasmuch as there were no major secular trends in 12th grade data, evenings out is not compared to the average high school senior class data for each year range.

terms of the new responsibilities that emerge during young adulthood. We provide evidence in support of this proposition later in the chapter. First, however, let us consider changes in several other more specific behaviors and note how each of these behaviors is related to substance use.

Going Out With a Date or Spouse

One of the questions asked of all Monitoring the Future respondents was this: "On the average, how often do you go out with a date (or your spouse, if you are married)?" Dating is, of course, one of the things that high school students and young adults do when they spend an evening out for fun and recreation. For respondents in 1990–1998, the dating and evenings-out measures correlated .35 among high school seniors (shown in Table A.2.1), and the correlations rose to .47 for the last four follow-ups (modal ages 25–32, shown in Table A.2.3). It thus appears that going out with a date or spouse represents a larger portion of total evenings out as young adults reach their late twenties and early thirties.

Further evidence is available in Fig. 5.2, which shows how answers to the dating question changed between ages 18 and 31–32; it is clear that the trajectory is distinctly different from that for total evenings out shown in Fig. 5.1. As high school seniors, about 2 out of 3 respondents (65% of young men and 67% of young women) reported dating 1 to 3 times per month, or more often, on average (bottom four categories in Fig. 5.2 combined). Among men, this rose to 72% at ages 21–22, stayed nearly the same through ages 25–26 (70%), and then declined gradually to 58% by ages 31–32. Among women, it rose to 73% at ages 21–22 and then declined steadily to 47% at ages 31–32. In other words, by their later twenties and early thirties, men were dating somewhat more often than women, on average.

Who were the men in the later follow-ups dating if fewer of the women at that age were dating? A closer look at Fig. 5.2 suggests the answer. During their late teens and early twenties, higher proportions of young women than young men were dating frequently (2–3 times a week, or over 3 times a week); clearly, at least some of these women were dating men who were (at least slightly) older. Two other age differences between men and women are consistent with, and help explain, the differences in dating frequencies. First, at any given age throughout the late teens and twenties, higher proportions of women than men are married; indeed, in our samples the marriage rates for men lagged behind those for women by almost 2 years (see Table A.1.4). Second, the women in our samples also became parents at an earlier age, on average, than the men (Table A.1.5); this is particularly important because, as we spell out later in this chapter, it is parenthood rather than marriage that sharply reduces the frequency of dating. In sum, it appears that by their late twenties and early thirties fewer women than men go out often with a date or spouse, because larger proportions of women at that age are "tied down" by parenthood.

Going to Parties or Other Social Affairs

One of the Monitoring the Future questionnaire forms (administered to one fifth, and in later years, one sixth, of the total samples) includes a question series asking how often the respondent does each of a number of things. One

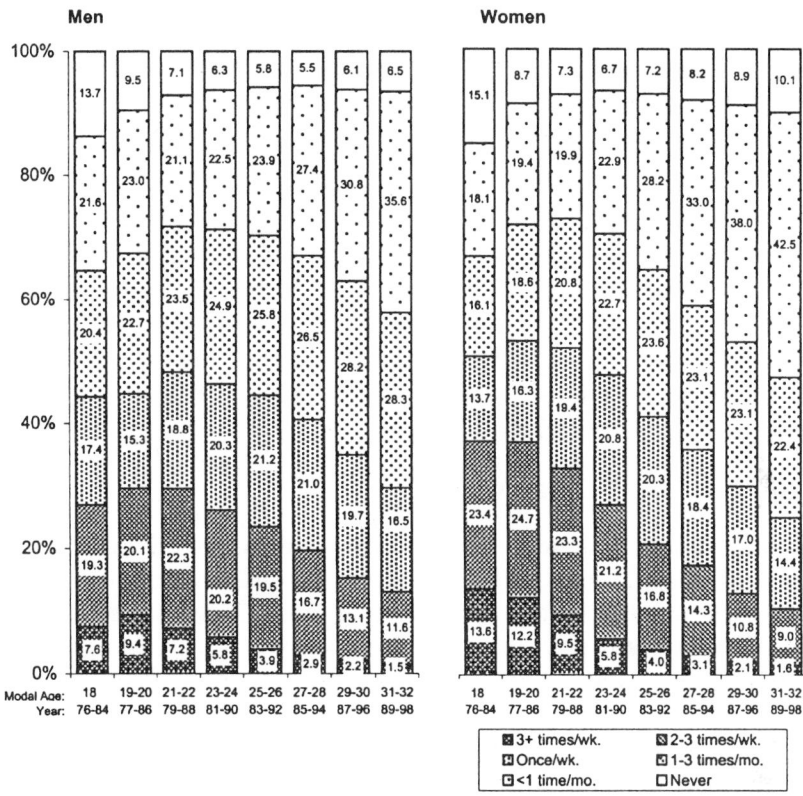

FIG. 5.2. Frequency of going out with a date (or spouse if married) for panel respondents followed from age 18 to ages 31–32. Bar percentages are based on high school senior data, plus follow-ups 1–7, from class years 1976–1984; one person could contribute up to seven follow-up observations (see Additional Panel Analysis Issues and Strategies section in chap. 3). The sample is restricted to those respondents who answered this question at follow-up 6 and/or follow-up 7. Approximate numbers of observations per age group for men: 4,400; for women: 5,400. Inasmuch as there were no major secular trends in 12th grade data, dating is not compared to the average high school senior class data for each year range.

item is "Go to parties or other social affairs"; another is "Get together with friends, informally." We view these two items as capturing related but distinguishable portions of a "socializing" continuum, one informal and the other somewhat more structured. As Tables A.2.1–A.2.3 show, responses to the two items were fairly highly correlated with each other and with frequency of evenings out (r values range from .35 to .49), and all three items showed similar patterns of relations with substance use and other measures. We focus on the measure of going to parties and other social affairs because it showed somewhat stronger correlations and also larger changes over time. Further findings for the measure of informal getting together with friends can be seen in Tables A.2.1–A.2.3 and also in Bachman et al. (2001).

Figure 5.3 shows, for both men and women, a strong and steady age-related decline in attending parties and other social affairs; combining the bottom two categories in the figure, 74% of men and 71% of women at age 18 attended at least 1–2 times a month on average, whereas by ages 31–32 only 29% of men and 25% of women did so. Getting together with friends informally occurred more frequently than going to parties and other social affairs, but the informal get-togethers also declined steadily from age 18, when 90% of men and 86% of women reported doing so at least once a week on average, to ages 31–32, when only 41% (of both men and women) reported doing so (data not shown, but available in Bachman et al., 2001).

Going to Taverns, Bars, and Nightclubs

Another item included in the question series previously described asks how often respondents "Go to taverns, bars, or nightclubs." Figure 5.4 shows that when our respondents were high school seniors (classes of 1976–1984), 41% of the men and 31% of the women reported that they visited such establishments 1–2 times monthly or more often (bottom two categories combined). Several years later, by the time they were 21–22, the proportions visiting 1–2 times monthly increased to 68% of the men and 55% of the women. Thereafter, the rates declined steadily, and by ages 31–32 only 38% of men and 23% of women went to taverns, bars, or nightclubs as often as 1–2 times per month. It is not surprising that visits to such establishments increased as respondents reached ages 21–22; increasing numbers of states during that period (late 1970s to late 1980s) had minimum ages of 21 for sale of alcoholic beverages, thus making it less attractive (and often less possible) for those ages 18–20 to visit taverns, bars, and nightclubs. Nor is it surprising that such visits began to decline, on average, once young adults passed ages 21–22; as we show later in this chapter, the same kinds of new responsibilities associated with a general decline in evenings out are associated also with declining visits to taverns, bars, and nightclubs.

It is worth noting that during the period in which respondents from the classes of 1976–1984 were moving through their twenties and into their thirties, the frequency of visits to bars, taverns, or nightclubs reported by successive classes of high school seniors declined, as shown by the X notations in Fig. 5.4. This is not, however, a broad historic trend applying to most ages; rather, it reflects the fact that increasing numbers of states adopted a minimum age of 21 for selling and serving alcohol (O'Malley & Wagenaar, 1991).

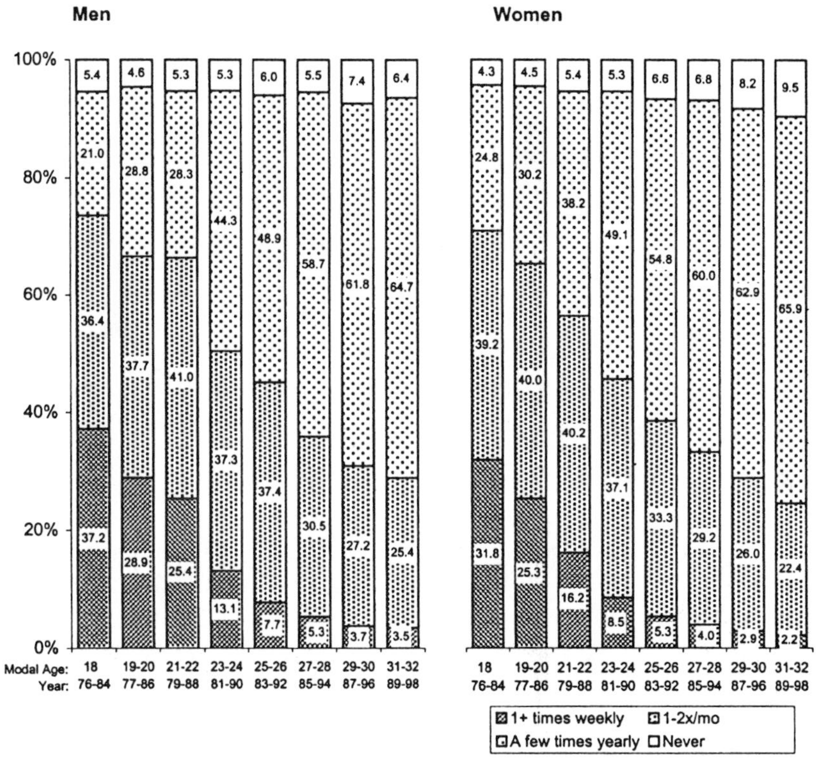

FIG. 5.3.   Frequency of attending parties or other social affairs for panel respondents followed from age 18 to ages 31–32. Bar percentages are based on high school senior data, plus follow-ups 1–7, from class years 1976–1984; one person could contribute up to seven follow-up observations (see Additional Panel Analysis Issues and Strategies section in chap. 3). The sample is restricted to those respondents who answered this question at follow-up 6 and/or follow-up 7. Approximate numbers of observations per age group for men: 880; for women: 1,090. Inasmuch as there were no major secular trends in 12th grade data, attending parties is not compared to the average high school senior class data for each year range.

HOW CHANGES IN EVENINGS OUT ARE LINKED WITH CHANGES IN SUBSTANCE USE

Now, having examined age-related changes in evenings out and other so-cial–recreational behaviors, we are ready to begin linking these possible me-diating variables with drug use and with post-high-school roles and responsibilities. As in chapter 4, we begin by working backward from sub-stance use (i.e., arrow c in Fig. 1.1).

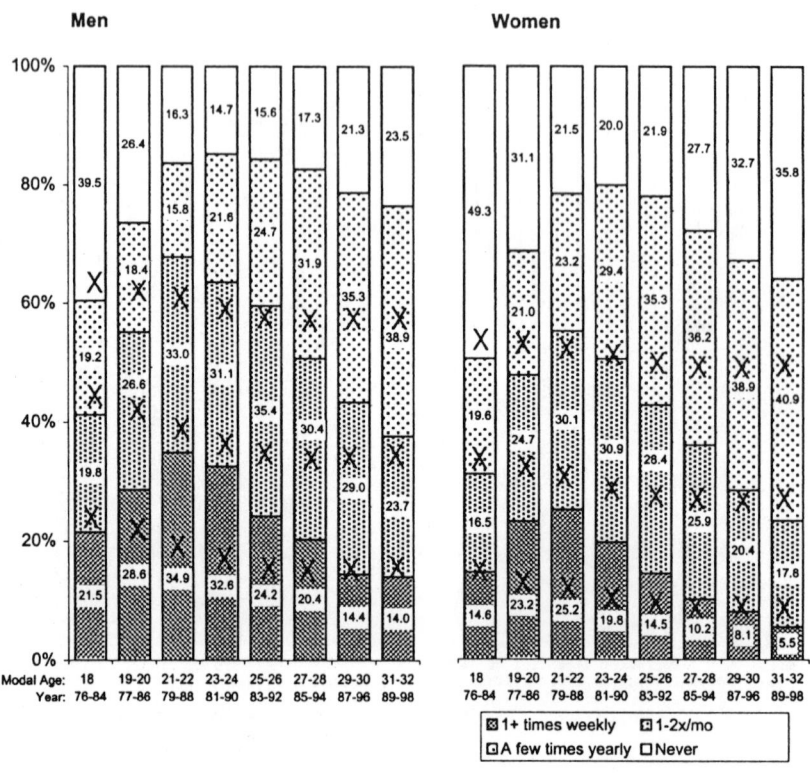

FIG. 5.4. Frequency of visits to bars, taverns, or nightclubs for panel respondents followed from age 18 to ages 31–32. Bar percentages are based on high school senior data, plus follow-ups 1–7, from class years 1976–1984; one person could contribute up to seven follow-up observations (see Additional Panel Analysis Issues and Strategies section in chap. 3). The sample is restricted to those respondents who answered this question at follow-up 6 and/or follow-up 7. Approximate numbers of observations per age group for men: 880; for women: 1,090. X notations demarcate the boundaries between the frequency of visits to bars, taverns, or nightclubs categories for the senior year data within the given year ranges. Senior samples include approximately 69,000 men and 72,000 women in each year grouping.

As noted earlier, high school seniors who spend the most evenings out for fun and recreation are also most likely to smoke, drink, and use illicit drugs. Do these positive relationships between evenings out and various types of substance use continue to hold true during young adulthood? In the previous chapter we noted that the negative relationships between religiosity and substance use held fairly strong, but for somewhat different reasons depending on the substance. In the case of cigarette use, the links remained strong primarily because of the very high stability of smoking and of religiosity. For alcohol use and illicit drug use, on the other hand, religiosity apparently made some ongoing contribution; its impact was not limited to initial distinctions evident at the end of high school.

In this chapter we find that the positive relationships between evenings out and substance use eventually decline somewhat as young people go through their twenties. Here again, the patterns differ by substance, with the highly stable behavior of cigarette use standing in contrast to the other kinds of substance use. We also see that evenings out for fun and recreation shows less stability during young adulthood than religiosity.

Change and Stability in Evenings Out

Simple structural equation models introduced in the preceding chapter showed 2-year stability estimates for the religiosity measures starting near .90 and growing even stronger during the mid-twenties, thus indicating very high stability indeed. Not surprisingly, models involving evenings out yield distinctly lower estimates. The estimated stability (i.e., "true" or error-free correlation) for evenings out between the end of high school (modal age 18) and the first follow-up 1 or 2 years later is about .68; for subsequent 2-year intervals the coefficients rise to about .71, .79, and .91 (with minor variations depending on which drug use behavior is included in the model). There is thus a lot more shifting around in patterns of evening recreational behavior during young adulthood than in religiosity—again, not a surprising finding.

It is interesting to note that by the last 2-year interval included in the stability models, between modal ages 23–24 and 25–26, young adults seem to become settled when it comes to frequency of evenings out for fun and recreation. As we see later, frequency of evenings out seems strongly influenced by marriage and parenthood; because these role responsibilities tend to be relatively stable and because increasing proportions of young adults assume these roles as they move from early to mid-twenties, it is understandable that evenings out and related behaviors tend to become more stable. During the first few years after high school, in contrast, living arrangements are apt to change relatively frequently, with many young adults leaving their parents' homes, often to enter college or military service.

Cigarette Use Linked to Evenings Out

High school seniors who spend 6–7 evenings a week out for fun and recreation are about three times as likely to be cigarette smokers compared to those who spend one or fewer evenings out per week; between these extremes, the higher the number of evenings out, the higher the proportion of seniors who smoke. Figure 5.5 shows this strong positive association among seniors; it also shows that with increasing age the link becomes weaker and weaker, so that by the time young adults reach their mid-twenties there is no longer any clear correlation between the two measures.

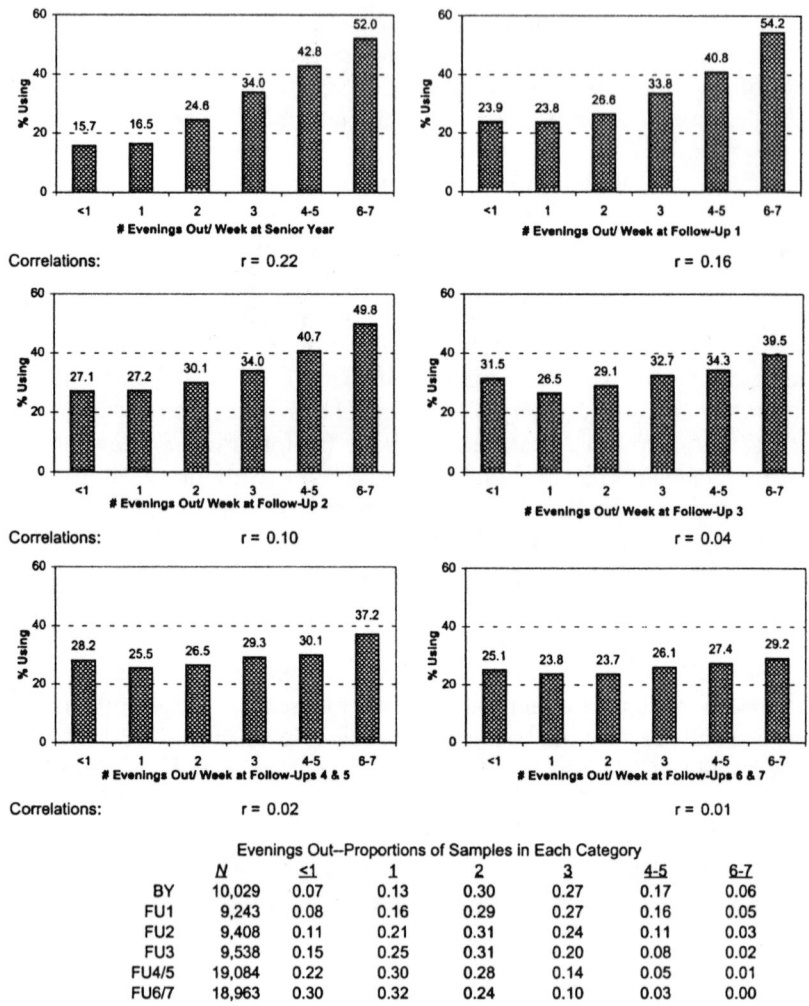

	N	≤1	1	2	3	4-5	6-7
Evenings Out–Proportions of Samples in Each Category							
BY	10,029	0.07	0.13	0.30	0.27	0.17	0.06
FU1	9,243	0.08	0.16	0.29	0.27	0.16	0.05
FU2	9,408	0.11	0.21	0.31	0.24	0.11	0.03
FU3	9,538	0.15	0.25	0.31	0.20	0.08	0.02
FU4/5	19,084	0.22	0.30	0.28	0.14	0.05	0.01
FU6/7	18,963	0.30	0.32	0.24	0.10	0.03	0.00

FIG. 5.5. Thirty-day prevalence of cigarette smoking related to frequency of evenings out. Percentages are based on the classes of 1976–1984 followed from age 18 to ages 29–32 (follow-ups 6 and 7, combined). The sample is restricted to those respondents who answered the questions on both 30-day cigarette use and evenings out at follow-up 6 and/or follow-up 7. Correlations are based on the drug use measure recoded as a dichotomy.

Another perspective is provided by the structural equation model in Fig. 5.6, linking evenings out with cigarette use. This shows the moderate and then increasing stability in evenings out described in the preceding section, as well as the very high stability of cigarette use described in the previous chapter (see Fig. 4.4). Here, similar to what we found for religious attendance in chapter 4, there is an initial senior-year relationship (which, of course, also captures any relationship prior to the senior year), but then no further impact of evenings out on smoking behavior.

How shall we interpret the patterns shown in Figs. 5.5 and 5.6? Our first observation, consistent with our commentary in chapter 4 and in previous work (Bachman et al., 1997), is that smoking behavior after high school is very stable across time because most regular smokers have become nicotine dependent. But why is smoking during high school linked with evenings out, whereas in later years this link disappears? One obvious explanation is that some students use their evenings out (for fun and recreation) as opportunities for smoking (away from parents' eyes and restrictions); in contrast, young adult smokers have less need to go out because they are likely to be free to smoke at home.

An additional, more fundamental, explanation may help to account for why high school students who are frequently out for fun and recreation are also more likely to be smokers. Other analyses of Monitoring the Future data (Bachman, Safron, & Schulenberg, under review; Schulenberg et al., 1994) have shown that, among adolescents, smoking and frequent evenings out both seem to be part of a broader syndrome that includes relatively low educational interest and performance (see also Jessor, Donovan, & Costa, 1991). It may well be the case that adolescents who do poorly in their roles as student may compensate by seeking "adult-like" status in a variety of ways, including going out in the evenings (instead of doing home-

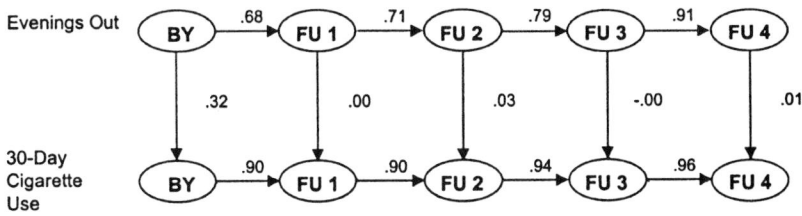

Note: This simplified model shows only the structural portion of the model; the measurement portion is not shown.

FIG. 5.6.   Impacts of evenings out on 30–day cigarette use, shown at five points in time: senior year of high school (BY, for base year) and the first four follow-ups (FU1–FU4).

work), smoking, drinking, and participating in other substance use and other problem behaviors.

Alcohol Use Linked to Evenings Out

Just as being out in the evenings is correlated with smoking among high school seniors, so also is it correlated with alcohol use and instances of heavy drinking—and probably for many of the same reasons. Among seniors from the classes of 1976–1984, those who were out 6–7 nights per week were twice as likely to have used alcohol during the past 30 days (about 85% did so) compared with those who were out fewer than one night per week (about 41%; data in Bachman et al., 2001). When it comes to instances of heavy drinking (5 or more drinks in a row anytime during the past 2 weeks), the relationship is even more pronounced; as shown in Fig. 5.7, those seniors who went out most frequently were about six times as likely to drink heavily as those who went out least often. It should be noted that these patterns based on the classes of 1976–1984 were largely replicated with later classes (1990–1998), except that overall proportions of drinkers were lower in the later classes (reflecting, in large part, higher minimum drinking age laws). Nevertheless, it continued to be true that seniors who went out nearly every evening were more than twice as likely to be current drinkers, and they were about five times as likely to have used heavily, compared to those who went out least often.

Figure 5.7 also shows that as young adults grew older and reached their early thirties, the proportions involved in instances of heavy drinking continued to be higher among those who spent many evenings out for fun and recreation. (This pattern contrasts fairly sharply with the findings for cigarette use; see Fig. 5.5.) The relationship between evenings out and occasional heavy drinking gradually weakened after the second follow-up (modal ages 21–22), when drinking at home was likely to be easier (and going out less likely to be a necessary condition). Nevertheless, even by the sixth and seventh follow-ups (modal ages 29–32), reports of occasional heavy drinking were twice as likely among those who went out four or more times a week for fun and recreation as among with those who went out one or fewer evenings per week (see Fig. 5.7).

We carried out structural equation modeling in which evenings out was linked with monthly alcohol use and with instances of heavy drinking. The results were quite similar for the two alcohol measures; thus we focus on the findings for the more general measure, frequency of drinking during the past month, shown in Fig. 5.8. Our first observation based on Fig. 5.8 is that the initial senior-year relationship between evenings out and frequency of drinking is quite strong—a path coefficient of .56. This is our best estimate

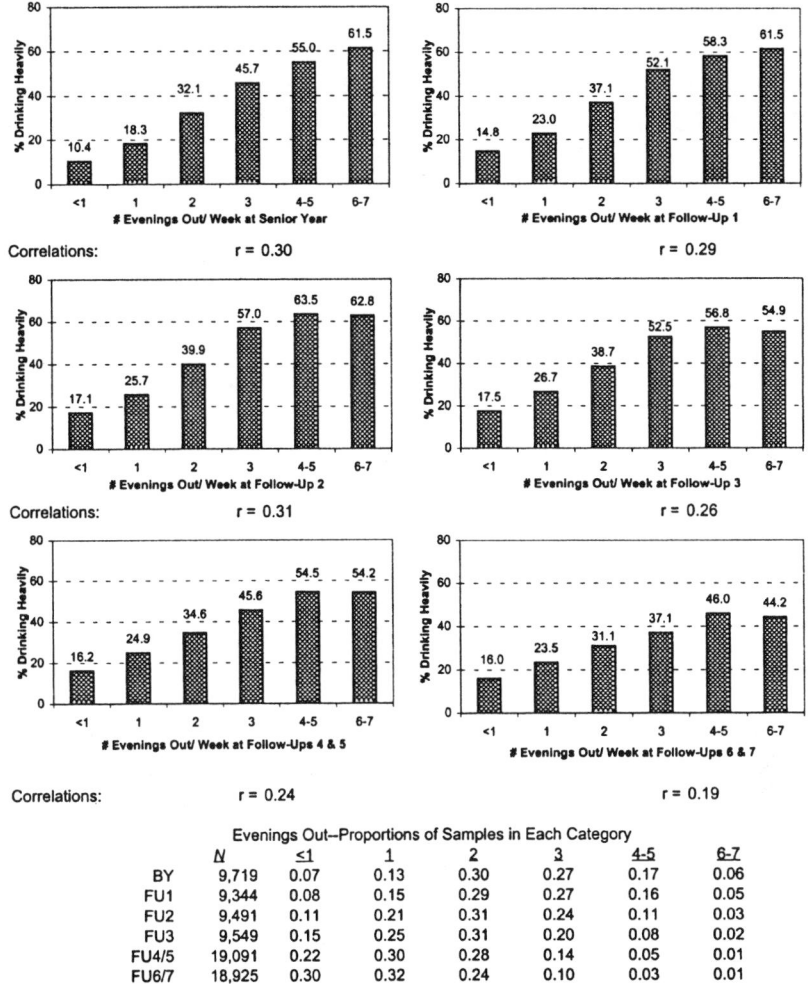

FIG. 5.7. Two-week prevalence of occasional heavy drinking (5 or more drinks in a row) related to frequency of evenings out. Percentages are based on the classes of 1976–1984 followed from age 18 to ages 29–32 (follow-ups 6 and 7, combined). The sample is restricted to those respondents who answered the questions on both 2-week heavy drinking and evenings out at follow-up 6 and/or follow-up 7. Correlations are based on the drug use measure recoded as a dichotomy.

(given this very simple model) of the "true" (i.e., error-free) correlation between seniors' frequency of evenings out and their frequency of drinking. (The model shows this correlation as a causal path running from evenings out to drinking. This is an assumption, of course, and we discuss later that such an assumption cannot be taken at all literally. However, it is not unreasonable to describe the coefficient as an estimated true *correlation*, with causal interpretations left to further discussion and interpretation.)

Our second observation is that the model estimates that drinking tendencies are quite stable by the time young people reach their late teens and become even more stable by their mid-twenties. Indeed, the same sort of increase in stability is shown for evenings out.

Our third observation based on Fig. 5.8 is that evenings out continue to make some contribution to drinking behaviors, above and beyond the initial contribution by the end of high school. This is in sharp contrast to the data for cigarette use, but the contrast is consistent with what we found for religiosity in chapter 4, and our interpretation is essentially the same: By the end of high school most cigarette use reflects habituation and dependence, whereas most alcohol use does not. As we suggested earlier, by the time young adults reach their mid-twenties it is usually not necessary for them to go out in the evening in order to drink. Nevertheless, the data in Fig. 5.8 clearly indicate that drinking among young adults is facilitated by evenings out for fun and recreation.

A final set of observations prompted by Fig. 5.8 has to do with causal directions. When we introduced this sort of model in chapter 4, we argued that in spite of the oversimplifications, such models can give us more information than a simple table of correlations. However, it is still the case that the assumptions involved should not be taken literally, and that is particularly true for the dimensions introduced in this chapter. In chapter 4 we were willing to assume that differences in religiosity contribute a good deal more to differences in drug use than the other way around; however, in this chapter dealing with time spent in fun and recreation, the causal interpreta-

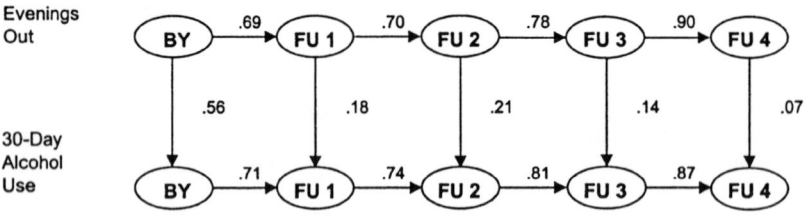

Note: This simplified model shows only the structural portion of the model; the measurement portion is not shown.

FIG. 5.8.   Impacts of evenings out on 30-day alcohol use, shown at five points in time: senior year of high school (BY, for base year) and the first four follow-ups (FU1–FU4).

tions are more complicated. Again recalling Carson's dictum ("You buy the premise, you buy the sketch"), we must acknowledge that it is now very hard to buy the premise of one-way causation. To be sure, being out in the evening for fun and recreation may provide opportunities for, and thus contribute to, alcohol use, but it is also the case that many young people go out in the evenings precisely for the purpose of drinking. To put a finer point on it, should we say that the tendency to go to bars contributes to the tendency to drink, or that the tendency to drink contributes to the tendency to go to bars, or some of each? Some of each is the only safe conclusion, of course, but we are left with questions of how much of each, and so on. More elaborate causal modeling could be undertaken to try to deal with such issues, but that is not our purpose here. Rather, we are content to acknowledge the limitations and attempt to deal with them constructively.

One way of acknowledging the limitations while keeping the modeling simple is merely to rerun the model with the arrows pointing in the other direction. When we did that for the models involving evenings out, the cigarette findings were virtually unchanged whereas the results for the alcohol use measures were changed appreciably. As Fig. 5.9 illustrates, if the causal arrows are reversed so that drinking is treated as the "cause" of evenings out, the coefficients linking evenings out and drinking (i.e., the vertical lines in the figure, now with arrows reversed) remain much the same; however, the stability estimates are shifted upward for drinking behavior and downward for evenings out. In other words, if we were to "buy the premise" that desire for drinking opportunities influences evenings out (rather than the other way around), then some of the stability that we would otherwise attribute to tendencies concerning evenings out would be attributed instead to what now appear to be very stable tendencies concerning whether or not to drink.

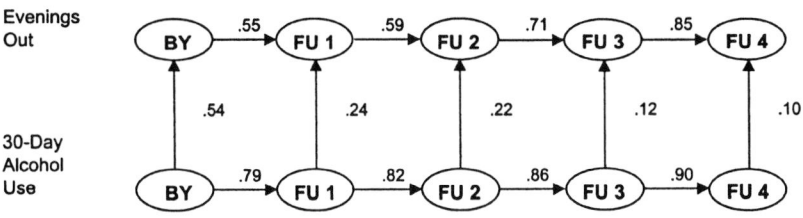

Note: This simplified model shows only the structural portion of the model; the measurement portion is not shown.

FIG. 5.9.   Impacts of 30-day alcohol use on evenings out, shown at five points in time: senior year of high school (BY, for base year) and the first four follow-ups (FU1–FU4).

Marijuana Use Linked to Evenings Out

Among high school seniors from the classes of 1976–1984, more than half of those who spent 6 or 7 evenings per week out for fun and recreation reported current use of marijuana (some use during the preceding 30 days), whereas among those who averaged less than one evening out, fewer than 1 in 10 were current users. As can be seen in Fig. 5.10, the relationship among seniors was strong and linear; the more evenings they spent out for fun and recreation, the more likely they were to use marijuana. The figure shows that the same was true for young adults from these classes during their late teens and early twenties, although the strength of association weakened somewhat and overall use declined by their mid-twenties and early thirties.

As we noted in chapter 4, during the 1980s—the period during which most of these changes in age occurred—there was an overall downward trend in marijuana use (Bachman et al., 1997; Johnston et al., 2000a; O'Malley et al., 1988a, 1988b). Accordingly, the age progression shown for those from the classes of 1976–1984 are not necessarily due entirely to age or to factors associated with age. They correspond also to population-wide shifts in attitudes about marijuana (Bachman et al., 1988; Bachman, Johnston et al., 1990; Bachman et al., 1997; Johnston, 1982). In order to check whether the age differences shown for the classes of 1976–1984 were still applicable, we examined additional data for the same ages as shown in Fig. 5.10 but this time obtained from respondents during only the years 1990–1998. We were thus able to avoid secular trends, although we were not tracking the same individuals across time. This analysis of different ages during the period 1990–1998 revealed lower overall levels of marijuana use than those shown in Fig. 5.10 and also somewhat weaker relationships with evenings out; nevertheless, we again found stronger relationships among high school seniors and very young adults than among those in their mid-twenties or older. Accordingly, we conclude that it is still true that evenings out for fun and recreation make more of a contribution to marijuana use among seniors and those just out of high school than among those who have reached their mid-twenties.

The structural equation modeling linking evenings out with marijuana use produced results somewhat similar to those for alcohol use. As Fig. 5.11 shows, the link at the senior year of high school was quite strong, although not quite as strong as that for alcohol. Links for subsequent years were much weaker, and by the third follow-up (modal ages 23–24) the model indicates no further contribution from evenings out to marijuana use (although, of course, they continue to be correlated because of the high stability of both evenings out and marijuana use among young adults in their mid-twenties).

How should we interpret the shifts in relationship between evenings out and marijuana use as young people move from the end of high school into

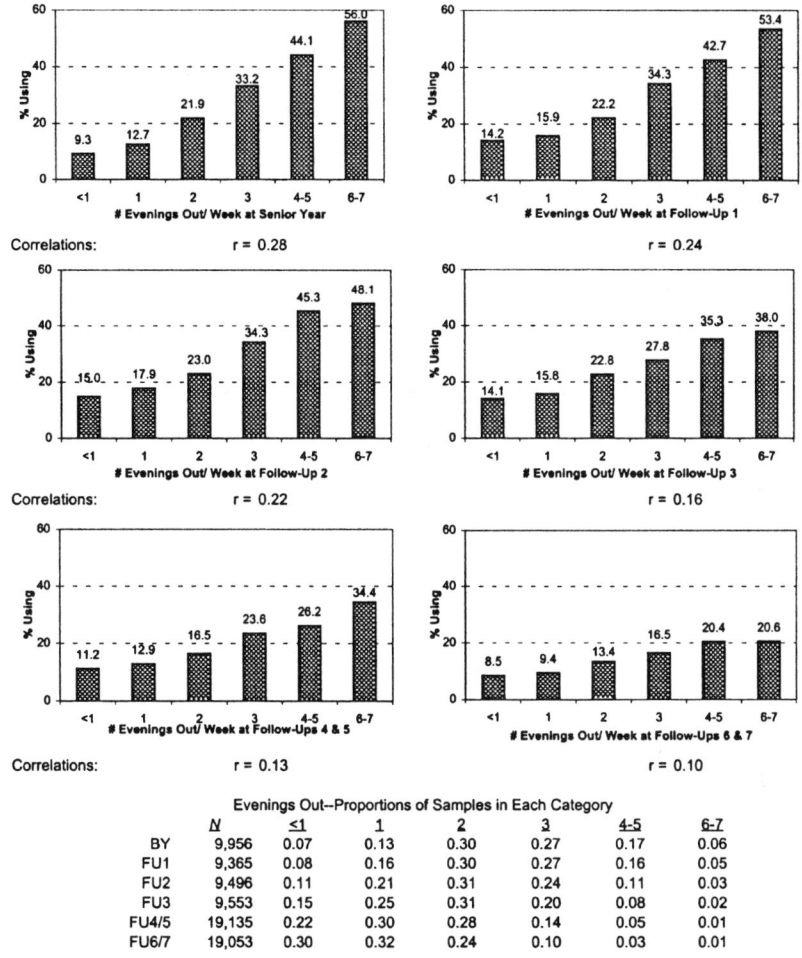

FIG. 5.10.   Thirty-day prevalence of marijuana use related to frequency of evenings out. Percentages are based on the classes of 1976–1984 followed from age 18 to ages 29–32 (follow-ups 6 and 7, combined). The sample is restricted to those respondents who answered the questions on both 30-day marijuana use and evenings out at follow-up 6 and/or follow-up 7. Correlations are based on the drug use measure recoded as a dichotomy.

their early twenties and then their mid-twenties and later? The strong positive correlation at the end of the senior year no doubt reflects many of the same processes as underlie the positive correlations between evenings out and both alcohol use and cigarette use. One specific factor is that most high school students find it easier to use substances (cigarettes, alcohol, and il-

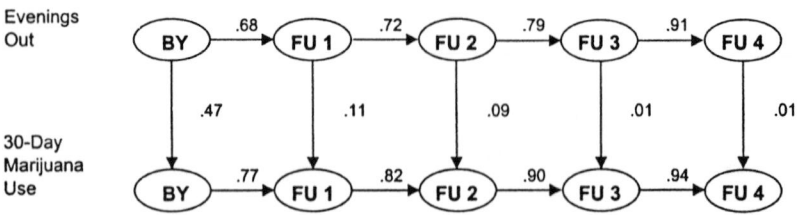

Note: This simplified model shows only the structural portion of the model;
the measurement portion is not shown.

FIG. 5.11.   Impacts of evenings out on 30–day marijuana use, shown at five points in time: senior year of high school (BY, for base year) and the first four follow-ups (FU1–FU4).

licit drugs) outside of home and away from parental supervision. A more general explanation for at least part of the correlation is that being away from home in the evenings for fun and recreation seems to be part of a broader syndrome that we have described as "premature adulthood" (Bachman et al., under review). The continuing contribution during young adulthood, shown in Figs. 5.10 and 5.11, suggests that much of the marijuana use by young adults continues to be a part of social activities—that is, evenings away from home for fun and recreation. Of course, in all of this we must keep in mind the cautions raised in the earlier section linking evenings out with drinking: Although spending an evening out for fun and recreation can directly facilitate substance use, it is also the case that young people can choose to spend an evening out for exactly that purpose. Thus, interpretation of causal direction remains very complicated, no matter how simple the model may look.

Cocaine Use Linked to Evenings Out

As we noted in chapter 4, cocaine usage rates shifted appreciably during the time since 1976. Accordingly, the changes shown in Fig. 5.12 include secular trends—most notably a sharp decline after 1986 in response to increased perceptions of risk (see O'Malley et al., 1988a, 1998b, for an extensive treatment of these issues; see also Bachman, Johnston et al., 1990; Johnston et al., 2000a). But the patterns shown in the figure also reflect age-related differences—especially rising rates of use during late teens and early twenties. Figure 5.12 shows that only small proportions of young adults used any cocaine in the 30 days preceding any of the surveys; however, use was positively correlated with number of evenings out for fun and recreation. Although the overall size of these correlations was modest because of the limited numbers of users, Fig. 5.12 shows that throughout ages 18–28, it was consistently true that those who spent most evenings out for fun and recreation were roughly five times more likely to have used cocaine than those

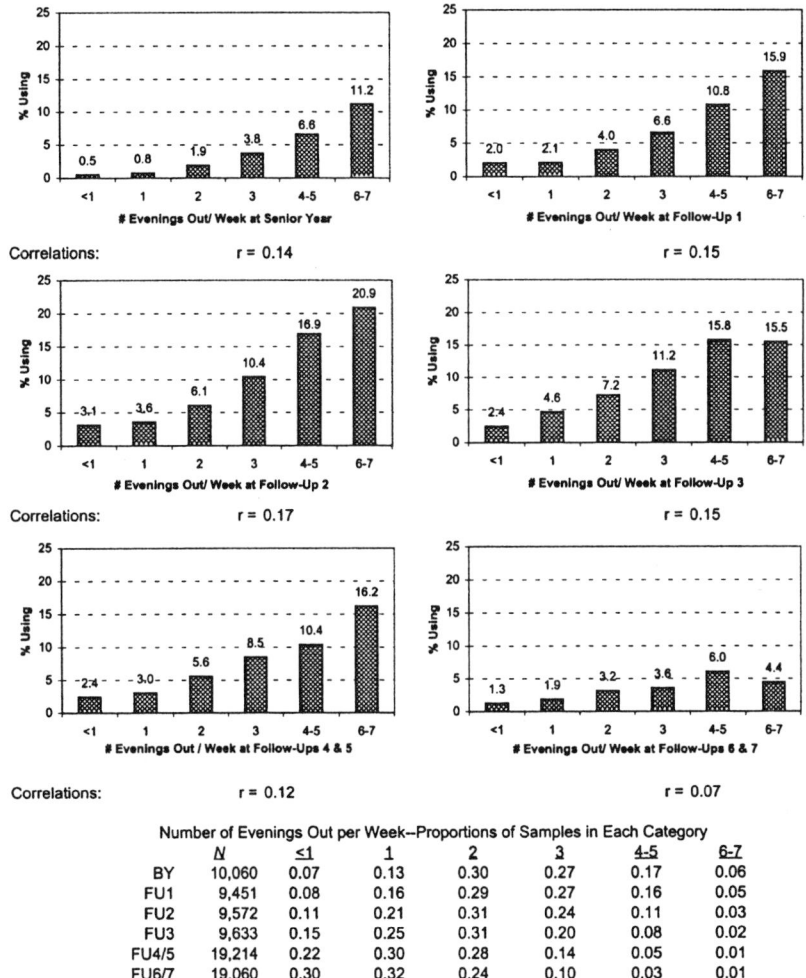

Number of Evenings Out per Week--Proportions of Samples in Each Category

	N	≤1	1	2	3	4-5	6-7
BY	10,060	0.07	0.13	0.30	0.27	0.17	0.06
FU1	9,451	0.08	0.16	0.29	0.27	0.16	0.05
FU2	9,572	0.11	0.21	0.31	0.24	0.11	0.03
FU3	9,633	0.15	0.25	0.31	0.20	0.08	0.02
FU4/5	19,214	0.22	0.30	0.28	0.14	0.05	0.01
FU6/7	19,060	0.30	0.32	0.24	0.10	0.03	0.01

FIG. 5.12. Thirty-day prevalence of cocaine use related to frequency of evenings out. Percentages are based on the classes of 1976–1984 followed from age 18 to ages 29–32 (follow-ups 6 and 7, combined). The sample is restricted to those respondents who answered the questions on both 30-day cocaine use and evenings out at follow-up 6 and/or follow-up 7. Correlations are based on the drug use measure recoded as a dichotomy.

who were out one or fewer nights per week. Separate analyses of the same age band, limited to the years 1990–1998, showed lower overall use and thus lower correlations, but also showed the same rough five-to-one ratio (data not shown).

Consistent with the descriptive data in Fig. 5.12, the structural equation model in Fig. 5.13 shows a fairly strong initial relationship between evenings out and cocaine use and then continuing contributions throughout the first four follow-ups (modal ages 19–26). The pattern is fairly similar to that for marijuana, except that the coefficients are generally smaller (due to overall lower usage rates for cocaine). Our interpretation of why the relationships appear as they do is essentially the same as our interpretation for the marijuana relationships and need not be repeated here.

Substance Use Linked to Evenings Out: Summary

The findings presented here show that high school seniors who spent frequent evenings out for fun and recreation were more likely than their classmates to be involved in smoking, drinking, and illicit drug use. This is consistent with prior research on students, summarized in chapter 2, including earlier studies of the high school seniors in the Monitoring the Future samples. The new data presented here show that substantial relationships between evenings out and substance use continue during young adulthood, although the reasons for those continuing connections vary somewhat from one substance to another.

The findings further show that those who went out frequently during high school were also likely to go out frequently as young adults. However, although young adults showed considerable stability in their tendencies to

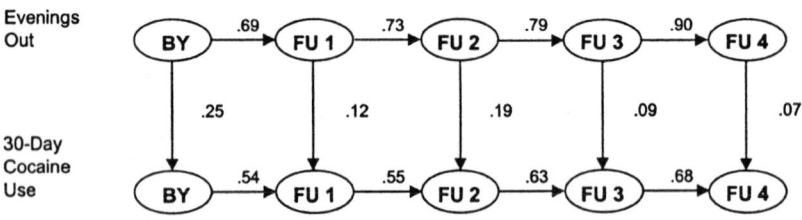

Note: This simplified model shows only the structural portion of the model;
the measurement portion is not shown.

FIG. 5.13.   Impacts of evenings out on 30-day cocaine use, shown at five points in time: senior year of high school (BY, for base year) and the first four follow-ups (FU1–FU4).

spend evenings out for fun and recreation, these estimated stabilities were distinctly lower than the estimates for religiosity and also somewhat lower than the estimates for most substance use.

Given our overarching goal of learning how and why the new freedoms and responsibilities of young adulthood affect substance use, it is particularly important to understand the extent to which *changes* in patterns of evenings out during young adulthood may contribute to *changes* in substance use. Here is where our findings show sharp differences between cigarette use and other forms of substance use. As noted in chapter 4, cigarette use is highly resistant to change once young adults have left high school. Thus, a positive correlation between evenings out and cigarette use continued into very early adulthood, due only to the moderate stability of the evenings out behavior coupled with the very high stability of cigarette use; however, by the time the respondents reached their mid-twenties the relationship had disappeared (a product–moment correlation of 0.02). For alcohol use, instances of heavy drinking, marijuana use, and cocaine use, the evidence (cross-sectional analyses as well as structural equation models using panel data) indicates that at least during early adulthood, changes in patterns of evenings out were linked with changes in substance use. The causal interpretations are complicated, but at a minimum our findings indicate that the changes are related to each other.

Why should evenings out make a difference? We explore a number of possibilities in the next section as we look at some of the specific activities that evenings out can involve.

HOW CHANGES IN OTHER SOCIAL–RECREATIONAL BEHAVIORS ARE LINKED WITH CHANGES IN SUBSTANCE USE

Earlier in this chapter we reported age-related changes in dating, going to parties or other social affairs, and going to bars (we use "bars" hereafter as a shorthand for "taverns, bars, and nightclubs"). In this section we present relatively brief summaries of analyses linking each of these social–recreational behaviors to substance use, following the same procedures as those reported earlier in this chapter for evenings out (and in chap. 4 for religiosity). Fuller details of these analyses are provided elsewhere (Bachman et al., 2001); correlational data for years 1990–1998 appear also in Tables A.2.1–A.2.3.

Substance Use Linked to Going Out With a Date or Spouse

High school seniors who dated most frequently were somewhat more likely than average to smoke, drink alcohol, occasionally drink heavily, use marijuana, and use cocaine. Among those from the high school classes of 1976–1984, the raw correlations were .17 for cigarette use, .16 for each of the alcohol and marijuana use measures, and .08 for cocaine use. Among seniors in the classes of 1990–1998, whose overall use rates were lower for these substances, the correlations (shown in Table A.2.1) also were lower but still positive (and statistically significant).

Does dating, including "dates" with a spouse, continue to relate to substance use during young adulthood? As we found for evenings out in general, the link between dating and smoking reduced quickly during the early twenties and had disappeared by the mid-twenties. But alcohol use, including occasions of heavy drinking, remained linked to frequency of dating. Drinking was least likely among those who reported never dating and somewhat below average among those who dated less than once a month. Among the rest, there was little further difference in alcohol use linked with whether they dated 2–3 times a month or several times a week. Marijuana use and cocaine use were also somewhat less likely among those who never dated and a bit more likely than average among those who dated frequently. None of these relationships were as large as those shown in the preceding section for evenings out.

Substance Use Linked to Going to Parties or Other Social Affairs

Among high school seniors and young adults from the classes of 1976–1984, going to parties or other social affairs was strongly and positively associated with alcohol use and use of illicit drugs. Positive correlations with cigarette use were moderately strong in senior year ($r = .25$) and declined thereafter, consistent with other findings in this chapter.

Alcohol use and instances of heavy drinking showed especially strong correlations with attendance at parties and other social affairs; the links with the heavy drinking measure are shown in Fig. 5.14. During the senior year of high school and the first few years thereafter, about two thirds of those who attended parties or other social affairs once a week or more often also reported having consumed five or more drinks in a row at least once during the preceding 2 weeks; this contrasts with about one fifth of those who attended parties a few times a year or less. The correlation between party-going and instances of heavy drinking was highest ($r = .44$ to $.42$) during late teens and early twenties, gradually declined ($r = .32$ to $.30$) during middle and later twenties, and was still lower by the last follow-ups at modal ages 29–32 ($r = .24$). The decline occurred in part because frequent party-going was a bit less likely to be associated with heavy drinking among older respondents and in part simply because there were fewer frequent attendees as respondents grew older (i.e., the variance in party-going de-

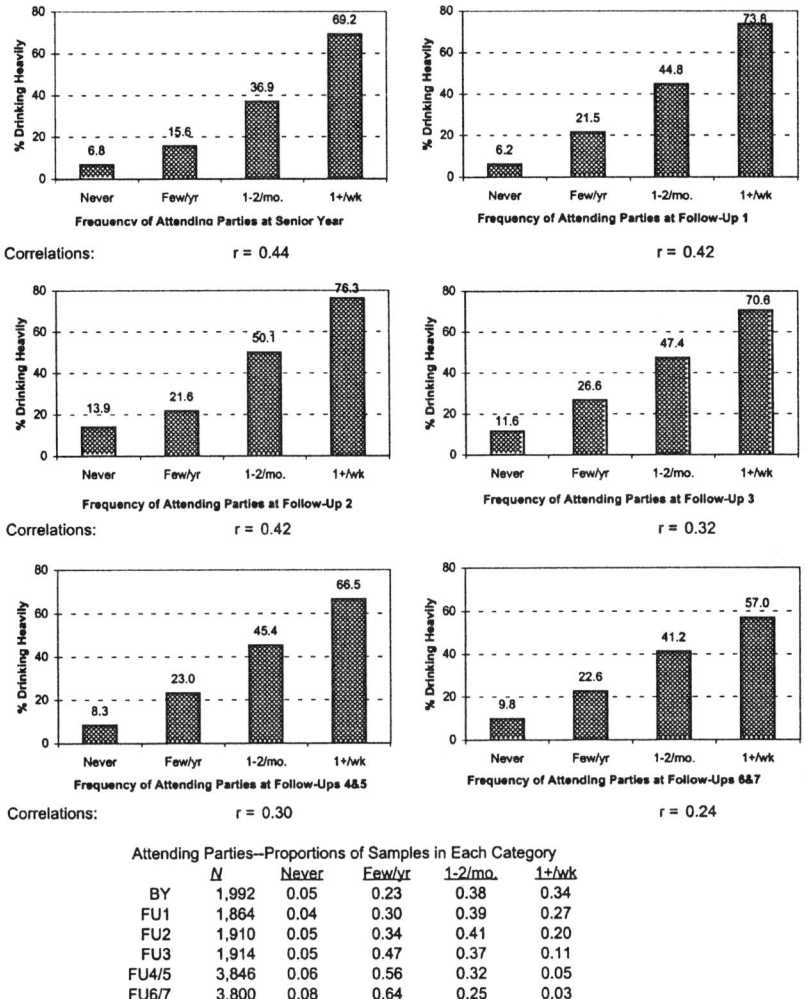

FIG. 5.14. Two-week prevalence of occasional heavy drinking (5 or more drinks in a row) related to weekly frequency of attending parties or other social affairs. Percentages based on the classes of 1976–1984 followed from age 18 to ages 29–32 (follow-ups 6 and 7, combined). The sample is restricted to those respondents who answered the questions on both 2-week heavy drinking and attending parties at follow-up 6 and/or follow-up 7. Correlations are based on the drug use measure recoded as a dichotomy.

clined sharply, as discussed earlier in this chapter and shown in Fig. 5.3). The data in Fig. 5.14 are based on the senior classes of 1976–1984 followed through time as they grew older; calculations based on the same ages all drawn from the period 1990–1998 yielded correlations just as strong, even though instances of heavy drinking were slightly less frequent among those ages 18–20 during the 1990s.

Marijuana use also was positively correlated with party-going, as shown in Fig. 5.15. Among seniors from the classes of 1976–1984, when marijuana use was at its peak, about half of those who partied once a week or more also reported current marijuana use (some use during the past month). Rates of marijuana use were lower among seniors during the 1990s; nevertheless, among those in the classes of 1990–1998 who partied weekly or more often, about 30% were current marijuana users (data available in Bachman et al., 2001). Figure 5.15 shows that as members of the classes of 1976–1984 grew older, the connection between party-going and marijuana use declined from $r = .35$ at the end of high school to $r = .10$ by modal ages 29–32. This reflects in part the overall decline in marijuana use during the period in which these individuals made their transitions through young adulthood. It also reflects more specific age-related processes, because comparisons of the same age bands using data collected in 1990–1998 also show a decline from $r = .29$ among seniors to $r = .10$ among those in modal ages 29–32 (data available in Bachman et al., 2001).

Cocaine use was higher among frequent party-goers from the high school classes of 1976–1984, as shown in Fig. 5.16, and, as the respondents aged, the relationships (and overall proportions of users) grew larger throughout most of their twenties. By modal ages 29–32, however, overall use dropped and the correlation with party-going shrank to .05. During the 1990s the link between party-going and cocaine use remained positive but smaller than the pattern shown in Fig. 5.16.

Substance Use Linked to Going to Bars

Of all the dimensions of social activities examined in this chapter, going to bars showed the strongest links with all forms of substance use studied. This is hardly surprising for alcohol use, but even cigarette use showed this connection throughout ages 18–32. Among those high school seniors in the classes of 1976–1984 who reported they went to bars almost daily, more than 60% were current cigarette smokers; and as they went through their twenties it remained true that more than 60% of those who went to bars almost daily were current smokers. The same was true for young adults at all of these ages during the 1990s (1990–1998; data available in Bachman et al., 2001).

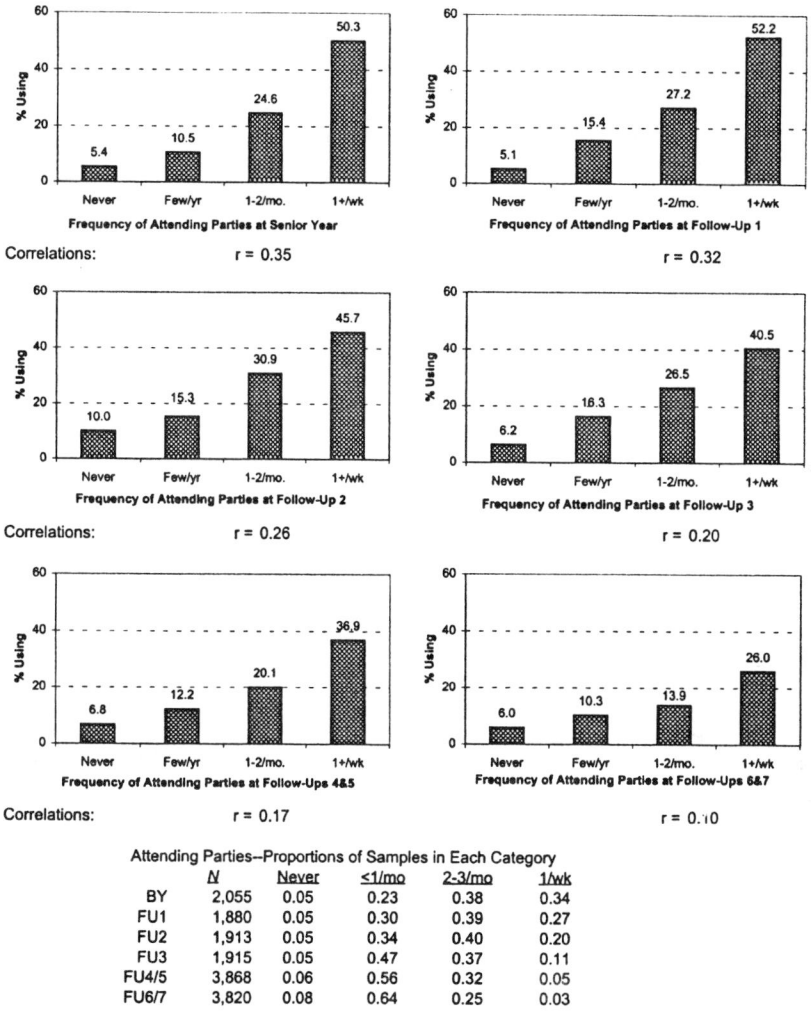

FIG. 5.15.   Thirty-day prevalence of marijuana use related to weekly frequency of attending parties or other social affairs. Percentages based on the classes of 1976–1984 followed from age 18 to ages 29–32 (follow-ups 6 and 7, combined). The sample is restricted to those respondents who answered the questions on both 30-day marijuana use and attending parties at follow-up 6 and/or follow-up 7. Correlations are based on the drug use measure recoded as a dichotomy.

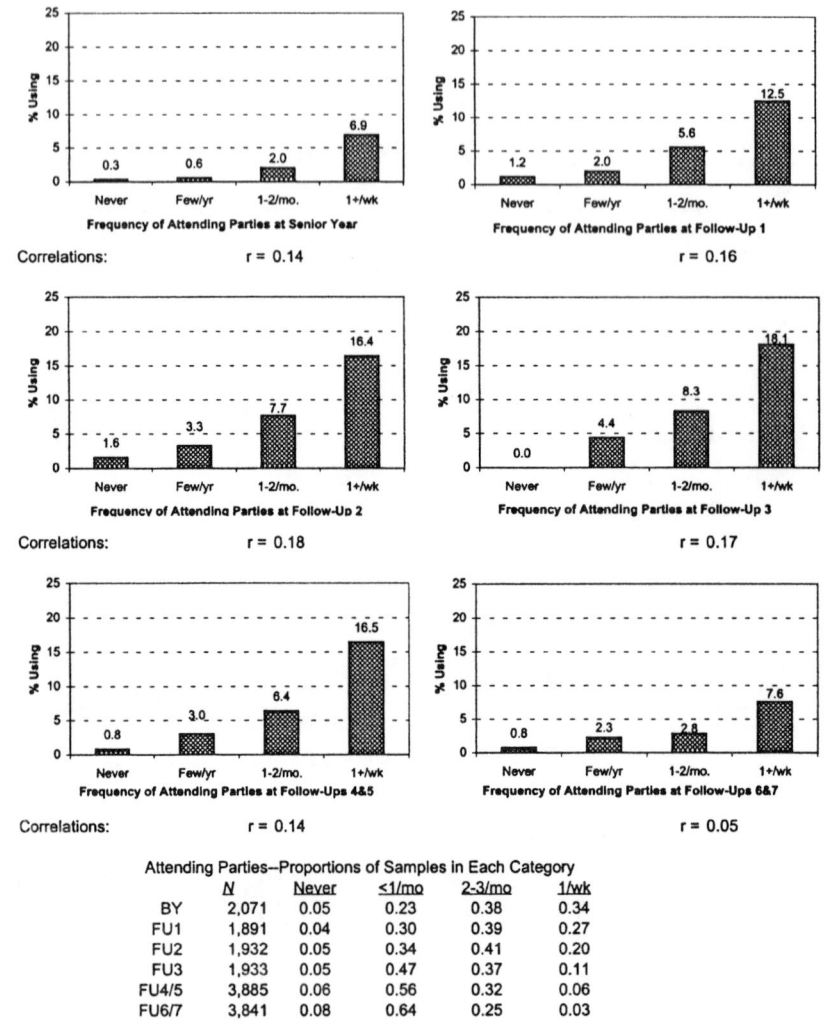

Attending Parties--Proportions of Samples in Each Category					
	_N_	Never	≤1/mo	2-3/mo	1/wk
BY	2,071	0.05	0.23	0.38	0.34
FU1	1,891	0.04	0.30	0.39	0.27
FU2	1,932	0.05	0.34	0.41	0.20
FU3	1,933	0.05	0.47	0.37	0.11
FU4/5	3,885	0.06	0.56	0.32	0.06
FU6/7	3,841	0.08	0.64	0.25	0.03

FIG. 5.16.   Thirty-day prevalence of cocaine use related to weekly frequency of attending parties or other social affairs. Percentages based on the classes of 1976–1984 followed from age 18 to ages 29–32 (follow-ups 6 and 7, combined). The sample is restricted to those respondents who answered the questions on both 30-day cocaine use and attending parties at follow-up 6 and/or follow-up 7. Correlations are based on the drug use measure recoded as a dichotomy.

Alcohol use, as well as instances of heavy drinking, showed very high correlations with going to bars (r = approximately .50) throughout ages 18–32. This held true for the classes of 1976–1984 followed through time, as well as for all age bands surveyed in 1990–1998. Use of marijuana and use of cocaine also were higher among those who frequently went to bars.

Substance Use Linked to Dating, Parties, and Bars: Summary

We have seen that among the socializing behaviors listed here, going to bars showed the strongest links with all forms of substance use examined here, whereas dating showed the weakest links. Differences between substances, noted earlier, continue to be evident in this section. Cigarette use was generally least strongly linked to the recreational behaviors after high school, whereas the alcohol use measures showed the strongest links.

Few of the findings here were especially surprising. We expected very strong links between going to bars and alcohol use, of course. Also, we were not surprised to find that dating showed relatively weak links with substance use; drinking might be incidental to dating, but there is less reason to suppose that smoking and illicit drug use would be linked to dating once young people reach full adulthood.

One of the most interesting findings in this section, in our view, is the continuing link between smoking and going to bars. Since smoking is such a highly stable behavior after high school, we are inclined to interpret this relationship as indicting primarily that smokers may feel especially comfortable going to bars—or, looking at the other side of the coin, nonsmokers may view bars (which often are quite smoky) as rather unappealing.

ANALYSES LINKING RECREATIONAL LIFESTYLE WITH POST-HIGH-SCHOOL EXPERIENCES[1]

This chapter dealing with time spent in social and recreational behaviors has examined a number of key measures. Evenings out for fun and recreation is a measure obtained from all respondents in senior-year surveys and follow-ups. It can be viewed as the most "general" of the measures treated in this chapter; most of the other social and recreational behaviors involve evenings out and thus represent specific subsets of the total evenings out. For these reasons, in this section we continue our practice of focusing primarily on the evenings-out measure.

We have just shown in the previous section that evenings out and other social and recreational behaviors are linked with substance use (corre-

---

[1]The different dimensions of post-high-school experiences and the proportions of respondents in each category at each follow-up are documented in the appendix, Tables A.1.1–A.1.5.

sponding to arrow *c* in Fig. 1.1). Now we turn to the other causal link (arrow *b*). We examine in some detail how various post-high-school roles and experiences may influence frequency of evenings out, and we note whether the possible impacts of the other social and recreational behaviors are similar or different. (Further detail on the other measures is provided in the appendix and in Bachman et al., 2001.)

Student Status Related to Recreational Lifestyle

During the first few years after high school, the frequency of evenings out changes rather little, overall. Those who became full-time students during the first two follow-ups had reported slightly lower than average frequencies of evenings out during their senior year of high school, but several years later those small differences had narrowed. Those who became full-time students also were slightly lower than average in frequency of dating during high school, and those differences continued while they were in college.

During the first few years after high school, the samples as a whole showed some decline in frequency of attending parties and other social affairs and in frequency of getting together informally with friends. Among the full-time students, however, attendance at parties and informal get-togethers did not decline. Multivariate analyses indicate that this "party effect" did not apply to all full-time students; rather, the students living in dormitories actually increased their rates of partying and getting together informally, as we will see, whereas other full-time students did not. (The multivariate analyses for attending parties and other social affairs are documented in Table A.5.3; those for getting together informally are in Table A.5.4.)

Going to taverns, bars, and nightclubs increased during the first few years after high school, among both students and nonstudents. Not surprisingly, the multivariate analyses indicate that the increases were most pronounced among students living in dormitories and among those (both students and nonstudents) in "other living conditions" (documented in Table A.5.5). Here again, once we take account of living arrangements, there appears to be nothing inherent in student status that predisposes to going to bars.

Employment Status Related to Recreational Lifestyle

Most of the variations in recreational lifestyle linked to employment status are explainable primarily in terms of other more fundamental factors. For example, those who reported that they were full-time homemakers showed greater than average declines, but such distinctions largely disappeared once marital status was controlled in the multivariate analyses (documented in Tables A.5.1–A.5.5). One employment distinction was not eliminated, or even reduced, when living arrangements and marital status were controlled: Those who were in military service at the time of follow-up reported more than average evenings out in general, and they were particularly more likely to report going to bars. This finding is consistent with our earlier finding that rates of alcohol use increased somewhat more than average among those who were in military service (Bachman et al., 1997). It should be kept in mind, however, that other analyses, focusing on a broader range of high school classes but dealing with only the first follow-up, have shown that *recent* high school graduates who entered military service did not show greater than average increases in instances of heavy drinking (Bachman et al., 1999).

Living Arrangements Related to Recreational Lifestyle

As noted in chapter 4, we included marriage in comparisons with five other categories of living arrangements because we considered being married (and thus living with a spouse) to be the most important of the living arrangements in terms of interpersonal relationships. The next three figures show that frequencies of evenings out in general (Fig. 5.17), dating (Fig. 5.18), and going to bars (Fig. 5.19) changed between senior year and follow-up for those in each of the six living arrangements (at the time of follow-up).

Being Married. Those married at the time of follow-up had been just about average in frequency of evenings out when they were high school seniors, as shown in Fig. 5.17; similarly, as seniors they had been about average in likelihood of going to bars (see Fig. 5.19), in rates of attending parties and other social affairs, and in frequency of getting together with friends informally. By the time of follow-up, however, those who were married showed the largest declines along all four of these dimensions. Of course, the fact that these social activities declined among those who were married might be attributable to a number of other factors associated with marriage, particularly the fact that many of those married were also parents. Indeed, the multivariate analyses (see appendix) revealed that some portion of the "marriage effect" on social and recreational activities did overlap with other factors, most notably parenthood (as discussed and illustrated later).

It is perhaps not surprising that those who were married at follow-up had been above average in frequency of dating when they were high school seniors, as shown in Fig. 5.18. The figure also shows that married respondents *on average* had the largest declines in dating—recall that the question wording was "… go out with a date (or your spouse, if you are married)." The multivariate analyses are particularly important for this dimension, because the results show quite clearly that the reduction in dating was limited al-

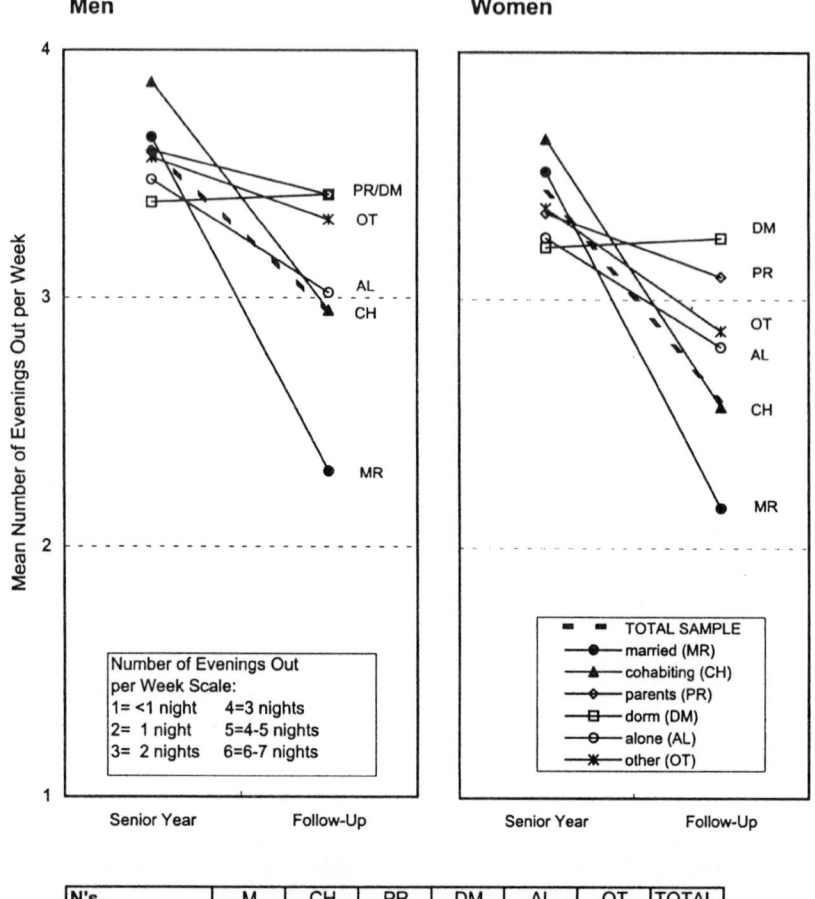

N's	M	CH	PR	DM	AL	OT	TOTAL
Men	15,357	3,043	11,363	2,211	4,453	7,611	44,038
Women	23,178	4,268	11,600	2,520	3,727	7,339	52,632

FIG. 5.17. Change in mean numbers of evenings out for fun and recreation per week related to living arrangement at the time of follow-up. High school seniors from the classes of 1976–1984 were followed up as many as seven times between modal ages 19 and 32. In this figure, one person could contribute up to seven follow-up observations (see Additional Panel Analysis Issues and Strategies section in chap. 3). The approximate standard deviations for evenings out at senior year were 1.13 for males and 1.17 for females.

most entirely to those who were parents.[2] It thus appears that married couples continue to date at about the same rate as others their age, until children enter the picture.

Cohabiting. Like those who were married at follow-up, those who were cohabiting at follow-up had been somewhat above average in frequency of dating while still in high school; however, in contrast to the married category taken as a whole (i.e., including those who were parents), the cohabitants did not show a decline in frequency of dating between senior year and follow-up (see Fig. 5.18). The cohabitants had also been above average in most of the other social and recreational activities during their senior year, but along some of these dimensions (e.g., evenings out—Fig. 5.17, but not going to bars—Fig. 5.19) the cohabitants showed greater than average declines. Such declines were not as large as those for the total married category, but it seems likely that the cohabitants' changes paralleled fairly closely those of married respondents who did not have children. It should be kept in mind, of course, that some individuals who were cohabiting at one of the earlier follow-ups were married without children at a later follow-up and then married *with* children at a subsequent follow-up. That said, it must also be kept in mind that many of those who married did not precede their marriage with a period of cohabitation, and this helps to account for some of the senior-year differences between these two categories.

Living With Parents. As Fig. 5.17 shows, those who were living with their parents at time of follow-up were somewhat above average in frequency of evenings out, although they had been just about average when they were seniors. This difference was reduced by nearly half in the multivariate analyses but by no means eliminated (documented in Table A.5.1). Similarly, those living with parents showed slightly larger than average increases in frequency of dating (see Fig. 5.18), although these also were reduced (this time by about two thirds; documented in Table A.5.2) when other factors were controlled in the multivariate analyses. Those living with parents also showed slightly larger than average increases in going to bars (see Fig. 5.19), and these differences were not reduced when other factors were controlled (documented in Table A.5.5).

---

[2]This is indicated by the fact that when married parenthood was included in the analyses along with marital status, the parenthood effect remained very strong, whereas the marriage effect was nearly eliminated among women (from a bivariate unstandardized coefficient of $-.53$ to a multivariate unstandardized coefficient of $-.11$, shown in Table A.5.2a) and entirely eliminated among men (from $-.41$ to $.01$, Table A.5.2b).

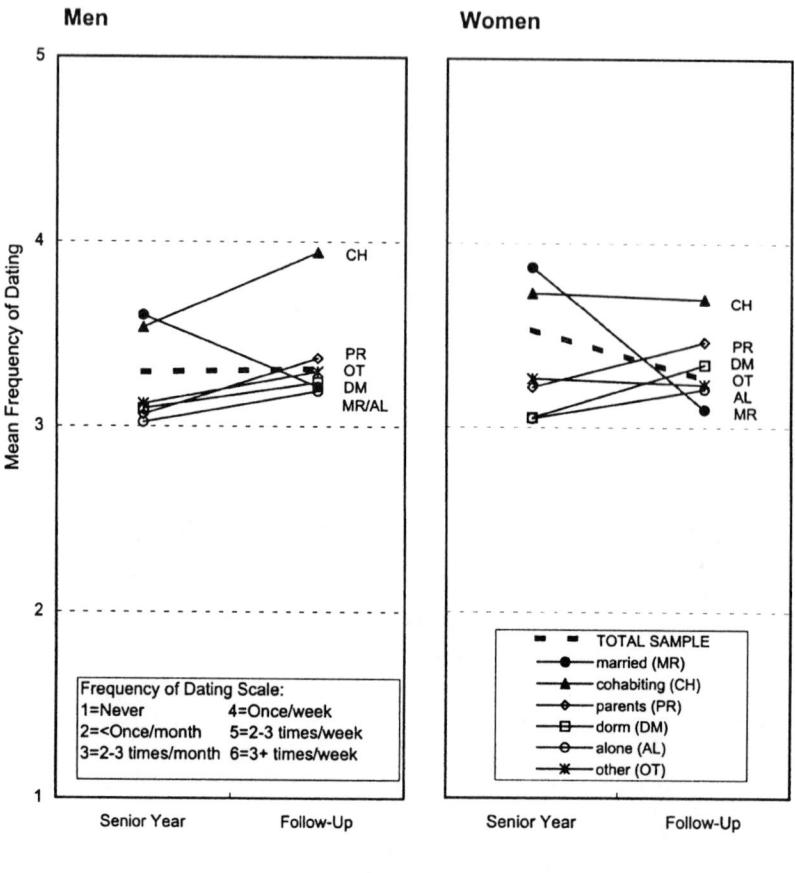

N's	M	CH	PR	DM	AL	OT	TOTAL
Men	15,237	3,017	11,104	2,168	4,412	7,484	43,422
Women	23,069	4,232	11,382	2,498	3,675	7,250	52,106

FIG. 5.18.   Change in mean frequency of going out with a date (or spouse if married) related to living arrangement at the time of follow-up. High school seniors from the classes of 1976–1984 were followed up as many as seven times between modal ages 19 and 32. In this figure, one person could contribute up to seven follow-up observations (see Additional Panel Analysis Issues and Strategies section in chap. 3). The approximate standard deviations for dating at senior year were 1.36 for males and 1.49 for females.

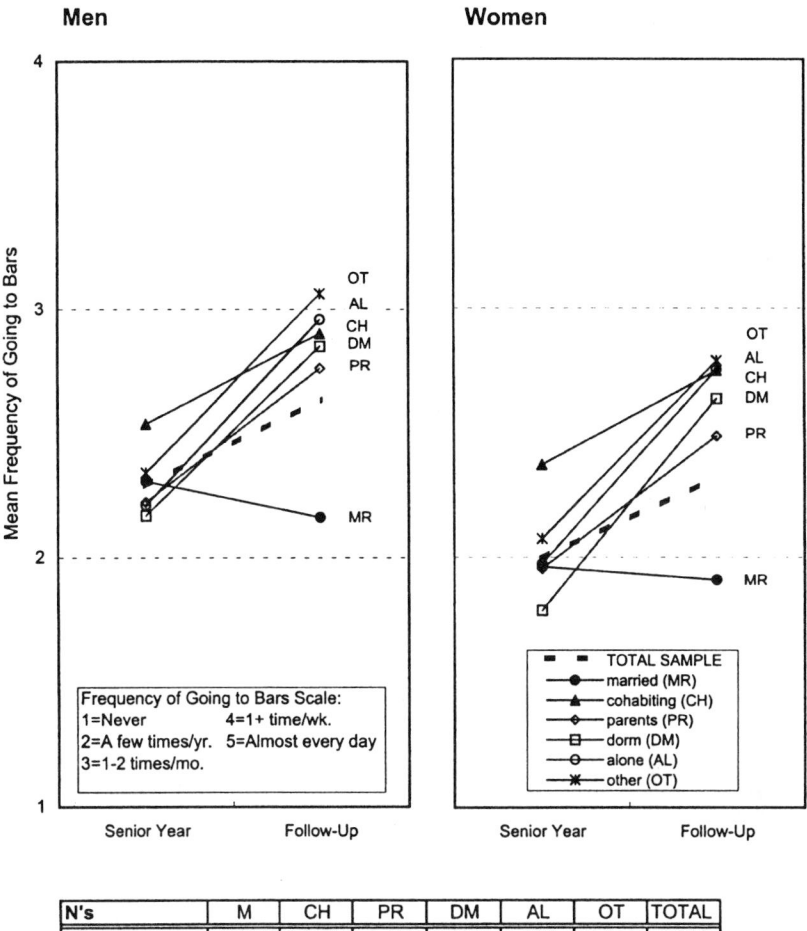

Men **Women**

Mean Frequency of Going to Bars

Frequency of Going to Bars Scale:
1=Never   4=1+ time/wk.
2=A few times/yr. 5=Almost every day
3=1-2 times/mo.

- ■ TOTAL SAMPLE
—●— married (MR)
—▲— cohabiting (CH)
—◆— parents (PR)
—▣— dorm (DM)
—○— alone (AL)
—✳— other (OT)

Senior Year   Follow-Up   Senior Year   Follow-Up

N's	M	CH	PR	DM	AL	OT	TOTAL
Men	3,194	657	2,466	464	895	1,584	9,260
Women	4,749	838	2,527	529	760	1,513	10,916

FIG. 5.19.   Change in mean frequency of going to taverns, bars, or nightclubs related to living arrangement at the time of follow-up. High school seniors from the classes of 1976–1984 were followed up as many as seven times between modal ages 19 and 32. In this figure, one person could contribute up to seven follow-up observations (see Additional Panel Analysis Issues and Strategies section in chap. 3). The approximate standard deviations for going to bars at senior year were 1.02 for males and 0.95 for females.

All of these observations, including the data shown in Figs. 5.17–5.19, are based on analyses that combined respondents from all seven follow-ups. In fact, however, most of the living with parents occurred during the first two or three follow-ups; therefore, these analyses to some extent confound age with living arrangements (unavoidably). Perhaps a more useful perspective is provided by analyses based on only the first two follow-ups (the approach used to examine student status). When these younger adults living with parents were compared only with other young adults (modal ages 19–22), the patterns described in the previous paragraph were diminished or eliminated. Most notably, when analyses were limited to the younger adults, it turned out that those living with their parents were actually a bit less likely than average to go to taverns, bars, or nightclubs (see Bachman et al., 2001, for details).

Living in a Dormitory. As indicated in earlier comments (see also Figs. 5.17 and 5.19), living in a dormitory was associated with more frequent than average evenings out, going to parties, getting together with friends informally, and going to bars—at least when the comparisons are made across all follow-ups (i.e., modal ages 19–32). But, of course, most of those in dormitories were in their late teens and early twenties, and comparing them with all others (including many in their late twenties and early thirties) carried the risk that any broader differences associated with age might masquerade as dormitory effects. In order to avoid this confounding with age, we reexamined the relationships, focusing exclusively on younger adults (i.e., the multivariate analyses of the first two follow-ups only—modal ages 19–22); the findings already described were still clearly evident, but given the younger comparison group, the departures from average were somewhat reduced in magnitude. Again in comparison with other young adults (modal ages 19–22), those in dormitories dated a bit less than average and also a bit less than full-time students in general; the same was true when they were seniors in high school (see Bachman et al., 2001).

Previous analyses led us to conclude that there was a "dormitory effect," largely independent of other aspects of living arrangements or student status, that seemed to contribute to a rise in alcohol use in general and instances of heavy drinking in particular (Bachman et al., 1997). The findings shown here suggest some of the reasons that dormitory life may contribute to such increases in drinking. As shown earlier in this chapter, frequent evenings out and especially going to parties or bars were strongly associated with alcohol use. Now we see that these particular behaviors increased among young adults living in dormitories. In contrast, dating was not so strongly linked to alcohol use, and it did not show unusually high increases among those living in dormitories.

Living Alone and in Other Living Arrangements. The remaining two living arrangements show some similarities to each other, as well as some understandable differences. The greatest similarity is that young adults living alone and those in other arrangements (mostly shared housing with other young adults) were the ones most likely to frequent bars (see Fig. 5.19). This holds true whether we focus on the full age range shown in the figure (modal ages 19–32) or limit attention to the first two follow-ups (modal ages 19–22). Not surprisingly, those in the "other living arrangements" category were a bit more likely to attend parties and other social affairs than those living alone.

Pregnancy and Parenthood Related to Recreational Lifestyle

Pregnancy. Our previous book showed sharp declines among pregnant women in alcohol use and illicit drug use and even some declines in cigarette smoking (Bachman et al., 1997). The present analyses suggest that little or none of these declines are attributable to overall changes in recreational lifestyle. Pregnant women, and also men with pregnant wives, did report somewhat lower than average frequencies of evenings out, party-going, and visits to bars; however, those data matched almost perfectly the data for marriage, and after controls for marital (and parental) status, the multivariate analyses revealed practically no effect attributable to pregnancy (documented in Tables A.5.1a, A.5.2a, A.5.3a, A.5.4a, and A.5.5a).

Parenthood. If pregnancy did not put much of a crimp in the recreational lifestyle of young adults, the subsequent parenthood clearly did. Figure 5.20 illustrates how married parenthood reduced evenings out—it dropped from 2–3 nights a week in high school to only about 1 night a week for married parents, versus about 2 nights a week for nonparents. This effect of married parenthood was somewhat larger than the effect for marriage alone, and in multivariate analyses it remained a stronger predictor than marriage (shown in Table A.5.1). Figure 5.20 also suggests that among women, but not men, being a single parent has effects very similar to married parenthood. The multivariate analyses, which control for other aspects of lifestyle, provide some additional perspective: among women, single motherhood actually reduced evenings out even more than married motherhood did (unstandardized multivariate coefficients of –.65 and –.43, respectively, from Table A.5.1a), whereas among men single fatherhood reduced evenings out by about two thirds as much as married fatherhood did (unstandardized multivariate coefficients of –.27 and –.42, respectively, from Table A.5.1b). Thus, among all nonmarried people, single parenthood tended to reduce evenings out for fun and recreation, and the effects were stronger for

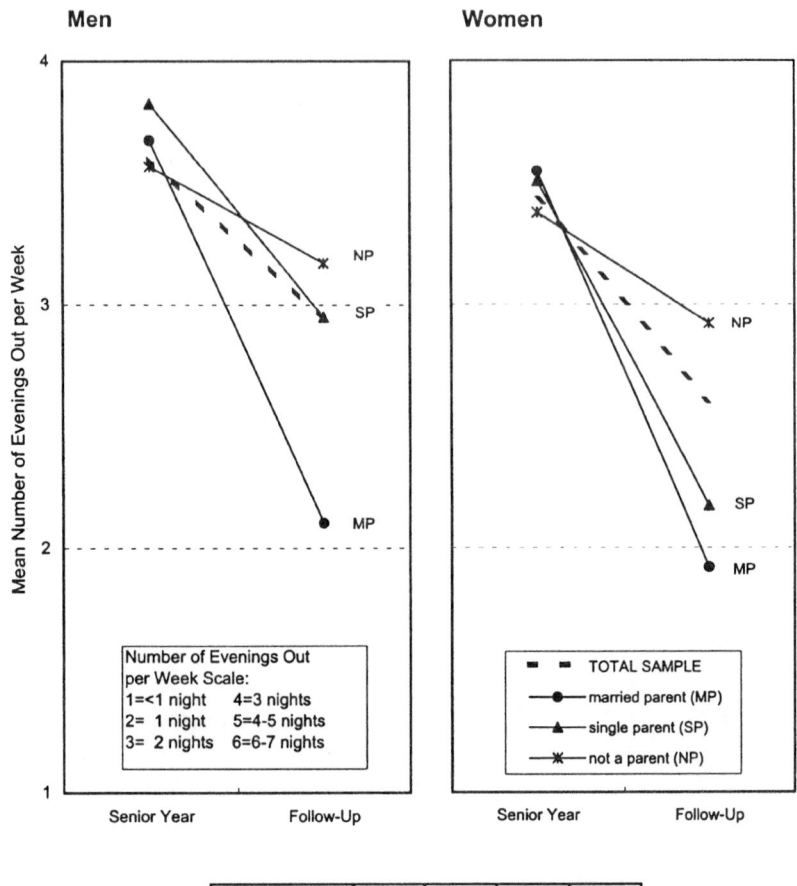

N's	MP	SP	NP	TOTAL
Men	9,295	1,909	32,834	44,038
Women	14,327	3,507	34,798	52,632

FIG. 5.20.   Change in mean numbers of evenings out for fun and recreation per week related to parenthood status at the time of follow-up. High school seniors from the classes of 1976–1984 were followed up as many as seven times between modal ages 19 and 32. In this figure, one person could contribute up to seven follow-up observations (see Additional Panel Analysis Issues and Strategies section in chap. 3). The approximate standard deviations for evenings out at senior year were 1.13 for males and 1.17 for females.

single mothers than for single fathers. The gender difference is quite understandable; single mothers are much more likely than single fathers to have primary custody of their children, and it appears that child care is a major factor interfering with evenings out.

Much the same observations apply to other activities such as going to parties or other social affairs or getting together with friends informally. Married parents were also substantially less likely than nonparents to go to bars, although for this dimension the multivariate analyses show somewhat stronger impacts for marriage than for parenthood (documented in Table A.5.5).

All of these reductions in social activities linked to parenthood may help to explain our earlier reported "parenthood effect" in reducing alcohol use and illicit drug use (Bachman et al., 1997). Parents busy caring for their children apparently have less time for socializing, and that in turn leaves them with fewer opportunities for substance use.

Interestingly, the social costs of parenthood were most pronounced along the dimension least closely linked with substance use: going out with a date or spouse. As mentioned earlier, the multivariate analyses (see Table A.5.2) indicate that the reductions in dating associated with marriage were almost entirely due to parenthood. This, of course, will come as no news to those who are, or once were, young parents.

Further Findings on Marital Status and Recreational Lifestyle

Engagement. Our earlier research showed "engagement effects" on drug use, especially heavy drinking and marijuana use, that were similar to but weaker than the "marriage effects." We found somewhat similar changes in frequency of evenings out and also in attendance at parties; those engaged (whether cohabiting or not) showed declines that were somewhat smaller than the declines associated with marriage, whereas those who were single showed the smallest declines (data in Bachman et al., 2001). The clearest set of findings is shown in Fig. 5.21, where it can be seen that going to bars increased most sharply (compared with senior year) among those who were single, did not increase among those who were married, and rose somewhat among those who were engaged (whether cohabiting or not). It thus appears that the "engagement effects" on substance use may be attributable, at least in part, to the shifts in recreational lifestyle that tend to accompany engagement.

Divorce. In chapter 4 we found few differences in religiosity linked to divorce, using data from 2-year follow-up intervals. In this chapter, however, we see that divorce seemed to make a difference in frequency of evenings out, as well as attendance at parties and going to bars. Figure 5.22 shows a

number of marital transitions (or nontransitions) occurring from one follow-up survey to the next, and for each transition pattern the figure shows
"before" and "after" mean frequencies of evenings out.

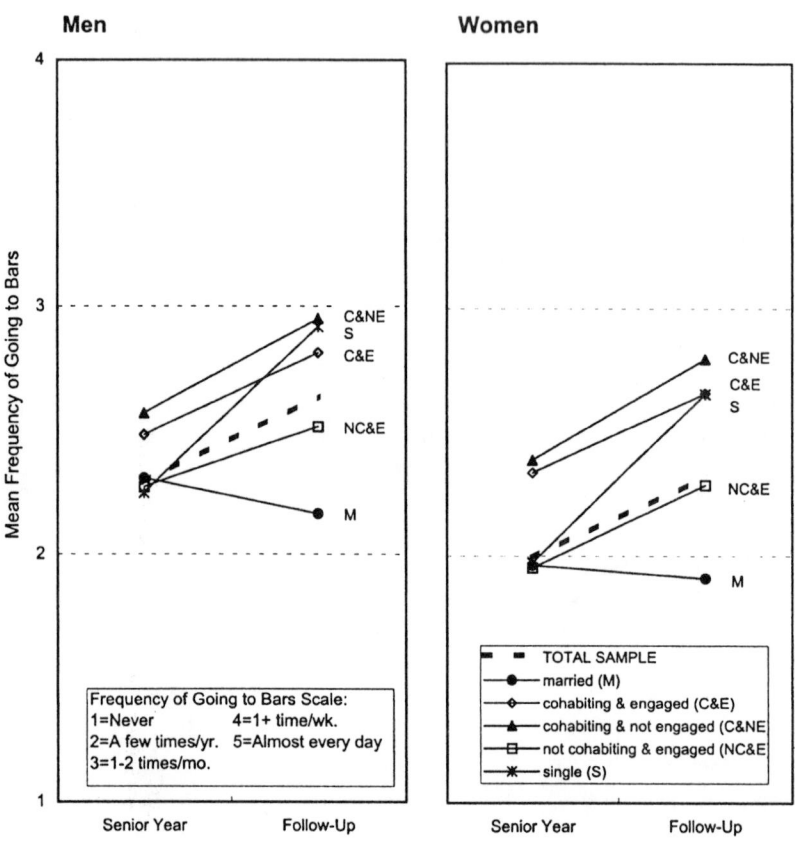

N's	M	CE	CNE	NCE	S	TOTAL
Men	3,194	209	448	366	5,043	9,260
Women	4,749	298	540	475	4,854	10,916

FIG. 5.21. Change in mean frequency of going to taverns, bars, or nightclubs related to engagement, cohabitation, and marriage at the time of follow-up. High school seniors from the classes of
1976–1984 were followed up as many as seven times between modal ages 19 and 32. In this figure,
one person could contribute up to seven follow-up observations (see Additional Panel Analysis
Issues and Strategies section in chap. 3). The approximate standard deviations for going to bars
at senior year were 1.02 for males and 0.95 for females.

We begin our examination of Fig. 5.22 by noting that this new analysis approach (which focuses on 2-year transitions) yields a number of findings consistent with the marriage and engagement findings reported earlier in this chapter (which were based on our usual analysis approach—i.e., treating senior-year surveys as "before" data and all follow-ups as "after" data). Figure 5.22 shows that: (a) Individuals married at both points reported the lowest frequencies of evenings out; these are also the individuals who were most likely to have been married long enough to have children and thus have fewer evenings available to go out. (b) Individuals single at both points reported the most frequent evenings out. (c) The transition from single to engaged involved some decline in evenings out. (d) The transition from engaged to married also involved some decline. (e) The full transition from single to married involved a larger decline, roughly the equivalent of declines c and d combined.

Turning now to the new data on divorce, Fig. 5.22 shows that the transition from married to divorced was associated with an increase in evenings out—in effect, a reversal of the negative "marriage effect" on evenings out. The increase was more pronounced among men than among women, perhaps because the divorced women were more likely than the divorced men to be tied down by having primary custody of young children. Individuals who went from divorced to married, on the other hand, showed a decline in evenings out roughly parallel to the decline experienced by those who went from single to married. Those who were divorced at both times showed little change; their frequencies of evenings out were lower than those consistently single but higher than those consistently married. Consistently divorced women reported fewer evenings out than consistently divorced men, perhaps again because more of the divorced women had primary custody of children.

Two-year transitions in frequency of going to parties or other social affairs showed patterns fairly similar to those for evenings out. Most notably, those who went from married to divorced showed an increase in party-going, which likely contributed to their increased use of alcohol and illicit drugs.

Two-year transitions in frequency of going to bars, shown in Fig. 5.23, showed sharp increases among the recently divorced. The figure also shows declines among those who went from divorced to married, parallel declines among those who went from single to married, and smaller declines among those who went from single to engaged or from engaged to married.

Another Look at Marriage Linked to Evenings Out and to Dating. We have shown in this chapter that marriage was associated with a decline in frequency of evenings out. This held true in the examination of 2-year transitions between follow-ups, as well as in the analyses that contrasted se-

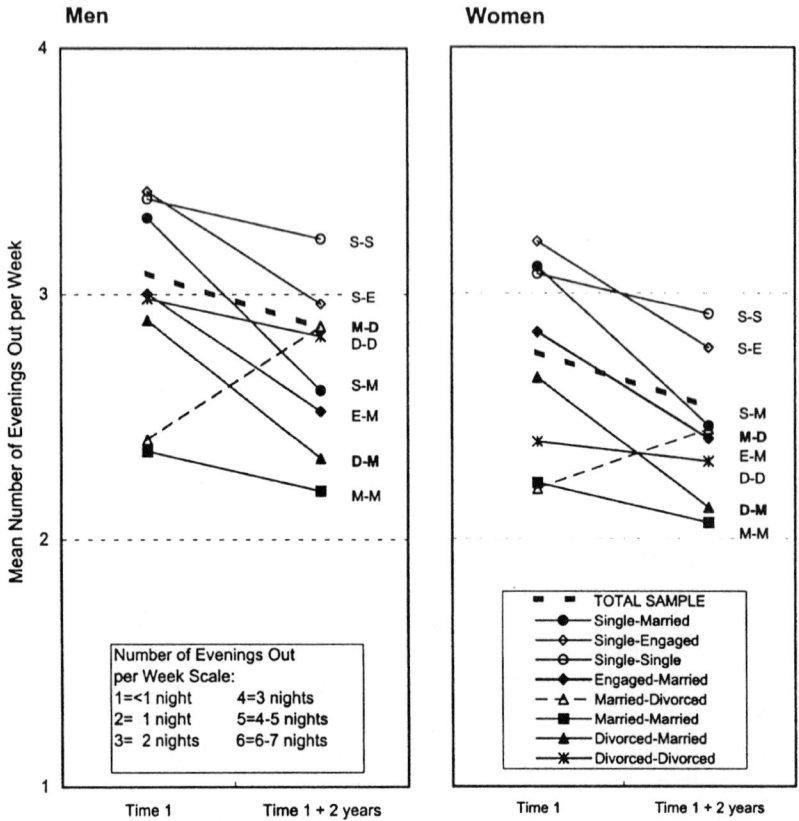

FIG. 5.22.   Mean change in numbers of evenings out for fun and recreation per week related to marriage–divorce transitions for the classes of 1976–1997. Time 1 is any follow-up (1–6); Time 1 + 2 years is the adjacent follow-up. In this figure, one person could contribute up to seven follow-up observations (see Additional Panel Analysis Issues and Strategies section in chap. 3). The approximate standard deviations for evenings out at senior year were 1.13 for males and 1.17 for females.

nior-year evenings out with any follow-up. As we pointed out at some length in chapter 3, utilizing these relatively simple two-point "before–after" comparisons made it feasible for us to deal with a variety of possible transitions at once, especially in multivariate analyses. When we focused on just the one transition from single to married, however, we found it workable to consider longer sequences of follow-ups. Doing so still required that we streamline the analysis by limiting our attention to individuals who remained single and individuals who made the transition from single to married and then continued to report being married in subsequent follow-ups. In this analysis approach we

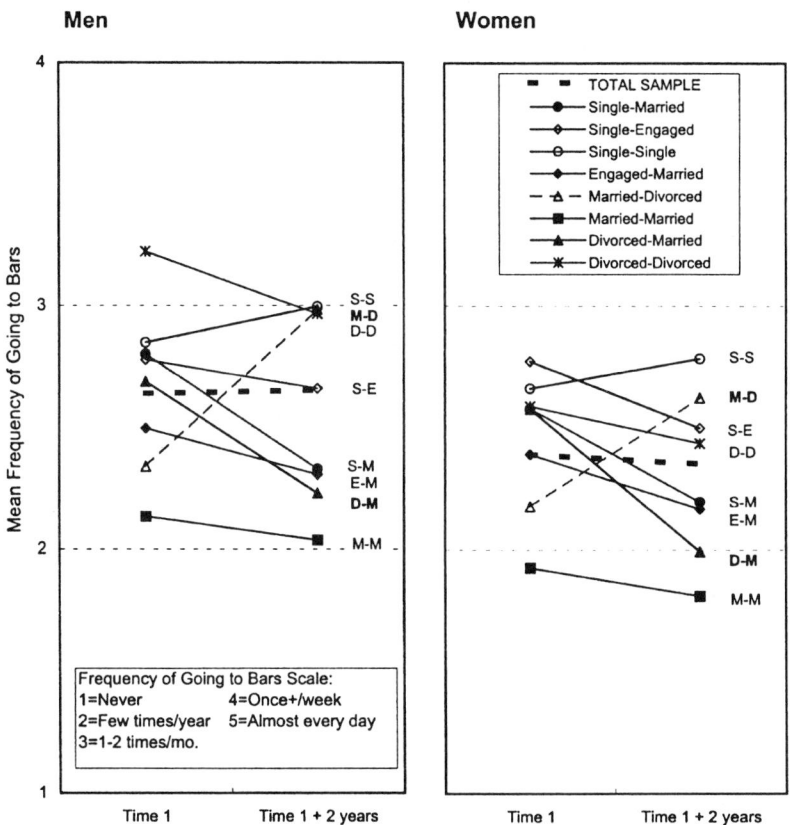

N's	S-M	S-E	S-S	E-M	M-D	M-M	D-M	D-D	TOTAL
Men	664	589	5,455	471	207	2,570	62	145	10,163
Women	847	794	5,289	721	313	4,161	131	272	12,528

FIG. 5.23.   Mean change in frequency of going to taverns, bars, or nightclubs related to marriage–divorce transitions for the classes of 1976–1997. Time 1 is any follow-up (1–6); Time 1 + 2 years is the adjacent follow-up. In this figure, one person could contribute up to seven follow-up observations (see Additional Panel Analysis Issues and Strategies section in chap. 3). The approximate standard deviations for going to bars at senior year were 1.02 for males and 0.95 for females.

excluded individuals who reported divorce, because pattern sequences incorporating divorce would have yielded far too many possible patterns—many having very few cases. For much the same reasons, we ignored the "engaged" category in this analysis approach and simply treated engaged individuals as "single." Figure 5.24 shows an 8-time-point analysis linking marriage transitions to frequency of evenings out.

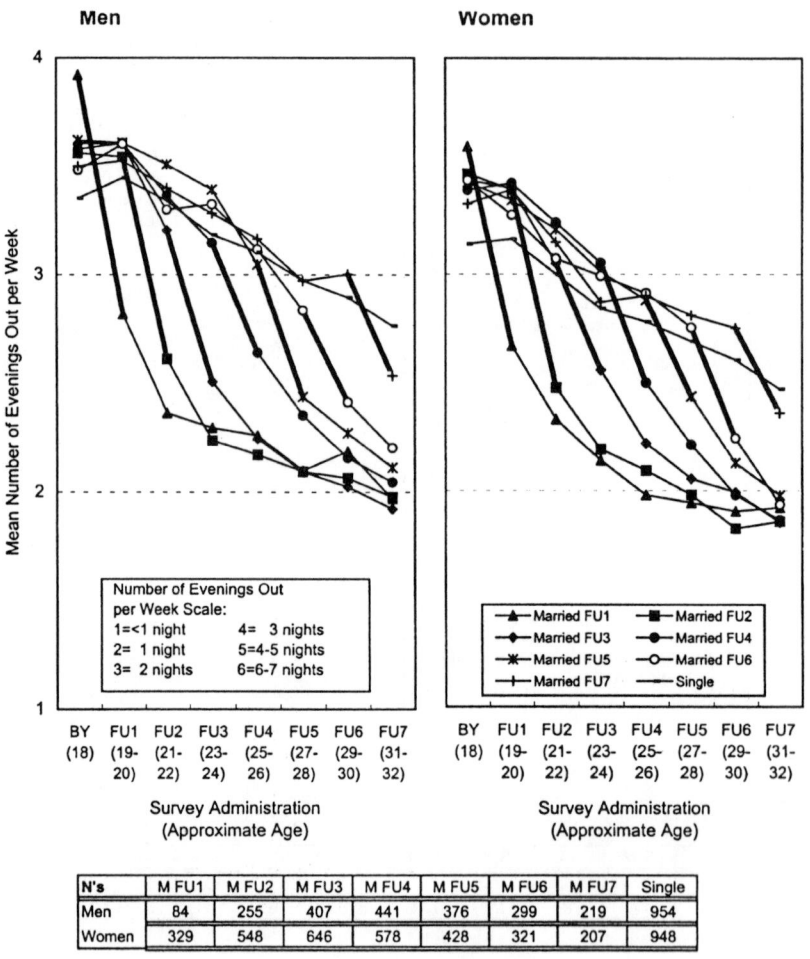

FIG. 5.24. Mean change in numbers of evenings out for fun and recreation per week related to marital status for the classes of 1976–1984 across eight time points. No missing data were allowed. Respondents who were engaged were considered single. Bold line indicates the time interval during which marriage occurred.

The first thing about Fig. 5.24 that strikes the eye is the fact that no matter whether respondents made the transition from single to married in their late teens, twenties, or early thirties, the "marriage effect" was much the same—a distinct drop in average number of evenings out for fun and recreation (transitions from single to married are shown by the heavier lines in the figure). In earlier research we have shown a similar "marriage effect" of reduced alcohol use and illicit drug use. Indeed, the pattern for evenings out shown in Fig. 5.24 shows many similarities to the pattern shown in Fig. 3.2 for marijuana use.

Another observation based on Fig. 5.24 is that there was some age-related decline in evenings out above and beyond that associated with marriage. In the years after marriage, of course, some of the decline in evenings out may be attributable to "parenthood effects" described earlier in this chapter. But those who remained single for several follow-ups also showed modest declines in evenings out, on average. These may reflect a number of the other factors documented earlier in this chapter; for example, as they grew older fewer respondents lived in dormitories or in other "dorm-like" settings.

Do marital transitions affect dating in the same way as they affect evenings out in general? The answer, as shown in Fig. 5.25, is partly yes and partly no. When it comes to frequency of going out with a date or spouse, once again the transition from single to married is marked by a reduction; however, in other respects the patterns for dating are different from those shown in Fig. 5.24 for evenings out. Not surprisingly, just *prior* to the interval in which marriage occurred, the frequency of dating tended to increase. Also not surprisingly, those who remained single through all seven follow-ups showed lower overall frequencies of dating. It is of interest to note that frequency of dating continued to decline fairly steeply in the years after marriage occurred. This is quite consistent with the observation, based on analyses earlier in this chapter, that becoming a (married) parent was associated with substantial decreases in going out on dates (with spouse).

One other observation based on Fig. 5.25 is that the patterns for dating do not match the patterns for alcohol use and illicit drug use nearly as closely as do the patterns for evenings out (as shown in Fig. 5.24). This is nicely consistent with the finding that dating shows relatively weak correlations with substance use.

Conclusions Based on Multivariate Analyses

All of the relationships between recreational lifestyle measures and post-high-school experiences, described bivariately in the preceding sections, were included also in multivariate analyses (following the approach

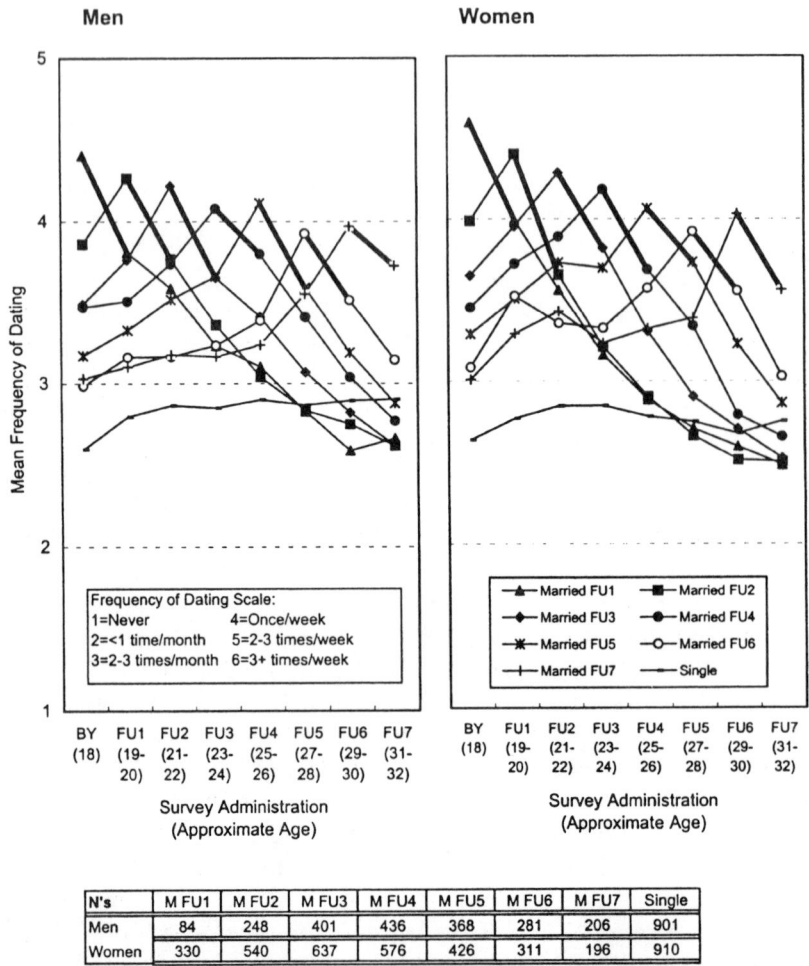

FIG. 5.25. Mean change in frequency of going out with a date (or spouse if married) related to marital status for the classes of 1976–1984 across eight time points. No missing data were allowed. Respondents who were engaged were considered single. Bold line indicates the time interval during which marriage occurred.

outlined in chap. 3). Key multivariate findings are included in the appendix (Tables A.5.1–A.5.5 for chap. 5), and more detailed information is provided in Bachman et al., 2001. We have already referred to some of the specific multivariate findings earlier in this chapter as we described and interpreted the bivariate findings; this section is limited to reporting general observations and conclusions.

The first general observation is that the multivariate findings for frequency of evenings out (Table A.5.1) are fairly closely matched by the findings for frequency of attending parties or other social affairs (Table A.5.3), frequency of getting together with friends informally (Table A.5.4), and frequency of going to bars, taverns, or nightclubs (Table A.5.5). Because these dimensions show similar patterns, we focus primarily on the evenings-out findings. However, the multivariate findings for frequency of dating (Table A.5.2) are in several respects different; accordingly, we discuss them separately.

The next general observation is that the focal variables in this chapter, in contrast to the religiosity measures in chapter 4, were quite predictable from the set of post-high-school experiences included in the multivariate analyses. The multiple correlations predicting follow-up evenings out were .44 for women and .42 for men (see bottom of sixth column in Tables A.5.1a and A.5.1b); including base-year evenings out in the equations increased the multiple correlations only modestly (to .48 and .47, respectively; see bottom of seventh column). Indeed, the simple (bivariate) correlations between senior-year and follow-up evenings out were only .19 for women and .22 for men, indicating that follow-up evenings out were influenced much more by current roles and circumstances than by senior-year recreational patterns.

Another general observation is that when student status and work status were combined with living arrangements, engagement, pregnancy, and parental status as predictors of evenings out and the other recreational activities, most contributions of student and work status were greatly reduced or eliminated. The one interesting exception is that those in military service, both men and women, showed greater than average increases in frequencies of evenings out and particularly in frequencies of going to bars; the controls for living arrangements diminished these relationships only slightly for women and actually enhanced them slightly for men (documented in Tables A.5.1 and A.5.5).

One other general observation involves the strong "predictive contribution" of follow-up number in the multivariate analyses. The follow-up number is, of course, a fairly close proxy for age; the modal ages were 19–20 for the first follow-up, 21–22 for the second, and so on up to 31–32 for the seventh follow-up. We showed at the start of the chapter how evenings out and other recreational behaviors tended mostly to decline with increasing age, and we suggested that some of the factors examined herein could account for much of the declines. Including follow-up numbers in the multivariate analyses thus was important not only to control for age differences while examining the contribution of other factors, but also because the analyses provide some insight into the extent to which age-related differences may be explainable by other factors. We turn to that next.

Accounting for Age-Related Changes in Evenings Out and Dating.
Figure 5.1 showed that immediately after high school among young women, and soon after high school among young men, average frequencies of evenings out began a steady decline that continued through modal ages 31–32. Now we are in a position to consider to what extent these average changes in frequencies of evenings out are explainable in terms of the responsibilities of young adulthood, as examined in this chapter. We have already shown that a number of particular experiences, most notably marriage and parenthood, were associated with declines in evenings out. The multivariate analyses provide an opportunity to estimate the total impact of these experiences by looking at age-related differences *adjusted to take account of all other factors included in the analyses.* The results, shown in Fig. 5.26, suggest that half or more of the age-related change observed in evenings out is attributable to the other factors included in our research, and Table A.5.1 shows that the strongest among these other factors were living arrangements (including marital status and parenthood). It thus appears that the increasing proportions of young adults who marry and become parents account for a good deal of the declines in evenings out that occur during the twenties and early thirties.

Figure 5.27 shows a similar analysis for frequency of going out with a date (or spouse, if married), with more dramatic results. The overall negative relationship between age and dating was completely eliminated (indeed, it was very slightly reversed) when the responsibilities of adulthood were taken into account. As noted earlier in the chapter (and shown in Table A.5.2), parenthood was the most important factor decreasing dating, whereas being engaged tended to increase frequency of dating. Age per se, on the other hand, seemed to make virtually no difference once these other factors were taken into account.

SUMMARY

Compared with the measures of religiosity treated in chapter 4, the measures of time spent in fun and recreation treated in this chapter proved to be much less stable over time and also much more responsive or reactive to a variety of post-high-school experiences. There were other fundamental differences, of course, between religiosity and the topics treated in this chapter: they were related in opposite directions to substance use and *generally* in opposite directions to post-high-school experiences. For example, married parenthood tended to increase attendance at religious services, whereas it reduced evenings out for fun and recreation. Nevertheless, it is of interest to note that the religiosity measures were not at all strongly correlated with frequency of evenings out (product–moment correlations at senior year and

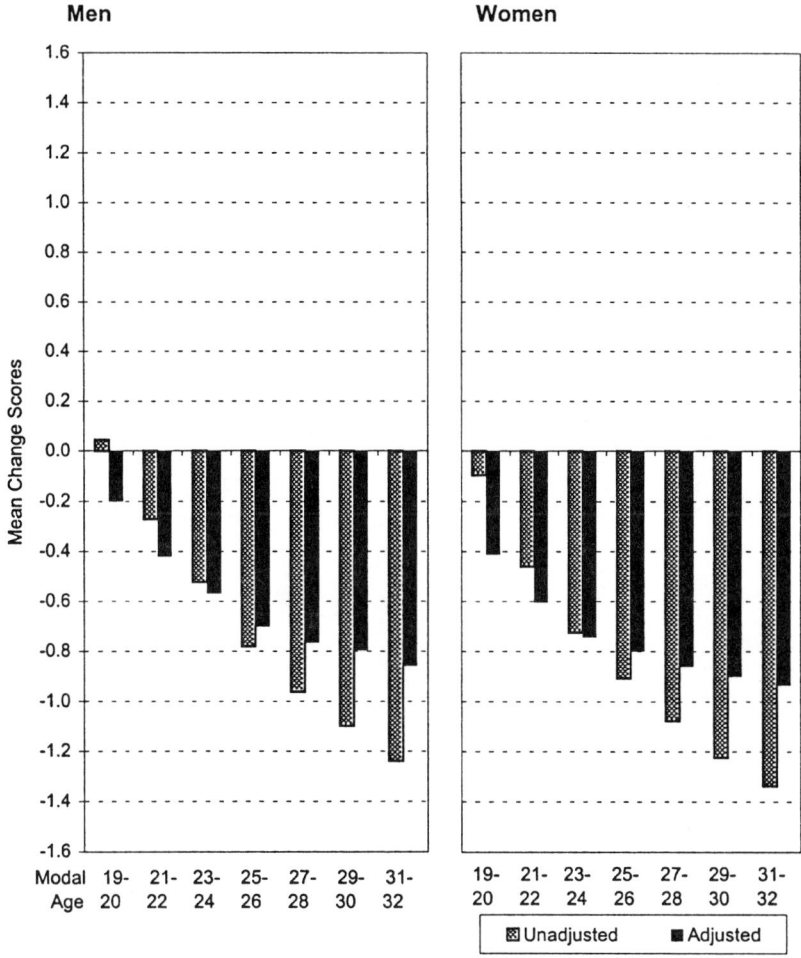

Men   **Women**

Mean Change Scores

Modal   19- 21- 23- 25- 27- 29- 31-   19- 21- 23- 25- 27- 29- 31-
Age   20   22   24   26   28   30   32   20   22   24   26   28   30   32

☒ Unadjusted   ■ Adjusted

FIG. 5.26.   Mean change scores in evenings out, unadjusted and adjusted, related to modal age. The mean change score is the predicted amount of change in evenings out between the senior year and the modal age indicated. The unadjusted mean change score only controls the follow-up survey interval (or, modal age). The adjusted mean change score controls all the predictor variables. Calculation of change scores is discussed in detail in the appendix.

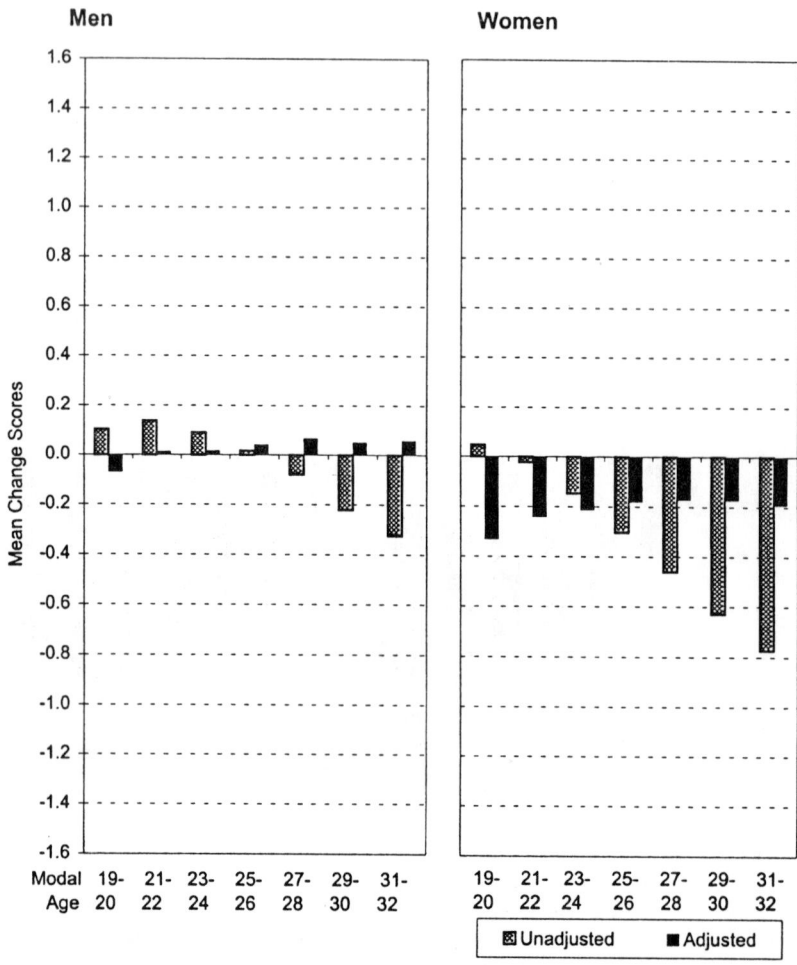

FIG. 5.27. Mean change scores in dating, unadjusted and adjusted, related to modal age. The mean change score is the predicted amount of change in dating between the senior year and the modal age indicated. The unadjusted mean change score only controls the follow-up survey interval (or, modal age). The adjusted mean change score controls all the predictor variables. Calculation of change scores is discussed in detail in the appendix.

across all 7 follow-ups ranged from –.04 to –.09; see also Table A.2). So it would seem that, to the extent that frequency of evenings out and other recreational activities treated in this chapter mediated the relationship between post-high-school experiences and substance use, those mediating effects were rather different from (and nonoverlapping with) any mediating effects of religiosity.

Time spent in the recreational behaviors examined in this chapter tended to decline as young people left high school and gradually assumed more and more of the responsibilities of young adulthood. For most of the recreational behaviors, the largest declines seemed attributable to marriage and parenthood. But these and other post-high-school experiences did not explain or account for all of the age-related declines in evenings out (see Fig. 5.26) or in attendance at parties or other social affairs, getting together with friends informally, or going to bars. This suggests some residual effects that were more directly age-related rather than attributable to marriage and parenthood. We suspect that some of the age-linked decline was due simply to the declining proportions of age-mates who remained unmarried and nonparents. Thus, as unmarried young adults moved from age 19 to age 32, they were likely to have fewer and fewer friends who remained unencumbered by the responsibilities of marriage and parenthood, and this reduction in potential companions may have reduced the opportunities or incentives for evenings out for fun and recreation.

All of these findings concerning frequency of evenings out and of going to parties and to bars showed patterns rather similar to those found in our earlier book for alcohol use, marijuana use, and cocaine use (Bachman et al., 1997). These similarities in reactions to post-high-school experiences provide further evidence that evenings out and the other recreational activities may be important mediators of some of the impacts of those post-high-school experiences on drug use. Nevertheless, problems remain in sorting out causal interpretations.

We noted such problems of causal interpretation at several points in this chapter, but it is worth illustrating them again here. Evenings out for fun and recreation, especially those that involve parties or going to bars, involve added opportunities and perhaps temptations to drink or possibly to use an illicit substance. Sometimes such opportunities prompt individuals to indulgences that they did not plan or anticipate; indeed, it occasionally happens that such indulgences are regretted afterward. All of these scenarios seem consistent with the highly plausible causal interpretation that going to parties and bars contributes to substance use. However, it is also true that young adults are usually aware in advance of such opportunities and temptations; indeed, those opportunities quite often may constitute the primary motivation for going to parties or bars. Thus there is also strong support for the causal interpretation that people desiring to use substances choose, *as a consequence of those desires,* to go to parties and bars. So we conclude that evenings out and going to parties and bars are importantly linked with substance use, while also acknowledging that a number of complexly interrelated causal processes underlie those linkages.

When it comes to frequency of going out with a date or spouse, the story is somewhat different. The explanation of age-related changes is simpler and more complete: Those with children dated less, and there was little in the way of any residual age-related effect (see Fig. 5.27). Importantly, the relationships between dating and substance use were weaker than was the case for any of the other measures of fun and recreation treated in this chapter. So as a potential mediating variable, frequency of dating is not so strong a candidate.

6

Perceived Risks and Disapproval of Smoking, Heavy Drinking, and Illicit Drug Use

Young people's views about various substances are closely linked to whether and how much they use those substances. Individuals who see great risk of harm in cigarette use also are likely to disapprove cigarette use, and such individuals are unlikely to be smokers. The same connections between attitudes and behaviors hold for heavy drinking, marijuana use, and cocaine use.

It is hardly surprising that attitudes about substances correlate with actual use, of course, but much remains unsettled about the nature and direction of causal connections. Do drug-related attitudes cause or contribute to patterns of use? Undoubtedly they do. But opposite causal relationships also are plausible, as when someone tries using a substance and, as a direct consequence of that experience, has a change in opinion about the risks of such use. As one example, those trying marijuana and detecting no adverse effects might revise their perceived risks downward, and that would contribute to the overall negative correlation found between perceived risks and marijuana use. Alternatively, those experiencing negative consequences after drinking a lot might increase their perceived risks of drinking heavily, and that would tend to diminish the overall negative correlation between perceived risks and heavy drinking (at least, *past* heavy drinking).

There is fairly strong evidence that increases during the 1980s in perceived risks and disapproval regarding marijuana contributed to declines in
use, whereas the reverse explanation (that changes in marijuana use caused
the changes in attitudes) was not supported by the data (e.g., Bachman et
al., 1988; Bachman, 1994). Similar findings emerged for cocaine use
(Bachman, Johnston, & O'Malley, 1991). However, although these time
trend data support the view that the dominant causal direction runs from
attitudes to behaviors, we cannot rule out the possibility—indeed, the likelihood—that at least some causal effects at the individual level run in the
opposite direction, from behaviors to attitudes.

In sum, even though we have panel data tracking individuals over a
number of years, with repeated measurements of both attitudes and behaviors, it still is not possible to sort out just how much one causes the other.
This is especially true when we consider that the measurements are separated by 2-year intervals. However, given the nature of the survey measures
(e.g., present perceived risks of marijuana versus use during the previous 30
days or the previous 12 months), we think the problems of sorting out causal
direction would not be fully resolved even with much more frequent measurement. What we can do, however, is document how attitudes about a
particular substance are related to the use of that substance and whether
such relationships seem to change very much during young adulthood.

In this chapter we follow the general analysis pattern established in the
preceding two chapters. We begin by examining overall changes in respondents' perceived risks and in their levels of disapproval with respect to four
dimensions of substance use: smoking, heavy drinking, marijuana use, and
cocaine use. Next we consider how individuals' attitudes were related to
their behaviors. Then we explore the extent to which the changes in attitudes were linked to changes in roles and responsibilities during young
adulthood.

FOCUSING ON VIEWS ABOUT SPECIFIC SUBSTANCES RATHER THAN SUBSTANCE USE IN GENERAL

It would simplify matters from both conceptual and analytic standpoints if we
were able to focus on individuals' overall views about substance use, rather
than having to deal with each substance one at a time. Alas, that approach
simply does not work as well as one that treats the substances specifically.

It is true that individuals' disapproval ratings tend to correlate across
substances, as do their perceptions of risk. It is not hard to understand why.
One reason is that views about a variety of substances tend to have common
causes. For example, we saw in chapter 4 that religiosity is negatively correlated with actual use of cigarettes, alcohol, and illicit drugs; it is also the case

that religiosity is correlated (positively) with perceived risks and disapproval regarding each of these substances (illustrated in chap. 8). There is another important reason why attitudes about substances tend to be positively correlated: Personal experiences with one sort of substance (whether pleasurable or the opposite) may generalize to other substances. An example is that individuals who try marijuana and enjoy it may, as a direct consequence, lower their perceived risk and disapproval views regarding not only marijuana use, but also cocaine use and other illicit substance use. A converse example is that individuals who get high on alcohol and embarrass themselves (or worse) may increase their perceptions of the risks of getting high on any substance, not just alcohol.

In spite of these cross-drug relationships, however, it remains true (as documented later in this chapter and in Table A.2) that the *strongest* correlates of the use of any particular substance are the views about *that* substance, with views about other substances showing only weaker correlations. Accordingly, our approach in this chapter is to focus on views about each substance separately, noting a number of similarities as well as some distinctions.

PATTERNS OF AGE-RELATED CHANGE IN PERCEIVED RISKS AND DISAPPROVAL

As noted, the disapproval of any form of substance use examined here is strongly correlated with the perceived risk of that use. Although the existence of such correlations does not establish causal direction, a fairly straightforward conceptual argument can be made: One important reason for disapproving the use of a substance, but not necessarily the only reason, is the perception that such use is risky or dangerous to the user or to others or both. We find somewhat less plausible the reverse interpretation that disapproval causes something to be perceived as risky. In any case, the two perspectives on each drug—perceived risks of use and disapproval of use—are closely enough linked so that we discuss them together.

Consistent with our causal assumptions, we first present the findings for perceived risks of each substance use behavior, and we then present the findings for disapproval. We maintain the separation because the two dimensions are different conceptually and also because they differ in their strength of correlation with actual use (as we show later in this chapter). And if these reasons were not enough, there is a practical consideration for examining the two dimensions separately: Throughout much of the Monitoring the Future study, the perceived risk items and the disapproval items appeared on separate questionnaire forms, thus making it impossible to combine them. (In recent years some questionnaire forms included both dimensions, thereby providing the opportunity to show how strongly the dimensions are correlated. These correlations are included in Table A.2 and are discussed later in this chapter.)

Perceived Risks and Disapproval of Pack-a-Day Cigarette Use

Most high school seniors and young adults in recent years have perceived great risk in smoking one or more packs of cigarettes per day, and nearly all of the rest perceived moderate risk. As shown in Fig. 6.1, only 5% or fewer of young adults perceived slight risk or no risk. The "no risk" category is not shown separately in the figure because it is, quite literally, "vanishingly small" (less than 1% in all instances).

The figure also shows that as young adults from the high school classes of 1976–1984 grew older, there was a modest and gradual rise in the proportions who perceived great risk in pack-a-day smoking—an increase from 62% to 73% among men and from 64% to 83% among women. The X notations in the figure show that during the period when the classes of 1976–1984 grew older, there was a small overall increase in perceived risks of smoking among high school seniors, suggesting that a period effect (historic change) occurred during that time. But the upward trend in the X notations is only about half as steep as that shown as an age-related pattern among the young adults. Accordingly, we think that Fig. 6.1 reveals age-related increases in perceived risk in addition to the period effect. Further evidence of both age and period effects in young adults' perceived risks of smoking is available in our annual report of Monitoring the Future survey results; in particular, it is worth noting that throughout the 1990s, the proportions perceiving great risk in pack-a-day smoking averaged 77% among those aged 27–30 in contrast to 69% among high school seniors during the same period (adapted from Johnston et al., 2000b, pp. 159, 167, Table 6-1). Put differently, only 23% of those in their late twenties, compared with 31% of high school seniors, perceived anything less than great risk in pack-a-day smoking. Thus we conclude that perceived risks of smoking are large by the end of high school but grow even larger during young adulthood.

No clear patterns of change related to age—or, for that matter, change related to time period—were evident for *disapproval* of pack-a-day smoking (see Bachman et al., 2001, for data; see also Johnston et al., 2000a). The disapproval question asked respondents whether they disapproved of people (over age 18) smoking one or more packs of cigarettes per day, and it provided three response alternatives: don't disapprove, disapprove, and strongly disapprove. In spite of the fact that most young adults saw great *risk* in such smoking, fully 30–33% of men and 24–30% of women indicated that they "don't disapprove" the behavior, 31–38% indicated "disapprove," and

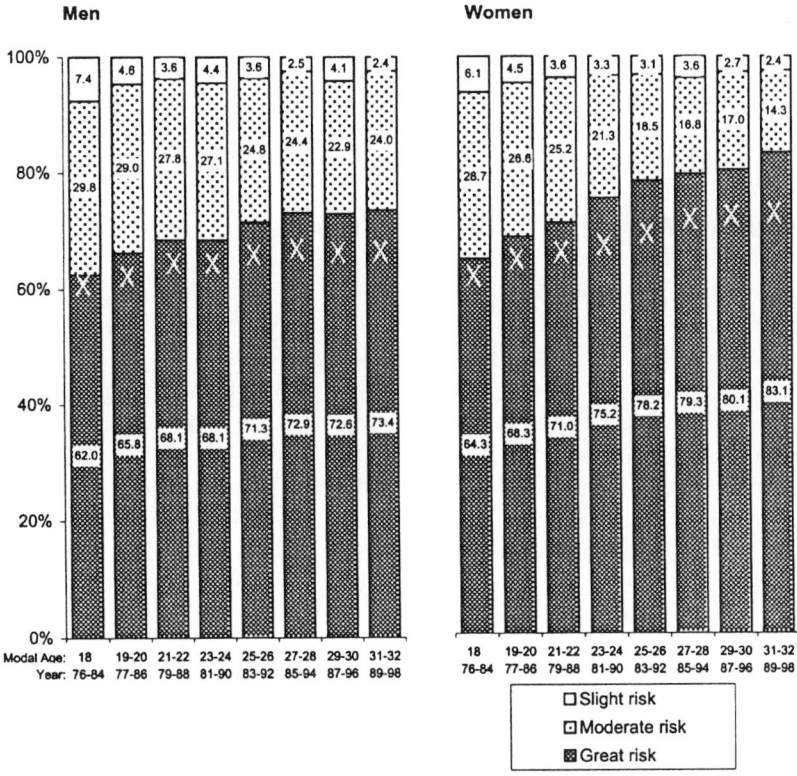

FIG. 6.1.   Perceived risk of smoking one or more packs of cigarettes per day for panel respondents followed from age 18 to ages 31–32. Bar percentages are based on high school senior data, plus follow-ups 1–7, from class years 1976–1984; one person could contribute up to seven follow-up observations (see Additional Panel Analysis Issues and Strategies section in chap. 3). The sample is restricted to those respondents who answered this question at follow-up 6 and/or follow-up 7. Percentages do not sum to 100. Fewer than 1% of respondents reported "no risk" and therefore were omitted. Approximate numbers of observations per age group for men: 850; for women: 1,030. X notations demarcate the boundaries between "great risk" and the three lower risk categories for high school seniors in the given year ranges. Senior samples include approximately 69,000 men and 72,000 women in each year grouping.

33–38% of men and 32–43% of women indicated "strongly disapprove." It thus appears that some young adults who saw great risk in smoking were nevertheless unwilling to condemn or "disapprove" the behavior—especially to the point of describing themselves as "strongly disapproving." Part of the explanation is that about 20% of those who perceived a "great risk" of pack-a-day smoking were themselves current smokers (i.e., had smoked during the past 30 days), and fully half of those who perceived "moderate risk" were current smokers. These individuals were apparently able to acknowledge the risks of smoking, but few went so far as to "strongly disapprove" it. These apparent inconsistencies between perceived risk levels and disapproval levels occurred to a much greater extent for cigarette use than for other substance use, as we subsequently show and discuss.

Perceived Risks and Disapproval of Occasional Heavy Drinking

The Monitoring the Future surveys include perceived risk and disapproval questions about several levels of alcohol use: trying alcohol, taking 1–2 drinks nearly every day, taking 4–5 drinks nearly every day, and having five or more drinks once or twice each weekend. Given that some research suggests positive health effects of 1–2 drinks daily, and given also that our primary measure of *problem* alcohol use is occasional heavy drinking (five or more drinks at a time), we focus our attention here on ratings of risks and disapproval associated with having five or more drinks once or twice each weekend (data on the other measures are available in Johnston et al., 2000a). The findings for perceived risks are presented in Fig. 6.2.

The most worrisome finding in Fig. 6.2 is that more than one third of male high school seniors from the classes of 1976–1984 perceived only slight risk or no risk in occasional heavy drinking, and nearly one fourth of the female seniors felt the same. (The gender differences here do not simply reflect the fact that consuming five drinks has a greater impact on the typical woman than the typical man. Similar gender differences were evident for the question about having 1–2 drinks daily.)

Figure 6.2 indicates some gradual increase in perceived risks after age 22; however, the X notations in the figure also provide evidence of period effects nearly as large as the age-related shifts. In other words, throughout much of the time period in which graduates of the classes of 1976–1984 were growing older, each new senior class was slightly more likely than previous ones to perceive risk in occasional heavy drinking. More detailed analyses of age-related differences, shown on a year-by-year basis, are provided by Johnston et al. (2000b). Those analyses show that the small year-by-year increases in perceived risks among high school seniors, and also among those aged 19–22, ended after about 1992. More important for present purposes, the analyses show that *for any particular calendar year*, the perceived risks of occasional heavy drinking were lowest among those aged 23–26 and only slightly higher among those aged 27–30. For example, averaged across the years 1990–1999, the proportions perceiving great risk in having five or more drinks once or twice each weekend were 46% of high school seniors, 40% of those aged 19–22, 39% of those aged 23–26, and 43%

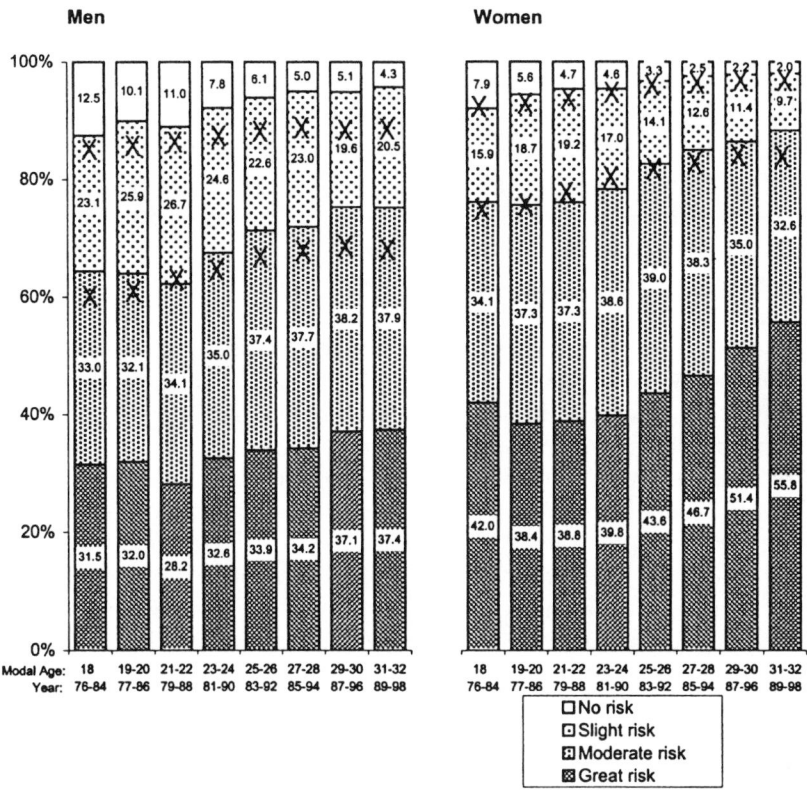

FIG. 6.2.   Perceived risk of having five or more drinks once or twice each weekend for panel respondents followed from age 18 to ages 31–32. Bar percentages are based on high school senior data, plus follow-ups 1–7, from class years 1976–1984; one person could contribute up to seven follow-up observations (see Additional Panel Analysis Issues and Strategies section in chap. 3). The sample is restricted to those respondents who answered this question at follow-up 6 and/or follow-up 7. Approximate numbers of observations per age group for men: 860; for women: 1,030. X notations demarcate the boundaries between the three highest risk categories for high school seniors in the given year ranges. Senior samples include approximately 69,000 men and 72,000 women in each year grouping.

of those aged 27–30 (adapted from Johnston et al., 2000b, p. 167, Table 6-1). We thus conclude that the apparent "age effect" shown in Fig. 6.2 is better interpreted as *primarily* a period effect, perhaps along with a slight curvilinear age effect.

The findings for disapproval of occasional heavy drinking parallel to some extent those for perceived risk shown in Fig. 6.2 (details are provided in Bachman et al., 2001). Only 22% of young men at modal ages 21–22 strongly disapproved such behavior, but that rose to 35% when they reached modal ages 31–32; among women the corresponding increase was from 32% to 51% who strongly disapproved. Other analyses (Johnston et al., 2000b, see especially tabular data on p. 170) show increases in disapproval among successive classes of high school seniors through about 1992, thus suggesting that a portion of the age-related trends in disapproval may best be interpreted as period effects; however, these same analyses (along with analyses done for this book) suggest that there were also modest age-related increases in disapproval of occasional heavy drinking.

It is important to note that with respect to occasional heavy drinking, disapproval ratings corresponded fairly closely to ratings of risk (whereas for smoking we noted some apparent inconsistency). The time trends in views about occasional heavy drinking very likely reflect the extensive media efforts begun during the 1980s to publicize the risks—*to others as well as to self*—when people drink heavily. Perhaps increased awareness of the risks to others, particularly when heavy drinkers drive, contributed to the increases in disapproval during the 1980s and early 1990s. So although some young adults may have been hesitant to "strongly disapprove" of smokers who were "harming only themselves" (apart from passive smoking effects), these same young adults may have been more willing to condemn heavy drinking because it includes risks to others—"innocent bystanders."

Perceived Risks and Disapproval of Marijuana Use

Three levels of marijuana use were included in the risk and disapproval measures: trying it once or twice, smoking it occasionally, and smoking it regularly. Two indexes were created, one summing the three perceived risk items and one summing the three disapproval items. Figure 6.3 presents the results for perceived risks of marijuana use.

Possible scores on the risk of marijuana use index ranged from 3 ("no risk" for any of the three levels of use) to 12 ("great risk" for use at any level). As is shown in Fig. 6.3, there were few respondents who saw no (or almost no) risk at any level of use (scores of 3 or 4); among seniors in the classes of 1976–1984, only about 18% of men and 14% of women were so sanguine about marijuana use, and by the time they reached their early thirties the proportions had dropped to 5% or less. On the other hand, there were also relatively few respondents who saw *great* risk in any level of marijuana use; only about 14% of seniors had highest scores (11 or 12), and by age 30, the proportion with such scores rose only to 21% among men and 24% among women. Most respondents assigned different risks to different levels of marijuana use; thus, the majority saw no or slight risk in trying the drug, slight or moderate risk in using it occasionally, but great risk in using it regularly (see Johnston et al., 2000b, p. 164, Table 6-1). As already indicated, there were some increases in perceived risks of marijuana use as graduates from the classes of 1976–1984 grew older; however, the X notations in Fig. 6.3 show that during the same time period, the perceptions of marijuana risk among new classes of high school seniors also rose—and at a steeper rate until the last few years. Another perspective on

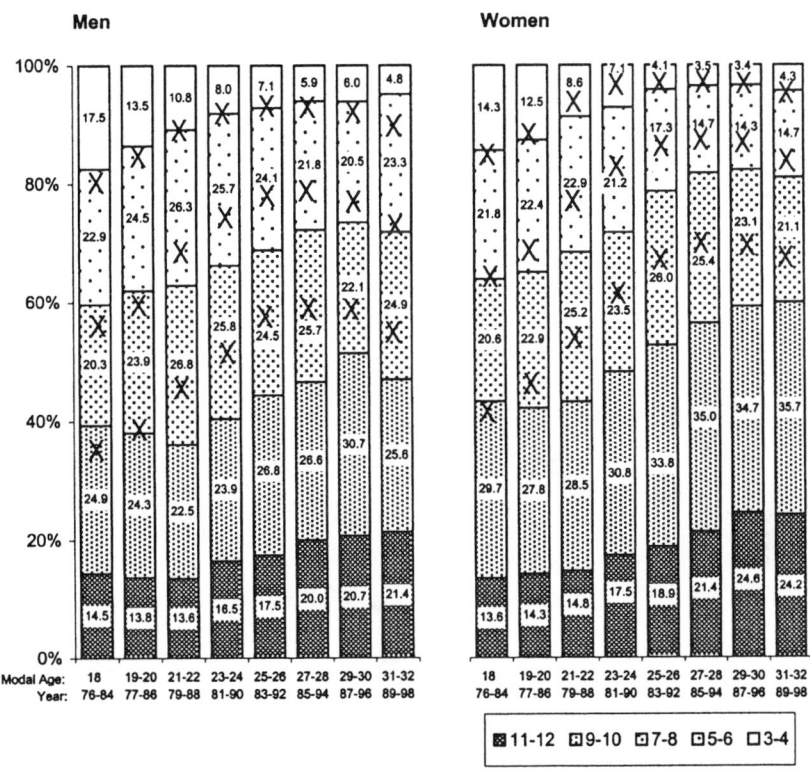

FIG. 6.3.   Perceived risk of marijuana use (index) for panel respondents followed from age 18 to ages 31–32. The index is the sum of responses for (a) trying marijuana once or twice, (b) smoking marijuana occasionally, and (c) smoking marijuana regularly, each with the following scale: 1 = no risk, 2 = slight risk, 3 = moderate risk, 4 = great risk. Bar percentages are based on high school senior data, plus follow-ups 1–7, from class years 1976–1984; one person could contribute up to seven follow-up observations (see Analysis Issues and Strategies section in chap. 3). The sample is restricted to those respondents who answered this question at follow-up 6 and/or follow-up 7. Approximate numbers of observations per age group for men: 840; for women: 1,010. X notations demarcate the boundaries between the four highest risk index categories for the senior year data from sets of years indicated; senior samples include approximately 69,000 men and 72,000 women in each year grouping.

changes over time is provided in Fig. 6.4 (adapted from Johnston et al., 2000b, p. 164–167, Table 6-1). This figure traces four age bands using data from 20 annual surveys (1980–1999) and shows changes over time in proportions perceiving "great risk" in (a) trying marijuana once or twice or (b) using it regularly. The data on perceived risks of regular use (upper portion of the figure) show most clearly how seniors' views shifted, rising from 50% in 1980 to 79% in 1991 and declining thereafter. The changes for the older

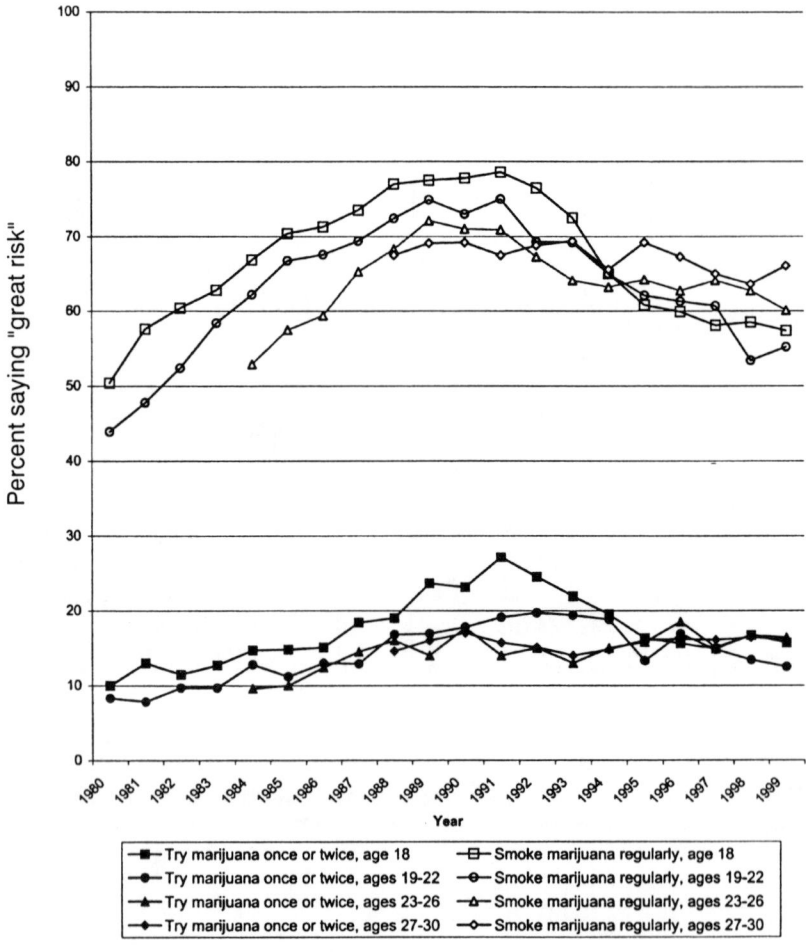

FIG. 6.4.   Perceived risk of marijuana among high school seniors (aged 18) and young adults in modal age groups of 19–22, 23–26, and 27–30 from the years 1980 to 1999. Ratings of occasional use are not shown; see Johnston et al. (2000b).

age groups were less pronounced, suggesting some cohort differences; in particular, perceptions of risk among those in their mid- or late twenties did not drop as much or as quickly during the 1990s as was true for the younger age bands. This is consistent with the data in Fig. 6.3, showing that among members of the classes of 1976–1984, the shifts in perceived risks of marijuana use were more gradual than the changes in views among seniors during the same time period (the X notations in the figure).

The findings for disapproval of marijuana use are fairly similar to those for the perceived risks shown in Figs. 6.3 and 6.4. Here again many respondents made distinctions linked to level of marijuana use; the modal response for trying marijuana was "don't disapprove," whereas the modal response for regular use was "strongly disapprove." When they were high school seniors, relatively few members of the classes of 1976–1984 strongly disapproved even trying marijuana (18% of men and 22% of women); however, the proportions who strongly disapproved increased over the years (to 28% of men and 33% of women by modal ages 31–32). Here, similar to our findings for perceived risks, disapproval increased at least as sharply from one senior class to another during the period in which our panel respondents grew from age 18 to ages 31–32 (detailed data are provided in Bachman et al., 2001, and Johnston et al., 2000a).

Perceived Risks and Disapproval of Cocaine Use

Two levels of cocaine use were included in the risk and disapproval measures: trying it once or twice and taking it regularly. Responses for the two levels were summed, creating one index for perceived risk and one for disapproval.[1]

Large majorities of high school seniors and young adults felt there was "great risk" in regular use of cocaine, and more than half also felt that even trying cocaine once or twice entailed "moderate risk" or "great risk." As shown in Fig. 6.5, such scores (7 or 8 on the perceived risk index) among members of the classes of 1976–1984 were lowest at modal ages 21–22 (51% of men, 62% of women), after which they rose fairly steadily through modal ages 31–32 (72% of men, 79% of women). Very few individuals saw "no risk" in trying cocaine and "slight risk" (or less) in regular use (scores of 2 or 3 on the index); the proportions dropped from 7% among male seniors and 5% among female seniors to less than 1% at modal ages 31–32.

Here, as we saw also for marijuana use, perceived risks among high school seniors increased during the period of study, as shown by the X notations in Fig. 6.5. It should be noted also that the shifts over time among successive

---

[1]Beginning with the 1986 surveys, an item on perceived risk of occasional use was added. Data on this measure can be found in Johnston et al. (2000a).

classes of high school seniors were greater than those shown by the members of the classes of 1976–1984 who were moving through their twenties and into their early thirties during the same period. In other words, it appears that young adults' perceived risks of cocaine use were somewhat lower than those of high school seniors during the 1980s and 1990s. This is consistent with the fact that at any year throughout the 1980s and the early 1990s, actual use of

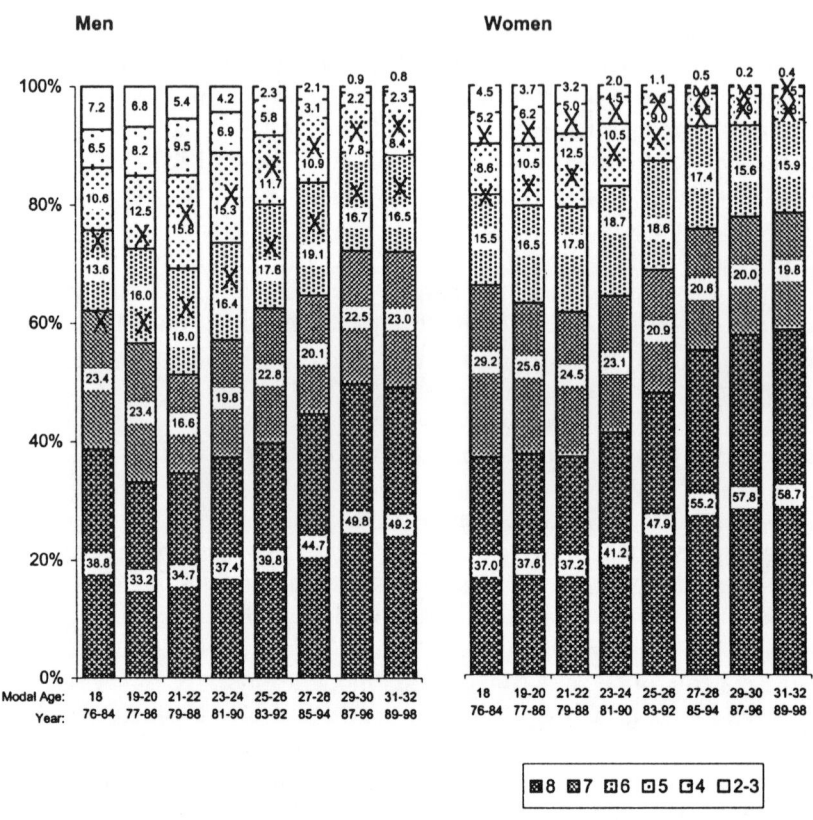

FIG. 6.5.   Perceived risk of cocaine use (index) for the classes of 1976–1984 followed from age 18 to ages 31–32. The index is the sum of responses for (a) trying cocaine once or twice and (b) using cocaine regularly, each with the following scale: 1 = no risk, 2 = slight risk, 3 = moderate risk, 4 = great risk. Bar percentages are based on high school senior data, plus follow-ups 1–7, from class years 1976–1984; one person could contribute up to seven follow-up observations (see Analysis Issues and Strategies section in chap. 3). The sample is restricted to those respondents who answered this question at follow-up 6 and/or follow-up 7. Approximate numbers of observations per age group for men: 820; for women: 980. X notations demarcate the boundaries between the three highest risk index categories for the senior year data from sets of years indicated; senior samples include approximately 69,000 men and 72,000 women in each year grouping.

cocaine was somewhat greater among those in their twenties than among high school seniors (see Johnston et al., 2000b, Fig. 5-9).

Although Fig. 6.5 reflects what happened, *on average*, to members of the classes of 1976–1984 combined, this averaging across time fails to reveal that a distinct and substantial increase in perceived risks of cocaine use occurred for young adults of all ages between the 1986 and 1987 surveys. The 1987 survey was the first to occur after the well-publicized cocaine-related deaths of athletes Len Bias and Don Rogers in 1986. As seen in Fig. 6.6, increases in perceived risk of cocaine use occurred at each of four age levels from 18 to 30. A closer look at Fig. 6.6 also shows that during the early 1990s, the percentages perceiving great risk in trying cocaine once or twice were somewhat higher among those 18–22 (about 59% in 1990–1991) than among those 23–30 (about 52%); by the late 1990s, however, these age-related differences were reversed (to about 54% among those 18–22 in 1998–1999, versus about 61% among those 23–30).

As was the case for perceived risks, disapproval of cocaine use showed increases from modal ages 21–22 onward, and successive classes of high school seniors also showed increased disapproval (data provided in Bachman et al., 2001; see also Johnston et al., 2000b, for year-by-year trends in seniors' disapproval). Disapproval, like risk, increased sharply for all age groups in 1987. It is noteworthy that disapproval of cocaine use was quite high, far more so than was the case for marijuana. From 1987 onward, about half or more of the respondents in all age groups strongly disapproved even trying cocaine, and about 90% disapproved regular use (see Johnston et al., 2000b, Table 6-2).

HOW PERCEIVED RISKS AND DISAPPROVAL ARE CORRELATED WITH SUBSTANCE USE

It is already well known that perceived risks and disapproval of using a substance are positively correlated with each other and negatively correlated with actual use of the substance. But does the strength of those correlations vary from one substance to another? Do the patterns of correlation shift as individuals move through young adulthood? We address each of these questions in the sections that follow.

Most of our discussion is focused on one substance at a time; however, we also note some contrasts between substances. We begin with a few general observations, based on intercorrelations involving all (pairwise) combinations of perceived risk, disapproval, and actual use measures for smoking, drinking, marijuana use, and cocaine use. The appendix presents product–moment correlations among these measures for three age groups: Table A.2.1 shows high school seniors in years 1990–1998 (modal age 18), Table

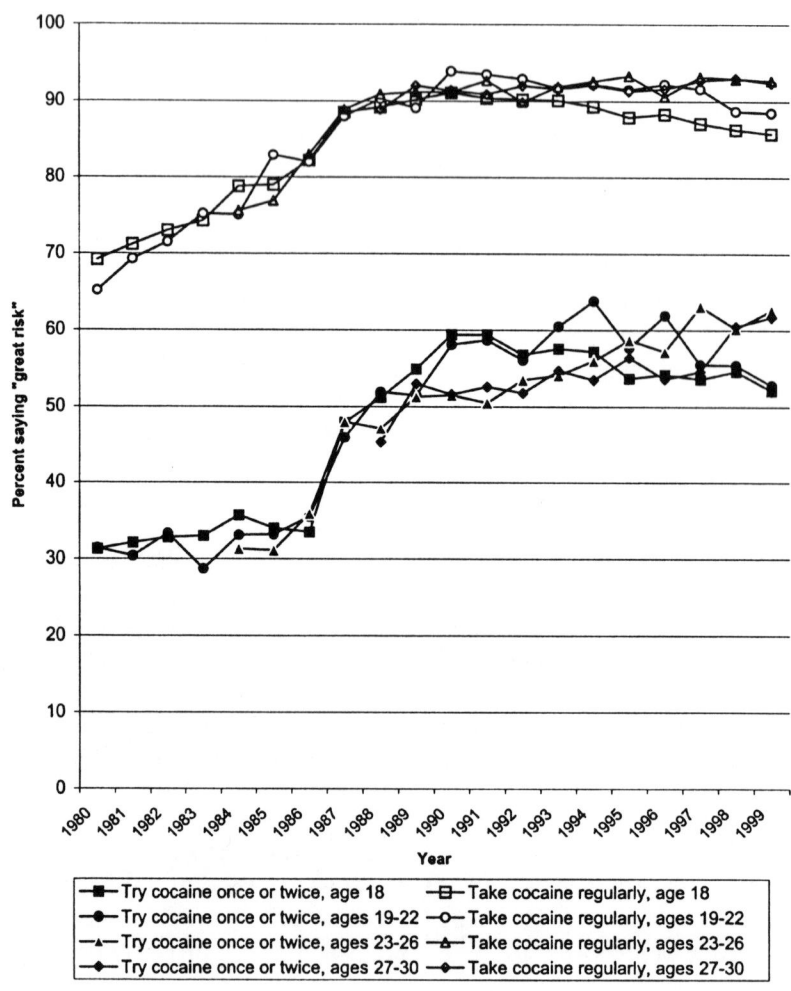

FIG. 6.6. Perceived risk of using cocaine once or twice or using cocaine regularly among high school seniors (aged 18) and young adults in modal age groups of 19–22, 23–26, and 27–30 from the years 1980 to 1999.

A.2.2 shows those who responded to the first three follow-ups during 1990–1998 (modal ages 19–24), and Table A.2.3 shows those who responded to the fourth through seventh follow-ups during 1990–1998 (modal ages 25–32). We thus can compare cross-sections of three different age bands: senior year of high school, late teens and early twenties, and late twenties and early thirties, all studied during the same time period: the

1990s. As we illustrate, these correlational findings for the years 1990–1998 are generally quite consistent with correlational data tracking the classes of 1976–1984 through the last quarter of the century, but the 1990–1998 data have the advantage of eliminating (or at least greatly reducing) the complications introduced by secular trends (period effects).[2] The 1990–1998 data also permit us to show how perceived risks and disapproval are correlated (because those measures appeared together on some questionnaire forms from 1990 onward).

The first general observation based on the data in Tables A.2.1–A.2.3 is that each of the substance use measures was positively correlated with every other substance use measure, across all three age bands. The size of these correlations across substances varies greatly, however; the range is from .10 to .47. We discuss some of these variations and their implications.

The second general observation is that all of the perceived risk and disapproval measures were positively related at all ages, again with wide variations in size of correlations (from .08 to .68). In particular, it is of interest that correlations among the disapproval ratings were generally a good deal stronger (range = .34 to .67; median correlation = .46) than the corresponding correlations among the perceived risk ratings (range = .14 to .55; median correlation = .27). That finding supports the notion that disapproval is caused by factors in addition to perceptions of risk, and such factors may be fairly consistent across the several substances studied here. For example, we expected that aspects of religiosity (both attendance and importance) would relate more strongly to the disapproval measures than to the perceived risks measures. The tables show that to be the case without exception; for each of the four types of substance use shown, the disapproval measure correlated more strongly with the religiosity measures than did the perceived risk measure. This difference was fairly large for pack-a-day smoking (median difference = .10 correlation points); however, for the other substance use dimensions, the correlations with religiosity were nearly as strong for perceived risk as for disapproval (median difference = .03 correlation points).

---

[2]We must acknowledge panel attrition, however, as a different sort of complication that is introduced when comparisons are made among the three sets of samples in Table A.2 in the appendix. The base-year (senior year of high school) samples consist of all those chosen for follow-up, but we know that a subset of such individuals do not participate in the follow-ups. In contrast, individuals who participated in follow-ups 4–7 (modal ages 25–32) are those who were willing to extend their participation in the study for a number of years. The loss of some individuals due to panel attrition is generally more of a problem when examining mean levels or frequencies of drug use, whereas correlations (as in Table A.2) generally seem less affected. Indeed, when one considers that comparisons across age groups in Table A.2 also involve somewhat different sets of birth cohorts, as well as the panel attrition noted here, the strong similarities across the three sets of correlations is all the more impressive. It seems clear that the interrelations among the variables in the table are quite robust.

The third general observation is that all perceived risk measures and all disapproval measures correlated negatively with all substance use measures. However, these negative correlations were far from equal. Thus the fourth general observation confirms a point made earlier in this chapter: The strongest predictors of any drug use dimension were disapproval and perceptions of risk associated with that particular drug.

The fifth general observation is that although we noted age-related changes in the various perceived risk and disapproval measures, along with corresponding age-related changes in levels of substance use, the *correlations* between the attitudes and the behaviors were quite similar across the three age bands. That said, it is worth adding that correlations were slightly lower among those aged 25–32, probably reflecting their lower rates of use (and thus lower variance).

The first general observation—that all of the substance-using behaviors were correlated positively at all ages—is, of course, consistent with a great deal of research indicating a number of common causes for the various kinds of substance use (e.g., Bachman, Johnston, et al., 1981; Clayton, 1992; Hawkins et al., 1992). But within that general pattern of positive correlations, a variety of distinctions can be drawn. Some of the correlations were strongest among the high school seniors and least strong among those in their later twenties and early thirties. Most notably, correlations between cigarette use and other substance use, especially 30-day alcohol use, dropped off more markedly with age. We see this as consistent with our earlier findings that cigarette use in the years following high school seemed less influenced by other post-high-school experiences, presumably because of the relatively high levels of dependency experienced by cigarette smokers.

Cigarette Use Linked to Perceived Risks and Disapproval

Figure 6.7 shows that as members of the high school classes of 1976–1984 moved through the seven follow-up surveys (reaching modal ages 31–32), there was a good deal of consistency in the negative relationship between perceived risk of pack-a-day smoking and current cigarette use (any use during the past 30 days). Among those who saw only "slight risk," 60% or more were current smokers, except that by the late twenties and early thirties that dropped to about 50%. Among those who saw "moderate risk," 40% or more were current smokers. Large majorities of all respondents saw "great risk" in pack-a-day smoking, but even among these individuals about 20% were current smokers.

The picture is a bit different for disapproval of pack-a-day smoking, as shown in Fig. 6.8. Only a little more than one third of respondents reported that they "strongly disapprove" pack-a-day smoking, and only about 10% or

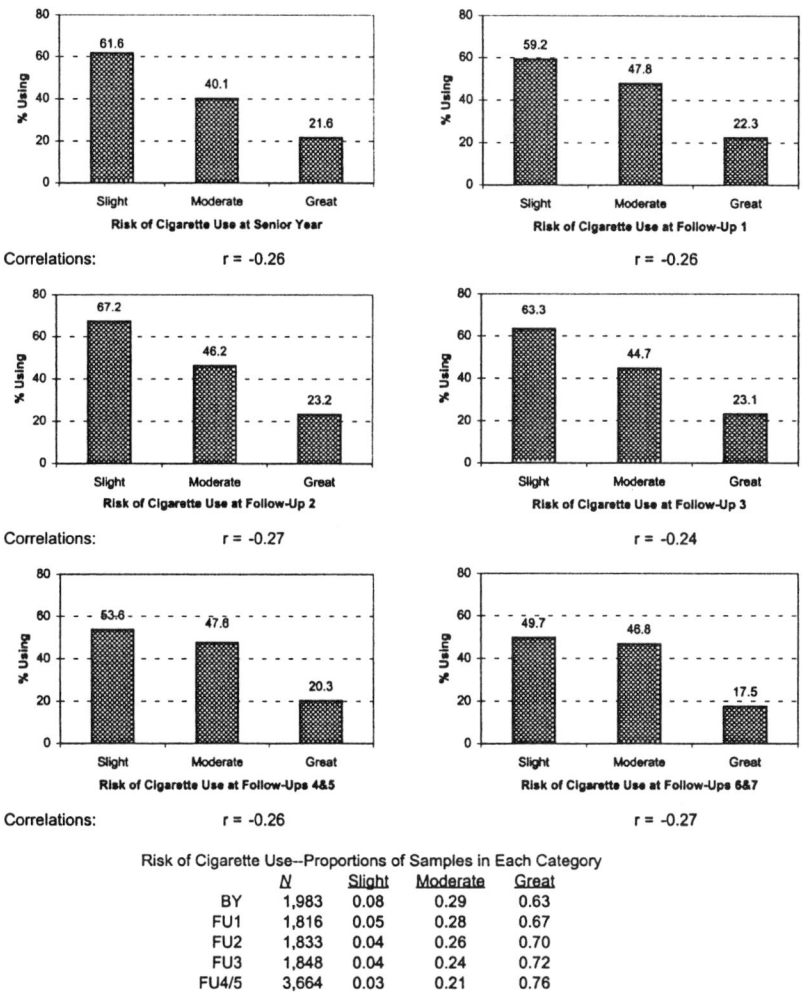

| Risk of Cigarette Use—Proportions of Samples in Each Category | | | |
	N	Slight	Moderate	Great
BY	1,983	0.08	0.29	0.63
FU1	1,816	0.05	0.28	0.67
FU2	1,833	0.04	0.26	0.70
FU3	1,848	0.04	0.24	0.72
FU4/5	3,664	0.03	0.21	0.76
FU6/7	3,701	0.03	0.19	0.78

FIG. 6.7.   Thirty-day prevalence of cigarette smoking related to risk of cigarette use. Percentages based on the classes of 1976–1984 followed from age 18 to ages 29–32 (follow-ups 6 and 7, combined). The sample is restricted to those respondents who answered the questions on both 30-day cigarette use and risk of cigarette use at follow-up 6 and/or follow-up 7. Correlations are based on the drug use measure recoded as a dichotomy. Fewer than 1% of respondents reported "no risk" and therefore were omitted.

fewer of these individuals were themselves current smokers. Fewer than one third of respondents indicated that they "don't disapprove" pack-a-day smoking, and about 60% or more of these individuals were current smokers. Among the roughly one third of respondents who chose the middle "disap-

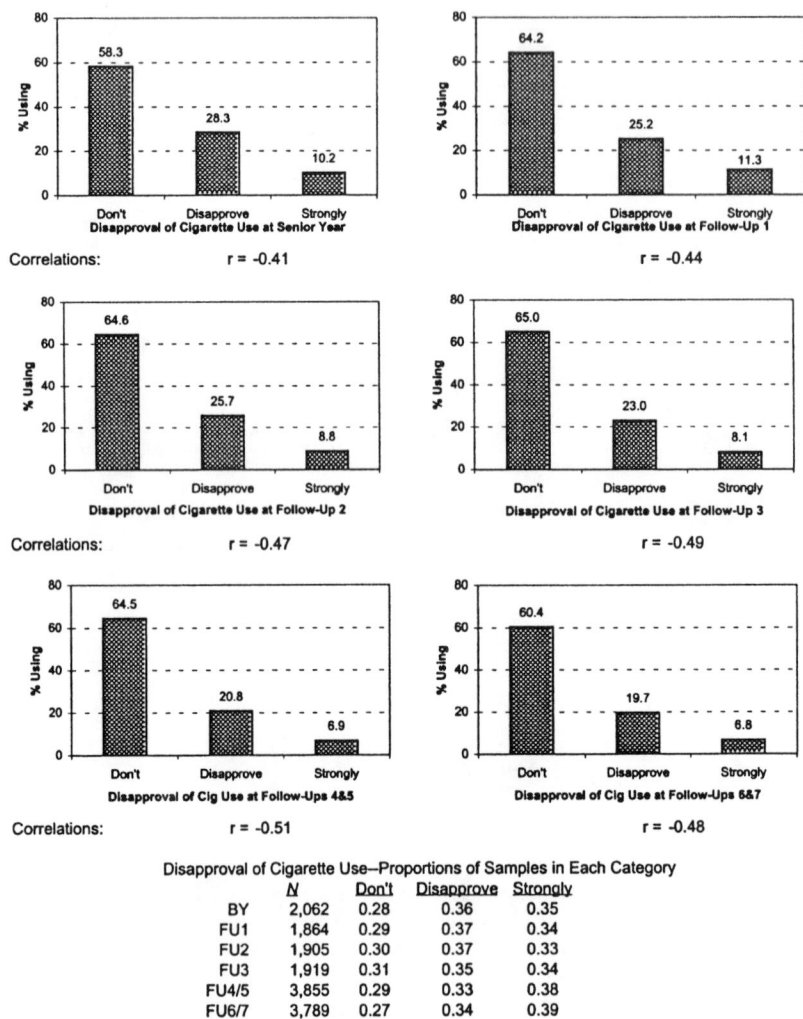

	N	Don't	Disapprove	Strongly
BY	2,062	0.28	0.36	0.35
FU1	1,864	0.29	0.37	0.34
FU2	1,905	0.30	0.37	0.33
FU3	1,919	0.31	0.35	0.34
FU4/5	3,855	0.29	0.33	0.38
FU6/7	3,789	0.27	0.34	0.39

FIG. 6.8. Thirty-day prevalence of cigarette smoking related to disapproval of cigarette use. Percentages based on the classes of 1976–1984 followed from age 18 to ages 29–32 (follow-ups 6 and 7, combined). The sample is restricted to those respondents who answered the questions on both 30-day cigarette use and risk of cigarette use at follow-up 6 and/or follow-up 7. Correlations are based on the drug use measure recoded as a dichotomy.

prove" category, the proportions of current smokers gradually declined with increasing age—from about 28% to about 20%.

Putting the findings from the two figures together, and taking into account that proportions perceiving "great risk" were much larger than proportions "strongly disapproving," one might conclude the following: Many individuals who perceived risks in the behavior were nevertheless willing to smoke, but fewer of those who disapproved the behavior would smoke—especially if they disapproved it strongly. The conclusion might be stated differently, however, and with somewhat different causal implications: It appears that most smokers were willing to acknowledge "moderate risk" or even "great risk" in the behavior (especially at the pack-a-day level), but only a minority of smokers could bring themselves to "disapprove" and very few could "strongly disapprove" such smoking.

These observations illustrate the difficulty of determining to what extent the attitudes shaped the behavior, or vice versa. In general, we believe that perceptions of risk have been important factors shaping substance use behavior, and we consider that causal interpretation to be valid for smoking behavior as well as for the other types of substance use examined in this book. That said, it still seems plausible to suppose that some causation operates in the other direction. Especially when it comes to disapproval, it may be that individuals modify their views to some extent to conform more comfortably with their own behaviors. This causal direction seems quite plausible in the case of cigarette smoking, because smokers can well appreciate the extent to which many cigarette users (perhaps including themselves) find it difficult or impossible to quit. Indeed, this may be an important reason why many respondents, and particularly smokers, were unwilling to indicate "strong disapproval" of pack-a-day smoking, even though they saw "great risk" in the behavior.

Occasional Heavy Drinking Linked to Perceived Risks and Disapproval

Among high school seniors in the classes of 1976–1984, about 10% of students felt there was "no risk" in having five or more drinks once or twice each weekend; and of those individuals, 80% reported having engaged in occasional heavy drinking—that is, they reported having five or more drinks in a row at least once during the past 2 weeks. About 37% of the seniors felt there was "great risk" in such behavior; nevertheless, even among these individuals about 16% reported having done so themselves. Still, the negative correlation between perceived risk and occasional heavy drinking was quite strong among the seniors ($r = -.45$), and the relationship remained nearly as strong through young adulthood (as shown in Fig. 6.9

based on the classes of 1976–1984: Table A.2 shows almost identical results for samples limited to the years 1990–1998).

As we reported earlier in this chapter, by the time members of the classes of 1976–1984 reached their late twenties and early thirties, the proportions seeing "no risk" declined and the proportions seeing "great risk" increased. Instances of heavy drinking also declined with age, as could be expected given the shifts in perceived risks. However, it is important to note that instances of heavy drinking also declined *within each perceived risk category*, as is shown in Fig. 6.9. It thus appears that although increased perceptions of risk probably contributed to the age-related decline in heavy drinking, those changes in perceptions do not account for all of the decline.

The story was much the same for disapproval of occasional heavy drinking, except that the negative correlations with the actual behavior were just slightly stronger for the disapproval measure than for the risk measure, as shown in Table A.2 (see also Bachman et al., 2001, for additional data). The fact that the two sets of correlations involving occasional heavy drinking were only slightly different stands in contrast to the findings for cigarettes, in which the disapproval measure correlated nearly twice as strongly with the behavior as did the risk measure. Table A.2 provides further evidence that risk and disapproval were much more closely linked for heavy drinking than for cigarette use: For instances of heavy drinking, correlations between the risk and disapproval measures ranged from .57 to .61; for pack-a-day smoking, correlations between the risk and disapproval measures ranged from .30 to .33—only about half as large.

Marijuana Use Linked to Perceived Risks and Disapproval

The index of perceived risk of marijuana use ranged from 3 ("no risk" in trying it, occasional use, or regular use) to 12 ("great risk" for all such behaviors). As Fig. 6.10 shows, majorities of those who saw no risk in any use or at most slight risk of regular use (scores of 3 or 4) were themselves current users of marijuana (i.e., reported some use during the past 30 days). Here, as we saw in the previous section on heavy drinking, the figure shows that the proportions of users among individuals perceiving low risk declined with age—from 73% among high school seniors to 55% among those in their late twenties and early thirties. So here again, it appears that increased perceptions of risk very likely contributed to age-related declines in use but did not account for all of the decline.

The findings for disapproval of marijuana use were quite similar to those for perceived risks (further details are available in Bachman et al., 2001). Here, as was true for heavy drinking, the negative correlations with the drug-using behavior were very slightly stronger for the disapproval measure than for the risk measure, as shown in Tables A.2.1–A.2.3 (for all ages in years

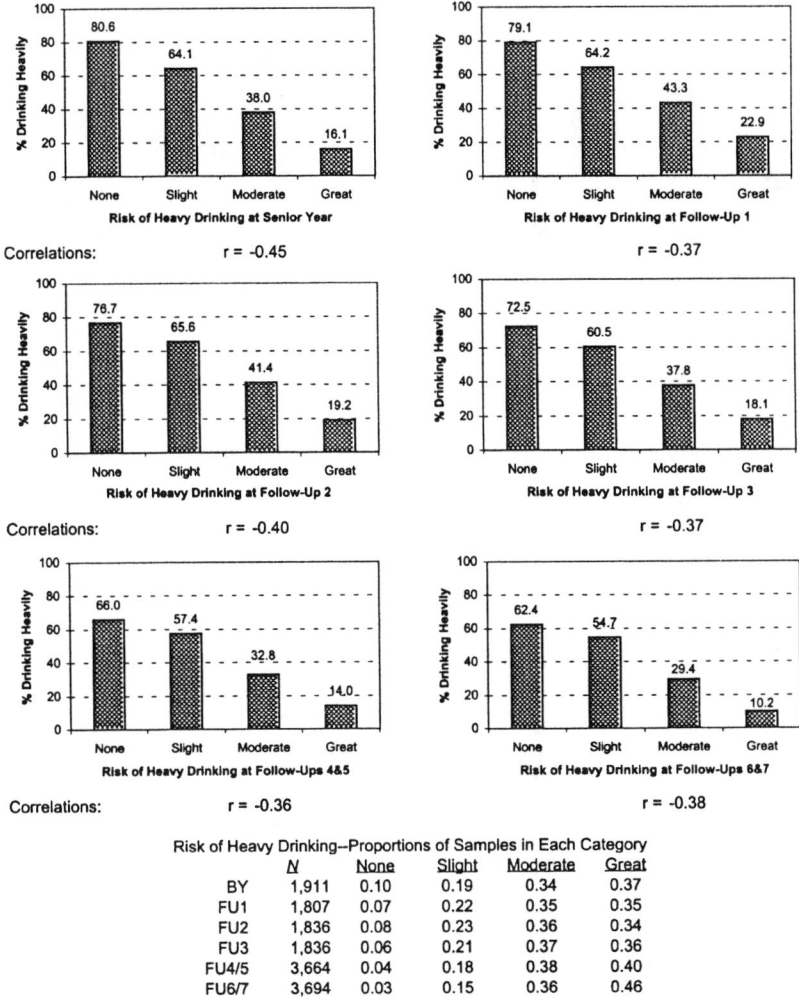

FIG. 6.9. Two-week prevalence of occasional heavy drinking (5 or more drinks in a row) related to risk of occasional heavy drinking. Percentages based on the classes of 1976–1984 followed from age 18 to ages 29–32 (follow-ups 6 and 7, combined). The sample is restricted to those respondents who answered the questions on both 2-week binge drinking and risk of binge drinking at follow-up 6 and/or follow-up 7. Correlations are based on the drug use measure recoded as a dichotomy.

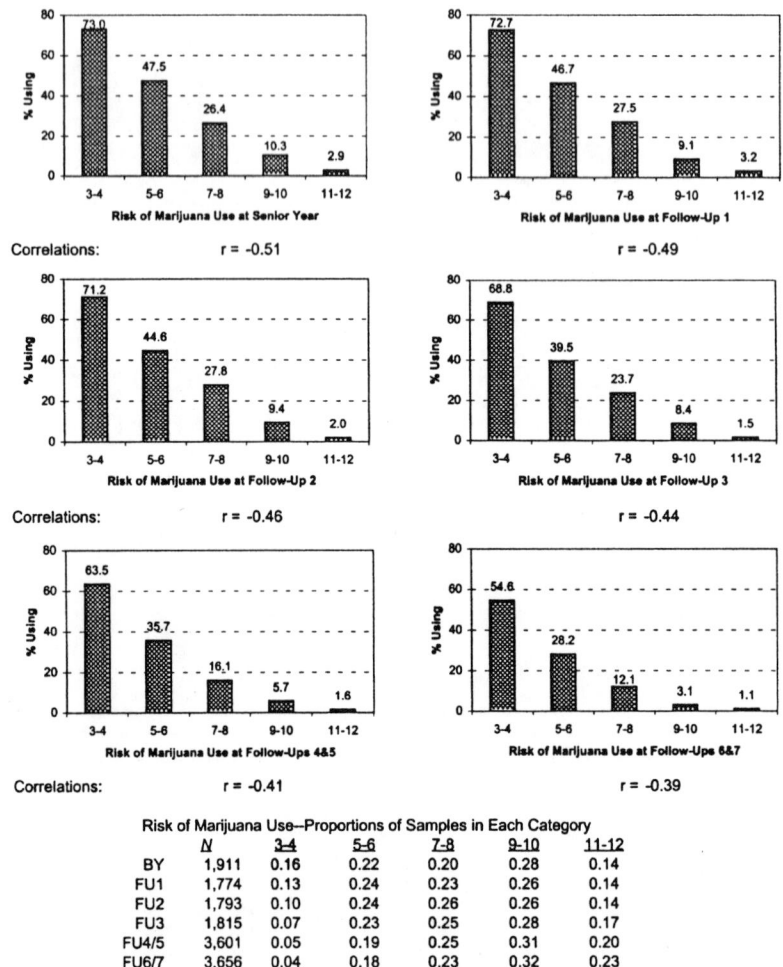

Risk of Marijuana Use--Proportions of Samples in Each Category					
	_N_	3-4	5-6	7-8	9-10	11-12
BY	1,911	0.16	0.22	0.20	0.28	0.14
FU1	1,774	0.13	0.24	0.23	0.26	0.14
FU2	1,793	0.10	0.24	0.26	0.26	0.14
FU3	1,815	0.07	0.23	0.25	0.28	0.17
FU4/5	3,601	0.05	0.19	0.25	0.31	0.20
FU6/7	3,656	0.04	0.18	0.23	0.32	0.23

FIG. 6.10. Thirty-day marijuana use related to risk of marijuana use (index). The index is the sum of responses for: (a) trying marijuana once or twice, (b) smoking marijuana occasionally, and (c) smoking marijuana regularly, each with the following scale: 1 = no risk, 2 = slight risk, 3 = moderate risk, 4 = great risk. Percentages based on the classes of 1976–1984 followed from age 18 to ages 29–32 (follow-ups 6 and 7, combined). The sample is restricted to those respondents who answered the questions on both 30-day marijuana use and risk of marijuana use at follow-up 6 and/or follow-up 7. Correlations are based on the drug use measure recoded as a dichotomy.

1990–1998). The tables also show that the perceived risk and disapproval measures for marijuana use were very strongly correlated: $r = .64$ to .68.

Correlations between the risk and disapproval measures were slightly higher in the case of marijuana use than for occasional heavy drinking, perhaps because the three-item indexes for marijuana use contained less error than the single-item measures concerning occasional heavy drinking. We are far more impressed by the similarities in the marijuana and occasional heavy drinking findings than by the differences. In our previous book, we saw rather similar dynamics for the two kinds of behavior, and now we also see fairly similar patterns for the attitudes related to the behaviors. (Further data on the similarities, for both the behaviors and the attitudes, are available in Tables A.2.1–A.2.3.)

Cocaine Use Linked to Perceived Risks and Disapproval

The index of perceived risk of cocaine use ranged from 2 ("no risk" in trying it or in regular use) to 8 ("great risk" in both trying and regular use). In Fig. 6.11 we combined the bottom two risk categories because there were very few cases in each, and we combined the top two categories (although they contained the majority of cases) because the cocaine use rates for both were near zero. As the figure shows, even among the small proportion (about 6%) of seniors in the classes of 1976–1984 who saw slight or no risk in regular cocaine use, just over one quarter (27%) were current users (i.e, reported any use during the preceding 30 days); and as perceived risk levels increased, use rates dropped sharply. By the second and third follow-ups (modal ages 21–24), the proportions perceiving slight or no risk dropped further (to 3–4%); however, among these individuals about 40% were current cocaine users. By the sixth and seventh follow-ups (modal ages 29–32), fewer than 1% saw little or no risk, and even in this very small group the current usage rates had dropped to one quarter (25%). As discussed earlier, these age-related trends for members of the classes of 1976–1984 have a great deal to do with the important secular shift in cocaine attitudes and use after the 1986 survey. Among individuals of different ages surveyed in the years 1990–1998, there were very few who saw little or no risk in cocaine, and overall usage rates were distinctly lower than in prior years; given this reduced variance along both dimensions, it is not surprising that during the 1990s, the correlations between these measures were consistently fairly low (ranging from −.15 to −.20).

The findings for disapproval of cocaine use (detailed in Bachman et al., 2001, and summarized in Tables A.2.1–A.2.3) were very similar to those for perceived risk, although once again the disapproval correlations were slightly higher. Among seniors from the classes of 1976–1984, only 6% did

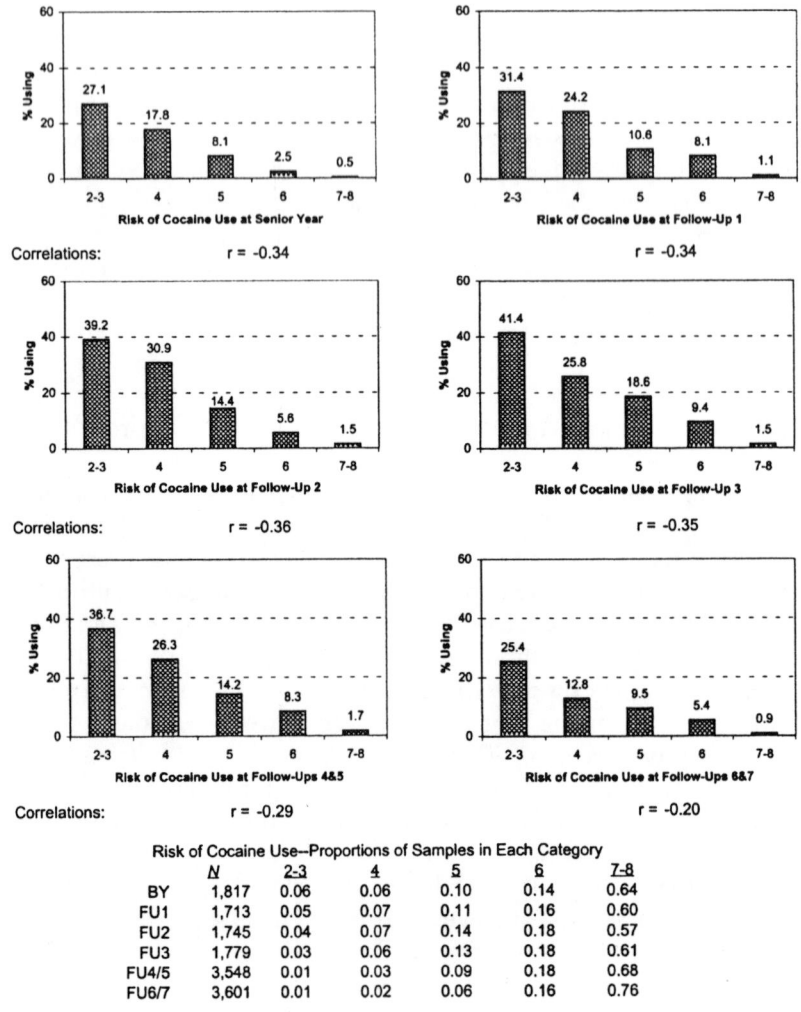

	N	2-3	4	5	6	7-8
BY	1,817	0.06	0.06	0.10	0.14	0.64
FU1	1,713	0.05	0.07	0.11	0.16	0.60
FU2	1,745	0.04	0.07	0.14	0.18	0.57
FU3	1,779	0.03	0.06	0.13	0.18	0.61
FU4/5	3,548	0.01	0.03	0.09	0.18	0.68
FU6/7	3,601	0.01	0.02	0.06	0.16	0.76

FIG. 6.11. Thirty-day prevalence of cocaine use related to risk index of cocaine use. The index is the sum of responses for: (a) trying cocaine once or twice and (b) smoking cocaine regularly, each with the following scale: 1 = no risk, 2 = slight risk, 3 = moderate risk, 4 = great risk. Percentages based on the classes of 1976–1984 followed from age 18 to ages 29–32 (follow-ups 6 and 7, combined). The sample is restricted to those respondents who answered the questions on both 30-day marijuana use and risk of marijuana use at follow-up 6 and/or follow-up 7. Correlations are based on the drug use measure recoded as a dichotomy.

not disapprove of regular cocaine use and about one third of them were themselves current users. One to 4 years later (first and second follow-ups, modal ages 19–22), there were again 5–6% who did not disapprove regular use, but 40% or more of these individuals were current users. Disapproval rates increased thereafter, and proportions of users within each category of disapproval also dropped.

Tables A.2.1–A.2.3, focusing on just the years 1990–1998, show an interesting additional age-related difference: correlations between the risk and disapproval ratings were .37 among high school seniors, .45 among those aged 19–24, and .52 among those aged 25–32. This might suggest some tendency for disapproval ratings to come more fully into accord with perceptions of risk as individuals become older, except that none of the other substances showed this convergence of risk and disapproval with increasing age. A more likely explanation, in our view, focuses on cohort differences: during the 1990s, disapproval ratings showed a bit more variance among older respondents compared with younger ones. Specifically, among those older respondents, all of whom finished high school before the major shift in cocaine attitudes and use occurred, there were slightly more individuals who did not condemn *trying* cocaine use, compared with those who "came of age" after that shift in 1987. There were no such differences with respect to *regular* cocaine use; by the 1990s virtually everyone disapproved of such use. (For further details, see Johnston et al., 2000b, Table 6-2.)

Substance Use Linked to Perceived Risk and Disapproval: Summary

We stated at the outset of this section that it is already well known that perceived risks of using a substance and disapproval of using a substance are positively correlated with each other and negatively correlated with actual use of the substance. But we were interested in whether the strength of those correlations varied from one substance to another and whether the patterns of correlation shifted as individuals moved through young adulthood.

The analyses reported here indicate a number of differences from one substance to another. In general, we found that actual use of a substance correlated a little more strongly with disapproval of that substance than with perceived risks. For cigarettes, this distinction was much more pronounced: Most smokers saw moderate or great risk in pack-a-day smoking, whereas relatively few individuals who strongly disapproved the behavior were themselves smokers; thus the correlations with disapproval were distinctly stronger. Consistent with this, perceived risks and disapproval of pack-a-day smoking correlated with each other only .30 to .33, whereas the risk–disapproval correlations ranged from .57 to .61 for occasional heavy drinking and from .64 to .68 for marijuana use. The risk–disapproval correlations were somewhat lower for cocaine, attributable perhaps to the very low variance in both dimensions: Cocaine use in recent years has been seen as very risky and has been strongly disapproved. (All of these correlations are based on surveys from the years 1990–1998 and are shown in Tables A.2.1–A.2.3.)

Most patterns of correlation shifted little across ages 18–32. We noted higher correlations among the older cohorts of respondents with respect to their views about cocaine and attributed them primarily to cohort differences. Members of the older cohorts were more likely to have used cocaine or to have known users; perhaps because of that, they were slightly less likely to disapprove of trying the drug once or twice, and the greater range of variation in their responses permitted slightly higher correlations.

Although the correlations among *attitudes* remained largely the same across the different age bands examined, there were some age-related declines in the extent to which *actual usage rates* were correlated across substances (see Tables A.2.1–A.2.3). This age-related decline was particularly pronounced in the correlations between current use of cigarettes and current use of alcohol (see also chap. 5); during 1990–1998, the two behaviors correlated .40 among those aged 18, .27 among those aged 19–24, and only .16 among those aged 25–32. Correlations between current smoking and occasional heavy drinking dropped somewhat less, from .37 to .24. This is consistent with earlier findings that drinking behaviors were influenced by a variety of new post-high-school roles and experiences, whereas smoking was much more resistant to change—presumably because many smokers found themselves unable to quit (Bachman et al., 1997).

ANALYSES LINKING PERCEIVED RISKS AND DISAPPROVAL WITH POST-HIGH-SCHOOL EXPERIENCES[3]

We have established thus far that there have been some age-related increases in perceived risks and disapproval associated with occasional heavy drinking, with marijuana use, and with cocaine use; however, along each of these dimensions there was also evidence of secular trends, thus raising questions about interpretation. Nevertheless, it remains true that those individuals from the high school classes of 1976–1984 did show some changes in their views about drugs as they went through their twenties and into their thirties. So it will be useful, in this section, to ask whether certain post-high-school experiences tended to be associated with greater-than-average increases in perceived risks and disapproval, smaller-than-average increases, or even decreases.

---

[3]The different dimensions of post-high-school experiences and the proportions of respondents in each category at each follow-up are documented in the appendix, Tables A.1.1–A.1.5.

We examine the same set of post-high-school experiences in this chapter as in previous ones. Tables A.6.1–A.6.8 summarize extensive bivariate and multivariate analyses linking these experiences to the perceived risk and disapproval measures for pack-a-day smoking, occasional heavy drinking, marijuana use, and cocaine use. In the text we are much more selective.

We are able to be selective in our reporting in this section because, to the extent that views about substance use seem to change in response to post-high-school experiences, the changes tend to be in similar directions for the several different substances. In particular, the findings for views about occasional heavy drinking, marijuana use, and cocaine use tend to parallel each other. So we will generalize to the extent we can and invite the reader to see the appendix for further details as desired.

Individual views about pack-a-day cigarette use seemed relatively unaffected by the post-high-school experiences studied herein and thus are mentioned only occasionally in this section. Putting it more precisely, we did not find many substantial changes in views about cigarettes that could be linked to specific roles and experiences after high school. This is not altogether surprising, given our earlier finding that actual use of cigarettes was similarly unaffected by most of the post-high-school experiences we studied (Bachman et al., 1997). That said, it is important to add that smoking behaviors, as well as views about smoking, were clearly correlated with a number of important variables in our study, but these were stable relationships, not changes. Thus, for example, those who were full-time students at the time of the follow-up survey were more likely than average to see great risks in pack-a-day smoking and more likely to disapprove the behavior; however, those same individuals were equally more likely to have held such views while they were seniors in high school. Significantly, it is also the case that views about smoking were negatively correlated with high school grades and college plans; such relationships were clearly in place by the senior year of high school and diminished very little during the subsequent years (as can be seen in Tables A.6.1–A.6.2).

Student Status Related to Perceived Risks and Disapproval

Those who were full-time students during the first two follow-ups (modal ages 19–22) did not differ substantially from their age-mates in terms of perceived risks and disapproval of occasional heavy drinking, marijuana use, or cocaine use. When they were high school seniors, however, these college-bound individuals had been somewhat above average in their perceptions of risk and their disapproval. It thus appears that something about their experiences caused the full-time students to decrease slightly their perceptions of risk and their disapproval. The multivariate analyses (Tables

A.6.3–A.6.8) suggest that these changes had to do primarily with the different living arrangements associated with student status—a conclusion consistent with our earlier findings that changes in occasional heavy drinking and in illicit drug use among students were traceable primarily to their living arrangements (Bachman et al., 1997).

Full-time students were above average in their disapproval and perceived risks associated with pack-a-day cigarette smoking, but the differences were equally in evidence before they left high school. In sum, before they left high school the college-bound seniors were above average in perceived risks and disapproval associated with all substances, but after entering college only their views about smoking remained distinctive.

Employment Status Related to Perceived Risks and Disapproval

There was little change in views that could be linked to employment status. Women who were full-time homemakers showed greater than average increases in perceived risks and disapproval ratings; however, the multivariate analyses revealed this to be related primarily to marital and parental status rather than being a homemaker per se.

One finding worth noting is that disapproval of having five or more drinks once or twice each weekend declined somewhat among males who entered military service. This finding was evident for analyses based on all seven follow-ups (see Table A.6.4a). A similar but stronger pattern was evident when analyses were limited to the first two follow-ups, thereby comparing young recruits with other young men in their late teens and early twenties (data available in Bachman et al., 2001). This finding points to an area of continuing concern for U.S. military leadership; efforts to prevent illicit drug use and reduce cigarette use in the armed forces have met with considerable success in recent years, but modifying views and behaviors involving occasional heavy drinking remains a challenge (Bachman et al., 1999).

Living Arrangements and Marital Status Related to Perceived Risks and Disapproval

Living arrangements, including marital status, were shown earlier to be important correlates of changes in alcohol and illicit drug use (Bachman et al., 1997). They are also related, in largely similar ways, to changes in perceived risks and disapproval associated with the use of these substances. We present the findings for perceived risks of marijuana use as an illustration, shown in Fig. 6.12 (figures for the other dimensions are available in Bachman et al., 2001).

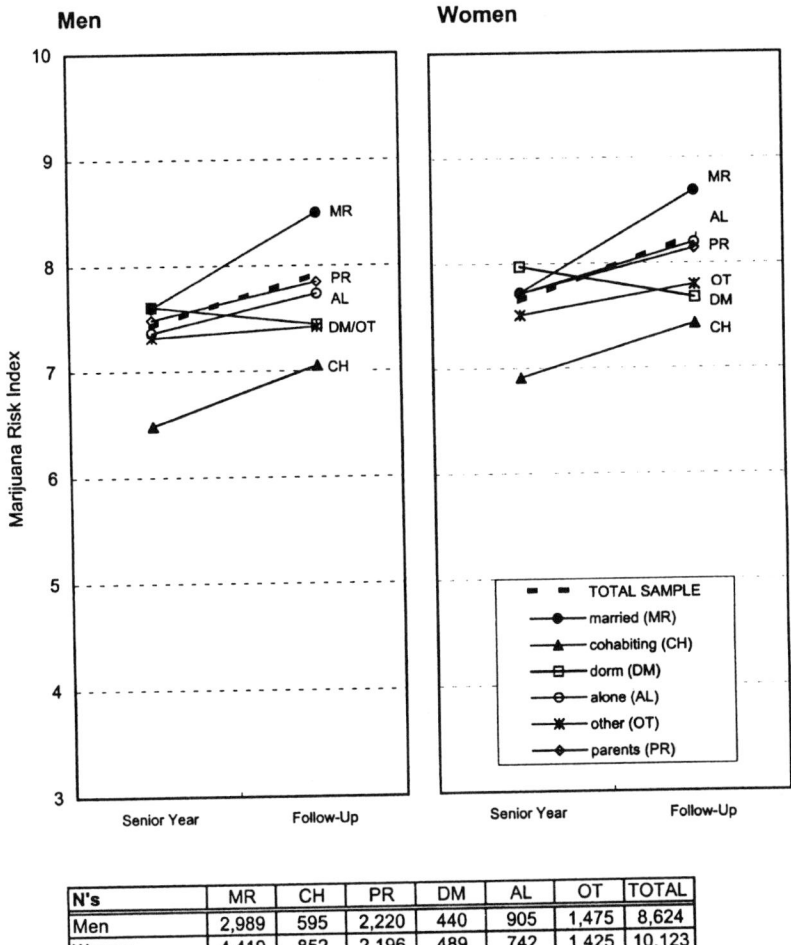

N's	MR	CH	PR	DM	AL	OT	TOTAL
Men	2,989	595	2,220	440	905	1,475	8,624
Women	4,419	852	2,196	489	742	1,425	10,123

FIG. 6.12.   Change in mean risk of marijuana use (index) related to living arrangement at the time of follow-up. The index is the sum of responses for: (a) trying marijuana once or twice, (b) smoking marijuana occasionally, and (c) smoking marijuana regularly, each with the following scale: 1 = no risk, 2 = slight risk, 3 = moderate risk, 4 = great risk. High school seniors from the classes of 1976–1984 were followed up as many as seven times between modal ages 19 and 32. In this figure, one person could contribute up to seven follow-up observations (see Additional Panel Analysis Issues and Strategies section in chap. 3). The approximate standard deviations for perceived risk of using marijuana at senior year were 2.26 for males and 2.11 for females.

Being Married.   Respondents married at the time of follow-up showed average levels of perceived risk and disapproval that were higher than those of any other category of living arrangements. This can be seen with respect to marijuana risks in Fig. 6.12; it was equally true for risks of cocaine use and of weekend heavy drinking and for disapproval of all three types of substance use. When they were high school seniors, these same individuals were quite close to the overall average along each of these dimensions. Generally half or more of these "marriage effects" contributing to perceived risks and disapproval remained after other factors were controlled in the multivariate analyses (see Tables A.6.3–A.6.8). There was also a slight rise in disapproval (but not perceived risk) of pack-a-day smoking among married women, but not among married men (see Table A.6.2).

Cohabiting.   Our earlier research showed that those who were cohabiting at the time of follow-up tended to be above average in substance use, but the same had been the case when they were high school seniors (and not cohabiting—all were living with parents or guardians). As shown in Fig. 6.12, cohabitants were also below average in their perceptions of the risks involved in marijuana use, both at the time of follow-up and also when they were seniors in high school. The multivariate analyses (see Table A.6.5) reveal that cohabitants were further below average at the follow-up than they were in high school, and these differential changes were actually enhanced by controls for other factors.[4] The same pattern of findings was evident for disapproval of marijuana; cohabitants, especially females, were distinctly below average in disapproval. Much the same was true also for perceived risks and disapproval associated with cocaine use and with weekend heavy drinking. These findings, like our earlier ones concerning actual substance use, fit into a broader picture of cohabitants as persons more willing than average to disagree with (and depart from) conventional restrictions on individuals' behaviors.

Living With Parents.   Among those who did not leave home to attend college, the majority of young adults continued to live with parents for several years after high school. Follow-up respondents living with their parents were just about average in their ratings of perceived risks and disapproval of pack-a-day smoking, weekend heavy drinking, marijuana use, and cocaine use. The findings for risk of marijuana use are shown in Fig. 6.12 (and other findings can be found in Tables A.6.1–A.6.8). It should be noted that the

---

[4]The multivariate analyses in the appendix show a bit more differential change than is apparent in Fig. 6.12. That may be due to the fact that the figure is based only on members of the high school classes of 1976–1984, whereas Table A.6.5 is based on all available respondents (Fig. 3.1 illustrates this distinction).

findings were just about the same when analyses were restricted to first and second follow-ups (data provided in Bachman et al., 2001).

Given that they constitute a large proportion of all young adults in their late teens and early twenties, it follows necessarily that those continuing to live with parents would be about average in their ratings of perceived risks and disapproval. However, there are additional reasons to expect these individuals to be about average in their drug views, as well as their drug use. Our earlier research showed that during the period that young high school graduates continued to live with their parents, they were less likely than others to experience dramatic changes in interpersonal contacts and social activities. They tended not to experience as much freedom from constraints or as many new peer pressures as those who moved to dormitories or apartments, but neither did they have the new responsibilities that accompany marriage. "The result seems to be that their drug use change patterns fall neatly in between the patterns for others with different mixes of freedoms and responsibilities" (Bachman et al., 1997, p. 174)—and the same can now be said for their *views* about drug use.

Living in a Dormitory. Figure 6.12 shows that marijuana risk ratings among those who were living in dormitories at the time of follow-up had actually declined slightly from their ratings when high school seniors, whereas for the total samples the marijuana risk ratings had increased on average. Similar patterns were in evidence (see appendix tables; see also Bachman et al., 2001) for disapproval of marijuana use, as well as for perceived risks of weekend heavy drinking, of marijuana use, and of cocaine use (but not pack-a-day smoking). As we noted in the previous chapter, however, living arrangement comparisons of the sort shown in Fig. 6.12 employ the full range of follow-up data (extending across modal ages 19–32), whereas most of those living in dormitories were in just the first or second follow-up (modal ages 19–22). Therefore, the more appropriate analyses for exploring possible "dormitory effects" are those restricted to the first two follow-ups.

Focusing on just the first two follow-ups, we begin by recalling that risk and disapproval ratings (for weekend heavy drinking, marijuana use, and cocaine use) increased little or not at all during the late teens and early twenties; the increases began only after the second follow-up. Based on that, we could expect those living in dormitories to be not so different from others in the same age range. That said, it must be added that the bivariate and multivariate analyses based on just the first two follow-ups still showed evidence of "dormitory effects" on risk and disapproval ratings, albeit somewhat smaller than would be suggested by the pattern in Fig. 6.12. Young men and women living in dormitories had risk and disapproval ratings (for heavy drinking, marijuana use, and cocaine use) that were not much different on average from those of others aged 19–22, whereas when they were high school seniors, those students heading for dormitory life tended to be somewhat above average in their risk and disapproval ratings. In general, these modest declines in risk and disapproval ratings, which occurred among young people moving from home to dormitories, remained evident to some extent even after controls for all other predictors included in our multivariate analyses (data provided in Bachman et al., 2001).

Living Alone and in Other Living Arrangements.   Relatively small numbers of individuals lived alone, especially during the first few years after high school. Perhaps in part because of the lack of reliability due to small numbers of cases, the risk and disapproval findings for this subgroup were not very strong or consistent. Moreover, along a number of dimensions the findings limited to the first two follow-ups were not the same as findings based on all follow-ups. Overall, those living alone were about average or slightly below average in their ratings of risk; they tended to be below average in their disapproval ratings.

The findings for those in the "other living arrangements" category (mostly those in shared housing with other young adults) were a good deal clearer and more consistent. In general, being in this category was associated with lower than average risk and disapproval ratings of heavy drinking and illicit drug use. This held true for bivariate and multivariate analyses based on all seven follow-ups (see Tables A.6.3–A.6.8), as well as those based on just the first two follow-ups (see Bachman et al., 2001, for tables). Among many young men and women in their late teens and early twenties, the "other living arrangements" were similar to dormitory life, except with fewer institutional constraints. Our earlier research showed that those in the "other living arrangements" category equaled or exceeded dormitory residents in frequency of occasional heavy drinking and in illicit drug use (Bachman et al., 1997). We were thus not surprised to find that individuals in this category also averaged among the lowest in ratings of risk and disapproval (only those in the cohabiting category were lower).

Pregnancy and Parenthood Related to Perceived Risks and Disapproval

Pregnancy.   Substance use by a pregnant woman carries risks for the fetus and thus is widely disapproved. However, our questionnaire items dealing with perceived risk and disapproval made no mention of pregnancy, nor did they ask respondents about risks or disapproval involving their own use. Therefore, we would expect differential changes to be attributable to pregnancy only if there were some sort of generalization involved. Apparently there was. There were rises in risk and disapproval ratings associated with being pregnant or having a pregnant spouse that often equaled and sometimes exceeded those associated with being married. Moreover, when marriage and pregnancy were included together as predictors in the multivariate analyses (along with many other predictors), the "pregnancy effects" were diminished but did not disappear and sometimes were larger than those that remained for marriage.[5]

Parenthood. Married parents tended to show greater than average increases in risk and disapproval ratings; however, in most instances these were roughly comparable to the increases shown by married respondents in general, and they fell short of statistical significance in the multivariate analyses (see Tables A.6.1–A.6.8). The only exceptions involved perceived risks and disapproval of marijuana use; mothers, both married and single, showed substantial increases that remained sizeable and significant in the multivariate analyses. Married fathers also showed increases in perceived risks and disapproval of marijuana use, but these fell short of statistical significance.

Further Findings on Marital Status Related to Perceived Risk and Disapproval

Engagement. The multivariate analyses revealed "engagement effects" roughly comparable in size to the "marriage effects" described earlier. Compared with nonengaged single respondents, those who were engaged were more likely to perceive risks in weekend heavy drinking, marijuana use, and cocaine use; they were also more likely to disapprove such behaviors (see Tables A.6.3–A.6.8).

Divorce. Our examination of divorce patterns over 2-year follow-up intervals showed some tendency for those who were divorced to be lower than average in their disapproval ratings for pack-a-day smoking, weekend heavy drinking, and illicit drug use. The patterns involving perceived risks were not very strong or consistent. (Data are available in Bachman et al., 2001.)

---

[5]Our evaluation of possible "pregnancy effects" was complicated to some extent by the fact that the pregnancy question was not included in follow-up surveys prior to 1984. This, plus the relatively small numbers of women (or spouses) pregnant at any particular time, limited the numbers of cases for this dimension in our multivariate analyses. It thus took fairly large effects to be statistically significant, and some of those involving perceived risks and disapproval fell short of our criteria. Nevertheless, the findings show a good deal of consistency (including replication with separate subsamples—those asked the risk items and those asked the disapproval items). Accordingly, we are inclined to accept the findings, albeit with some caution.

Conclusions Based on Multivariate Analyses

The multivariate analyses in Appendix Tables A.6.1–A.6.8, along with more extensive data in Bachman et al. (2001), provide a number of interesting comparisons with the multivariate findings in the previous two chapters. We saw in chapter 4 that *change scores* along the religiosity dimensions were not very predictable from post-high-school roles and experiences, and the same can now be said for the risk and disapproval ratings examined in this chapter. The post-high-school predictors could account for very little variance in change scores for views about pack-a-day smoking or perceived risks of weekend heavy drinking. For most of the other change scores, the post-high-school predictors were able to explain about 1–2% of the variance; this is roughly similar to the findings for the religiosity measures but far below the levels of explained variance for the measures treated in chapter 5. So our most general conclusion is that post-high-school experiences have only limited impacts on views about drugs.

Nevertheless, there were some impacts. The multivariate analyses indicate that these had to do primarily with living arrangements and marital and parental status; student and employment status made little or no contribution to prediction once the other variables were included in the equations. The multivariate analyses also indicated that some of the age-related differences were attributable to living arrangements, particularly marital and parental status (see Tables A.6.1–A.6.8; see also Bachman et al., 2001, for further details).

SUMMARY

The findings reported in this chapter confirm what we stated at the outset: young adults' views about various substances are closely linked to whether and how much they use those substances. Perceived risks of marijuana use were strongly correlated with disapproval of such use, and both showed strong negative relationships with actual marijuana use. The relationships involving heavy drinking were closely parallel to those for marijuana use. The relationships for cocaine use were similar but weaker. For cigarette use, perceived risks showed rather little variation and weaker correlations, because most respondents perceived "great risk" in pack-a-day smoking and nearly all others rated the risk at the next highest level ("moderate"). However, disapproval of pack-a-day smoking showed strong negative correlations with smoking. All of these patterns of interrelationship between perceived risks, disapproval, and the use (or nonuse) of a substance were fairly consistent across the range of ages from senior year of high school to late twenties and early thirties.

It seems quite likely that perceptions of risks associated with the use of various substances are important contributors to disapproval of such use. Our correlational findings cannot prove that this is the dominant causal direction, but they certainly demonstrate close connections between the two views. Correlational findings also cannot prove that disapproval and perceived risks are among the direct causes of actual substance use (or nonuse), but again our findings clearly demonstrate very close associations between the views and the behaviors. Thus the correlational findings are fully consistent with our conceptualization that perceived risks help shape disapproval and that both of these factors heavily influence actual substance use.

Our findings also show that views about one kind of substance tend to correlate with views about other substances. Thus, for example, those with high risk and disapproval ratings regarding marijuana use tend also to be above average in their risk and disapproval ratings regarding cocaine use, weekend heavy drinking, and pack-a-day smoking. Nevertheless, the strongest correlates of the use of any particular substance are the views about *that* substance; views about other substances show weaker correlations.

Views about the various substances changed during young adulthood. Specifically, among graduates of the high school classes of 1976–1984, risk and disapproval ratings increased to some extent from their early twenties onward. However, those age-related changes in views coincided in time with broader historical changes during the 1980s and 1990s. In our earlier book we confronted similar problems, because age-related changes in actual usage rates coincided with historical changes in use. In spite of these complications, the findings suggest that a portion of the age-related changes is attributable to some of the new responsibilities associated with young adulthood, rather than merely secular trends.

The responsibilities of young adulthood that tended to increase ratings of risk and disapproval included engagement, marriage, pregnancy, and parenthood. Commitment to another person (fiance or spouse) may lead individuals toward more critical views of substance use. Additionally, concerns about risks to the fetus may contribute to increased risk and disapproval ratings on the part of pregnant women and their spouses. Finally, parents face the additional responsibility of providing good examples for their children, and this responsibility probably contributes to their increased concerns about substance use.

7

Friends' Use of Substances, and Perceived Availability of Illicit Drugs

"Birds of a feather flock together." Such truisms are not always true, but in the case of substance use the old saying is largely valid. Earlier research, summarized in chapter 2, showed consistently that drug-using youth and young adults are likely to have friends who use the same substances. We thus expected that respondents who engaged in various substance use behaviors, and especially those who did so fairly often, would report that relatively high proportions of their friends also engaged in such behaviors. That is exactly what we found, as is detailed in this chapter.

That individuals' self-reported substance use was correlated with their perceptions of friends' use is a relatively straightforward finding, but understanding just why those correlations occur is much less straightforward. The problem is not that we cannot think of reasons for the correlations; rather, the problem is that there are too many good reasons, as we noted in chapter 2 and discuss briefly here.

First, individuals with friends who use a particular substance are more likely to have the opportunity to use the substance themselves, because the friends may offer to share (whether cigarettes, alcohol, or illicit drugs). In addition, the friends may actively encourage use both positively ("Try this, you'll love it") and negatively ("Don't be so timid"—or words to that effect).

And the higher the proportion of friends who use a substance, the greater the frequency of such opportunities and influence attempts.

Second, individuals who use substances themselves are likely also to encourage friends to use. The mechanisms are those just outlined—substance users sharing and encouraging use by their friends. It can be argued, of course, that any particular individual's initiation into substance use is likely to be facilitated by friends (often slightly older friends) who are already users; however, by the time an individual is a senior in high school, it is likely that both directions of causation have come into play. In any case, correlational data are unlikely to permit a clear resolution of this chicken–egg problem.

There are still other reasons for expecting positive correlations between friends' use and own use of any of the substances studied here. One such reason, really a whole collection of such reasons, can be labeled *common prior causes*. An important example is the tendency for those doing poorly in school to smoke cigarettes. People not doing well in school tend to associate with each other—by their own choices, by the (negative) choices of some of their age-mates, and also by classroom grouping practices (including their own tendency to avoid the most challenging classes). So in addition to the mutual influence processes just mentioned, we could expect smokers to associate with other smokers just because of the strong negative links between educational success and cigarette use.

If all that were not complicated enough, we must acknowledge the problem that our surveys rely on individuals' *perceptions* of their friends' substance use, rather than having independent measures of friends' behaviors. There is a possibility of distortion resulting from respondents shaping their perceptions of friends' use so as to be more in line with their own use (a process that could occur without the respondents' awareness). A different sort of inaccuracy could occur because not all respondents are aware of all substance use by their friends. In general, adolescents tend to overestimate the extent of peer substance use, but some underestimation is likely as well. For example, if a respondent has a friend who gets drunk most weekends, but does so privately or with a different set of friends and does not tell the respondent about it, then the respondent might "undercount" the number of friends who get drunk. Some such underreporting surely occurs at random, but other underreporting would be systematic—substance users would be more likely to mention their own use to friends they knew (or assumed) also to be users.

In sum, there are multiple reasons for expecting respondents' reports of their friends' use to correlate positively with the respondents' own self-reports of use. Our correlational findings can confirm that such relationships did occur, and we can (and do) point out and discuss differences in the sizes of the relationships, but we are not willing to make strong assumptions about which of the several possible causal processes dominate. In the previous chapter we were willing to assert that perceived risks and disapproval concerning particular forms of substance use were among the important causes of actual use (more so than vice versa); here, however, it does not seem feasible to extricate one direction of causation from another in explaining that substance usage patterns correlate positively among friends. Rather, we focus on documenting the linkages, noting especially the ways in which the new freedoms and responsibilities following high school seem related not only to individuals' own drug use, but also the usage patterns they perceive among their friends.

PATTERNS OF AGE-RELATED CHANGE IN (PERCEIVED) FRIENDS' USE OF SUBSTANCES AND IN PERCEIVED AVAILABILITY OF ILLICIT DRUGS

It should be kept in mind that throughout this chapter, when we refer to friends' use of substances, we are really reporting respondents' perceptions of such use. We asked respondents (in some, but not all, of our questionnaire forms) to estimate how many of their friends did each of the following: smoke cigarettes, smoke marijuana, take cocaine, use alcohol, or "get drunk at least once a week." For each substance use dimension, the response scale was "none, a few, some, most, all." As we show in this section, distributions of responses to these simple and straightforward questions correspond consistently with the age-related changes in self-reported drug use that we detailed in our earlier volume (Bachman et al., 1997). Thus, for example, just as proportions of marijuana users declined as young adult cohorts moved from age 18 through age 32, so also did the proportions of reported friends using marijuana decline. Later in this chapter we show also that, at the individual level of analysis, these ratings of friends' use correlate highly with self-reported use. Both sorts of findings provide evidence of the *construct validity* of these measures of friends' use.

Friends' Use of Cigarettes

Current cigarette consumption, and especially consumption at the rate of a half-pack or more per day, tends to increase among young adults during their first few years after high school and then decline slightly beginning in their mid-twenties (Bachman et al., 1997; Johnston et al., 2000b). Figure 7.1 shows a somewhat similar age-related pattern of decline in proportions of friends perceived to be smokers. For example, when the members of the classes of 1976–1984 were in high school, only about 44% reported that a

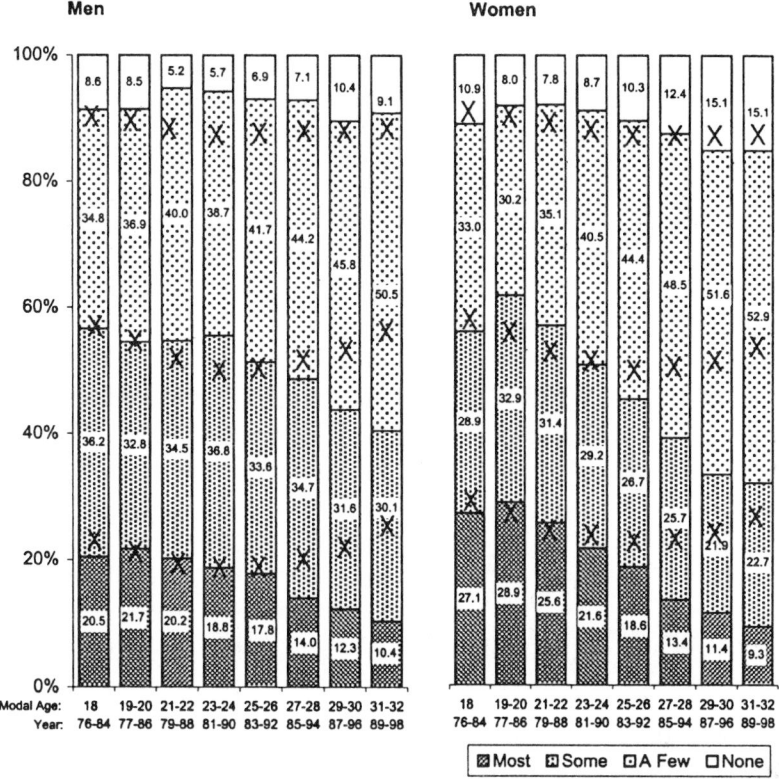

FIG. 7.1. Estimated proportion of friends who use cigarettes for panel respondents followed up from age 18 to ages 31–32. Bar percentages are based on high school senior data, plus follow-ups 1–7, from class years 1976–1984; one person could contribute up to seven follow-up observations (see Additional Panel Analysis Issues and Strategies section in chap. 3). The sample is restricted to those respondents who answered this question at follow-up 6 and/or follow-up 7. Approximate numbers of observations per age group for men: 860; for women: 1,070. X notations demarcate the boundaries between the quantity categories for the senior year data within the given year ranges.

few or none of their friends used cigarettes (top two categories in Fig. 7.1 combined); by the time they reached their early thirties, these proportions had grown to 60% among the men and 68% among the women. The X notations in the figure show some shifts during the same time period in high school seniors' perceptions of friends' smoking; however, those shifts are modest and are not consistent with the age-related trends for members of the classes of 1976–1984. Thus we are inclined to view the age-related changes shown in the figure as largely uninfluenced by secular trends.

Friends' Use of Alcohol, and Drunkenness

As is shown in Fig. 7.2, about two thirds of the high school seniors in the classes of 1976–1984 reported that most or all of their friends used alcohol (bottom two categories combined), and the figure rose to three quarters or more by the time they reached age 21. The proportions declined thereafter, and by their early thirties less than two thirds of the men and just over half of the women reported that most or all of their friends used alcohol. These figures correspond fairly closely to our earlier findings on self-reported alcohol

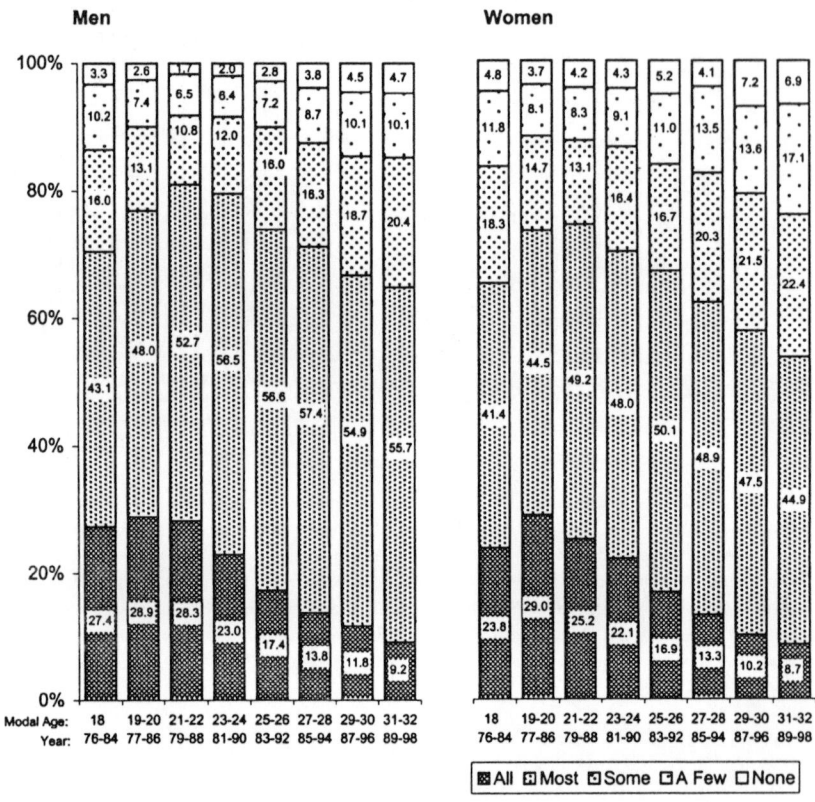

FIG. 7.2.   Estimated proportion of friends who drink alcohol for panel respondents followed up from age 18 to ages 31–32. Bar percentages are based on high school senior data, plus follow-ups 1–7, from class years 1976–1984; one person could contribute up to seven follow-up observations (see Additional Panel Analysis Issues and Strategies section in chap. 3). The sample is restricted to those respondents who answered this question at follow-up 6 and/or follow-up 7. Approximate numbers of observations per age group for men: 860; for women: 1,070. Inasmuch as there were no major secular trends in 12th grade data, friends' use is not compared to the average high school senior class data for each year range.

use among members of the classes of 1976–1981; users (those who reported any use in past 30 days) declined from 85% of men and 76% of women at modal ages 21–22, to 76% of men and 64% of women at modal ages 31–32 (Bachman et al., 1997, p. 80). So at least some alcohol use was the norm among majorities of young adults, although the proportions of users declined somewhat during their twenties and into their thirties.

Moderate use of alcohol usually does not create problems, but consumption of sufficient quantities to produce drunkenness is a matter of serious concern. Figure 7.3 shows that the proportions of friends perceived as "getting drunk at least once a week" declined fairly steadily as members of the classes of 1976–1984 went through their twenties. When they were high school seniors, only 41% of the men and 49% of the women reported that few or none of their friends got drunk weekly or more often (top two categories in Fig. 7.3 combined); however, by the time they reached their early thirties, fully 70% of the men and 84% of the women reported few or no friends who got drunk on such a regular basis. Here again, the reports of friends' behaviors correspond with age-related trends in self-reported use—in this case substantial declines in proportions who reported taking five or more drinks in a row at least once during the past 2 weeks (Bachman et al., 1997, p. 80).

Friends' Use of Marijuana

Our previous analyses showed that marijuana use declined substantially among members of the high school classes of 1976–1981. We also noted that downward secular trends that were widespread among young adults may have accounted for much of that decline, leading us to the tentative conclusion that there were only modest age-related declines in use above and beyond the secular trends (Bachman et al., 1997, pp. 114–115). Figure 7.4, which extends coverage to the classes of 1976–1984 and adds 3 more years of data beyond our earlier book, shows similar age-related declines in young adults' reports of friends' use. However, the figure also shows that the declines among high school seniors (X notations in the figure) ended around 1990 (see also Johnston et al., 2000a, p. 337, for more detailed data on high school senior trends), whereas the age-related declines among our panel respondents continued fairly steadily. We are thus more confident, given the three additional years of data, that some age-related declines in marijuana use occurred beyond the downward secular trends that occurred during the 1980s.

Friends' Cocaine Use

Earlier analyses reported age-related shifts in cocaine use among members of the classes of 1976–1981 that were explainable partially in terms of

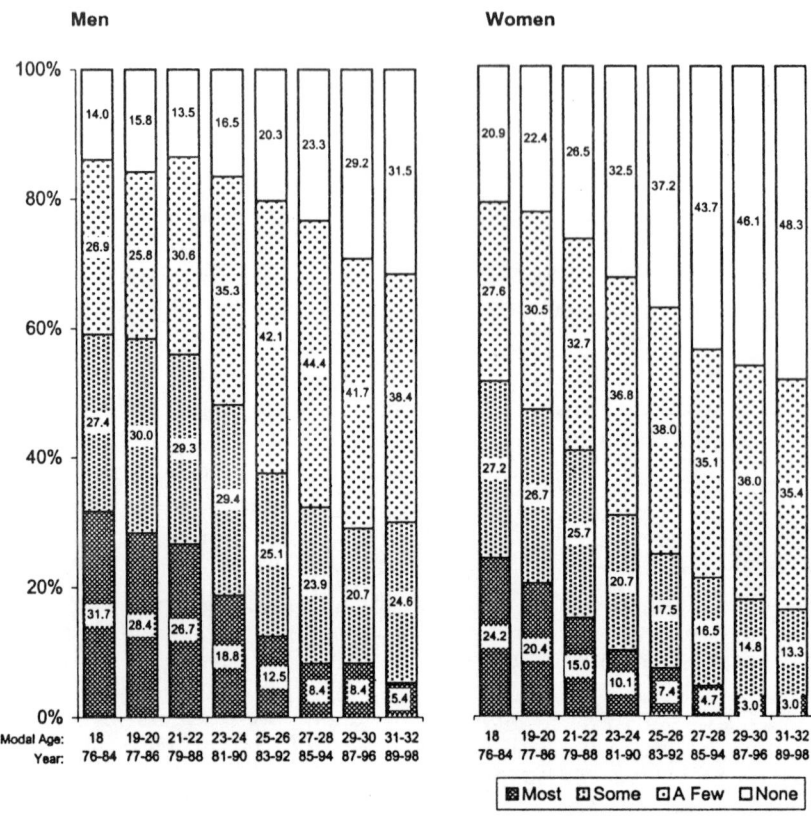

FIG. 7.3. Estimated proportion of friends who get drunk for panel respondents followed up from age 18 to ages 31–32. Bar percentages are based on high school senior data, plus follow-ups 1–7, from class years 1976–1984; one person could contribute up to seven follow-up observations (see Additional Panel Analysis Issues and Strategies section in chap. 3). The sample is restricted to those respondents who answered this question at follow-up 6 and/or follow-up 7. Approximate numbers of observations per age group for men: 860; for women: 1,070. Inasmuch as there were no major secular trends in 12th grade data, friends' use is not compared to the average high school senior class data for each year range.

post-high-school experiences and partially in terms of secular trends (Bachman et al., 1997, pp. 136, 150). Figure 7.5 tells a fairly similar story: Among members of the classes of 1976–1984, perceived cocaine use by friends rose during their early twenties and thereafter declined, with the changes in both directions somewhat larger than the shifts among succeeding sets of senior-year samples (as shown by the X notations in the figure).

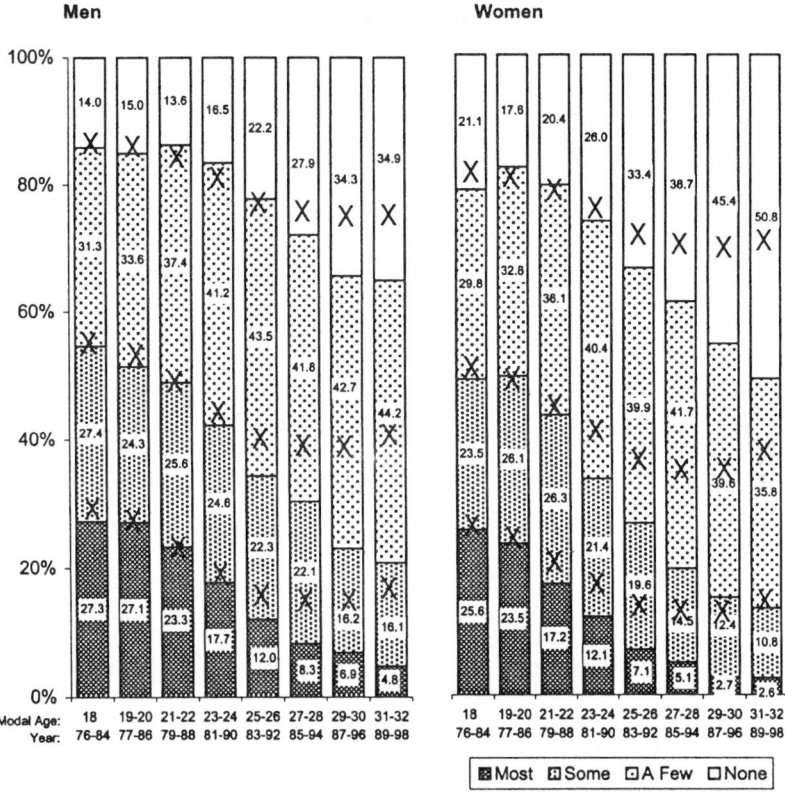

FIG. 7.4.   Estimated proportion of friends who use marijuana for panel respondents followed up from age 18 to ages 31–32. Bar percentages are based on high school senior data, plus follow-ups 1–7, from class years 1976–1984; one person could contribute up to seven follow-up observations (see Additional Panel Analysis Issues and Strategies section in chap. 3). The sample is restricted to those respondents who answered this question at follow-up 6 and/or follow-up 7. Approximate numbers of observations per age group for men: 860; for women: 1,070. X notations demarcate the boundaries between the estimated number of friends using marijuana categories for the senior year data within the given year ranges.

Perceived Availability of Illicit Drugs

Earlier research using Monitoring the Future high school senior data consistently showed that trends in perceived availability of the illicit drugs marijuana and cocaine had very little connection with trends in use of either drug (Bachman, Johnston, et al., 1990; Bachman et al., 1991; Johnston et al., 2000a). The major reason for this lack of relationships among trends is that

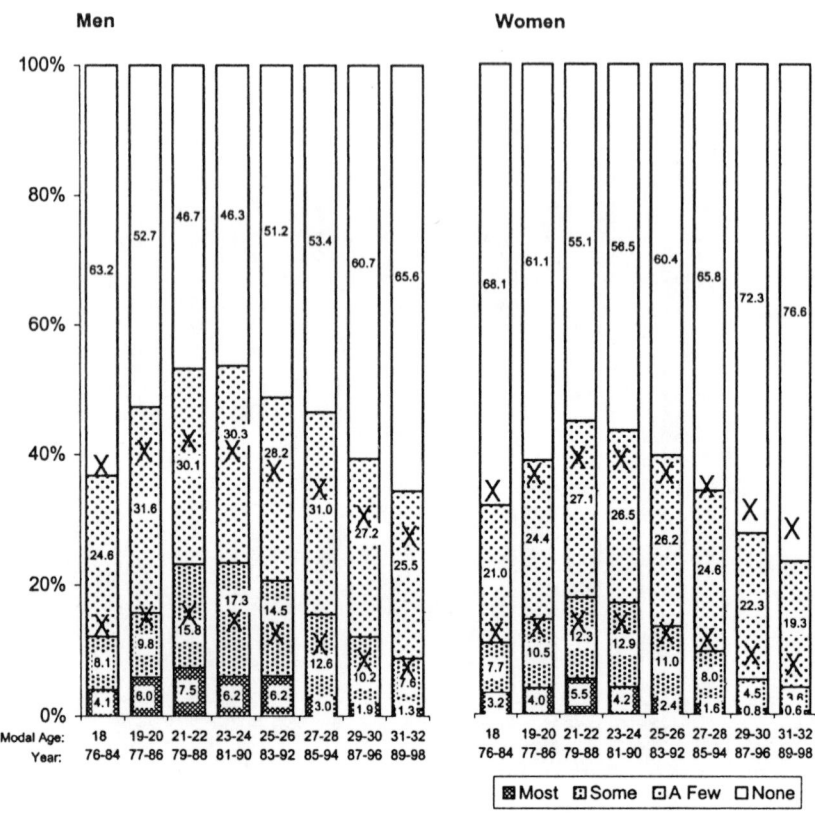

FIG. 7.5.   Estimated proportion of friends who use cocaine for panel respondents followed up from age 18 to ages 31–32. Bar percentages are based on high school senior data, plus follow-ups 1–7, from class years 1976–1984; one person could contribute up to seven follow-up observations (see Additional Panel Analysis Issues and Strategies section in chap. 3). The sample is restricted to those respondents who answered this question at follow-up 6 and/or follow-up 7. Approximate numbers of observations per age group for men: 860; for women: 1,070. X notations demarcate the boundaries between the lowest quantity categories (Most–Some and Some–A few) for the senior year data within the given year ranges.

the trend lines for perceived availability have been relatively flat; throughout the years, large proportions of high school seniors have considered it very easy or fairly easy to obtain marijuana, and roughly half of seniors in recent years have also considered it easy or fairly easy to obtain cocaine.

However, even though trends in perceived availability have not been large or closely linked with trends in use, it seems entirely likely that those who use an illicit drug would generally perceive it as available, whereas at least some nonusers might think that *they* would have considerable difficulty obtaining the illicit drug. Thus, we expected to find individuals' perceived availability of an illicit drug to be positively correlated with their use of that drug.

Here again chicken–egg problems abound. Does availability of a drug contribute to its use? Undoubtedly it does; after all, an individual cannot very well use a drug unless it is available. But if a substance is widely available, then relatively small variations in *perceived* availability may not make much of a difference. Conversely, do individuals who periodically use illicit drugs learn more about availability and take steps to assure their supply? Undoubtedly many or most of them do. So we have more than enough reasons to expect correlations, but we have little basis for deciding among competing hypotheses about causal direction(s).

Marijuana Availability. Figure 7.6 shows that after young adults from the high school classes of 1976–1984 graduated, their perceptions of marijuana availability increased slightly on average; then, as they moved through their twenties, the perceived availability of marijuana declined gradually. Nevertheless, even in their early thirties, 87% of the men and 78% of the women believed it would be "very easy" or "fairly easy" to get marijuana if they wanted some (bottom two categories in Fig. 7.6 combined). These age-related changes in perceived availability are consistent with age-related declines in use (Bachman et al., 1997), albeit much smaller. Trends in perceptions of high school seniors, shown by the X notations in Fig. 7.6, were weak and not consistent with the age-related declines. Thus, we believe the shifts in adult perceptions of availability—which were largely shifts from "very easy" to "fairly easy"—were linked to individual declines in use. Moreover, given the high perceptions of availability contrasted with lower levels of actual use, we suspect that age-related declines in use eventually contributed to the declines in perceived availability more than the reverse. But that causal interpretation cannot be proved by our correlational data.

Cocaine Availability. Figure 7.7 reveals that fewer respondents perceived cocaine as readily available, compared with the findings for marijuana. Moreover, the age-related changes were clearly different for the two illicit drugs. Among members of the high school classes of 1976–1984, perceived availability rose throughout their mid-twenties and declined somewhat thereafter. Specifically, about 42% of the men and 40% of the women considered cocaine "fairly easy" or "very easy" to get when they were high school seniors; by modal ages 25–26, the figures had risen to 72% among men and 63% among women; and by modal ages 31–32, they had declined

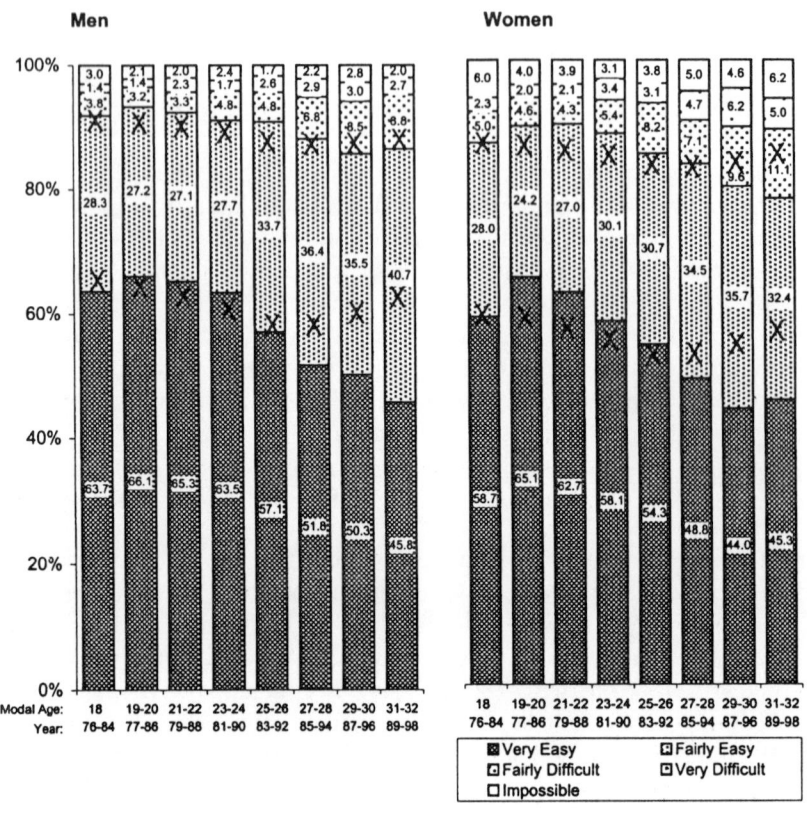

Men   **Women**

FIG. 7.6. Perceived availability of marijuana for panel respondents followed up from age 18 to ages 31–32. Bar percentages are based on high school senior data, plus follow-ups 1–7, from class years 1976–1984; one person could contribute up to seven follow-up observations (see Additional Panel Analysis Issues and Strategies section in chap. 3). The sample is restricted to those respondents who answered this question at follow-up 6 and/or follow-up 7. Approximate numbers of observations per age group for men: 870; for women: 1,070. X notations demarcate the boundaries between the three easiest availability categories for the senior year data within the given year ranges.

to 61% among men and 53% among women. Responses of high school seniors, shown by the X notations in the figure, indicate some secular trends in perceptions of cocaine availability; however, these are not nearly as pronounced as the age-related shifts. Also, the perceptions of availability were far higher than reports of use. So we are again inclined to view the age-related shifts in perceived availability as probably primarily responsive to, rather than causative of, the increases in actual cocaine use that occurred during our respondents' early twenties and the decreases in use during their

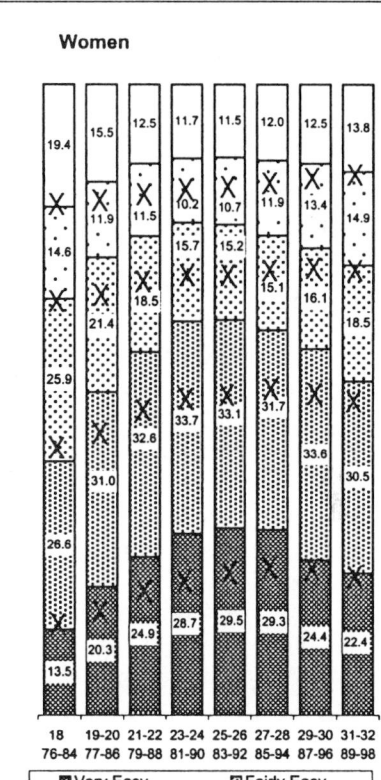

FIG. 7.7.   Perceived availability of cocaine for panel respondents followed up from age 18 to ages 31–32. Bar percentages are based on high school senior data, plus follow-ups 1–7, from class years 1976–1984; one person could contribute up to seven follow-up observations (see Additional Panel Analysis Issues and Strategies section in chap. 3). The sample is restricted to those respondents who answered this question at follow-up 6 and/or follow-up 7. Approximate numbers of observations per age group for men: 860; for women: 1,060. X notations demarcate the boundaries between the five availability categories for the senior year data within the given year ranges.

later twenties (see Bachman et al., 1997, p. 136, for a figure showing these shifts in cocaine use).

HOW PERCEPTIONS OF FRIENDS' USE ARE CORRELATED WITH SUBSTANCE USE

Here, as in chapter 6, we rely on summary correlational data in Tables A.2.1–A.2.3 in the appendix—in this section the correlations of interest are those between self-reported use and perceptions of friends' use. It is worth recalling that the tables present product–moment correlations for three separate groups: Table A.2.1 includes high school seniors in years 1990-1998 (modal age 18), Table A.2.2 includes individuals who responded to the first three follow-ups during 1990–1998 (modal ages 19–24), and Table A.2.3 includes individuals who responded to the fourth through seventh follow-ups during 1990–1998 (modal ages 25–32). Inspection of data from the classes of 1976–1984 (available in Bachman et al., 2001) revealed generally high levels of similarities between those findings (which incorporate some secular trends) and the findings in Tables A.2.1–A.2.3 (which incorporate cohort differences and some effects of panel attrition).

The correlations between (self-reported) own behavior and (perceived) friends' involvement in the same behavior were consistent across age bands. In general these correlations were quite high—especially taking into account that both kinds of dimensions were estimated using single-item measures that unavoidably included appreciable amounts of measurement error.

Just as self-reported usage rates were positively correlated across all substances, so also were perceived proportions of friends using correlated positively across all substances. Further, own use of any substance and friends' use of any *other* substance were positively correlated (e.g., the more an individual smoked cigarettes, the more friends used marijuana—correlations ranged from .26 to .34). However, the strongest correlations involved the same substances (e.g., rates of cigarette use correlated .42 to .47 with proportions of friends perceived to use cigarettes).

As Tables A.2.1–A.2.3 show, correlations between own use and friends' use of the same substance ranged from .42 to .49 for cigarette use, alcohol use, and instances of heavy drinking (correlated with friends' drunkenness) across all age bands. Differences between age bands were small and did not reveal any consistent pattern.

For each of the illicit drugs marijuana and cocaine, two measures are shown in the tables—current use (i.e., use during the past 30 days) and annual use (i.e., use during the past 12 months). The current use measures involve a narrower and more recent sample of behavior, which has advantages from a conceptual standpoint but limitations from a measurement standpoint. Other things equal, we prefer the recent sample of behavior because it corresponds more closely in time with the other measures (e.g., *current* perceptions, attitudes, marital and parental status). Earlier research also indicated that the current use measures are likely to be more accurate (less subject to forgetting) than the annual use measures (Bachman & O'Malley, 1989). All that notwithstanding, the annual use measures yield consistently higher correlations than the current use measures. This is because most of the illicit drug use reported by our respondents was infrequent, and the

30-day time samples missed most of those who reported some use during the 12-month time samples.[1]

As shown in Tables A.2.1–A.2.3, self-reported annual marijuana use correlated very highly with perceived friends' marijuana use (r values ranged from .57 to .61 across the three age bands). The corresponding figures for annual cocaine use were not as high among the young adults ($r = .45$ for modal ages 25–32; $r = .43$ for modal ages 19–24) and were distinctly lower among high school seniors ($r = .33$). These differences between the marijuana and cocaine correlations reflect the relatively low rates of cocaine use, especially among high school seniors.

In sum, this section demonstrates quite clearly what we asserted at the outset of this chapter: Drug-using youth and young adults are likely to have friends who use the same substances. More precisely, the findings shown in Tables A.2.1–A.2.3 and highlighted here indicate that the more an individual used a particular substance, the higher the proportion of friends he or she perceived as using that substance. The correlations were large and were much the same across ages ranging from senior year of high school to the late twenties and early thirties. The links between own use and friends' use were particularly strong for marijuana, perhaps because the drug was (and is) illicit and thus especially salient to respondents, but perhaps also because illicit drug users are especially likely to associate with each other to an even greater degree than cigarette and alcohol users. The correlations involving the illicit drug cocaine were not as strong as those involving marijuana, but we think that may be due largely to the fact that cocaine use was much less widespread, especially among high school seniors.

HOW PERCEPTIONS OF AVAILABILITY ARE CORRELATED WITH SUBSTANCE USE

Turning again to Tables A.2.1–A.2.3, we see that, as we expected, use of marijuana and cocaine correlated positively with perceived availability. Among high school seniors during the years 1990–1998, annual use of marijuana correlated .26 with perceived availability, among those in their early twenties the correlation was slightly lower at .21, but among those in their later twenties (fewer of whom used marijuana) the correlation was only .13. The corresponding correlations for annual cocaine use were lower but quite consistent across ages; the correlations were .15, .16, and .14. As we argued earlier, it seems reasonable that there should be some positive correlation,

---

[1]This is suggested by the standard deviations in Table A.2, and by the means (recall that a score of 1.0 indicates *no* use). Much more detailed data showing the higher proportions of annual users compared with current users can be found in Johnston et al. (2000a).

because users know by experience that they can (perhaps with some degree of difficulty) obtain the illicit drug in question; however, at least some non-users do not know whether and how readily they could obtain the drug if they wished. Given the fact that respondents in general, many of whom did not use marijuana and most of whom did not use cocaine, felt they could obtain marijuana easily and obtain cocaine easily or with moderate difficulty, it seems not surprising that the correlations between perceived availability and own use were rather low.

Another perspective on the relationships between perceived availability and use is provided by Fig. 7.8, which tracks the high school classes of 1976–1984 across seven follow-up surveys. Consistent with earlier observations, the figure shows some decline in correlations with increasing age, but it also permits several further observations. First, it is clear that perceived availability was a *necessary* condition for marijuana use; almost all use occurred among those who considered marijuana fairly easy or very easy to get. Second, it is clear that perceived availability was not a *sufficient* condition for marijuana use; most of those who thought it was very easy to get were not current users. Of particular interest for this book, the figure also shows that marijuana use declined with increasing age even among those who continued to believe that it would be very easy for them to get the drug if they wanted some. Parallel findings emerged for cocaine (as reported in Bachman et al., 2001): Actual use of cocaine (self-reported) was limited almost entirely to those who considered it fairly easy or very easy to get; however, relatively few of those who considered it easy to get actually used cocaine, and the proportions grew even smaller by their late twenties and early thirties. We thus conclude that perceived availability, although a necessary condition for most illicit drug use, is not a primary cause of such use—because substantial majorities of young adults who perceived easy access nevertheless opted not to be regular users of illicit drugs.

Returning again to Tables A.2.1–A.2.3, another set of interesting findings involves the relationships between perceived availability and perceived friends' use. To be sure, we are dealing with perceptions along both dimensions, and errors in one may be correlated with errors in the other (e.g., an individual who believes that cocaine is very easy to get may also believe that some of his friends use the drug, even if he has no direct evidence to support either belief). Nevertheless, it also seems plausible that individuals who know that some of their friends use an illicit drug may also know something about degree of availability—often because the friends told them about availability. In any case, the higher the proportions of friends perceived to use an illicit drug, the greater the perceived ease of availability of that drug. Moreover, these correlations were all substantially higher than the corresponding correlations between own use and perceived availability.

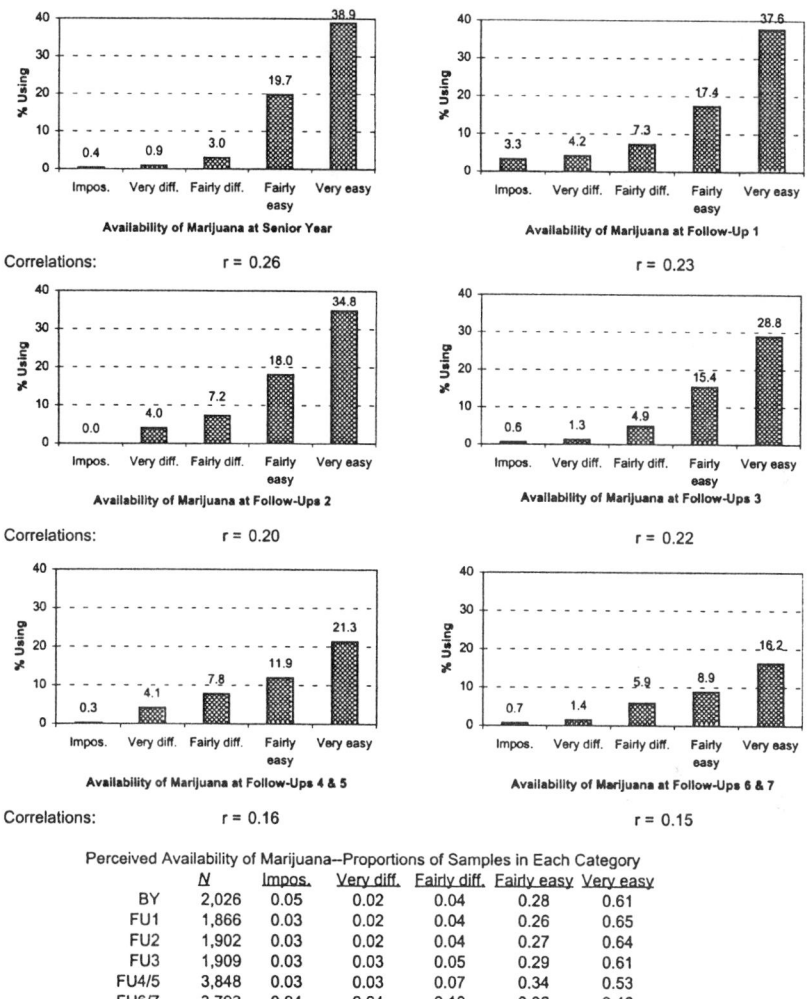

Perceived Availability of Marijuana--Proportions of Samples in Each Category

	N	Impos.	Very diff.	Fairly diff.	Fairly easy	Very easy
BY	2,026	0.05	0.02	0.04	0.28	0.61
FU1	1,866	0.03	0.02	0.04	0.26	0.65
FU2	1,902	0.03	0.02	0.04	0.27	0.64
FU3	1,909	0.03	0.03	0.05	0.29	0.61
FU4/5	3,848	0.03	0.03	0.07	0.34	0.53
FU6/7	3,793	0.04	0.04	0.10	0.36	0.46

FIG. 7.8.   Thirty-day prevalence of marijuana use related to perceived availability of marijuana. Percentages are based on the classes of 1976–1984 followed from age 18 to ages 29–32 (follow-ups 6 and 7, combined). The sample is restricted to those respondents who answered the questions on both drug use and marijuana availability at follow-up 6 and/or follow-up 7. Correlations are based on the drug use measure recoded as a dichotomy.

For marijuana use, the 1990–1998 correlations between friends' use and availability were .40 among seniors, .36 among those in their early twenties, and .27 for those in their later twenties and early thirties. For cocaine, the correlations were .30, .28, and .25 (respectively).

In sum, perceived availability of an illicit drug was not among the strongest correlates of actual (self-reported) use of that drug. Instead, it appears that young adults' perceptions of availability had a lot to do with perceived proportions of friends using the drug. Here we suspect that the dominant causal direction was as follows: Having friends who used a drug contributed to the perceptions of availability, often simply because the friends described how easy it was to get drugs. Of course, other causal processes also could be involved. For example, a respondent who used cocaine and knew it to be readily available might have introduced friends to cocaine use, thereby contributing to the correlation between perceived availability and friends' use. However, the fact that perceived availability consistently correlated much more strongly with friends' use than with own use suggests that the high proportions of individuals who perceived illicit drugs to be available were primarily the result of their having at least a few friends—or acquaintances—who reported that they used the drug and that it was easy to get.

ANALYSES LINKING FRIENDS' USE OF SUBSTANCES WITH POST-HIGH-SCHOOL EXPERIENCES[2]

Given the substantial correlations between self-reported use of a substance and perceived friends' use of the same substance, there was good reason to expect that links between friends' use and post-high-school experiences would parallel our earlier findings (Bachman et al., 1997) on the links between post-high-school experiences and drug use. That is exactly what we found. Tables A.7.1–A.7.4 summarize the bivariate and multivariate analyses showing how post-high-school experiences were associated with friends' cigarette smoking, occasional drunkenness, use of marijuana, and use of cocaine.

Student Status Related to Friends' Use of Substances

Just as college students were less likely than average to be smokers themselves, both in high school and when they became full-time, post-high-school students, so also did they tend to have fewer friends who smoked. So the story for smoking, whether own use or friends' use, was one of stable differences.

---

[2]The different dimension of post-high-school experiences and the proportions of respondents in each category at each follow-up are documented in the appendix, Tables A.1.1–A.1.5.

The story for alcohol use, and particularly for having friends who get drunk at least once a week, was quite different. During high school the college-bound students reported fewer friends, compared to their noncollege-bound classmates, who got drunk at least once a week; however, those differences disappeared after high school. Specifically, among the nonstudents there was a modest decline in proportions of friends who got drunk, whereas there was no such decline among the full-time students. In fact, the "student effect" on friends' drunkenness, like our earlier reported "student effect" on heavy drinking (Bachman et al., 1997), is explainable largely in terms of the living arrangements of students— particularly living in a dormitory.

Once living arrangements were controlled, student status appeared to have little relationship to changes in proportions of friends perceived to use marijuana or to use cocaine (documented in Tables A.7.3–A.7.4).

Employment Status Related to Friends' Use of Substances

There was generally little differential change in friends' use of substances related to employment status, with the important exception of those in military service. Men in military service and also the relatively small numbers of women in service were above average in proportions of friends who smoked and proportions of friends who got drunk at least once a week. Their friends' use of illicit drugs, on the other hand, was below average. (For further detail on drug use among military recruits, including changes during the past two decades, see Bachman et al., 1999.)

Living Arrangements and Marital Status Related to Friends' Use of Substances

Friends' use of alcohol and use of illicit drugs were related to respondents' living arrangements and marital status in much the same ways as the respondents' own use of these substances (see Bachman et al., 1997, for the latter data). Figure 7.9 presents findings for friends' marijuana use; findings for other dimensions of friends' use were similar (available in Bachman et al., 2001).

Being Married. As is shown in Fig. 7.9, respondents married at the time of follow-up reported fewest friends as marijuana users, whereas when these respondents were seniors in high school, they were just about average in terms of proportions of friends using marijuana. Those who were married also showed greater than average decreases in proportions of friends perceived as getting drunk at least once a week or as using cocaine. The multivariate analyses (reported in Tables A.7.2–A.7.4) showed that after other factors were controlled, fully half to three quarters or more of the relationships remained between being married and having fewer friends who got drunk or used illicit drugs. It thus seems likely that marriage contributed to these differential changes, most likely by contributing to shifting friendship

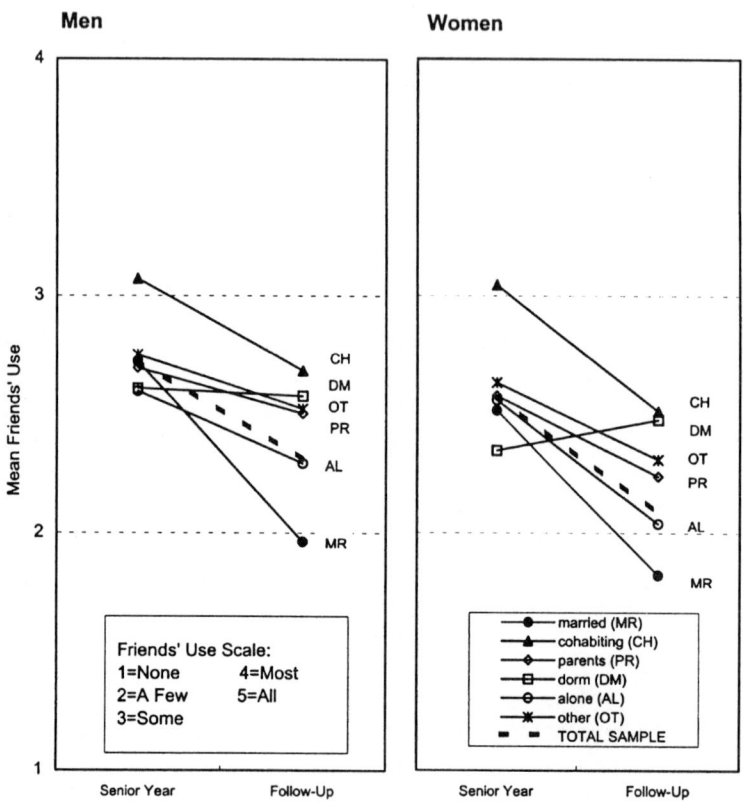

N's	MR	CH	PR	DM	AL	OT	TOTAL
Men	2,935	601	2,163	430	815	1,450	8,394
Women	4,490	793	2,284	513	724	1,400	10,204

FIG. 7.9. Change in mean estimated proportion of friends who use marijuana related to living arrangement at the time of follow-up. High school seniors from the classes of 1976–1984 were followed up as many as seven times between modal ages 19 and 32. In this figure, one person could contribute up to seven follow-up observations (see Additional Panel Analysis Issues and Strategies section in chap. 3). The approximate standard deviations for perceived friends' use of marijuana at senior year were 0.95 for males and 0.99 for females.

patterns, but perhaps also because increasing proportions of older friends also became married. (It seems less likely to us that an individual becoming married would cause that individual's long-term friends to stop using drugs.)

Cohabiting. Respondents who were cohabiting at the time of follow-up were above average in proportions of friends reported as smoking cigarettes, using marijuana, using cocaine, or getting drunk weekly or more often. But while in high school these same cohabiting respondents also tended to have more drug-using friends. These findings closely parallel our earlier findings that cohabitants were consistently above average in their own drug use, both while cohabiting (i.e., at the time of follow-up) and also prior to cohabiting (i.e., when they were high school seniors). Additionally, the multivariate analyses (Tables A.7.1–A.7.4) indicate that with other factors controlled, cohabitants (especially males) were less likely than average to experience decreases in friends' substance use.

Living With Parents. Respondents living with their parents at follow-up reported friends' substance use at proportions slightly above the overall averages at follow-up but equal to overall averages when they were seniors in high school. More importantly, analyses focusing on just the first two follow-ups (the period in which the young adults were most likely to be continuing to live with their parents) revealed that proportions of friends using various substances were just about average, both before and after controls for other factors in multivariate analyses (see Bachman et al., 2001, for multivariate analyses limited to the first two follow-ups).

Living in a Dormitory. As noted in the section on student status, college students were less likely to be smokers, were less likely to have been smokers during high school, and had fewer friends who smoked. This was particularly true for those students who lived in dormitories and thus indicates that dormitory life does not expose students to a lot of cigarette use. Dorm life does, however, involve many students in occasional heavy drinking, and thus it was not at all surprising to find that dorm residents were more likely than those in any of the other living arrangement categories to report having friends who were drunk at least once a week. The "dormitory effects" with respect to friends' drunkenness remained substantial after multivariate controls for other factors, both in analyses including all seven follow-ups (Table A.7.2) and those involving just the first two follow-ups (findings reported in Bachman et al., 2001). "Dormitory effects" linked to friends' marijuana use can be seen in Fig. 7.9 and in Table A.7.3; they were smaller among men than among women. For friends' cocaine use, there were no appreciable effects for men in dorms and only very modest effects for women in dorms. In sum, it appears that dormitory residents are exposed to a good deal of drunkenness among friends and are more likely than average to be heavy drinkers themselves. Dormitory life may also contribute to marijuana use, but not much to cocaine use.

Once again, sorting out causal contributions is exceedingly difficult. If living in dormitories increased exposure to substance-using friends, and if it also increased perceptions that such use was frequent and perhaps even "normative," then friends' use presumably was among the reasons that many dorm residents showed above-average increases in their own heavy drinking and marijuana use. But such individuals were, of course, part of the friendship group experienced by other dorm residents, and thus the chicken–egg problem in sorting out causation remains. It is perhaps worth noting, however, that students (and their parents) make decisions about whether students live at home or in dormitories; moreover, many colleges and universities offer students the option of living in "substance-free dorms." So students electing to live in dorms where substance use is widespread are, in many instances, not simply hapless victims of their living arrangements—rather, they have much to do with selecting such environments, and they themselves become part of friendship groups and thus do their own part to shape dormitory norms and environments with respect to substance use.

Living Alone and in Other Living Arrangements. We found little in the way of clear or consistent differences in patterns of friends' use that could be linked with living alone. Those in the "other living arrangements" category, however, showed shifts (relative increases) in proportions of friends who got drunk that were roughly comparable to those reported by students living in dorms (based on the multivariate analyses). These differences were particularly evident in the analyses that were limited to the younger adults (those in the first two follow-ups; reported in Bachman et al., 2001). Those in the "other living arrangements" category also had somewhat above-average proportions of friends who used marijuana (shown in Fig. 7.9 and Table A.7.3) and friends who used cocaine (Table A.7.4). All of these relationships remained, to at least some extent, after controls for other variables in the multivariate analyses.

Pregnancy and Parenthood Related to Friends' Use of Substances

Pregnancy. There is good evidence that most women reduce or eliminate their use of alcohol and other substances when they are pregnant. Do they also change their patterns of association so that they have fewer friends who use substances? Not so, according to our multivariate analyses (Tables A.7.1–A.7.4). Pregnant women and their spouses reported somewhat lower than average levels of substance use by their friends, but rather than being attributable to pregnancy, it appears that these differences were explainable in terms of age, marital status, and other aspects of living arrangements (e.g., few pregnant women or their spouses live in dorms).

Parenthood. Married parents showed greater than average reductions in proportions of friends who used substances. Single mothers showed smaller such reductions, whereas single fathers showed none. All of these changes, however, were explainable largely or entirely in terms of marriage and other factors (see Tables A.7.1–A.7.4).

Further Findings on Marital Status Related to Friends' Use of Substances

Engagement. The multivariate analyses showed engagement to be linked to some reductions in proportions of friends who got drunk, proportions who used marijuana, and proportions who used cocaine. Among women these "engagement effects" generally equaled or exceeded the corresponding "marriage effects," whereas among men they tended to be somewhat smaller (see Tables A.7.2–A.7.4).

Divorce. Divorce was associated with slight increases in proportions of friends who got drunk at least once a week and proportions of friends who used illicit drugs (data shown in Bachman et al., 2001). This is consistent with our earlier findings that those who divorced increased their own instances of heavy drinking and of marijuana use (Bachman et al., 1997), and with our present findings (in chap. 5, see especially Fig. 5.23) that those recently divorced sharply increased their frequency of going to bars (where they, along with some of their friends, could drink heavily).

Conclusions Based on Multivariate Analyses

In this section on friends' substance use, as we found also for religiosity in chapter 4 and perceived risks and disapproval in chapter 6, *change scores* were not highly predictable from post-high-school roles and experiences. The post-high-school predictors could account for relatively little variance in change scores for friends' cigarette use (see Table A.7.1) and for roughly 1–2% of the variance in the other change score dimensions (Tables A.7.2–A.7.4). That said, it must be added that prediction of change scores for respondents' own substance use, reported in our earlier book, was on the same order of magnitude and showed many of the same patterns as well as similar strengths of association (Bachman et al., 1997; Tables A.5–A.11). It thus seems highly likely that patterns of friends' substance use were affected by many of the same factors that affected patterns of own substance use. We think this interpretation of the findings is more broadly and generally plausible than one alternative interpretation: that the respondents' post-high-school experiences changed their friends' use which in turn changed the respondents' use. Another alternative interpretation is somewhat more plausible: that post-high-school experiences led to somewhat different sets of friends who also had different patterns of substance use. Overall, we are left with what we have been describing as a chicken–egg problem. We have clear evidence that substance use during young adulthood continues to be closely linked with friends' use, but we cannot determine with any confidence whether (and which) one of several possible causal processes is dominant.

ANALYSES LINKING PERCEPTIONS OF AVAILABILITY WITH POST-HIGH-SCHOOL EXPERIENCES

As noted earlier, problems of causal interpretation are present here also. Perceived availability was quite high for marijuana and fairly high also for cocaine; however, perceived availability of either substance was somewhat higher among those who used it compared with those who did not. Using and continuing to use an illicit substance is likely to maintain the perception (and reality) of availability, whereas at least some nonusers are likely to be less confident of their ability to gain access to a drug if they wished to do so. But that leaves unresolved the question of whether variations in perceived availability play any important role in determining use.

Our exploration of links between availability and post-high-school experiences, detailed in Tables A.7.5–A.7.6 and in Bachman et al. (2001) and summarized very briefly here, showed patterns consistent with the fact that use and perceived availability of either marijuana or cocaine were positively correlated. Specifically, post-high-school experiences were able to account for about 1% or less of the variance in change scores in the perceived availability of marijuana and of cocaine. The multivariate analyses suggested negative impacts on perceived availability among those in military service, those who were married, and (to a lesser extent) those who were engaged. The analyses also suggested positive impacts on perceived availability among those living in dormitories and those in the "other living arrangements" category (which often involved living with other young adults in dormitory-like conditions). In other words, the same post-high-school experiences that seemed to contribute to actual use of marijuana and of cocaine (Bachman et al., 1997) also seemed to contribute to perceived availability of those drugs.

SUMMARY

Young adults who smoked were more likely than average to report large proportions of their friends as smokers. Young adults who drank heavily on occasion reported larger than average proportions of friends as getting drunk at least once a week. Similarly, self-reports of marijuana use were correlated with perceptions of friends' marijuana use, and the same was true regarding cocaine. These correlations were quite strong, particularly considering that the perception measures are not very precise.

Young adults who used marijuana were more likely than average to consider it "very easy" to get the drug. It should be kept in mind, however, that even among nonusers, marijuana was generally considered at least "fairly easy" to get, if they wanted some. Similarly, cocaine users were more likely than nonusers to rate that drug as easy to get, although in general it was viewed as less accessible than marijuana.

Analyses examining post-high-school experiences suggested that patterns of friends' substance use were affected by many of the same factors that affected respondents' own substance use. Specifically, students living in dormitories or other group housing situations were more likely than their age-mates to have friends who got drunk. Individuals in military service had higher than average proportions of friends who smoked and who got drunk, but lower than average proportions of friends who used illicit drugs. Being engaged or married was associated with lower than average proportions of friends who got drunk or used illicit drugs, whereas becoming divorced was related to increases in such behaviors by friends. We consider it unlikely that becoming divorced causes the divorcee's friends to get drunk or use illicit drugs (at least not on a regular basis), but we consider it highly plausible that divorce is associated with some shift in friendship patterns, with the new friends more likely to be substance users.

As we said at the outset of this chapter, there is no lack of plausible causal interpretations for the relationships reported herein. Rather, our problem is that there are too many good reasons, and we cannot readily sort out the various alternative (and often complementary) explanations for why friends' use is related to own use. Friends encourage and facilitate each others' substance use, and intricate questions about whether an individual's influence over his friend's use is stronger than the reverse cannot be answered with the survey data available to us. Similarly, although availability of illicit substances is a necessary condition for their use, it is hardly a sufficient condition; and given the widespread availability of marijuana and cocaine (at least based on our respondents' perceptions), availability is probably a relatively minor causal factor.

For the reasons just cited, which were elaborated at the outset of this chapter and in chapter 2, we have opted not to try to incorporate friends' use or perceived availability in the causal modeling efforts reported in chapter 8. This is not because we consider friends' use to be unimportant, but because we cannot with confidence treat it primarily as a cause rather than a consequence of young adults' own substance use.

8

Putting the Pieces Together—
Structural Equation Models

In this chapter we attempt to show how a number of the relationships examined separately in previous chapters can fit together. "Putting the pieces together" is a bit of an overstatement, however; a more appropriate title for this chapter would be "Putting *some of* the pieces together." We begin this chapter by spelling out *which* of the pieces we put together, *why* we chose these particular ones, and *what rationale* we offer for the particular causal ordering we selected for our structural equation models.

In this book and the previous one, we examined a considerable range of post-high-school experiences, and we showed some of the ways in which they overlap. We found, for example, that increases in occasional heavy drinking among full-time college students could be explained primarily by their marital status and living arrangements. We were at pains, in our previous book, to make clear our interpretation that student status does indeed matter, albeit indirectly: "Our interpretation of these findings is that student status does indeed contribute to increased alcohol use, but only indirectly via the marital status and other living arrangements that generally go along with being a college student" (Bachman et al., 1997, p. 169).

It is one thing to look simultaneously at a number of potential causal factors that may be overlapping in their impacts, document some of those overlaps, and offer interpretations of underlying causal sequences. That is what we did in chapters 4–7. It is quite another matter to incorporate into analy-

181

ses a series of specific hypotheses about causal ordering. That is what we do in this chapter. Attempting to sort out such an ordering required us to limit sharply the number of variables to be considered. So it is important to keep in mind that we provide here just one set of examples of how the pieces fit together, examples that confirm the conclusions we reached after examining some of the pieces separately.

DECISIONS ABOUT VARIABLES, SAMPLES, AND MODELS

We examined a range of possible mediating variables in chapters 4–7, and we used a variety of subsamples of Monitoring the Future respondents in doing so. Our approach in the causal modeling reported in this chapter was to be as inclusive as we felt would be manageable and justifiable, in order to illustrate how several variables might work together to mediate the impacts of post-high-school experience on substance use. Our selection of variables and samples for these analyses was guided by conceptual considerations and results of previous studies (see chap. 2), as well as by findings from analyses presented in earlier chapters.

Selection of Variables for Inclusion

Most of the variables are based on single items from our questionnaires. Where multiple items are used as indicators, they are noted in the paragraphs that follow.

Marriage. In order to focus primarily on the mediating variables, we decided to focus on just one of the new roles and responsibilities of young adulthood: the transition into marriage—a post-high-school experience that involves a large proportion of young adults and that was found in previous research to have fairly large impacts on various types of substance use. We chose to contrast young adults who did and did not make the transition from single to married sometime between the first follow-up (modal ages 19–20) and the third follow-up (modal ages 23–24).

Religiosity. We showed in chapter 4 that negative associations between religiosity and substance use were strong among high school seniors and remained strong during young adulthood. Much of the connection during young adulthood was attributable to the very high stability of religiosity across time and the fairly high stability of substance use behaviors. In spite of the high stability of religiosity, however, chapter 4 also showed that marriage and other post-high-school experiences had at least some impacts on religiosity. Accordingly, we considered this dimension to be a good candidate for inclusion in our causal modeling.[1]

Evenings Out. Chapter 5 showed that frequency of evenings out for fun and recreation was positively associated with substance use among high school seniors and young adults. The chapter also showed that evenings out declined after marriage and that other post-high-school experiences also appeared to affect frequency of evenings out. This dimension was thus another very good candidate for the causal modeling. A number of other factors treated in chapter 5 also were correlated with substance use; these included frequency of going to parties and frequency of going to bars (or nightclubs or taverns). Although it would have been of interest to include these also in our causal modeling, it was not practical to do so because these items appeared only on a different questionnaire form than the items on perceived risks and disapproval. Moreover, the items about going to parties and to bars overlap with the evenings out measure, and that would have added complexity to the modeling exercise. Fortunately, that overlap means that the evenings out measure can be viewed as at least a partial proxy for the other more specific measures about parties and bars.

Disapproval/Perceived Risk. Chapter 6 showed that both perceived risks of using a substance and also disapproval of the substance were strongly and negatively correlated with actual use of the substance—relationships that held true among high school seniors and also among young adults. Although the disapproval and perceived risk measures were not as strongly affected by post-high-school experiences as were the evenings out and other measures in chapter 5, it was nevertheless true that marriage and some of the other experiences were associated with changes (increases) in perceived risks and disapproval of most substance use. Thus both of these dimensions of drug-related attitudes were considered good candidates for inclusion in the causal modeling.

We did some exploratory work in which both the perceived risk and the disapproval measures were included jointly in models predicting substance use. (In all instances, of course, the risk and disapproval measures were matched to the substance use dimension; thus, for example, perceived risk of marijuana use and disapproval of marijuana use were matched with actual marijuana use, and so on.) It was only in recent years that any of the Monitoring the Future questionnaire forms included both perceived risk and disapproval measures (in prior years they appeared on separate ques-

---

[1]In the causal models, two indicators are used for religiosity: frequency of attendance at services and importance of religion.

tionnaire forms); thus, modeling including both dimensions was restricted to recent surveys. The exploratory analyses led us to conclude that including both perceived risks and disapproval produced a complicated and unwieldy model, whereas using either one alone provided what we judged to be a clearer picture of the predictive value of drug-related attitudes and of the other dimensions included in the models. Accordingly, we opted to estimate models separately for perceived risks and for disapproval. The models for perceived risk and disapproval were very similar across the various substances. To keep the results as straightforward as possible, we focus primarily on disapproval because changes in disapproval compared to changes in perceived risks over the 4-year time period were associated with more change in substance use over the same time period.[2]

Marijuana Use/Cocaine Use/Heavy Drinking/Alcohol Use/ Smoking.   Each of these substance use dimensions was the subject of separate model estimations. The cigarette use measure dealt with use during the past 30 days. The measure of occasional heavy drinking involved only the past 2 weeks. For marijuana use and cocaine use, we had the option of focusing on use during the past 30 days or the past 12 months. The 30-day measures had several advantages: (a) probably more accurate recall, (b) a closer match in time to the other measures (i.e., we asked about *current* attitudes and behaviors regarding religion, evenings out, and views about drugs), and (c) a greater likelihood of not actually overlapping the point of transition from single to married. The 12-month measures had the advantage of a much longer time sample for what were relatively rare behaviors among most young adults, and the resulting relationships (even after adjustment for measurement errors) were generally stronger. Accordingly, we opted for the 12-month measures for the illicit drugs, after ascertaining that the results were similar but somewhat weaker for the 30-day measures.

Variables Not Included.   In chapter 7 we showed that perceptions of friends' drug-using behaviors were correlated quite strongly with self-reports of the same drug-using behaviors, but we also discussed in that chapter the considerable difficulties in sorting out causal processes underlying these correlations. We were left with the view that friends do indeed influence each

---

[2]The number of indicators varied by substance. Three indicators were available for attitudes about marijuana: trying it once or twice, using it occasionally, and using it regularly. Two indicators were available for attitudes about cocaine: trying it once or twice, and using it regularly. Three indicators were used for attitudes about alcohol use (when predicting use during the past 30 days): trying it once or twice, taking 1 or 2 drinks nearly every day, and taking 4 to 5 drinks nearly every day. A single indicator was used for attitudes about occasional heavy drinking: having 5 or more drinks once or twice each weekend. A single indicator was used for attitudes about smoking cigarettes: smoking one or more packs per day.

other when it comes to substance use, but for any particular individual the causation most likely runs both ways (i.e., an individual is influenced by friends but influences friends in turn, and also chooses friends and in turn is chosen by them, all in ways that tend to heighten the correlations). Accordingly, we opted not to try to incorporate friends' use into our causal models.

Similarly, we opted not to include perceived availability in models involving marijuana use and cocaine use. The correlations here were smaller, while the causal interpretations remained problematic.

As noted earlier, we chose to focus on just one of the new roles and responsibilities of young adulthood. Thus our models did not include student status, employment status, various other living arrangements, pregnancy, or parenthood. These were omitted not because they are unimportant, but because they would have produced too many complications in the modeling effort.

Selection of Samples

Focus on First and Third Follow-Ups. Our causal modeling uses just two points in time: a "before" point at which all respondents were single, and an "after" point at which some were married. (We achieved that degree of simplicity by the expedient of removing from the analyses all respondents who were not single at the first point and all who were something other than single or married at the second point; that excluded anyone who reported being divorced.) Other things equal, we would have preferred to carry out our causal modeling using two points fairly close in time—perhaps even closer than the 2-year intervals between our follow-ups. But other things seldom really are equal, and they certainly were not in this instance. Had we used a 2-year interval—the smallest available given our follow-up design—we would have had only a relatively small proportion who had made the transition from single to married. We thus opted for a longer interval—specifically, the 4-year interval between the first and third follow-up surveys.

We chose the first follow-up (modal ages 19–20) as a starting point because very few respondents were married this early in their lives, and thus we would be excluding very few individuals from our analysis. We chose the third follow-up (modal ages 23–24) as the ending point because a reasonable number were married by that point whereas not very many had already become divorced. We are thus examining the impacts of relatively early marriage (versus nonmarriage) among young adults in their early twenties. Because other analyses had satisfied us that marriage effects were fairly similar throughout the age span of our study (Figs. 3.2, 5.24, and 5.25 provide examples), we felt this particular sample of marriage effects would generalize to the effects of marriages of individuals during their later twenties or even early thirties.

Two Different Subsamples (Single Forms). As indicated earlier, we opted to examine the disapproval measures and the perceived risk measures in separate analyses. One of the reasons for preferring this approach was the very practical one that it permitted us to use our samples extending back to those from the high school class of 1976 (when the two sets of measures appeared on different questionnaire forms, thereby precluding the use of both measures in the same model). Specifically, the samples involved members of the 1976–1992 high school classes—all those who had participated in the study long enough to have completed the third follow-up survey, which occurred 5 or 6 years after graduation.

Because the risk and disapproval measures were on separate questionnaire forms for nearly all of the data collections involved, we had available for analysis two different sets of subsamples (each pooled across the classes of 1976–1992). We thus have independent samples for the disapproval analyses and the perceived risk analyses. This results in slightly different estimates due to sampling variation; however, there is a very close degree of replication across the two sets of pooled subsamples, and that heightens our confidence in the findings.

The Causal Model

Figure 8.1 outlines the causal model that we developed to explore whether and to what extent three variables—religiosity, frequency of evenings out, and disapproval—could be seen as mediating the "marriage effect" on substance use. We have already spelled out some of the specific decisions and the underlying rationales for selecting certain dimensions for inclusion in the model. We present next the rationale for the causal ordering shown in the model, and we also have more to say about how this causal model evolved and why we are able to use what is a relatively simple model (i.e., one that omits many other possible causal paths).

Rationale for Causal Ordering

Once we reduced the number of variables to a manageable number, based on the logic outlined earlier in this chapter, the remaining decisions about causal ordering were mostly straightforward, guided by conceptual and practical considerations. As illustrated in Fig. 8.1, each of our final causal models involved four variables measured at the first follow-up (modal ages 19–20), the same four variables remeasured at the third follow-up (modal ages 23–24), plus the marital status variable indicating whether a transition from single to married had occurred between the first and third follow-ups. An obvious early decision was to treat each of the initial four variables as

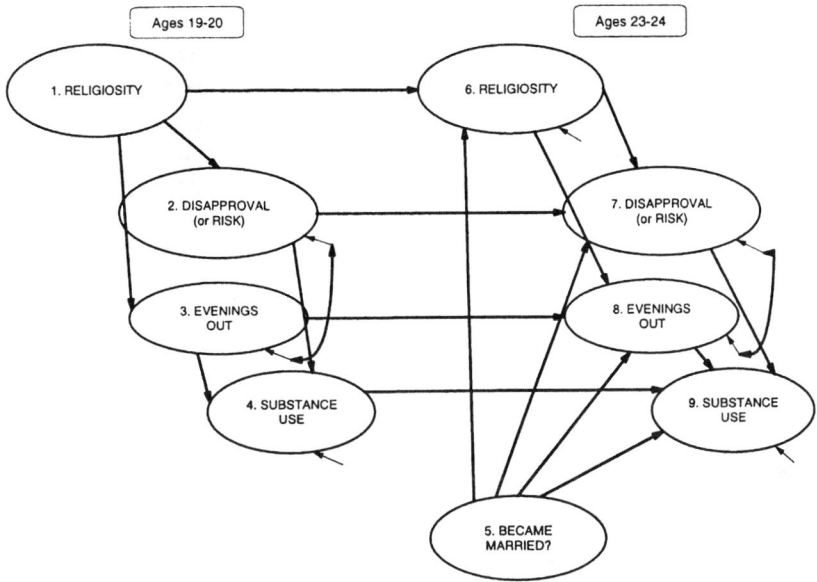

FIG. 8.1. Key to the structural models of the relations among religiosity, evenings out, disapproval of substance use, and substance use at ages 19–20 and 23–24 among young adults who became married or remained unmarried.

one "cause" of the later version of that same variable—thus the four horizontal arrows shown in Fig. 8.1, which really amount to indicators of stability over the 4-year interval between first and third follow-ups.

A closely related decision was to omit cross-lag causal arrows (e.g., disapproval at ages 19–20 "causing" changes in substance use at ages 23–24, or ages 19–20 substance use "causing" ages 23–24 disapproval), provided that omitting these cross-lags did not result in undue strain in the models. Our rationale is that we did not feel confident about sorting out possible reciprocal cross-lagged effects over a 4-year interval; moreover, we felt that our primary focus on possible mediation of the "marriage effect" did not require such a sorting out.

A key decision was to examine the marriage transition as a potential cause of changes in each of the other variables measured at the third follow-up. This would provide the basis for evaluating the extent to which changes in religiosity, frequency of evenings out, and disapproval (or perceived risk) mediated the impacts of marriage on substance use. We also preferred not to treat the marital transition as itself caused by the earlier levels of religiosity, evenings out, or disapproval/risk (provided this did not cause undue strain in the models); this was consistent with the findings shown in earlier chapters that there were not strong initial differences (as of senior year of high school) linked with subsequent marriage versus nonmarriage. Similarly, we preferred (again, provided it did not cause undue strain) not to treat earlier substance use as a cause of later marital status; this was consistent with our earlier findings (Bachman et al., 1997) that there were not strong initial differences in substance use linked with subsequent marriage versus nonmarriage. It is noteworthy that in some previous analyses we did find small but significant effects of alcohol and illicit drug use at age 18 on both evenings out and marriage at age 22 (Schulenberg et al., 1994). These relationships were not unexpected, especially given that the starting point in those analyses was senior year in high school. Nevertheless, we do not see those findings as conflicting with our current approach (and, as seen later, with our current findings).

We found it a bit more complicated to decide how to model the relationships among the key mediating variables: religiosity, evenings out, and drug-related attitudes (disapproval or perceived risk). We were willing to model each of these as primarily causes rather than consequences of substance use, although we were mindful that some causation might run in the opposite direction. But we had an initial preference to be more "agnostic" about how these three mediating variables related to each other; thus we undertook some exploratory analyses treating them simply as correlated predictors. The result of this exercise was that disapproval (or risk) and frequency of evenings out both emerged as direct causes of substance use, whereas religiosity merely showed intercorrelations with disapproval and evenings out but otherwise no impact on substance use. Those findings prompted us to reconsider the causal modeling as follows.

To put it simply, perhaps even amusingly, we concluded that we were being a bit *too* "agnostic" with respect to the role of religion as a factor influencing substance use. To show religiosity as merely a correlate of such causal factors as disapproval and evenings out seemed to us to misrepresent the likely realities. We considered it plausible that religiosity was one of the important factors influencing disapproval of substance use, whereas the opposite causal path (that disapproving of drug use makes one religious) seemed a good deal less plausible. In any event, we were certainly willing to assume that the *primary* causal pathway lay from religiosity to disapproval rather than the other way around. Similarly, we were willing to model religiosity as one of the factors influencing frequency of evenings out, rather than vice versa.

By treating religiosity as a causal factor contributing to the other mediating variables, we opened up the possibility of showing indirect effects as well as direct effects on substance use. We judged this a much more realistic model. On the other hand, we saw no reason to abandon our agnosticism about whether disapproval (or perceived risks) causes (less frequent) evenings out or vice versa. Accordingly, our model treats them simply as correlated and does not treat either as a cause of the other.

If model-making is a bit like sausage-making, we hope this brief review of our decision-making process was not too distasteful. Ideally, it should provide some justification for why the arrows in Fig. 8.1 are as they are. If it serves as a cautionary tale, so much the better. Certainly it would be appropriate for readers to recall Carson's dictum ("You buy the premise, you buy the sketch"). For our part, we have tried to keep firmly in mind that our premises are only that. Unavoidably, the models shown here greatly oversimplify the real world they are intended to represent. Nevertheless, we think the models presented herein can also provide some illumination.

ANALYTIC APPROACH

Structural equation modeling (SEM) analyses with latent variables were conducted to test the models and to provide a simultaneous estimation of the parameters while accounting for attenuation in the structural coefficients due to measurement error. The SEM analyses were conducted using EQS 5.7 (Bentler, 1995) with maximum likelihood estimation. Covariance matrices were used in all SEM analyses (pairwise deletion of missing data); results are presented in the standardized metric to facilitate interpretation. Covariance matrices included the indicators of the latent variables shown in Fig. 8.1 and already described.

Analyses proceeded by examining the model in Fig. 8.1 for each of the different substances separately; measurement models were incorporated as well as the structural relations. Initially, only the disapproval measures were examined; perceived risk measures were not included. Models were fit for the sample with males and females combined; then, in addition, two-group models were used to test for invariance between men and women. For both the combined sample models and the two-group models, the total marriage effects were decomposed into direct and indirect effects. The direct effects represented the marriage–substance use parameters (the path directly from 5 to 9 in Fig. 8.1), and the indirect effects represented the mediated effects of marriage on substance use through increased religiosity, increased disapproval, and decreased evenings out (the combination of all possible paths from 5 to 9 in Fig. 8.1 other than the direct effect). Significant indirect effects indicated that these mediating variables help to explain the effects of becoming married on change in substance use during the 4-year time period (ages 19–20 to ages 23–24). A marriage effect on changes in substance use was considered to be fully mediated by these variables when the indirect effects were significant and direct marriage effect was not. The combined sample modeling approach (but not the two-group approach) was then repeated, substituting perceived risk measures for the disapproval measures.

To determine the suitability of the models, several fit indices were used: Bentler and Bonett's Nonnormed Fit Index (BBNNFI), and the Root Mean Square Error of Approximation (RMSEA; Browne & Cudeck, 1993; see also MacCallum & Austin, 2000). For the BBNNFI, values between .95 and 1.0 indicate that the model provides a good fit to the data (Hu & Bentler, 1999). For the RMSEA, the lower limit of 0.00 is the ideal, and values less than .05 indicate a good fit to the data. In the two-group analyses, constraining parameters to be equal between males and females and observing the resulting change in chi-squares allow us to consider the extent of invariance across gender (Jaccard & Wan, 1996; Jöreskog & Sörbom, 1996).

FINDINGS FROM THE STRUCTURAL EQUATION MODELING

The model represented in Fig. 8.1 was examined using five different dimensions of substance use: annual marijuana use, annual cocaine use, 30-day alcohol use, 2-week heavy episodic drinking, and 30-day cigarette use; these examinations were carried out first using disapproval measures and then using perceived risk measures. Figures 8.2 through 8.6 present the structural equation results for the disapproval models for the different substances, and Table 8.1 summarizes the fit indices for the measurement models (in the combined sample) and the structural models (both for the combined sample and for the sample split by gender) for each of the substances.

The measurement models established the relations between the observed and latent constructs. In each of the measurement models, we used multiple indicators for each construct when possible and single indicators when necessary. For items that served as single indicators of constructs (evenings out, substance use, and in some cases disapproval/risk), unique variances were fixed based on previous reliability estimates for these variables; the errors were fixed at (1 – reliability) times the variance. All of the reliability estimates were judged to be acceptably high. Specifically, reliabilities for the substance use variables ranged between .65 (heavy drinking) and .87 (annual marijuana use); the reliabilities for the evenings out, disapproval, and perceived risk measures were between .58 and .63; and for marital status, we assumed no errors. When we used multiple indicators, the unique variances for the same items measured at both follow-ups were permitted to correlate. The measurement models allowed all possible correlations among the latent factors; therefore they provided a baseline comparison for the other models. Correlations between within-time error terms for indicators were fixed at zero.

Table 8.1

Fit Indices for Measurement Model, Structural Model for Total
Sample, and Structural Model for Males and Females

		Final Model		
Substance	df	χ^{2*}	BBNNFI	RMSEA
Measurement Model				
Marijuana Use (Annual)	54	1094.40	0.941	0.069
Cocaine Use (Annual)	30	127.94	0.986	0.028
Binge Drinking (2-week)	13	31.91	0.994	0.019
Alcohol Use (30-day)	54	697.69	0.939	0.054
Cigarette Use (30-day)	13	55.15	0.988	0.028
Structural Model (Total Sample)				
Marijuana Use (Annual)	72	1469.70	0.940	0.069
Cocaine Use (Annual)	48	215.12	0.985	0.029
Binge Drinking (2-week)	31	259.16	0.977	0.025
Alcohol Use (30-day)	72	972.52	0.936	0.056
Cigarette Use (30-day)	31	405.86	0.955	0.055
Structural Model (Gender Differences)				
Marijuana Use (Annual)	166	1516.05	0.949	0.045
Cocaine Use (Annual)	118	284.16	0.988	0.019
Binge Drinking (2-week)	85	307.36	0.977	0.025
Alcohol Use (30-day)	168	1143.40	0.939	0.038
Cigarette Use (30-day)	85	427.38	0.966	0.033

* All χ^2 values are significant at the p<.01 level.

Annual Marijuana Use

The first set of models that we considered were the annual marijuana use models. All of the other substance use models followed the same analytic approach, and results from these models follow. Compared to other substances, the measurement model for marijuana use, as indicated by Table 8.1, did not provide as good a fit to the data. Limited by the measurement model, the structural model also had lower fit indices than structural models for other substances. The measurement model fit for marijuana use could have been improved by allowing the within-time indicators of disapproval of marijuana use to correlate; however, to keep the models parsimonious and consistent across the different substances, these correlations were fixed at zero. That aside, the structural model (Fig. 8.2) illustrates how changes in religiosity, disapproval, and evenings out helped to explain the marriage effect on change in marijuana use between ages 19–20 and 23–24. It is notable that over this time period, reports of disapproval, evenings out, marijuana use, and, in particular, religiosity, were fairly stable. Highly stable factors reduced the explanatory power of changes in marital status or other factors because there was less to explain. Multigroup SEM analyses indi-

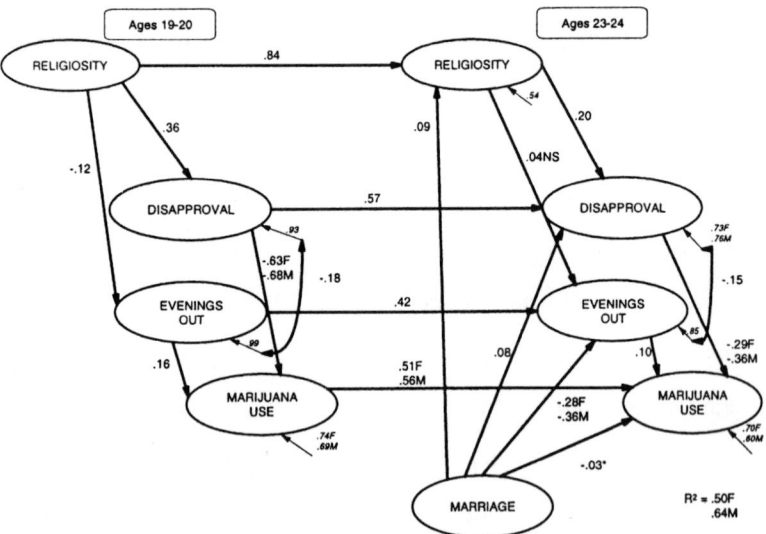

Note. Where two values are indicated for a parameter, gender differences exist: F = Females and M = Males.
All parameters are significant at p < .01 unless noted (p<.05*, NS = not significant). Error terms are in italics.

FIG. 8.2.   Structural model of the relations among religiosity, evenings out, disapproval of marijuana use, and annual marijuana use at ages 19–20 and 23–24 among young adults who became married or remained unmarried (females, $N = 2,250$; males, $N = 1,839$).

cated that males' reports of marijuana use were significantly more stable than females' reports from ages 19–20 to ages 23–24.

Figure 8.2 indicates strong associations among factors at ages 19–20— higher religiosity corresponded with higher disapproval and fewer evenings out, and higher disapproval and fewer evenings out corresponded with lower marijuana use. The path between disapproval and marijuana use at ages 19–20 was slightly stronger for males (–.68) than for females (–.63). This was also true at ages 23–24; the path between disapproval and marijuana use was –.36 for males and –.29 for females. In addition, at the second time point (ages 23–24), the indirect links remained significant (except for the religiosity–evenings out connection) and helped to mediate the effects of changes in marital status on marijuana use. Those who became married were more likely to increase their religiosity, increase their disapproval, and, most importantly, decrease their evenings out. The latter effect was stronger for men (–.36) than for women (–.28). With these mediating factors taken into account, there were significant indirect effects (–.062 for the total sample, $p < .01$) and fewer direct effects of marriage (see Table 8.2); respondents who became married were only marginally more likely to decrease their marijuana use (–.03, $p < .05$).

Annual Cocaine Use

The baseline measurement model for cocaine use, compared to marijuana use, provided a much better fit to the data (see Table 8.1). Likewise, the structural model fit the data well and, like marijuana use, illustrated how the mediating factors help to explain the marriage effect on change in cocaine use (see Fig. 8.3). Cocaine use was less stable than other reports of substance use, although the stability of disapproval of cocaine use was similar to disapproval reports of other substances.

The interrelations among the factors at ages 19–20 and the factors at ages 23–24 were similar to the patterns reported for marijuana use. For cocaine use, however, the links between evenings out and cocaine use were weaker than those between evenings out and marijuana use. In addition, the effect of marriage mediated through disapproval was stronger for cocaine use than for marijuana use. This may be because cocaine use was somewhat less stable. These mediated effects through evenings out and disapproval (and to a lesser extent, religiosity) were significant (–.074 for the combined sample, $p < .01$; see Table 8.2) and were strong enough to reduce the marriage effect to .00. That is, disapproval and evenings out completely mediate the marriage effect on cocaine use. Multigroup analyses revealed no important gender differences other than the one revealed also in the marijuana model (Fig. 8.2): males were somewhat more likely to reduce

Table 8.2
Decomposition of Marriage Effects on Marijuana Use, Cocaine Use,
Occasional Heavy Drinking, Alcohol Use, and Cigarette Use
for Males, Females, and the Total Sample

Substance	Total Effects[a]	Direct Effects	Indirect Effects
Marijuana Use (Annual)			
Males	-.080	-.026*	-.054**
Females	-.093	-.039*	-.053**
Total Sample	-.093	-.031*	-.062**
Cocaine Use (Annual)			
Males	-.052	.000	-.052**
Females	-.071	.000	-.071**
Total Sample	-.072	.002	-.074**
Heavy Drinking (2-week)			
Males	-.165	-.028	-.138**
Females	-.205	-.041	-.164**
Total Sample	-.193	-.033	-.160**
Alcohol Use (30-day)			
Males	-.129	-.003	-.126**
Females	-.270	-.156**	-.114**
Total Sample	-.219	-.094**	-.125**
Cigarette Use (30-day)			
Males	-.047	-.031**	-.016
Females	-.057	-.040**	-.018
Total Sample	-.054	-.034**	-.019**

[a]Significance tests are reported for indirect and direct effects only.
*p > .05 **p<.01

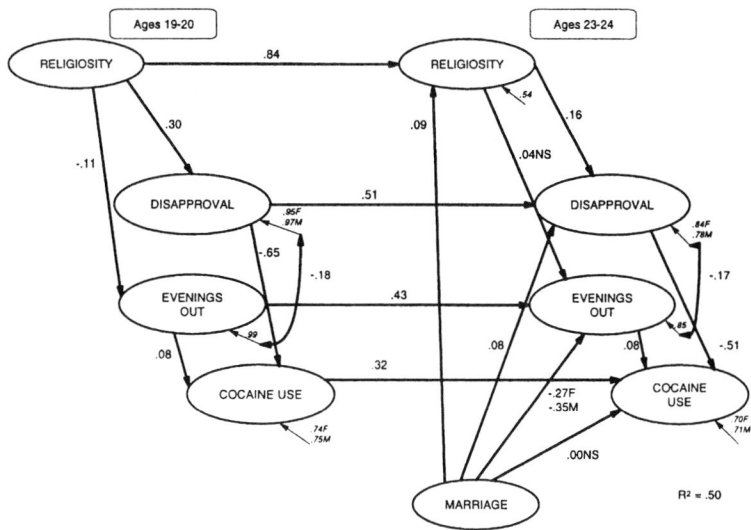

FIG. 8.3. Structural model of the relations among religiosity, evenings out, disapproval of co-caine use, and annual cocaine use at ages 19–20 and 23–24 among young adults who became married or remained unmarried (females, N = 2,238; males, N = 1,851).

their evenings out after marriage than females (–.35 for males, –.27 for females).

Heavy Drinking

The measurement model for respondents' reports of occasional heavy drinking during the previous 2 weeks provided the best fit to the data based on the indicators of goodness of fit from Table 8.1. The structural model also fit the data well, and the heavy drinking model showed the importance of the mediating factors in explaining the marriage effect (see Fig. 8.4). Heavy drinking was much less stable than were other reports of substance use, particularly for females (remember that it is based on reports over the previous 2 weeks rather than annual or 30-day use). The stability of reports of heavy drinking over the 4-year time period was .37 for males and only .10 for females.

Both at ages 19–20 and at ages 23–24, the links between evenings out and heavy drinking were stronger than between evenings out and marijuana or cocaine use. At ages 19–20, the association between disapproval of heavy drinking and reports of heavy drinking were stronger for males (–.76) than for females (–.61). The total effects of marriage on changes in substance use were higher for heavy drinking (–.193 for the combined sample)

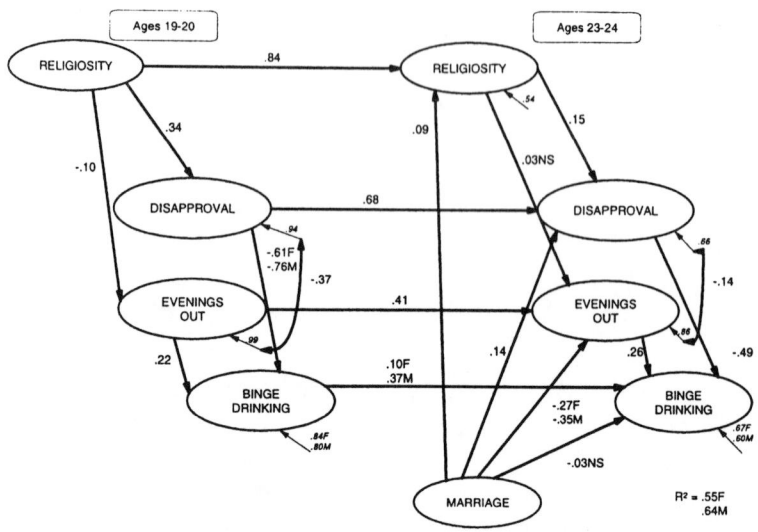

FIG. 8.4. Structural model of the relations among religiosity, evenings out, disapproval of occasional heavy drinking, and occasional heavy drinking at ages 19–20 and 23–24 among young adults who became married or remained unmarried (females, N = 2,223; males, N = 1,829).

than for marijuana use (–.093), cocaine use (–.072), or cigarette use (–.054), although the only significant effects occurred indirectly through the mediating variables (see Table 8.2). Disapproval and evenings out (and to a lesser extent, religiosity) mediated the effects of marriage on changes in heavy drinking, reducing the direct marriage effect so that it was nonsignificant (see Table 8.2). The significant indirect effects (–.160 for the combined sample, p < .01) indicated that respondents who married reduced their evenings spent out and increased their disapproval of heavy drinking, resulting in their decreased frequency of heavy drinking.

Monthly Alcohol Use

The results for 30-day alcohol use were very similar to those for occasional heavy drinking. The measurement model did not fit as well for 30-day alcohol use as for heavy drinking (see Table 8.1); therefore, the fit indices for the structural model were not as high as other models'. As with marijuana use, the measurement models could have been improved by adding correlations among within-time indicators of disapproval, which were excluded to keep

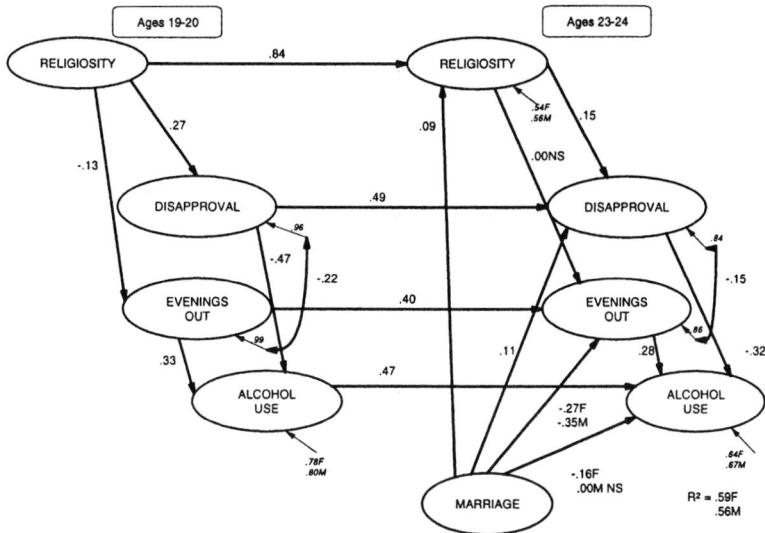

Note. Where two values are indicated for a parameter, gender differences exist: F = Females and M = Males. All parameters are significant at p < .01 unless noted (NS = not significant). Error terms are in italics.

FIG. 8.5. Structural model of the relations among religiosity, evenings out, disapproval of alcohol use, and 30-day alcohol use at ages 19–20 and 23–24 among young adults who became married or remained unmarried (females, $N = 2,214$; males, $N = 1,819$).

the models consistent and parsimonious. Notably, the stability of 30-day alcohol use was much higher than that of heavy drinking over the 4-year interval (see Fig. 8.5).

The evenings out measure was linked even more strongly with 30-day alcohol use than with heavy drinking. According to Table 8.2, respondents' disapproval and evenings out significantly mediated the effects of marriage on changes in 30-day alcohol use, reducing the direct marriage effect to −.003 (nonsignificant) for males and −.156 ($p < .01$) for females. The total effects of marriage on 30-day alcohol use were much stronger for females (−.270) than for males (−.129). For females, the indirect effects, though significant, were smaller than the direct effects of marriage on 30-day alcohol use (indirect effects = −.114); in contrast, for males, the total effects (−.129) consisted entirely of indirect effects (−.126).

Monthly Cigarette Use

The baseline measurement model for 30-day cigarette use was a much better fit to the data than were the structural models (see Table 8.1), which offer fewer explanatory mechanisms than for previous substances. This may be related to the fact that the stability of respondents' reports of use and disapproval of use were higher for cigarettes than for other substances (see Fig. 8.6). There was less change in cigarette use over time and thus less to explain. Males reported slightly greater stability in cigarette use over the 4-year period compared to females (.71 for males, .67 for females), as indicated by the multigroup analyses.

In contrast with the alcohol use models, at both time points the links between evenings out and cigarette use were lower, and at ages 23–24 the relation was not significant. As in the other models, the marriage link to changes in evenings out was significant (and slightly stronger for males); however, with the cigarette models there was no connection with changes in evenings out and changes in cigarette use. Because the connection between marriage and changes in disapproval also was not significant, both of the indirect effects of marriage on cigarette use (through increased disapproval and decreased evenings out) were less tenable for cigarette use models compared to alcohol use or illicit drug models. This was confirmed by decomposition of the total marriage effects (see Table 8.2), which indicated that the indirect effects were not significant for males and females tested separately ($p < .01$ when the entire sample was tested). For both males and

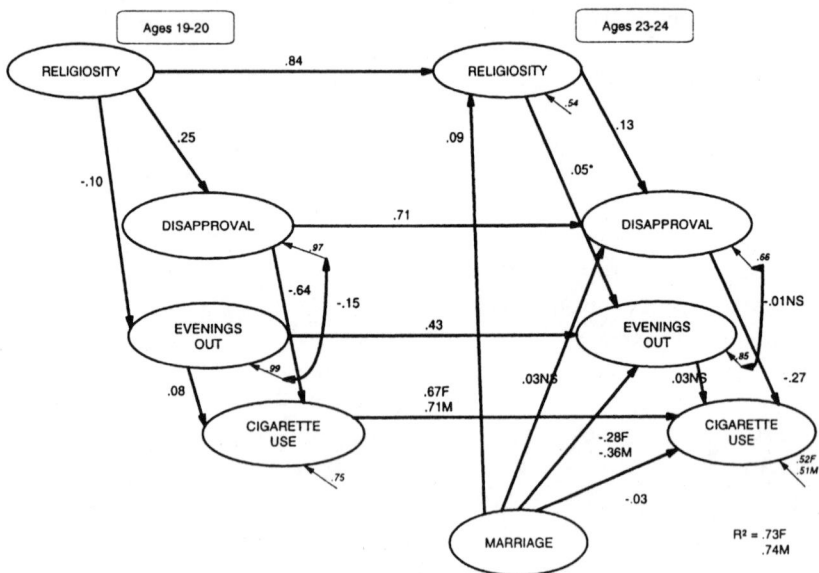

Note. Where two values are indicated for a parameter, gender differences exist: F = Females and M = Males. All parameters are significant at p < .01 unless noted (*p<.05, NS = not significant). Error terms are in italics.

FIG. 8.6. Structural model of the relations among religiosity, evenings out, disapproval of cigarette use, and 30–day cigarette use at ages 19–20 and 23–24 among young adults who became married or remained unmarried (females, $N = 2,222$; males, $N = 1,817$).

females, the direct marriage effects were significant and greater than the indirect effects.

Results From Perceived Risk Models

As noted in chapter 6, in many years of data collection the measures of perceived risk and disapproval appeared only on different questionnaire forms. We thus have a second independent subsample that could be used for replication purposes, in which the only difference in the models was the use of perceived risk rather than disapproval. Results from the structural equation modeling analyses using only the combined (male plus female) sample are summarized in Table 8.3. Figure 8.1 can be used as a guide.

Table 8.3 shows very similar results in parameter estimates for the various models. The differences that exist in parameters not associated with risk or disapproval were likely due to sampling error. The results at ages 19–20 suggested stronger associations between religiosity and disapproval rather than risk, and stronger links between disapproval and substance use rather than perceived risk and use. This was true at ages 23–24 as well. Accordingly, the marriage effects on substance use were slightly higher in the perceived risk models because the mediated effects were less strong via risk than via disapproval.

SUMMARY

In this chapter we attempted to "put some of the pieces together" by looking specifically at how three variables—religiosity, frequency of evenings out, and disapproval of substance use—play a role in mediating the marriage effects on changes in substance use. These effects were examined in a series of structural equation models, considering each type of substance use separately; the models were restricted to respondents who were single at the first follow-up (ages 19–20) and contrasted those who were and were not married by the third follow-up (ages 23–24).

The total marriage effects were strongest for changes in heavy drinking and monthly alcohol use. These effects, as Table 8.2 indicates, were explained to a large extent indirectly through mediating factors, such as increased disapproval of alcohol use and decreased frequency of evenings out. The monthly alcohol use model indicates that for women, however, these changes in evenings out and attitudes toward alcohol use do not fully explain the marriage effects on alcohol use. This suggests that other factors such as pregnancy may also be important.

Change in marital status had smaller effects on marijuana use and cocaine use compared to those on alcohol use and heavy drinking. For mari-

Table 8.3

Summary of Parameter Estimates for Final Structural Models for the Total Sample Using Either Risk or Disapproval Measures

Model	BBNNFI	RMSEA	1→2	1→3	2→4	3→4	1→6	5→6	2→7	5→7	6→7	3→8	5→8	6→8	4→9	5→9	7→9	8→9
Marijuana Use (Annual)																		
Disapproval	0.940	0.069	0.36	-0.12	-0.65	0.16	0.84	0.09	0.57	0.08	0.20	0.42	-0.32	0.04	0.54	-0.03	-0.31	0.10
Risk	0.952	0.057	0.28	-0.17	-0.52	0.21	0.83	0.07	0.57	0.10	0.18	0.51	-0.35	0.07	0.64	-0.03	-0.22	0.09
Cocaine Use (Annual)																		
Disapproval	0.985	0.029	0.30	-0.11	-0.65	0.08	0.84	0.09	0.51	0.08	0.16	0.43	-0.32	0.04	0.32	0.00	-0.51	0.08
Risk	0.981	0.031	0.22	-0.15	-0.62	0.09	0.83	0.07	0.55	0.06	0.14	0.51	-0.35	0.06	0.40	-0.03	-0.39	0.12
Binge Drinking (2-Week)																		
Disapproval	0.970	0.043	0.34	-0.10	-0.68	0.22	0.84	0.09	0.68	0.14	0.15	0.41	-0.32	0.03	0.26	-0.03	-0.49	0.26
Risk	0.972	0.041	0.28	-0.16	-0.56	0.34	0.83	0.07	0.59	0.08	0.13	0.49	-0.34	0.05	0.43	-0.06	-0.34	0.31
Alcohol Use (30-Day)																		
Disapproval	0.936	0.056	0.27	-0.13	-0.47	0.33	0.84	0.09	0.49	0.11	0.15	0.40	-0.31	0.00	0.47	-0.09	-0.32	0.28
Risk	0.934	0.056	0.17	-0.19	-0.32	0.43	0.83	0.07	0.45	0.07	0.14	0.48	-0.34	0.04	0.53	-0.10	-0.20	0.32
Cigarette Use (30-Day)																		
Disapproval	0.955	0.055	0.25	-0.10	-0.64	0.08	0.84	0.09	0.71	0.03	0.13	0.43	-0.33	0.05	0.68	-0.03	-0.27	0.03
Risk	0.962	0.047	0.12	-0.16	-0.36	0.17	0.83	0.07	0.50	-0.02	0.07	0.51	-0.35	0.08	0.78	-0.04	-0.17	0.02

juana use and cocaine use, much of this influence could be explained by mediation through evenings out and through disapproval. After accounting for indirect marriage effects, no direct effects remained on changes in cocaine use, and only a small direct marriage effect remained on change in annual marijuana use.

Change in marital status had a very small total effect on cigarette use, and little or none of the effect seemed to be mediated through evenings out and disapproval.

We largely replicated the mediated pathways by examining structural equation models that included perceived risk instead of disapproval. Across all of the substances, changes in disapproval were more closely tied to changes in substance use than were changes in perceived risk. Changes in disapproval were, therefore, somewhat better mediators of the marriage effects. This replication used independent samples (because the perceived risk measures involved a different questionnaire form, and thus different subsamples, than were used for the disapproval measures), thereby strengthening our findings and conclusions.

9

Summary, Conclusions, and Implications

Chapter 1 provided a conceptual overview showing the variables and linkages to be examined in this book (see Fig. 1.1), and chapters 4–7 examined many of the specific linkages illustrated in that figure. Then chapter 8 fitted together many of the pieces in simplified structural equation models (illustrated in Fig. 8.1). Now, building on the specific coefficients and other findings in previous chapters, and sometimes moving a bit beyond those findings, we summarize what we think we have learned.

We approach this summary and integration with the same sort of caution expressed earlier in the book. Models are always incomplete; they are not fully or accurately specified. In spite of that, we find them useful. We follow Carson's dictum (see p. 27), but only with caution. We "buy the premise" to some extent, and thus we "buy the sketch"—but only to some extent.

In Fig. 9.1 we attempt a summary and interpretation of key findings. All classes of variables first introduced in chapter 1 (Fig. 1.1) are included again here, but now we are willing to reach many more detailed conclusions about *dominant* directions and patterns of causation. Fig. 9.1 is largely an extrapolation from the structural equation models in chapter 8 (see Fig. 8.1 and Figs. 8.2–8.6), and all of the causal assumptions in those models reappear in Fig. 9.1. The major difference is that Fig. 9.1 is expanded to include the full range of variables, albeit in a somewhat general and simplified fashion.

Before we review our major findings and conclusions, we need to address briefly several important aspects of Fig. 9.1: (a) the meanings of "earlier time" and "later time" as shown at the bottom of the figure, (b) the distinctions and interrelationships among the drug-using behaviors studied herein, (c) the interrelationships among the several new freedoms and new responsibilities in young adulthood, and (d) the causal ordering linking religious behaviors to evenings out (and related factors) and to drug attitudes.

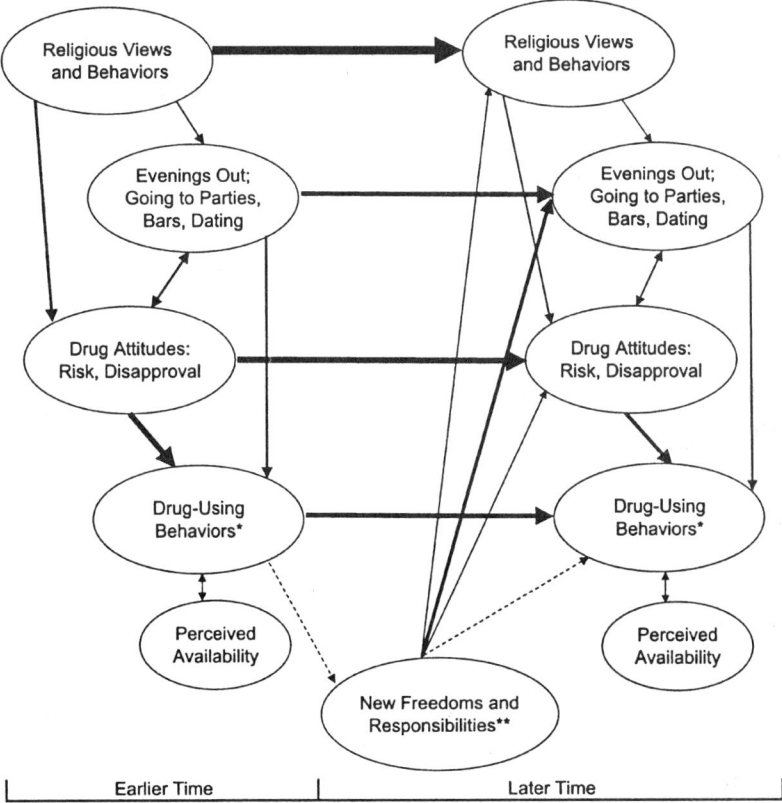

*Cigarette use, alcohol use, episodic heavy drinking, marijuana use, cocaine use
**Student status, work status, marital status and living arrangements, pregnancy, parenthood

FIG. 9.1.   Summary and interpretation of key findings. Arrows denote conclusions about dominant direction of causation. Strength of relationship is indicated by the thickness of each arrow (extrapolated from findings in chap. 8).

"Earlier Time," "Later Time," and Stability

There is no single definition for "earlier time" and "later time" as shown in Fig. 9.1. Rather, our purpose is to denote 2 points that are sufficiently separated in time so that some changes in roles and responsibilities can occur between the earlier time and the later time. Many of the analyses in this book, like most of the analyses in our earlier book, treated the base-year data collected at the end of the senior year of high school as the earlier time or "before" measure and treated any of the seven follow-up measures as the later time or "after" measure. The time span for these analyses ranged from 1 to 14 years, although certain post-high-school experiences (e.g., living in a dormitory) usually involved an earlier point after high school, whereas other experiences (e.g., married parenthood) generally involved a later period. The structural equation modeling in chapter 8 also focused on just two points in time, but for those analyses the points were the first and third follow-ups, separated by a period of 4 years. Some other analyses focused on multiple points in time.

One set of notions illustrated in Fig. 9.1 is that drug-using behaviors show a good deal of stability across time, religious views and behaviors are even more stable, and other factors also show some degree of stability. Matters of stability and variations in degree of stability are central to our analyses and conclusions. It is thus worth keeping in mind that the longer the time period between the earlier time and the later time, the more opportunities there are for change and the lower will be the overall stability (defined as the estimated "true" or "error-free" correlation between the earlier and the later measure).

Differences, Similarities, and Interrelationships Among Drug-Using Behaviors

There are a number of important differences among the substance-using behaviors studied in this book:

1. There have been different historical trends: gradual declines in marijuana use during the 1980s followed by some increases in the 1990s, sharp declines in cocaine use after 1986, and lesser changes in alcohol use and cigarette use.

2. There are different patterns of age-related change, although use of all substances eventually declines by the time young adults reach their late twenties and early thirties.

3. There are dramatic distinctions among substances in terms of proportions of users and the amount of their use: Most young adults use alcohol at least occa-

sionally, fewer use cigarettes but most who do tend to engage in the behavior multiple times each day, and the minorities who currently use illicit drugs generally do so infrequently.

4. The several forms of substance use involve different degrees of stability across time, with cigarette use the most stable (reflecting the high rates of dependency among users).

Given all of these differences, this book has followed our usual practice of treating the different drugs separately rather than trying to analyze "drug use in general."

There are also important overlaps among the several types of substance use. Smokers are more likely also to be alcohol users and to be occasional heavy drinkers, and individuals who use cigarettes and alcohol (substances legally available to adults) also are more likely than average to use illicit drugs. Moreover, alcohol use, illicit drug use, and, to a lesser extent, cigarette use are correlated in similar ways with indicators of religiosity, evenings out, and other mediating variables. All of these intercorrelations (documented in Table A.2) tend to be a bit stronger among high school seniors than among those in their early twenties (first three follow-ups), and all are weakest among those in their later twenties and early thirties (fourth through seventh follow-ups). The correlations grow weaker in later years because by then many individuals cease or reduce their substance-using behaviors; the evidence presented here points to certain common causes—particularly when it comes to reductions in occasional heavy drinking, in marijuana use, and in cocaine use. Some of the important common causes of declines in substance use are the new responsibilities of young adulthood, as analyzed in our earlier book. Another set of common causes are the mediating variables examined in this book. Before turning to the mediating variables, however, let us consider briefly how the new freedoms and new responsibilities of young adulthood are interconnected.

Interrelationships Among New Freedoms and New Responsibilities

In this book we examined a number of post-high-school experiences including student status, work status, marital status, other living arrangements, pregnancy, and parenthood. Our multivariate analyses examined these factors simultaneously (with background factors also included); additional multivariate analyses (reported in Bachman et al., 2001) also involved separate examinations of (a) the student and work status variables (along with background factors) and (b) marital status and other living arrangements, pregnancy, and parenthood (again, along with background factors). Our earlier work predicting to drug use and also our present work predicting to mediating variables showed that the student status and work status measures overlap with the other predictors in their effects and in general provide little or no unique prediction. However, those findings leave considerable room for interpretation.

Let us consider as an example our finding, reported in the earlier book, that college students showed above-average increases in instances of heavy drinking. When we asked what it was about the college experience that caused those increases in heavy drinking, we traced the answer to living arrangements and marital status. Specifically, full-time students are much less likely than their age-mates to be married but more likely to have left their parents' homes and to be living in dormitories or other housing involving roommates—all factors that are linked with increased instances of heavy drinking. We did not conclude, however, that student status is irrelevant. Instead, we interpreted our findings as follows: "...student status does indeed contribute to increased alcohol use, but only indirectly via the marital status and other living arrangements that generally go along with being a college student" (Bachman et al., 1997, p. 169). In other words, we view student status as an important factor influencing marital status and living arrangements. True enough, preferences about marriage and living arrangements can also influence choices about whether to become a full-time student; however, we believe that for most individuals, the plans and decisions about post-high-school education come first and are dominant.

We think that this causal interpretation of the indirect impacts of student status on instances of heavy drinking is equally applicable to some of our current findings, such as the students' above-average frequencies of evenings out in general and going to bars in particular. Choosing to be a student leads many individuals to defer marriage, to leave parental homes, and to live in dormitories or in other settings involving roommates. People in such living arrangements are more likely than average to spend evenings out, more likely to frequent bars, and more likely to be immersed in a culture of frequent heavy drinking (Schulenberg & Maggs, in press).

Some other interrelationships can be noted more briefly. For example, marriage can be viewed as contributing importantly to pregnancy and parenthood. Even though marriage is neither a necessary nor a sufficient condition for becoming a parent, our findings indicate that most young adults still take on these two sets of responsibilities in the order that society encourages—marriage first, then parenthood.

Causal Ordering Among Mediating Variables

In chapter 8 we presented a rationale for the causal ordering used in our structural equation modeling. That same causal ordering appears in Fig. 9.1

based on the same rationale but now also supported by the results of the modeling exercise. One general point to be made is that we do not view the interrelationships among the mediating variables as reflecting long-delayed impacts, and thus there are no "cross-lagged" causal connections shown in Fig. 9.1. To the contrary, we think that the causal impacts of one mediating variable on another tend to occur fairly promptly. Thus, for example, the impacts of high religiosity on drug-related attitudes (e.g., greater-than-average disapproval of smoking and heavy drinking) are likely to be fairly immediate; there is little reason to suppose they would be delayed for any considerable period of time.

Drug Attitudes as Strong Proximal Causes of Drug Use. The greater the risks young adults associate with any form of drug use, the more they disapprove of such use and the less likely they are to engage in such use. Perceived risks are strongly correlated with disapproval, especially for heavy drinking and for marijuana use. Heavy drinking and marijuana use are both strongly (negatively) correlated with perceived risks and just a little more strongly correlated (negatively) with disapproval; for the less widely used drug cocaine, the patterns of correlations are weaker but otherwise similar.

These findings support our view that perceived risks contribute very strongly to disapproval of various forms of substance use and that disapproval in turn plays a crucial—and very proximal—role in preventing substance use. Nothing else in our analyses shows so strong and direct a relationship with actual substance use as does disapproval.

Risk is not the only factor influencing disapproval; religiosity, above and beyond its impact on perceived risks, seems to contribute also to disapproval. Indeed, religiosity consistently correlates slightly more strongly with disapproval than with perceived risks.

The findings are just a bit different with respect to cigarette use; perceived risks of pack-a-day smoking show rather low variance and relatively weak correlations (compared with correlations involving disapproval). This is because nearly all young adults see at least moderate risk in pack-a-day smoking, and most young adults perceive great risk in such behavior. If there were wider variation in perceived risks of smoking (i.e., if more saw it as involving slight risk or no risk), then no doubt these correlations would be stronger—and the smoking problem among young adults would be even more serious than it already is.

Social–Recreational Behaviors as Proximal Causes of Drug Use. Young adults who frequently go out in the evening for fun and recreation are more likely than average to drink and occasionally drink heavily, and they are somewhat more likely to use illicit drugs (although the latter relationship grows weaker as they become older). Among high school seniors, the frequency of evenings out is correlated also with cigarette use, but after high school there is little correlation—presumably most graduates who smoke at all are habituated, and their cigarette consumption is unaffected by whether or not they go out in the evenings.

Figure 9.1 displays evenings out and other social–recreational behaviors as only modestly correlated with drug-related attitudes, and the correlations grow weaker from senior year through the early twenties and still weaker in the later twenties and early thirties. The correlations are negative; those who spend more evenings out for fun and recreation are somewhat less likely to see drug-using behaviors as risky and to disapprove of such behaviors. To a considerable extent, however, it appears that the impacts of social–recreational behaviors on substance use are nonoverlapping with the impacts of drug-related attitudes.

In sum, we conclude that social–recreational behaviors have moderate impacts, tending to encourage and facilitate substance use, and that these effects are largely independent of the effects of drug-related attitudes.

Religiosity as a Prior Cause.   For reasons discussed in chapter 8, we view religiosity as among the causes of drug-related attitudes and of social–recreational behaviors. Young adults who consider religion very important in their lives and who frequently attend religious services are a little less likely than average to spend evenings out for fun and recreation; they are also a lot more likely than average to perceive substance use as risky and to disapprove of such behaviors.

The fact that religiosity is positively correlated with disapproval, as well as negatively correlated with actual substance use, is hardly surprising. As discussed in chapter 2, many religious traditions specifically proscribe most or all of the substance-using behaviors studied here, and broader religious teachings call for respecting one's body and avoiding behaviors that put self and others at risk. So the negative correlation between religiosity and substance use is entirely understandable. What we can add are some conclusions about the causal pathways that are involved.

The findings presented here suggest that the negative impacts of religiosity on substance use are almost entirely indirect, via two quite unequal pathways. First, and most important, religiosity contributes positively to perceived risks and disapproval, which in turn contribute negatively to actual use. Second, it also appears that religiosity slightly inhibits frequent evenings out and party-going, which are positively linked to actual substance use.

Our findings also suggest that these indirect impacts of religiosity on substance use tend to occur relatively early in the lives of young people. The linkages are in place by the end of high school, and they remain strong primarily due to the very high stability of religiosity and the fairly high stability of the other factors.

IMPACTS OF THE NEW FREEDOMS
AND NEW RESPONSIBILITIES IN YOUNG ADULTHOOD

The analyses in this book were guided by the fundamental assumption that post-high-school role statuses and the corresponding new freedoms and responsibilities have impacts on levels of post-high-school drug use and that many of those impacts are indirect via mediating variables such as religiosity, social–recreational activities, and attitudes about drugs. But we are well aware of the difficulties in studying causal relationships in natural settings. Even with panel data spanning many years, correlational studies cannot prove causation. So when we use the terms *impacts* or *effects,* we are stating what we consider to be the most *plausible* interpretation, not asserting that our data *prove* that causal interpretation.

In the sections that follow we review the post-high-school experiences treated in detail in chapters 4–7, this time summarizing what we consider to be their impacts on the mediating variables examined in this volume as well as on the various types of substance use. For each post-high-school experience, we spell out to what extent we think the impacts on substance use operate via one or more of the mediating variables.

Student Status

Our earlier research (Bachman et al., 1997) showed that when high school graduates become college students, there is relatively little change in their cigarette use; during high school the college-bound are far less likely than average to be regular smokers, and that remains the case after high school graduation. College students' alcohol use, on the other hand, and especially their instances of heavy drinking show greater than average increases. The same is true to some extent for marijuana use, although not for cocaine use.

What accounts for college students' increases in heavy drinking and marijuana use? As noted earlier in this chapter, we trace the changes to the living arrangements associated with being a college student: moving out of parents' homes, living in dormitories or other sorts of student housing, and not being married.

How do the new mediating variables studied in this volume fit into the picture? Does going to college (and the accompanying changes in living arrangements) diminish religiosity? Does it lead to increased partying and to reduced inhibitions about heavy drinking and marijuana use? The answers are (respectively) "Not at all" and "Yes, to some extent."

Going to college does not seem to produce any general loss of religiosity. High school students bound for college are a bit more likely than average to attend religious services, and that does not change after they get to college. Thus, increases in heavy drinking and in marijuana use among college students cannot be attributed to any wholesale throwing off of religious constraints.

What does seem to happen is that college students on average, compared with their age-mates who do not go to college, are more likely to go to parties and to spend time informally with friends, and they are a bit more likely also to go to bars, taverns, and nightclubs. So the increases in students' drinking and probably also the smaller increases in their marijuana use appear to have a lot to do with the social life associated with their new living arrangements.

Going to college is associated also with modest shifts in views about heavy drinking and about marijuana use. Whereas during high school the college-bound are more likely than average to perceive risks and to disapprove, a year or two later (when they are full-time college students) their risk and disapproval ratings are just about average. In other words, consistent with the view among many college students that this is their time for youthful excess (e.g., Schulenberg & Maggs, in press), there is a net relative decline in perceived risks and disapproval, and we believe that these shifts in views contribute to the changes in actual use.

Employment Status: Military Service

Drug use was not strongly related to employment status in our earlier research, especially after other factors were included in multivariate analyses (Bachman et al., 1997). The one important exception to that general conclusion involved those in military service. Over the total time period studied in our earlier book, and consistent with findings of other researchers (Bray et al., 1991; Kroutil et al., 1994), we found military service to be associated with above-average use of the licit substances alcohol and cigarettes and below-average use of the illicit substances marijuana and cocaine. Recent trend analyses of Monitoring the Future data have shown important shifts over the period 1976–1996, indicating that the armed forces have made considerable progress in reducing substance use among new recruits (Bachman et al., 1999). Accordingly, our present findings must be viewed as somewhat historical, summarizing patterns across the last quarter century. That limitation notwithstanding, these historical findings may help to illuminate the role of some of the mediating variables.

Among our graduates from the high school classes of 1976–1997 combined, those in military service at follow-up showed greater than average increases in evenings out in general, and in going to bars in particular. They also showed greater than average declines in their disapproval of having five or more drinks in a row once or twice each weekend, and they were more likely than average to report having friends who got drunk at least once a week. So here again we see changes in social behaviors and situations, as well as changes in attitudes, as consistently linked with changes in substance use—in this case heavy drinking among those in military service.

Marital Status and Other Living Arrangements

Our earlier research showed that living arrangements during the post-high-school years, including marriage, are linked with changes in alcohol use, marijuana use, and cocaine use; however, living arrangements show relatively little impact on cigarette use (Bachman et al., 1997). In the earlier book we suggested that living arrangements provide many opportunities for individuals sharing a residence to be aware of and often influence each other's behaviors. Now we are able to document some of those influences.

Being Married. Marriage, among all the living arrangements studied here, has the most pervasive and long-lasting impacts on individuals' lives. Our earlier research showed that marriage is linked to significant reductions in alcohol use, marijuana use, cocaine use, and even cigarette use.

We found marriage to be associated with only very modest increases in religiosity. Therefore, marriage effects on substance use do not seem to occur primarily via changes in religiosity.

Some of the marriage effects on substance use occur via changes in attitudes about such use. Married respondents show larger increases in perceived risks and disapproval than respondents in any of the other living arrangements categories, and generally half or more of these marriage effects on drug attitudes remain after other factors are controlled in multivariate analyses. These attitudes are, of course, strongly linked with actual drug use. It therefore appears that one of the ways that marriage contributes to reductions in drug use is via increasingly negative attitudes about drugs.

Other important ways in which marriage leads to reduced drug use involve changes in social–recreational activities and probably also shifts in friendship patterns. Among all the living arrangements, marriage is associated with the largest declines in frequencies of (a) evenings out for fun and recreation, (b) attendance at parties and other social affairs, (c) getting together with friends informally, and (d) going to bars, taverns and nightclubs.

Indeed, one reason that many young adults engage in these activities is to find a partner—a motivation that presumably subsides considerably after marriage. Married respondents also are less likely than average to have friends who get drunk or use illicit drugs. Other factors such as parenthood contribute to some of these changes, as shown by the multivariate analyses, but substantial portions of the relationships seem directly attributable to marriage per se.

Cohabiting. Our earlier research showed that individuals who choose to cohabit are more likely to have been drug users during high school, consistent with other studies reporting selection into cohabitation based on early substance use and unconventional beliefs (DeMaris & MacDonald, 1993; Newcomb, 1987; Nock, 1995; Thornton et al., 1992; Yamaguchi & Kandel, 1985a). Our new findings provide further evidence that those who will become cohabitants are different from their classmates, on average, before they leave high school.

Young people with a history of low religious involvement and commitment are more likely than average to spend some of their early adulthood in unmarried cohabitation; moreover, those who cohabit show greater than average declines in religious attendance and importance. Cohabitants are also below average in their perceptions of risk and their disapproval associated with heavy drinking and illicit drug use, and they are above average in friends' substance use and abuse; all of these differences are in evidence during the high school years (before cohabitation occurs), and thus indicate primarily selection effects (i.e., preexisting differences).

Living With Parents. Young adults who continue to live with their parents during their first years after high school show substance use levels very close to average. We presumed, in our earlier report, that this lack of departure from the average is because these individuals "... are much less likely to experience dramatic changes in interpersonal contacts and social activities" (Bachman et al., 1997, p. 174). Our new findings confirm those earlier presumptions.

Importance of religion, frequency of religious attendance, views about drug use, and friends' use of substances are all just about average among individuals who continue to live with their parents after high school, and the same is true earlier when they are high school seniors. When we focus on young adults in the first 4 years after high school, we find that compared with others their age (many of whom are living in dormitories or similar arrangements), those continuing to live with their parents are just a bit less likely to go to taverns, bars, or nightclubs. In sum, the overall lack of dramatic changes in substance use among young adults living with their parents seems to reflect the lack of dramatic change in their interpersonal and social lives.

Living in a Dormitory. Our earlier research showed increased instances of occasional heavy drinking and some increases in marijuana use among students living in dormitories. We considered socialization effects of dormitory living to be the likely explanation. Our new findings show that dormitory life is not associated with any declines in religiosity; however, it is associated with frequent evenings out (especially going to parties or bars), with increased proportions of friends who get drunk at least once a week and proportions of friends who use marijuana, and with attitudes more accepting of marijuana use and weekend heavy drinking.

We noted in chapter 7 that individuals living in dormitories are increasingly exposed to substance-using friends and to perceptions that substance use is commonplace, and these factors in their social environments probably contribute to their own likelihood of heavy drinking and marijuana use. But we noted also that most individuals living in dorms are part of the friendship group experienced by other dorm residents, and thus they may themselves be or become "part of the problem." Because students (and their parents) make choices about where they live and because many colleges and universities offer students the option of "substance-free dorms," we can hardly view students who elect to live in substance-using dorms as hapless victims of their living arrangements. The causal process is a good deal more complicated than that.

Living Alone and in Other Living Arrangements. Our earlier research showed that among the relatively few young adults who live alone (and not in a dormitory), cigarette smoking and alcohol use increase slightly more than average. The "other living arrangements" is a residual category including those living in apartments or houses shared with several others, those living with a partner of the same sex, and military personnel living in barracks or in shared off-base housing. Young adults in "other living arrangements" show increases in alcohol use, occasional heavy drinking, and marijuana use roughly comparable to the changes associated with living in a dormitory, but they also show some increases in cigarette use and in cocaine use.

Our new findings again illustrate the importance of social factors. Individuals living alone and those in the "other living arrangements" category are more likely than average to frequent taverns, bars, and nightclubs; they also show lower than average perceived risks and disapproval associated with heavy drinking and illicit drug use. Those in the "other living arrangements" category also are more likely than average to attend parties and to have friends who get drunk at least once a week. Here, as for those living in dormitories, the causal processes are complex, because each individual helps to shape the social climate in which he or she lives.

Pregnancy and Parenthood

In this book, as in the previous one, we treated pregnancy and parenthood as two distinct dimensions, while recognizing that they obviously are very closely related. Most notably, any effects of pregnancy on drug use that remain permanent (e.g., a woman who quits smoking during pregnancy and then remains a nonsmoker) would show up in our analyses also as "parenthood effects."

Pregnancy. Our earlier research showed that pregnant women are more likely than average to decrease cigarette use and marijuana use and much more likely than average to reduce or stop their use of alcohol. These changes very likely occur as a direct consequence of health warnings about possible risks to fetuses. The changes do not, in any case, seem to reflect shifts in religiosity, overall changes in recreational lifestyle, or specific changes in friends' substance use (based on the multivariate analyses, which take into account that most pregnant women are married and some are already parents).

Our questionnaire items dealing with risk and disapproval of various forms of substance use do not mention pregnancy, nor do they ask respondents about risks or disapproval involving their own personal use. Nevertheless, pregnant women and also men with pregnant spouses show increases in perceived risk and disapproval ratings, and these "pregnancy effects" do not disappear when marriage and other factors are controlled statistically. So even in the absence of questionnaire items specific to pregnancy, our present findings provide some support for the view that increased concerns about health consequences underlie the reductions in substance use that occur among pregnant women and men with pregnant spouses.

Parenthood. Most parents in our study were married, but a significant proportion were not. In our earlier work we opted to analyze married and single motherhood and fatherhood separately "... because we considered the social environments of married and single parents to be different in potentially important ways, and also because most single fathers do not live with their children" (Bachman et al., 1997, p. 177). Our present analyses provide some specific evidence on how much the two kinds of parenthood differ from each other and how they differ from nonparenthood.

Although pregnancy does not show an impact on religiosity, married parenthood apparently does. Married parents are above average in religious attendance and importance, above and beyond any differences when they were in high school or any changes attributable to marriage. It thus appears that some married parents tend to heed religious teachings to raise their children "in the faith." Single parents, on the other hand, are below average in religiosity; however, this seems not to be a result of parenthood, because the same differences were evident when they were in high school (and before they became parents).

Parenthood has other important impacts on the social lives of young adults—often larger than the impacts of marriage. Compared with nonparents, married fathers and mothers spend fewer evenings out for fun and recreation, they less often go to parties or other social events, they less often get together with friends informally, they are less likely to go to bars, and they are much less likely to go out "with a date or spouse." The effects are somewhat similar for unmarried mothers, but much less so for unmarried fathers. All these findings are quite understandable if we take the view that child care is a major factor inhibiting these social activities; married parents generally share the burdens of child care, whereas single mothers are much more likely than single fathers to have primary custody. Married parents also show greater than average reductions in proportions of friends who use substances, although these changes are largely explainable in terms of marriage and other factors. Certainly these changes in social activities and social contacts help to explain the reduced alcohol use and illicit drug use of young parents, as found in our earlier research.

Further Findings on Marital Status

Engagement. Our earlier research showed that young adults who become engaged, whether cohabiting or not, tend to decrease alcohol use, occasional heavy drinking, and illicit drug use to a greater extent than those who are single and not engaged. These "engagement effects" are similar to the "marriage effects" on drug use, but generally not as large.

Our present analyses show further parallels between marriage and engagement. Specifically, young adults who are engaged show declines in evenings out, attendance at parties, going to bars, and friends who get drunk or use illicit substances; "engagement effects" along these dimensions are somewhat smaller than the corresponding "marriage effects." But when it comes to increased perceptions of risk and disapproval of heavy drinking and illicit drug use, engagement and marriage are roughly equal in their contributions.

So it appears that some of the effects of marriage are anticipatory (i.e., precede marriage), as is clearly evidenced by these findings on engaged individuals. Their social activities and contacts change, as do their views about drugs. Largely as a consequence, we believe, their actual drug-using behaviors also change.

Divorce. Further evidence on marriage effects is provided by the findings on divorce. Our earlier research showed quite clearly and consistently that transitions from married to divorced are marked by increased proportions using tobacco, alcohol, marijuana, and cocaine—exactly the reverse of the "marriage effects" on substance use. Moreover, transitions from divorced to remarried are marked by changes in the opposite direction—decreases in substance use. We earlier suggested that "Divorced singles may be likely to reenter the 'singles scene'—the world of bars and parties frequented by singles" (Bachman et al., 1997, p. 179).

Our new findings fully support our earlier proposition. The transition from married to divorced is associated with increases in evenings out, party-going, and going to bars; conversely, remarriage is associated with decreases in each of these behaviors (i.e., similar to the "marriage effect" described earlier). Divorce also is associated with slight increases in proportions of friends who get drunk at least once a week and proportions of friends who use illicit drugs. Not surprisingly, divorced individuals also tend to be lower than average in their disapproval ratings for pack-a-day smoking, weekend heavy drinking, and illicit drug use.

CONCLUSIONS AND IMPLICATIONS

What are we to conclude from all the findings presented in this book and summarized in this chapter? In this final section we revisit some of the issues treated in our earlier book, and extend some of our earlier observations. This book includes several years of additional data, but the primary contribution is that we now include a wide variety of variables that mediate the impacts of post-high-school roles and responsibilities on substance use. Our new findings generally confirm our earlier ones; more important, the new research helps to explain *why* young adults' new freedoms and responsibilities cause them to alter their use of substances.

Stability and Change

Longitudinal research using panel data, in which the same individuals are tracked over a number of years, provides opportunities to consider two complementary phenomena: stability and change. Our research on drug use and its correlates among young adults has provided considerable evidence of both.

The new freedoms and responsibilities of young adulthood represent major life changes with far-reaching implications. As we documented here, changes in marital status, in living arrangements, and in parental status have impacts on many other aspects of life ranging from religious views and behaviors to friendships and social activities. And all of these changes are connected with changes in attitudes about drugs and actual use of drugs.

But the other side of the coin is stability. Our research has provided much evidence that even when many aspects of life are changing, there are other aspects that, for many individuals, remain constant. Many young people leave home to go to college or take jobs in other places, and some of them acquire new friends and new ideas. Nevertheless, many of those who experience such changes also retain old friendships as well as earlier ideas and behavior patterns that involve religion, social activities, and drug use.

Our findings on stability suggest that the views and behaviors studied here tend not to shift around capriciously—at least not for most young people. The dimensions vary in their stability, as illustrated by the horizontal arrows in Fig. 9.1. Religious views and behaviors are especially stable among young adults; to be sure, they are affected to some extent by certain post-high-school experiences, but far more impressive is the degree to which they remain constant over the years. Attitudes and behaviors concerning drugs are not as stable as those concerning religion, but they too show a fairly high degree of consistency from year to year. Somewhat less stable are the social behaviors we examined; here is where the impacts of the new freedoms and new responsibilities of young adulthood are most apt to be evidenced.

In addition to stabilities across fairly long periods of time (shown by the horizontal arrows previously noted), Fig. 9.1 also illustrates a variety of processes contributing to change. First, the arrows showing relationships at earlier times indicate that factors usually well developed by the end of high school—religious views and behaviors, views about drugs, and, to a lesser extent, patterns of friendship and recreational behaviors—are important contributors to drug-using behaviors by late adolescence and continue to operate during young adulthood. Second, the figure also depicts that new experiences affect social behaviors, have some impacts on views about drugs, and even influence religiosity to a limited degree. Each of these factors in turn contributes to drug-using behaviors, helping to account for the fact that stability is less than perfect and that stability declines over longer periods of time (during which more of these other changes occur).

Stability and change: we saw a good deal of evidence of both, and we think we learned more about the interplay between the two. On average, the best predictor of a behavior at any given time is likely to be that same sort of behavior at a (slightly) earlier time. However, the longer the period of time, the greater the opportunities for the forces of change to operate. One of our conclusions in the earlier book can thus be repeated and expanded as follows: When we track individuals over longer intervals of time, we find that more and more of them move into the adult roles of marriage and parenthood; and we find that with each passing year the consistencies with earlier, youthful patterns of drug use and its correlates grow weaker.

CONCLUDING COMMENTS ON DECLINING SUBSTANCE USE IN YOUNG ADULTHOOD: IMPACTS OF SOCIAL ACTIVITIES, ROLES, AND BELIEFS

In our previous book we concluded that the new freedoms in the first years of young adulthood contribute to some increases in substance use and that the new responsibilities that typically come a little later in young adulthood contribute to declining substance use. We also pointed out that it was hard to draw policy implications from those conclusions. We would not discourage young adults from leaving home and going to college, in spite of increased risks of alcohol abuse; neither would we recommend early marriage, pregnancy, and parenthood as means for reducing substance use.

The findings in this book do not change these earlier conclusions; neither do they change our unwillingness to discourage new freedoms or hasten new responsibilities in young adulthood. But our current findings clarify some of the mediating processes through which the new freedoms and responsibilities of young adulthood lead to changes in substance use, and these findings may suggest some policy implications—often relevant to adolescence as well as young adulthood.

The present findings confirm earlier research indicating that religiosity—measured here as importance of religion and frequency of attendance at services—is an important protective factor when it comes to drug use. Religiosity contributes to higher levels of perceived risk and disapproval associated with substance use and thus to lower levels of actual use. Our findings also show that religious views and patterns of attendance, although marginally influenced by later experiences such as marriage and parenthood, are pretty well established by the end of high school and quite stable thereafter. So for those who view religious involvement as an important factor in the prevention of substance use, the message would seem to be: Start early.

The present findings also confirm earlier research showing that views about drugs—especially perceived risks and disapproval—are strongly linked with actual use. And in spite of all the problems in using correlations to sort out causal directions, we feel entirely confident in asserting that perceiving a substance as risky makes adolescents and young adults more likely to avoid use of that substance. Engagement, marriage, pregnancy, and parenthood all tend to heighten both disapproval and perceptions of risks of substance use; however, there are many other ways in which views about drugs can be influenced long before the new responsibilities of adulthood make their contribution. Given the fairly high stability of such views, as shown in this research, it seems clear that prevention efforts should target adolescents even more than young adults. We do not believe in scare tactics as a means of preventing drug use, but the large body of research linking perceptions of risk to lower drug use certainly suggests that known dangers of various kinds of drug use should be publicized widely, realistically, and also dramatically.

Frequent evenings out for fun and recreation, especially those involving parties or visits to bars, are among the behaviors that seem to be encouraged by the new freedoms of very young adulthood and then later discouraged by the new responsibilities that very often follow. Adult responsibilities to spouses and children appear to crowd out these kinds of recreation most likely to encourage substance use; thus, the implications for prevention may be to continue the quest to find constructive alternative ways for youth and younger adults to spend their leisure time. Activities that readily come to mind include tutoring younger children in school and in sports, serving as caregivers for those with disabilities, or working with other volunteers in shared community activities (e.g., Habitat for Humanity, Food Gatherers, etc.). If marriage and parenthood are constructive alternatives a bit later in adulthood—and our findings clearly suggest that they are—then perhaps among youth and younger adults, the most promising parallels would also involve close contacts with other people, especially contacts that include a genuine sense of responsibility.

Appendix

This appendix includes several kinds of supplementary material. First, it presents information on sampling and data-collection procedures used in the Monitoring the Future project. Second, it briefly describes the samples utilized in these analyses in terms of the respondents' patterns of post-high-school experiences (education, work, living arrangements, marriage, and parenthood) during the first 14 years after high school. Third, it provides a description of the multiple classification analysis (MCA) procedures and the reporting format, along with guidelines for interpreting the results.

The appendix also provides a number of supplementary tables, including: (a) distributions of respondents in the various post-high-school experiences by modal age (Tables A.1.1–A.1.5); (b) response scales and question wordings (Table A.1.6); (c) product–moment correlations among drug use variables and mediating variables for three age bands (Tables A.2.1–A.2.3); (d) numbers of cases in various categories (Table A.3); and (e) multivariate analysis (MCA) findings (Tables A.4.1–A.7.6).

SAMPLING AND DATA-COLLECTION PROCEDURES

A separate technical report spells out the design and procedures for the Monitoring the Future project and includes considerable detail on sampling methods, response rates, measurement content, and issues of validity in self-reports of drug use (Bachman, Johnston, & O'Malley, 1996). The annual monographs on trends in drug use and related factors (e.g., Johnston et (e.g., Johnston et al., 2000a) also provide considerable detail on methods. Our discussion here is limited to key features of the design, plus matters specific to the present analyses.

Sample Design and Methods

From its outset, the Monitoring the Future project was designed with two interrelated components: (a) annual nationwide surveys of high school seniors using group-administered questionnaires and (b) periodic follow-up questionnaires mailed to subsamples of each senior-class cohort. This cohort-sequential design (Labouvie, 1976; Schaie, 1965) permits a wide range of analyses, including the study of longitudinal changes reflecting the differential impacts of various post-high-school environments and role transitions.

Multistage Samples of High School Seniors. Samples of seniors are drawn by a multistage procedure: the first stage consists of geographic areas (the Survey Research Center's primary sampling areas located throughout the coterminous United States); the second stage is the selection of one or more schools in each primary sampling area (generating a total of 130 to 140 schools); and the third stage is the random selection of up to about 350 seniors per school (yielding nationally representative cross-sections totaling about 16,000 to 18,000 high school senior respondents each year).

Follow-Up Samples of Young Adults. For reasons of cost control and sampling efficiency, only a subset of each senior class sample is selected for follow-up. Two subsamples from each senior class are drawn, each numbering about 1,200; members of one group are invited to participate in a follow-up survey 1 year after graduation, and every 2 years after that; those in the other group are invited to participate 2 years after graduation, and every 2 years after that. The follow-up samples are drawn using stratified random procedures; they are self-weighting, with one important exception as noted in the following section.

Use of Sample Weights in These Analyses. Because the primary focus of the Monitoring the Future project is drug use, those who used illicit drugs as seniors are oversampled by a factor of 3 to 1. Our analyses assign a weight of 1/3 to each of these individuals (with all others weighted 1), thereby removing any bias that would have resulted from the oversampling. The numbers of cases reported herein are always the weighted Ns, which we consider to be a reasonably good indicator of the levels of accuracy provided by these samples.

Samples Included in These Analyses. Extensive follow-up data are available from all senior-class cohorts from 1976 onward. At the time the final sets of analyses were initiated, the 1998 follow-up data were the latest available. We chose to analyze up to seven follow-ups (if available) for each cohort. Accordingly, most of the present analyses include the senior classes of 1976 through 1997, with each class followed for up to 14 years but no later than 1998, as shown in Fig. 3.1.

In summary, these analyses made use of all of the follow-up data available at the time they were completed. As discussed in chapter 3, the decision to use all available panel data means that there is a 13- or 14-year follow-up span for the classes of 1976 through 1984, whereas for each successive class the available span is smaller.

Focus on Unmarried Seniors Living With Parents. A small portion of the cases for whom we had data were excluded from the present analyses in order to give all respondents much the same starting point in terms of primary role responsibilities. Specifically, we restricted these analyses to include only those who *as seniors* were unmarried, living with parents (or guardians), and not living with any children of their own; the fewer than 7% who did not meet those three criteria as seniors were excluded from the present analyses.

Representativeness of Samples. We have already noted that the samples used for these analyses were restricted to fall short of representing the full cohorts of young adults in the periods studied. First, the base-year data collections sampled high school seniors and thus omitted individuals who left high school before the end of the senior year. Second, we could not include a full 13- or 14-year span of follow-up data for later cohorts, simply because those data were not yet available. Third, we excluded from the present panel analyses those few who as seniors were already married, had children, were no longer living with parents or guardians, or any combination thereof.

In addition to the aforementioned systematic exclusions from the samples, representativeness is affected by nonparticipation at several points in the sampling process. First, about 35% of the schools initially invited to participate in the surveys each year declined to do so; however, in almost every such instance a similar school was recruited as a replacement. Second, about 15–20% of sampled seniors in participating schools did not complete questionnaires; this was largely due to absenteeism, and other analyses indicated that this produced only modest amounts of bias in estimates of drug use (Johnston et al., 2000a). Third, some individuals targeted for follow-up either could not be reached or did not choose to participate. At the first follow-up, an average of about 77% returned completed questionnaires. By

the seventh follow-up (13–14 years after high school), the total panel reten-
tion remained high, at about 63%. Nevertheless, this panel attrition generated a degree of bias. Fortunately, along most background dimensions the
bias was small, as documented in Bachman, O'Malley, et al. (1996), and we
suspect that any bias in *relationships* is even smaller. (For more extensive
treatments of Monitoring the Future participation rates, representativeness, and validity, see Bachman, Johnston, & O'Malley, 1996, and Johnston
et al., 2000a.)

In summary, there are limitations to our ability to generalize because (a)
several restrictions had to be imposed in defining target samples, (b) there
were some losses sustained in the senior-year surveys, and (c) there was
panel attrition. Nevertheless, the panel data cover a broad spectrum of the
high school senior population and a wide range of post-high-school behaviors. Moreover, the numbers of cases are sufficiently large that we are able to
analyze subgroups constituting small proportions of the total samples. Obviously, it is impossible for small subgroups to account for large portions of
the total variance in drug use; nevertheless, we report a number of instances
where the findings for such subgroups stand in sharp contrast to the rest of
the sample. Our analysis methods were designed to take advantage of the
sample size and to display subgroup differences clearly.

Survey Methods

Base-Year Surveys of High School Seniors. Each spring the surveys of seniors are administered during regularly scheduled class periods by
locally based Institute for Social Research representatives and their assis-
tants. Respondents are asked to provide their names and addresses on forms
that are then separated from the questionnaires (but linkable by code numbers accessible only to research staff). The self-completed questionnaires
are formatted for optical scanning.

Follow-Up Surveys of Young Adults. Follow-up questionnaires,
similar in most respects to the base-year questionnaires, are sent in the
spring by certified mail accompanied by a respondent payment check (initially $5, increased to $10 beginning in 1992). Additional reminder mailings
are sent to nonrespondents, and after several weeks attempts are made to
telephone all outstanding cases to encourage their participation.

PATTERNS OF POST-HIGH-SCHOOL EXPERIENCES

Dramatic role changes occur during the years after high school graduation.
In all cases, the role of high school student comes to an end and is replaced

by other roles such as college student, civilian employee, member of the armed forces, or various combinations of these and other roles. There also are changes in living arrangements for the majority of young adults; they leave their parents' homes to begin married life, to live in a dormitory or apartment while attending college, to live with friends, or simply to be on their own. Within the first few years of high school graduation, substantial numbers have earned college degrees, and substantial numbers also have taken on the responsibilities of parenthood. The timings of these changes vary across individuals; however, some general patterns are worth noting, especially because they have implications for interpreting some of the multivariate analyses documented later in this appendix.

Tables A.1.1–A.1.5 describe the respondents in our samples in terms of their patterns of role experiences during the first 14 years after high school. Table A.1.1 shows, for example, that more than half were full-time students at the time of the first follow-up (modal ages 19–20); the percentages of full-time students dropped somewhat by the time of the second follow-up (modal ages 21–22), dropped much more sharply by the third follow-up, and continued to decline thereafter. Corresponding closely to the decline in proportions of full-time students, the proportions in full-time civilian employment increased substantially to about 63% by the third follow-up (modal ages 23–24), as shown in Table A.1.2. Thereafter (i.e., during the later twenties), the proportions in full-time civilian employment continued to rise among men, whereas among women a more substantial rise occurred in the proportions describing themselves as full-time homemakers with no outside job.

Table A.1.3 shows, among other things, that more than half of the young adults in our sample were married within 10 years of graduation from high school, and by 14 years after high school (modal ages 31–32) two thirds were married, with marriage rates for men lagging behind those for women by almost 2 years. (Table A.1.4 shows the proportions at each follow-up point who reported that they were engaged to be married.) Table A.1.3 also shows that living with parents was the most typical arrangement for recent high school graduates (especially those who did not go to college); even 5 or 6 years after high school, about one in three men and one in four women (comprising nearly half of the men and women who were not married or cohabiting) continued to live with one or both parents.

As is shown in Table A.1.5, by the first or second year after high school, only a few of our panel respondents reported being parents—about half of them married and the other half unmarried. Then with each succeeding follow-up the proportion of parents rose. By ages 31–32, nearly two thirds of all women were parents, as were more than half of all men, and most of these parents were married.

TABLE A.1.1

Percentages of panel respondents who were in post-high-school education, by gender

	FU1	FU2	FU3	FU4	FU5	FU6	FU7	Total Observations
Modal ages:	19-20	21-22	23-24	25-26	27-28	29-30	31-32	19-32
Class years included:	76-97	76-95	76-93	76-91	76-89	76-87	76-85	76-98

Males
Student Status

	FU1	FU2	FU3	FU4	FU5	FU6	FU7	Total Observations
Number of cases (Wtd.):	13,090	11,391	9,751	8,085	6,761	5,492	4,406	58,977
Full-time student	57.3	44.8	20.8	11.4	6.8	4.7	2.4	
Part-time student	7.8	9.2	11.5	10.7	9.9	9.1	7.2	

Females
Student Status

	FU1	FU2	FU3	FU4	FU5	FU6	FU7	Total Observations
Number of cases (Wtd.):	16,150	13,955	11,911	9,973	8,356	6,836	5,422	72,603
Full-time student	59.2	44.3	16.9	8.4	5.5	3.9	3.1	
Part-time student	8.1	9.0	11.1	10.9	9.5	9.5	7.9	

TABLE A.1.2

Percentages of panel respondents in various employment statuses, by gender

	FU1	FU2	FU3	FU4	FU5	FU6	FU7	Total Observations
Modal ages:	19-20	21-22	23-24	25-26	27-28	29-30	31-32	19-32
Class years included:	76-97	76-95	76-93	76-91	76-89	76-87	76-85	76-98

Males
Employment Status:

	FU1	FU2	FU3	FU4	FU5	FU6	FU7	Total Observations
Number of cases (Wtd.):	13,296	11,530	9,865	8,177	6,841	5,550	4,456	59,716
Full-time civilian	31.4	43.9	65.0	76.6	82.1	84.5	86.4	
Full-time military	5.0	6.1	5.0	4.5	4.0	3.6	3.0	
Part-time job	28.0	23.1	13.6		5.3	3.8	2.9	
Full-time homemaker	0.4	0.3	0.2	0.2	0.3	0.3	0.4	
Not employed, not a student	4.3	4.4	5.3	4.2	3.8	3.6	3.7	

Females
Employment Status:

	FU1	FU2	FU3	FU4	FU5	FU6	FU7	Total Observations
Number of cases (Wtd.):	16,356	14,090	12,026	10,067	8,427	6,902	5,473	73,341
Full-time civilian	28.5	41.9	62.1	68.1	68.0	66.2	63.2	
Full-time military	0.7	0.8	0.8	0.6	0.5	0.5	0.3	
Part-time job	34.4	29.4	16.7	11.7	11.5	11.6	13.6	
Full-time homemaker	2.9	4.7	7.1	8.6	10.7	12.0	13.5	
Not employed, not a student	4.2	4.7	5.0	5.0	4.8	5.3	5.3	

Note: Employment status percentages for each follow-up add to less than 100 percent because full- and part-time students who were not in any of the above employment statuses are omitted.

TABLE A.1.3

Percentages of panel respondents in various living arrangements, by gender

	FU1	FU2	FU3	FU4	FU5	FU6	FU7	Total Observations
Modal ages:	19-20	21-22	23-24	25-26	27-28	29-30	31-32	19-32
Class years included:	76-97	76-95	76-93	76-91	76-89	76-87	76-85	76-98

Males
Current Living Arrangements:

	FU1	FU2	FU3	FU4	FU5	FU6	FU7	Total
Number of cases (Wtd.)	13,296	11,530	9,865	8,177	6,841	5,550	4,456	59,716
Married	3.5	11.9	24.2	38.3	49.9	59.2	64.5	
Partner of opposite sex	3.2	6.7	8.4	9.3	8.6	7.5	6.6	
Parents	51.2	37.5	31.1		13.2	8.5	6.6	
Dormitory	22.8	9.9	2.2	0.9	0.3	0.3	0.1	
Alone	2.7	5.8	10.8	13.2	13.7	13.8	13.7	
All other arrangements	16.7	28.3	23.3	18.5	14.4	10.8	8.4	

Females
Current Living

	FU1	FU2	FU3	FU4	FU5	FU6	FU7	Total
Number of cases (Wtd.)	16,356	14,090	12,026	10,067	8,427	6,902	5,473	73,341
Married	8.2	20.4	35.1	48.5	57.8	64.8	68.8	
Partner of opposite sex	6.1	9.0	10.9	10.3	9.0	7.2	6.6	
Parents	47.7	33.5	26.1	16.4	10.4	7.4	5.7	
Dormitory	24.8	9.8	1.5	0.4	0.3	0.1	0.0	
Alone	1.7	4.5	8.5	9.4	10.1	9.5	8.8	
All other arrangements	11.5	22.8	17.9	14.9	12.5	11.2	10.1	

TABLE A.1.4

Percentages of panel respondents married or engaged, by gender

	FU1	FU2	FU3	FU4	FU5	FU6	FU7	Total Observations
Modal ages:	19-20	21-22	23-24	25-26	27-28	29-30	31-32	19-32
Class years included:	76-97	76-95	76-93	76-91	76-89	76-87	76-85	76-98

Males
Married or Engaged

	FU1	FU2	FU3	FU4	FU5	FU6	FU7	Total
Number of cases (Wtd.):	13,296	11,530	9,865	8,177	6,841	5,550	4,456	59,716
Married	3.5	11.9	24.2	38.3	49.9	59.2	64.5	
Engaged	6.0	8.6	9.4	8.1	5.8	4.2	3.3	

Females
Married or Engaged

	FU1	FU2	FU3	FU4	FU5	FU6	FU7	Total
Number of cases (Wtd.):	16,356	14,090	12,026	10,067	8,427	6,902	5,473	73,341
Married	8.2	20.4	35.1	48.5	57.8	64.8	68.8	
Engaged	10.4	12.1	10.4	8.2	5.7	3.9	3.3	

TABLE A.1.5
Percentages of panel respondents who were married or unmarried parents, by gender

	FU1	FU2	FU3	FU4	FU5	FU6	FU7	Total Observations
Modal ages:	19-20	21-22	23-24	25-26	27-28	29-30	31-32	19-32
Class years included:	76-97	76-95	76-93	76-91	76-89	76-87	76-85	76-98

Males
Parental Status

	FU1	FU2	FU3	FU4	FU5	FU6	FU7	Total Observations
Number of cases (Wtd.):	13,296	11,530	9,865	8,177	6,841	5,550	4,456	59,716
Married parent	1.5	5.2	11.4	19.1	28.8	39.4	48.7	
Single parent	1.9	3.1	3.9	4.7	5.5	5.7	6.7	

Females
Parental Status

	FU1	FU2	FU3	FU4	FU5	FU6	FU7	Total Observations
Number of cases (Wtd.):	16,356	14,090	12,026	10,067	8,427	6,902	5,473	73,341
Married parent	2.5	9.0	16.9	26.2	35.6	46.0	54.5	
Single parent	2.8	5.4	6.8	7.6	8.4	9.2	9.7	

TABLE A.1.6
Response Scales and Question Wording

Core Drug Measures

Score	Cigarette Use (30 Days)	Alcohol, Marijuana, Cocaine Use (30 Days or 12 Months)	5 Drinks in a Row (2 Weeks)
1	Not at all	None	None
2	Less than 1 cigarette per day	1-2 occasions	Once
3	1-5 cigarettes per day	3-5 occasions	Twice
4	About 1/2 pack per day	6-9 occasions	3-5 times
5	About 1 pack per day	10-19 occasions	6-9 times
6	About 1 1/2 packs per day	20-39 occasions	10 or more times
7	2 packs or more per day	40 or more occasions	

Values, Attitudes, and Lifestyle Behaviors: The Mediating Variables

Chapter 4

The next three questions are about religion. How important is religion in your life?
1="Not important"
2="A little important"
3="Pretty important"
4="Very important"

The next three questions are about religion. How often do you attend religious services?
1="Never"
2="Rarely"
3="Once or twice a month"
4="About once a week or more"

Table continues

228

Chapter 5

During a typical week, on how many evenings do you go out for fun and recreation?

1="Less than one" 4="Three"
2="One" 5="Four or Five"
3="Two" 6="Six or Seven"

On the average, how often do you go out with date (or your spouse, if you are married)?

1="Never" 4="Once a week"
2="Once a month or less" 5="2 or 3 times a week"
3="2 or 3 times a month" 6="Over 3 times a week"

The next questions ask about the kinds of things you might do.
How often do you do each of the following?
• Go to parties or other social affairs
• Go to taverns, bars or nightclubs
• Getting together with friends, informally
1="Never"
2="A few times a year"
3="Once or twice a month"
4="At least once a week"
5="Almost every day"

Chapter 6

The next questions ask for your opinions on the effects of using certain drugs and other substances. How much do you think people risk harming themselves (physically or in other ways), if they . . .
• Smoke one or more packs of cigarettes per day
• Try one or two drinks of an alcoholic beverage (beer, wine, liquor)
• Take one or two drinks nearly every day
• Take four or five drinks nearly every day
• Have five or more drinks once or twice each weekend
• Try marijuana (pot, grass) once or twice
• Smoke marijuana occasionally
• Smoke marijuana regularly
• Try cocaine once or twice
• Take cocaine occasionally
• Take cocaine regularly
1="No Risk" 4="Great Risk"
2="Slight Risk" 5="Can't Say,
3="Moderate Risk" Drug Unfamiliar"

Individuals differ in whether or not they disapprove of people doing certain things. Do YOU disapprove of people (who are 18 or older) doing each of the following?
• Smoking one or more packs of cigarettes per day
• Trying one or two drinks of an alcoholic beverage (beer, wine, liquor)
• Taking one or two drinks nearly every day
• Taking four or five drinks nearly every day
• Having five or more drinks once or twice each weekend
• Trying marijuana once or twice
• Smoking marijuana occasionally
• Smoking marijuana regularly
• Trying cocaine once or twice
• Taking cocaine occasionally
• Taking cocaine regularly
1="Don't Disapprove"
2="Disapprove"
3="Strongly Disapprove"

Chapter 7

How many of your friends would you
• Smoke cigarettes?
• Drink alcoholic beverages (liquor, beer, wine)?
• Get drunk at least once a week?
• Smoke marijuana (pot, grass) or hashish?
• Take cocaine in powder form?
1="None"
2="A Few" 4="Most"
3="Some" 5="All"

How difficult do you think it would be for you to get each of the following types of drugs, if you wanted some?
• Marijuana (pot, grass)
• Cocaine in powder form
1="Probably Impossible"
2="Very Difficult"
3="Fairly Difficult"
4="Fairly Easy"
5="Very Easy"

TABLE A.2.1
Product-Moment Correlations Among Drug Use Variables and Mediating Variables:
High School Seniors, 1990-1998

	Variable	Mean	Std. Dev.	1.	2.	3.	4.	5.	6.	7.	8.	9.	10.	11.	12.	13.
1.	30 Day Cig	1.65	1.06													
2.	30 Day Alc	2.12	1.26	0.40												
3.	5+ Drks/2wks	1.63	1.04	0.37	0.79											
4.	Annual MJ	1.86	1.51	0.47	0.46	0.42										
5.	30 Day MJ	1.42	1.05	0.42	0.39	0.37	0.85									
6.	Annual Coke	1.08	0.45	0.23	0.21	0.22	0.36	0.38								
7.	30 Day Coke	1.02	0.23	0.16	0.15	0.15	0.22	0.27	0.73							
8.	Rel. Att.	2.69	0.95	-0.18	-0.16	-0.15	-0.20	-0.17	-0.08	-0.06						
9.	Rel. Imp.	2.71	0.93	-0.15	-0.16	-0.14	-0.18	-0.15	-0.07	-0.05	0.62					
10.	Evenings Out	3.51	1.19	0.23	0.29	0.27	0.25	0.23	0.11	0.08	-0.09	-0.09				
11.	Dating	3.41	1.46	0.12	0.14	0.11	0.10	0.07	0.05	0.03	-0.04	-0.03	0.35			
12.	Get Tgthr w/ Fr	4.30	0.71	0.17	0.25	0.23	0.21	0.17	0.08	0.05	-0.07	-0.09	0.38	0.18		
13.	Attend Parties	3.08	0.82	0.24	0.47	0.44	0.33	0.27	0.15	0.10	-0.07	-0.09	0.39	0.23	0.39	
14.	Going to Bars	1.92	0.95	0.26	0.43	0.39	0.27	0.21	0.15	0.10	-0.15	-0.11	0.27	0.18	0.23	0.45
15.	Risk Cigs	3.57	0.60	-0.24	-0.13	-0.13	-0.11	-0.11	-0.07	-0.06	0.07	0.07	-0.09	-0.03	-0.04	-0.07
16.	Dis Cigs	1.96	0.71	-0.45	-0.30	-0.25	-0.29	-0.24	-0.11	-0.07	0.15	0.17	-0.16	-0.07	-0.14	-0.19
17.	Risk 5+	3.21	0.83	-0.28	-0.45	-0.44	-0.33	-0.28	-0.14	-0.09	0.15	0.17	-0.20	-0.08	-0.15	-0.31
18.	Dis 5+	2.11	0.76	-0.33	-0.50	-0.46	-0.35	-0.28	-0.14	-0.09	0.16	0.20	-0.23	-0.09	-0.21	-0.36
19.	Risk MJ	8.85	2.16	-0.34	-0.37	-0.33	-0.55	-0.47	-0.19	-0.12	0.22	0.24	-0.20	-0.07	-0.16	-0.27
20.	Dis MJ	6.61	2.01	-0.39	-0.42	-0.35	-0.58	-0.48	-0.20	-0.12	0.24	0.26	-0.21	-0.06	-0.19	-0.30
21.	Risk Coke	7.28	0.98	-0.13	-0.14	-0.14	-0.19	-0.20	-0.22	-0.16	0.07	0.08	-0.06	0.00	-0.01	-0.09
22.	Dis Coke	5.35	0.99	-0.21	-0.22	-0.20	-0.29	-0.28	-0.25	-0.17	0.13	0.15	-0.10	0.01	-0.06	-0.15

Table A.2.1 (continued)

	Variable	Mean	Std. Dev.	1.	2.	3.	4.	5.	6.	7.	8.	9.	10.	11.	12.	13.
23.	Fr. Cig	2.69	0.91	0.47	0.33	0.29	0.35	0.29	0.15	0.09	-0.15	-0.15	0.20	0.14	0.15	0.27
24.	Fr. Alc	3.55	1.02	0.27	0.43	0.36	0.30	0.23	0.12	0.07	-0.14	-0.16	0.22	0.17	0.23	0.38
25.	Fr. Drunk	2.67	1.06	0.26	0.45	0.43	0.30	0.24	0.14	0.09	-0.12	-0.12	0.21	0.16	0.19	0.38
26.	Fr. MJ	2.25	0.96	0.34	0.37	0.32	0.57	0.49	0.21	0.14	-0.19	-0.16	0.22	0.12	0.18	0.32
27.	Fr. Coke	1.30	0.55	0.22	0.22	0.21	0.29	0.28	0.33	0.24	-0.08	-0.07	0.11	0.06	0.08	0.18
28.	Avail. MJ	4.34	0.90	0.19	0.24	0.19	0.26	0.19	0.09	0.05	-0.12	-0.11	0.17	0.12	0.20	0.22
29.	Avail Coke	3.26	1.13	0.10	0.11	0.09	0.15	0.13	0.15	0.10	-0.03	0.00	0.08	0.06	0.08	0.12

	Variable	14.	15.	16.	17.	18.	19.	20.	21.	22.	23.	24.	25.	26.	27.	28.
14.	Going to Bars															
15.	Risk Cigs	-0.10														
16.	Dis Cigs	-0.20	0.30													
17.	Risk 5+	-0.28	0.25	0.26												
18.	Dis 5+	-0.30	0.16	0.42	0.59											
19.	Risk MJ	-0.23	0.26	0.33	0.46	0.40										
20.	Dis MJ	-0.28	0.16	0.55	0.38	0.55	0.64									
21.	Risk Coke	-0.08	0.28	0.15	0.26	0.16	0.39	0.21								
22.	Dis Coke	-0.18	0.15	0.41	0.23	0.41	0.31	0.59	0.37							
23.	Fr. Cig	0.23	-0.14	-0.33	-0.23	-0.29	-0.29	-0.34	-0.06	-0.15						
24.	Fr. Alc	0.28	-0.05	-0.22	-0.31	-0.39	-0.30	-0.33	-0.04	-0.11	0.54					
25.	Fr. Drunk	0.30	-0.07	-0.21	-0.30	-0.37	-0.26	-0.30	-0.06	-0.14	0.50	0.67				
26.	Fr. MJ	0.27	-0.07	-0.24	-0.27	-0.32	-0.49	-0.53	-0.10	-0.22	0.57	0.53	0.51			
27.	Fr. Coke	0.17	-0.05	-0.13	-0.14	-0.15	-0.18	-0.22	-0.16	-0.24	0.33	0.27	0.34	0.45		
28.	Avail. MJ	0.19	0.01	-0.15	-0.13	-0.19	-0.29	-0.30	0.02	-0.07	0.27	0.32	0.26	0.40	0.16	
29.	Avail Coke	0.16	0.00	-0.04	-0.02	-0.05	-0.07	-0.10	-0.07	-0.13	0.13	0.15	0.15	0.21	0.30	0.52

TABLE A.2.2
Product-Moment Correlations Among Drug Use Variables and Mediating Variables: Follow-ups 1, 2, and 3, 1990-1998

	Variable	Mean	Std. Dev.	1.	2.	3.	4.	5.	6.	7.	8.	9.	10.	11.	12.	13.
1.	30 Day Cig	1.71	1.21													
2.	30 Day Alc	2.57	1.38	0.27												
3.	5+ Drks/2wks	1.77	1.10	0.27	0.73											
4.	Annual MJ	1.83	1.55	0.35	0.38	0.37										
5.	30 Day MJ	1.37	1.02	0.31	0.31	0.31	0.84									
6.	Annual Coke	1.10	0.52	0.18	0.19	0.21	0.39	0.37								
7.	30 Day Coke	1.02	0.21	0.10	0.13	0.15	0.22	0.25	0.66							
8.	Rel. Att.	2.49	0.91	-0.19	-0.22	-0.18	-0.23	-0.19	-0.10	-0.06						
9.	Rel. Imp.	2.76	0.93	-0.13	-0.22	-0.18	-0.20	-0.16	-0.09	-0.06	0.65					
10.	Evenings Out	3.14	1.15	0.09	0.30	0.31	0.20	0.18	0.10	0.07	-0.04	-0.07				
11.	Dating	3.38	1.34	0.02	0.10	0.06	0.04	0.02	0.02	0.01	0.00	-0.01	0.34			
12.	Get tgthr w/ Fr	3.97	0.80	0.11	0.29	0.29	0.20	0.18	0.08	0.05	-0.05	-0.09	0.45	0.11		
13.	Attend Parties	2.77	0.79	0.12	0.45	0.44	0.27	0.22	0.11	0.07	-0.07	-0.11	0.42	0.14	0.49	
14.	Going to Bars	2.49	1.02	0.19	0.58	0.48	0.25	0.18	0.12	0.08	-0.22	-0.20	0.30	0.13	0.30	0.49
15.	Risk Cigs	3.69	0.52	-0.26	-0.05	-0.07	-0.05	-0.05	-0.04	-0.03	0.07	0.07	-0.03	0.02	0.00	0.01
16.	Dis Cigs	2.01	0.72	-0.46	-0.22	-0.21	-0.24	-0.20	-0.11	-0.06	0.19	0.17	-0.08	0.00	-0.09	-0.09
17.	Risk 5+	3.09	0.83	-0.21	-0.45	-0.43	-0.28	-0.22	-0.12	-0.07	0.20	0.21	-0.18	-0.04	-0.18	-0.29
18.	Dis 5+	1.99	0.77	-0.24	-0.51	-0.48	-0.32	-0.24	-0.14	-0.08	0.25	0.25	-0.21	-0.05	-0.21	-0.32
19.	Risk MJ	8.61	2.21	-0.27	-0.38	-0.33	-0.52	-0.43	-0.20	-0.12	0.30	0.29	-0.15	-0.02	-0.19	-0.24
20.	Dis MJ	6.47	1.98	-0.33	-0.41	-0.36	-0.57	-0.45	-0.22	-0.13	0.33	0.31	-0.17	-0.03	-0.20	-0.27
21.	Risk Coke	7.29	0.93	-0.14	-0.19	-0.18	-0.28	-0.25	-0.25	-0.16	0.15	0.16	-0.07	0.00	-0.05	-0.07
22.	Dis Coke	5.39	0.93	-0.20	-0.24	-0.23	-0.36	-0.32	-0.30	-0.20	0.20	0.19	-0.09	0.00	-0.08	-0.12

Table A.2.2 (continued)

Variable	Mean	Std. Dev.	1.	2.	3.	4.	5.	6.	7.	8.	9.	10.	11.	12.	13.
23. Fr. Cig	2.57	0.87	0.46	0.26	0.26	0.32	0.27	0.16	0.09	-0.22	-0.16	0.15	0.05	0.14	0.17
24. Fr. Alc	3.71	0.98	0.19	0.46	0.36	0.27	0.19	0.12	0.07	-0.27	-0.24	0.18	0.09	0.22	0.33
25. Fr. Drunk	2.51	1.04	0.20	0.46	0.49	0.32	0.25	0.15	0.10	-0.21	-0.18	0.26	0.07	0.26	0.40
26. Fr. MJ	2.05	0.90	0.30	0.37	0.35	0.61	0.52	0.26	0.16	-0.27	-0.22	0.22	0.06	0.22	0.30
27. Fr. Coke	1.24	0.49	0.22	0.25	0.26	0.40	0.37	0.43	0.29	-0.15	-0.11	0.12	0.04	0.10	0.18
28. Avail. MJ	4.36	0.88	0.14	0.22	0.19	0.21	0.16	0.08	0.05	-0.15	-0.11	0.12	0.06	0.17	0.18
29. Avail Cocaine	3.31	1.14	0.10	0.09	0.09	0.14	0.12	0.16	0.10	-0.06	-0.03	0.05	0.03	0.05	0.06

Variable	14.	15.	16.	17.	18.	19.	20.	21.	22.	23.	24.	25.	26.	27.	28.
14. Going to Bars															
15. Risk Cigs	-0.03														
16. Dis Cigs	-0.19	0.31													
17. Risk 5+	-0.35	0.18	0.24												
18. Dis 5+	-0.42	0.10	0.35	0.61											
19. Risk MJ	-0.29	0.18	0.30	0.46	0.42										
20. Dis MJ	-0.35	0.11	0.49	0.38	0.53	0.68									
21. Risk Coke	-0.12	0.19	0.17	0.27	0.20	0.45	0.32								
22. Dis Coke	-0.19	0.09	0.38	0.22	0.37	0.36	0.59	0.45							
23. Fr. Cig	0.22	-0.18	-0.35	-0.22	-0.27	-0.28	-0.33	-0.13	-0.19						
24. Fr. Alc	0.43	-0.02	-0.19	-0.35	-0.42	-0.35	-0.37	-0.12	-0.15	0.40					
25. Fr. Drunk	0.40	-0.05	-0.20	-0.36	-0.43	-0.32	-0.36	-0.14	-0.20	0.42	0.58				
26. Fr. MJ	0.30	-0.06	-0.24	-0.29	-0.35	-0.51	-0.57	-0.22	-0.30	0.53	0.46	0.51			
27. Fr. Coke	0.19	-0.05	-0.15	-0.17	-0.19	-0.26	-0.31	-0.26	-0.33	0.32	0.24	0.33	0.49		
28. Avail. MJ	0.19	0.01	-0.14	-0.15	-0.20	-0.27	-0.28	-0.05	-0.10	0.22	0.30	0.27	0.36	0.17	
29. Avail Coke	0.09	0.00	-0.06	-0.04	-0.06	-0.10	-0.11	-0.09	-0.14	0.14	0.12	0.13	0.20	0.28	0.55

TABLE A.2.3
Product-Moment Correlations Among Drug Use Variables and Mediating Variables: Follow-ups 4, 5, 6, and 7, 1990-1998

	Variable	Mean	Std. Dev.	1.	2.	3.	4.	5.	6.	7.	8.	9.	10.	11.	12.	13.
1.	30 Day Cig	1.74	1.32													
2.	30 Day Alc	2.58	1.35	0.16												
3.	5+ Drks/2wks	1.51	0.89	0.24	0.63											
4.	Annual MJ	1.59	1.35	0.27	0.29	0.31										
5.	30 Day MJ	1.28	0.88	0.23	0.23	0.25	0.86									
6.	Annual Coke	1.12	0.55	0.18	0.20	0.26	0.37	0.32								
7.	30 Day Coke	1.03	0.24	0.12	0.14	0.19	0.22	0.20	0.72							
8.	Rel. Att.	2.59	0.90	-0.19	-0.25	-0.21	-0.21	-0.17	-0.11	-0.07						
9.	Rel. Imp.	2.87	0.89	-0.11	-0.24	-0.18	-0.17	-0.14	-0.08	-0.05	0.67					
10.	Evenings Out	2.30	0.99	-0.01	0.22	0.21	0.09	0.07	0.08	0.06	-0.06	-0.06				
11.	Dating	2.94	1.08	-0.04	0.17	0.10	0.05	0.03	0.03	0.01	-0.06	-0.07	0.47			
12.	Get tgthr w/ Fr	3.31	0.71	0.09	0.22	0.19	0.16	0.13	0.09	0.06	-0.06	-0.04	0.37	0.21		
13.	Attend Parties	2.25	0.56	0.02	0.28	0.24	0.10	0.07	0.08	0.06	-0.02	-0.05	0.35	0.29	0.38	
14.	Going to Bars	2.19	0.85	0.14	0.56	0.47	0.24	0.18	0.17	0.11	-0.29	-0.26	0.36	0.27	0.34	0.46
15.	Risk Cigs	3.76	0.44	-0.32	-0.05	-0.10	-0.08	-0.07	-0.07	-0.05	0.09	0.08	0.01	0.03	0.01	0.05
16.	Dis Cigs	2.04	0.70	-0.45	-0.17	-0.19	-0.20	-0.16	-0.10	-0.06	0.19	0.16	0.01	0.02	-0.08	-0.04
17.	Risk 5+	3.25	0.73	-0.16	-0.39	-0.37	-0.20	-0.16	-0.11	-0.07	0.22	0.21	-0.11	-0.09	-0.10	-0.13
18.	Dis 5+	2.14	0.71	-0.17	-0.44	-0.42	-0.23	-0.18	-0.13	-0.07	0.26	0.26	-0.13	-0.09	-0.15	-0.19
19.	Risk MJ	8.63	2.02	-0.19	-0.33	-0.25	-0.41	-0.34	-0.18	-0.11	0.31	0.30	-0.08	-0.09	-0.12	-0.11
20.	Dis MJ	6.43	1.89	-0.25	-0.37	-0.29	-0.47	-0.37	-0.21	-0.12	0.35	0.33	-0.09	-0.08	-0.16	-0.17
21.	Risk Coke	7.14	0.96	-0.12	-0.27	-0.22	-0.30	-0.23	-0.22	-0.14	0.23	0.24	-0.08	-0.07	-0.08	-0.10
22.	Dis Coke	5.24	0.98	-0.17	-0.28	-0.23	-0.35	-0.27	-0.25	-0.15	0.25	0.25	-0.08	-0.06	-0.12	-0.14

Table A.2.3 (continued)

	Variable	Mean	Std. Dev.	1.	2.	3.	4.	5.	6.	7.	8.	9.	10.	11.	12.	13.
23.	Fr. Cig	2.32	0.74	0.42	0.17	0.23	0.25	0.21	0.17	0.12	-0.21	-0.14	0.03	-0.01	0.09	0.02
24.	Fr. Alc	3.48	0.89	0.09	0.43	0.26	0.17	0.13	0.10	0.06	-0.26	-0.26	0.10	0.12	0.14	0.22
25.	Fr. Drunk	1.86	0.79	0.20	0.38	0.46	0.28	0.22	0.19	0.12	-0.24	-0.22	0.17	0.09	0.16	0.20
26.	Fr. MJ	1.73	0.72	0.26	0.31	0.31	0.58	0.49	0.28	0.17	-0.29	-0.22	0.10	0.06	0.16	0.13
27.	Fr. Coke	1.26	0.48	0.20	0.26	0.30	0.41	0.34	0.45	0.30	-0.19	-0.15	0.09	0.05	0.11	0.12
28.	Avail. MJ	4.13	0.90	0.10	0.12	0.11	0.13	0.11	0.07	0.04	-0.11	-0.08	0.04	0.04	0.09	0.07
29.	Avail Cocaine	3.40	1.10	0.08	0.07	0.09	0.10	0.09	0.14	0.10	-0.07	-0.04	0.04	0.03	0.07	0.07

	Variable	14.	15.	16.	17.	18.	19.	20.	21.	22.	23.	24.	25.	26.	27.	28.
14.	Going to Bars															
15.	Risk Cigs	-0.04														
16.	Dis Cigs	-0.18	0.33													
17.	Risk 5+	-0.33	0.18	0.20												
18.	Dis 5+	-0.39	0.13	0.34	0.57											
19.	Risk MJ	-0.30	0.17	0.24	0.40	0.35										
20.	Dis MJ	-0.36	0.12	0.48	0.32	0.49	0.65									
21.	Risk Coke	-0.23	0.14	0.18	0.31	0.28	0.55	0.45								
22.	Dis Coke	-0.28	0.08	0.37	0.22	0.43	0.42	0.67	0.52							
23.	Fr. Cig	0.20	-0.23	-0.34	-0.19	-0.22	-0.18	-0.25	-0.12	-0.17						
24.	Fr. Alc	0.44	-0.02	-0.14	-0.30	-0.35	-0.33	-0.32	-0.22	-0.19	0.25					
25.	Fr. Drunk	0.43	-0.10	-0.20	-0.32	-0.39	-0.27	-0.33	-0.22	-0.26	0.37	0.42				
26.	Fr. MJ	0.32	-0.10	-0.23	-0.24	-0.29	-0.43	-0.51	-0.30	-0.35	0.46	0.34	0.47			
27.	Fr. Coke	0.26	-0.07	-0.15	-0.17	-0.22	-0.28	-0.35	-0.31	-0.36	0.31	0.23	0.39	0.56		
28.	Avail. MJ	0.18	-0.03	-0.12	-0.09	-0.12	-0.18	-0.19	-0.09	-0.10	0.18	0.18	0.17	0.27	0.16	
29.	Avail Coke	0.15	-0.01	-0.07	-0.03	-0.07	-0.07	-0.10	-0.08	-0.12	0.14	0.08	0.14	0.19	0.25	0.66

MULTIPLE CLASSIFICATION ANALYSES PREDICTING
CHANGES IN MEDIATING VARIABLES

The relationships between mediating variables and change in roles and experiences constitute large portions of the substantive discussion in chapters 4 through 7. Arrow *b* of Fig. 1.1 connects the roles and experiences that constitute the new freedoms and responsibilities of young adulthood with a set of values, attitudes, and lifestyle behaviors that we treat as mediating variables—that is, variables that mediate the relationship between post-high-school experiences and roles and changes in substance use in young adulthood. Multiple classification analysis (MCA) was one type of analysis used to examine the relationships implied by arrow *b* of the model presented in Fig. 1.1. In this portion of the appendix, we provide additional information about MCA, and we provide guidelines for interpreting the MCA tables (A.4.1–A.7.6) included in this appendix.

MCA Procedures

MCA (Andrews, Morgan, & Sonquist, 1967) is a form of multivariate regression analysis very similar to ordinary least squares (OLS) multiple regression. MCA permits the analyst to predict one variable using a number of predictors simultaneously. Yet MCA differs from ordinary multiple regression in several crucial ways. MCA can meaningfully utilize predictors that are nominal or ordinal variables as well as predictors that are interval variables. That feature is essential to these analyses inasmuch as most of the post-high-school roles and experiences examined here cannot be operationalized as interval variables. Unlike dummy variable regression, in which coefficients for the nominal or ordinal predictors are departures from the omitted category of the predictor, MCA treats and displays all levels of any categorical predictor as departures from the mean of the dependent variable.

MCA results are very similar to OLS regression results. MCA results begin with the constant (an overall mean) of the dependent variable, which represents our best guess of any individual's score in the absence of any other information. Simple bivariate coefficients are given for each predictor, which estimate the average deviation from the overall mean associated with being in any particular category of the predictor variable. The multivariate coefficients in MCA consider predictors simultaneously and adjust each predictor to take some account of the other predictors. The multivariate coefficients estimate the specific effects of each predictor variable category *as if* the other predictors in the model were distributed within that single category as they are distributed for the total sample.

Variables Used in MCAs

Multiple regression procedures, including MCA, are designed to focus on one "dependent variable" at a time, and examine the "effects" on that variable of a number of "independent variables" or "predictors." We placed quotation marks around these terms because analyses of survey data, even longitudinal panel data, involve our *assumptions* about causal directions—assumptions that seem obvious for some variables, quite plausible for others, but sometimes debatable with respect to the post-high-school roles and experiences that are the focus of these analyses. Indeed, although the analysis methodology supposes only one direction of causation, our view of the underlying reality is sometimes more complex. However, having acknowledged that this approach involves assumptions and simplifications, we should add that it generally serves quite well as a means of summarizing complex relationships, and we have not felt inhibited from considering more complex causal interpretations than those implied by the terminology.

Mediating Variables—Values, Attitudes, and Lifestyle Behaviors—Treated as Dependent Variables. These analyses explore the ways in which a series of measures we call *mediating variables* differ according to post-high-school experiences and demographic background. We focus on one mediating variable at a time, each in turn now treated as the *dependent* variable in a series of MCAs. More specifically, the dependent variables in these MCAs consist of "change scores," as well as "before" scores and "after" scores, for each of the mediating variables. The complete question wordings and response scales for these measures appear in Table A.1.6. As discussed in chapter 3, each MCA was conducted separately for women and men. The appendix tables (one for each mediating variable) that present the results of these analyses follow the order established in chapters 4–7:

1. Chapter 4: Religious attendance and the importance of religion (Tables A.4.1–A.4.2).
2. Chapter 5: Frequency of evenings out for fun, frequency of going on dates, frequency of attending parties, frequency of getting together with friends informally, and frequency of visits to bars (Tables A.5.1–A.5.5).
3. Chapter 6: Perceived risks and disapproval of smoking, heavy drinking, marijuana use, and cocaine use (Tables A.6.1–A.6.8).
4. Chapter 7: Perceptions of friends' use of cigarettes, heavy drinking, marijuana use, and cocaine use (Tables A.7.1–A.7.4). Perceptions of the availability of marijuana and cocaine (Tables A.7.5–A.7.6).

Predictor Variables: Post-High-School Roles and Experiences.
The predictor variables of greatest interest in the MCA analyses are
post-high-school roles and experiences measured at the same time as the
"after" scores for the dependent variables. The post-high-school roles and
experiences, most of which were summarized earlier in this appendix (Tables A.1.1–A.1.5), included:

- Student status
- Work status
- Living arrangements/marriage
- Engagement
- Pregnancy
- Parenthood

These are "after" measures only, but they also represent changes, because
certain "before" characteristics as of the senior year of high school were held
constant for all respondents included in these analyses (i.e., none were married, none had children, all lived with their parents or guardians).

Additional Predictors: Control or Background Factors. In addition to the post-high-school experience variables, several other predictor
variables were included in our MCAs primarily as *controls*. Although the use
of change scores reduces the need for controlling background factors, we
view the inclusion of such variables as important safeguards—especially because the boundary between background and contemporaneous influences
cannot always be clearly drawn. Several background factors, measured at
the end of senior year, were included in these analyses: race, region,
urbanicity, high school grades, and college plans. Race may seem to be
clearly a background factor, yet social environments often differ considerably by racial subgroup, and such differences do not end with graduation
from high school. Similarly, region and urbanicity relate to differing social
contexts, and although some individuals move to different locations after
high school, many do not—thus these background factors may reflect contemporaneous influences as well as those in effect during high school. High
school grades and senior-year plans for college reflect a complex mixture of
endowment, ambition, and achievement, all of which can have continuing
impacts on individuals.

Two other variables were grouped with the background variables for
analysis purposes. The first and more important of these variables is the distinction between follow-up surveys, which serves as an indicator of the
number of years post-high-school as well as a close proxy for age (e.g., the
first follow-up occurred 1 or 2 years after high school when the modal age of
respondents was 19 or 20, and the seventh follow-up occurred 13 or 14 years
after high school when the modal age was 31 or 32). The second variable
distinguishes whether the first of the (otherwise biennial) follow-ups occurred 1 year versus 2 years after high school graduation.

Conventions Followed in Conducting and Reporting MCAs

All of the MCAs reported here were carried out in a manner consistent with usual conventions. That leaves room for many choices and options, and this section provides an overview and rationale for our choices. The next section provides specific detailed guidelines for interpreting the tables.

Numbers of Cases Specified for MCAs. We observed in chapter 3 that our fictional Jane Jones would have generated seven different "cases" for inclusion in the analyses because she participated in seven different follow-up surveys; and we noted that these seven observations would not be strictly independent of each other, because they are all from the same individual. For one thing, the change scores from any single individual share a common "before" measure (based on high school senior reports); moreover, the "after" measures are not entirely independent of one another. Therefore, for purposes of statistical significance testing, we specified the numbers of *cases* in the MCAs as equal to the total numbers of *separate individuals* rather than the total numbers of *observations*. Thus, the numbers of cases (weighted, as discussed earlier in the appendix) were specified (conservatively) as 12,000 for men and 15,000 for women. (The numbers of *observations* for the various subgroups are shown in Table A.3.)

Dummy Variables and Continuous Variables. Nearly all of the predictor variables used in these analyses are categorical rather than continuous, and many (such as work status and living arrangements) cannot be treated as ordinal variables in any meaningful sense. Accordingly, MCA treats such predictors as sets of dummy variables, which has the additional advantage of giving us detailed data on each of the predictor categories. Three of the background predictors—college plans, urbanicity, and high school grades—were treated as continuous variables to simplify interpretation (and conserve degrees of freedom):

1. *High-school grades* were reported on a 9-point scale ranging from 1 = D, to 9 = A. For women the mean was 6.33, and for men it was 5.79 (with 6.0 equal to a B).

2. *College plans* were responses to a question asking "How likely is it that you will ... graduate from college (4-year program)?" with the following response alternatives and codes: 1 = definitely won't; 2 = probably won't; 3 = probably will; 4 = definitely will. For women the mean was 2.89, and for men it was 2.90.

3. *Urbanicity* (based on residence during senior year of high school) was a five-category variable, scaled as follows: 1 = lived on a farm; 2 = lived in the country but not on a farm; 3 = lived in a (small) city (non-SMSA);[1] 4 = lived in

---

[1]SMSA is the abbreviation for *Standard Metropolitan Statistical Area* and is defined by the Census Bureau. For details, see Appendix B of Johnston et al. (2000a).

a (larger) city (SMSA, not self-representing); 5 = lived in a (very large) city (self-representing SMSA). For women the mean score on the urbanicity scale was 3.77, and for men it was 3.75.

Special Format for Reporting MCAs. The MCA findings are reported in the form of *unstandardized* regression coefficients, so that sizes of effects (i.e., changes in the mediating variables) can be interpreted directly. Moreover, unstandardized regression coefficients make it easy to observe when relatively rare situations (such as pregnancy) have impacts that equal or exceed more common situations (such as being married), even though the latter may account for more in the way of explained variance.

For those not familiar with Multiple Classification Analysis, we note here some of the features found in that form of regression analysis—features that make the output easier and more straightforward to interpret than is true of typical multiple regression output, especially when dummy variables are involved. In broad outline, the format used in our MCA tables has the following characteristics:

1. The starting point is a *constant* that consists of the mean of the dependent variable calculated across all respondents (i.e., all male cases, or all female cases). In effect, this represents our best guess about the dependent variable for any respondent if we knew nothing about any of the predictors.

2. For each of the predictor variables that are treated as interval scales (i.e., high school grades, plans to complete college, and urbanicity), the format presents a coefficient indicating the change or difference in the dependent variable that is associated with a 1-point shift in the predictor variable. It is important to note that to calculate the effect associated with any particular point on these three predictor dimensions, one must first calculate the difference between that point and the mean for all respondents for that predictor dimension, and then multiply that difference by the coefficient. (Although that may seem a bit awkward, it has the important advantage of maintaining the overall constant as a meaningful value, rather than a largely arbitrary one. Because there is little need to make the actual calculations for the three control variables in question, we considered the trade-off worthwhile.)

3. For each of the categorical predictors, the format provides a corresponding set of coefficients—one for each category. Each such coefficient indicates the extent of departure from the overall mean (i.e., the constant) associated with being in that category. Both bivariate and multivariate coefficients are displayed. Each bivariate coefficient indicates the average deviation from the overall mean for all cases in that particular category, without taking other variables into account. The multivariate regression coefficients show adjustments to the overall mean with all other predictors in the column included.

4. Summary statistics consist of the usual Multiple-R and R-squared values.

Detailed Guidelines for Interpreting MCA Tables[2]

Tables A.4.1 through A.7.6 are identical in the sets of predictor variables used and identical in format; they have different dependent variables. For illustrative purposes we concentrate on Table A.4.1, in which the dependent variable is religious attendance.

Each of the tables consists of two parallel parts, reporting results separately for women and for men, arranged on facing pages to permit easy comparison. Our illustrations focus on the data for women (i.e., Table A.4.1a).

Columns 1–3: Analyses Using Change Scores as Dependent Variables. The first three columns of data in both the female and male portions of each table are based on analyses predicting change scores. The entries in the first column are unstandardized bivariate regression coefficients, showing relationships between each predictor and the change score dependent variable, while taking no account of relationships with other predictor variables. The entries in the next two columns are unstandardized multivariate (MCA) coefficients, showing relationships between certain predictors and the dependent variable with certain other predictor variables included in the equation. The second column is limited to the background predictor variables; the third column includes background predictors, plus student status, work status, living arrangements (the first category of which is married), engagement status, pregnancy status, and parenthood status. Comparisons between the second and third columns permit an understanding of overlaps with predictors we treat as background factors.

Columns 4–7: Analyses Using "Before" and "After" Dependent Variables. The remaining four columns of data in both the female and male portions of each table are based on analyses predicting to static scores on the dependent variables. Entries in the fourth and fifth columns are unstandardized bivariate regression coefficients, taking no account of relationships with other predictor variables. The fourth column predicts the "before" (i.e., senior year of high school) measure of the dependent variable, whereas the fifth column predicts the "after" (i.e., follow-up) measure of the dependent variable. Subtracting the "before" score from the corresponding "after" score yields the change score shown in the first column; however,

---

[2]Most of the material in this section has been adapted directly from pp. 143–144 of Bachman, O'Malley, Johnston, Rodgers, and Schulenberg (1992), which was drafted originally by Willard Rodgers.

having the data separately for the two parts provides useful additional information beyond that shown by the change scores. For example, we can see in Table A.4.1a that women who were cohabiting at the time of follow-up (i.e., the "partner" category under "living arrangements") showed a greater-than-average decline in religious attendance (a change score coefficient of –0.151, combined with the constant of –0.284, as shown in the first column), but we can see also that these women were distinctly below average in religious attendance while in high school (a coefficient of –0.374, as shown in the fourth column) and that they were even further below average at the follow-up (a coefficient of –0.525, as shown in the fifth column). The findings are the same for men who were cohabiting, as is shown in the male portion of the table (i.e., Table A.4.1b).

Entries in the sixth column are unstandardized multivariate (MCA) coefficients, showing relationships with the full set of variables (the same ones as in the third column) now predicting the "after" (i.e., follow-up) measure of the dependent variable. Contrasting this sixth column with the fifth column provides further information on the shifts in relationships that occur when other variables are controlled. The sixth column, however, provides no control for earlier scores on the dependent variable. Accordingly, in the seventh column we add another predictor: the "before" (i.e., senior year) measure of the dependent variable. The coefficient for this predictor is 0.502 for women in Table A.4.1a; it can be interpreted as indicating that a difference of one scale point on religious attendance during the senior year of high school predicts a difference of 0.502 scale points at follow-up 1–14 years later (averaging roughly 6 years, taking into account that we have somewhat more earlier follow-up cases than later ones). This high coefficient, which involves no adjustment for measurement error, is consistent with the very high stability estimates (over shorter intervals) as reported in chapter 4, Fig. 4.4. The most important findings in the seventh column, however, are the other coefficients, which represent an alternative to the change score approach shown in the third column. To a large degree, the stories told by the data in the third and seventh columns are closely consistent. Our reporting has been informed by both sets of findings.

Multiple-R and Multiple-R-Squared Values. The bottom row entries in each of the tables (multivariate columns only) consist of multiple-R and R-squared values, the latter indicating the amount of variance explained by the predictor variables in that column. Comparing the R-squared values among columns permits an assessment of unique and overlapping explained variance.

Weighted Numbers of Observation by Variable Subgroup for the Total Sample[a]

	Maximum Weighted Numbers of Observations Available for any Analysis			
	Women		Men	
	Full Set of Obs. from Follow-Ups	Obs. from Follow-Ups	Full Set of Obs. from Follow-Ups	Obs. from Follow-Ups
VARIABLE[b]	1-7	1-2	1-7	1-2
SET#1 RACE				
WHITE	60,073	24,236	50,154	20,295
BLACK	6,626	2,958	3,967	1,797
OTHER	6,641	3,253	5,595	2,734
SET#2 REGION				
NORTHEAST	16,533	6,736	13,350	5,380
NORTH CENTRAL	22,621	9,147	18,732	7,539
SOUTH	22,171	9,506	17,649	7,538
WEST	12,016	5,057	9,985	4,370
HIGH SCHOOL GRADES	72,280	29,979	58,282	24,223
R WILL ATTEND 4YR COLLEGE	70,753	29,360	56,756	23,595
URBANICITY	73,341	30,447	59,703	24,823
SET#3 FOLLOW-UP NUMBER				
FU #1	16,356	16,356	13,296	13,296
FU #2	14,090	14,090	11,530	11,530
FU #3	12,026		9,865	
FU #4	10,067		8,177	
FU #5	8,427		6,841	
FU #6	6,902		5,550	
FU #7	5,473		4,456	
SET#4 ADMINISTRATION OF FIRST FOLLOW-UP				
ONE YEAR AFTER HIGH SCHOOL	38,130	15,783	31,264	12,848
TWO YEARS AFTER HIGH SCHOOL	35,211	14,664	28,452	11,979
SET#5 STUDENT STATUS AT FOLLOW-UP				
FULL-TIME STUDENT	19,472	15,738	16,375	12,601
PART-TIME STUDENT	6,840	2,555	5,540	2,061
NOT A STUDENT	46,291	11,813	37,061	9,819
SET#6 WORK STATUS AT FOLLOW-UP				
FULL-TIME CIVILIAN JOB	38,642	10,563	36,061	9,233
MILITARY SERVICE	477	231	2,830	1,362
PART-TIME JOB	15,461	9,769	9,076	6,390
HOMEMAKER	5,318	1,126	182	88
NONSTUDENT, NOT EMPLOYED	3,524	1,356	2,565	1,075
OTHER	9,918	7,401	9,003	6,679
SET#7 LIVING ARRANGEMENT AT FOLLOW-UP				
MARRIED	26,428	4,215	16,928	1,835
PARTNER	6,235	2,271	4,082	1,197
PARENT(S)	19,018	12,521	17,489	11,125
DORM	5,690	5,446	4,491	4,161
LIVE ALONE	4,852	904	5,482	1,031
OTHER	11,117	5,089	11,245	5,477
SET#8 ENGAGEMENT STATUS AT FOLLOW-UP				
ENGAGED	6,408	3,400	4,159	1,790
NOT ENGAGED	66,933	27,047	55,557	23,037
SET#9 IS R (or R'S SPS) PREGNANT AT FOLLOW-UP?				
YES	3,530	845	2,140	319
NO	59,435	21,502	47,817	17,194
DATA N.A. (1977-1983)	10,375	8,100	9,760	7,313
SET#10 PARENTHOOD STATUS AT FOLLOW-UP				
MARRIED PARENT	15,494	1,671	9,807	800
SINGLE PARENT	4,674	1,221	2,346	598
NOT A PARENT	53,173	27,555	47,563	23,429
TOTAL OBSERVATIONS	73,341	30,447	59,716	24,827

[a]Samples derived from items that appear on single forms are approximately 1/5th to 1/6th as large.

[b]Sets #1 and #2 were measured during the senior year of high school.
Sets #3 and #4 were determined by the timing of the follow-up.
Sets #5 - #10 were measured at follow-up.

Table A.4.1a
Regression Analyses Linking Post-High School Experiences to Changes in Religious Attendance
Females, Senior Years 1976-1997, Follow-ups 1977-1998

Regression Analyses Based on Full Set of Observations from Follow-Ups 1-7 (Wtd. N of Obs: 69,170) Unstandardized Regression Coefficients

| VARIABLE | Predicting to Change Scores | | | Bivariate Coeff. With Dependent Variable | | Multivariate Prediction of Dep. Var. at FU: Covarying BY Dep. Var? | |
	BIVARIATE COEFF.	Multivariate Coefficients BKGD.	ALL SETS	at BY	at FU	No	Yes
CONSTANT	-0.284	-0.284	-0.284	2.939	2.655	2.655	2.655
SET#1 RACE		**	**			**	**
WHITE	-0.014	-0.011	-0.010	-0.008	-0.022	-0.032	-0.021
BLACK	0.099	0.091	0.088	0.175	0.274	0.293	0.190
OTHER	0.038	0.016	0.005	-0.098	-0.059	0.016	0.010
SET#2 REGION						**	**
NORTHEAST	-0.020	-0.016	-0.010	-0.146	-0.166	-0.129	-0.070
NORTH CENTRAL	-0.018	-0.018	-0.014	0.064	0.046	0.061	0.023
SOUTH	0.021	0.014	0.006	0.127	0.148	0.090	0.048
WEST	0.023	0.029	0.029	-0.157	-0.134	-0.107	-0.039
HIGH SCHOOL GRADES/D=1 (Cov.)[a]		-0.005	-0.002			0.058 **	0.028 **
R WILL ATTEND 4YR COLLEGE (Cov.)[a]		-0.054 **	-0.041 **			0.023 **	-0.009
URBANICITY (Cov.)[a]		0.006	0.006			-0.059 **	-0.027 **
SET#3 FOLLOW-UP NUMBER		**	**			*	**
FU #1	0.113	0.117	0.127	-0.041	0.071	0.003	0.065
FU #2	0.001	0.004	0.025	-0.032	-0.031	-0.035	-0.005
FU #3	-0.051	-0.050	-0.036	-0.008	-0.059	-0.022	-0.029
FU #4	-0.062	-0.064	-0.064	0.006	-0.056	-0.011	-0.037
FU #5	-0.048	-0.051	-0.065	0.031	-0.016	0.015	-0.025
FU #6	-0.029	-0.034	-0.068	0.060	0.032	0.040	-0.014
FU #7	-0.002	-0.010	-0.058	0.086	0.084	0.075	0.008
SET#4 ADMINISTRATION OF FIRST FOLLOW-UP		*	*				*
ONE YEAR AFTER HIGH SCHOOL	0.014	0.015	0.016	0.005	0.019	0.014	0.015
TWO YEARS AFTER HIGH SCHOOL	-0.015	-0.016	-0.017	-0.006	-0.021	-0.015	-0.016
SET#5 STUDENT STATUS AT FOLLOW-UP							
FULL-TIME STUDENT	0.002		-0.025	0.065	0.067	0.028	0.002
PART-TIME STUDENT	-0.010		0.016	-0.017	-0.027	0.014	0.015
NOT A STUDENT	0.001		0.008	-0.025	-0.025	-0.014	-0.003
SET#6 WORK STATUS AT FOLLOW-UP			**			**	**
FULL-TIME CIVILIAN JOB	-0.048		-0.026	-0.013	-0.061	-0.020	-0.023
MILITARY SERVICE	-0.092		-0.077	-0.101	-0.193	-0.171	-0.124
PART-TIME JOB	0.024		0.007	0.033	0.057	0.023	0.015
HOMEMAKER	0.168		0.091	0.037	0.205	0.127	0.109
NONSTUDENT, NOT EMPLOYED	0.090		0.034	-0.133	-0.043	-0.029	0.003
OTHER	0.033		0.035	0.031	0.064	-0.008	0.014
SET#7 LIVING ARRANGEMENT AT FOLLOW-UP			**			**	**
MARRIED	0.036		0.011	0.083	0.119	0.082	0.046
PARTNER	-0.151		-0.146	-0.374	-0.525	-0.504	-0.324
PARENT(S)	0.092		0.077	-0.030	0.062	0.107	0.092
DORM	0.037		0.021	0.167	0.204	0.131	0.076
LIVE ALONE	-0.162		-0.064	-0.016	-0.177	-0.158	-0.111
OTHER	-0.105		-0.059	-0.020	-0.125	-0.095	-0.077
SET#8 ENGAGEMENT STATUS AT FOLLOW-UP			**			**	**
ENGAGED	0.033		0.086	-0.051	-0.018	0.197	0.141
NOT ENGAGED	-0.003		-0.008	0.005	0.002	-0.019	-0.013
SET#9 IS R PREGNANT AT FOLLOW-UP?						**	**
YES	0.056		0.033	0.071	0.127	0.067	0.050
NO	-0.010		0.004	-0.018	-0.028	-0.024	-0.010
DATA N.A. (1977-1983)	0.037		-0.034	0.083	0.120	0.120	0.043
SET#10 PARENTHOOD STATUS AT FOLLOW-UP			**			**	**
MARRIED PARENT	0.112		0.115	0.070	0.182	0.108	0.112
SINGLE PARENT	0.013		0.021	-0.188	-0.175	-0.070	-0.024
NOT A PARENT	-0.034		-0.035	-0.004	-0.038	-0.025	-0.030
RELIGIOUS ATTENDANCE AT BASE YEAR (Cov.)[a]							0.502 **
Multiple R		0.103	0.147			0.288	0.581
R Sqr.		0.011	0.022			0.083	0.337

Notes: * indicates statistical significance at .05 level. ** indicates statistical significance at .01 level. Statistical significance is not indicated for bivariate coefficients or constants. Ns used for significance testing were weighted to approximate the number of individuals (not the number of observations) since each individual could contribute up to seven observations. Sets #5-#10 were measured at follow-up. Sets #3 and #4 were determined by timing of follow-up. All others were measured at Base Year (BY).

[a] Means for covariates:

HIGH SCHOOL GRADES	6.331	URBANICITY	3.765
RELIGIOUS ATTENDANCE AT BASE YEAR	2.939	R WILL ATTEND 4YR COLLEGE	2.892

Table A.4.1b
Regression Analyses Linking Post-High School Experiences to Changes in Religious Attendance
Males, Senior Years 1976-1997, Follow-ups 1977-1998

Regression Analyses Based on Full Set of Observations from Follow-Ups 1-7 (Wtd. N of Obs: 55,191) Unstandardized Regression Coefficients

VARIABLE	BIVARIATE COEFF.	Predicting to Change Scores Multivariate Coefficients		Bivariate Coeff. With Dependent Variable		Multivariate Prediction of Dep. Var. at FU: Covarying BY Dep. Var?	
		BKGD.	ALL SETS	at BY	at FU	No	Yes
CONSTANT	-0.331	-0.331	-0.331	2.782	2.451	2.451	2.451
SET#1 RACE		**	**			**	**
WHITE	-0.018	-0.013	-0.012	0.010	-0.008	-0.015	-0.014
BLACK	0.088	0.073	0.078	0.089	0.177	0.200	0.139
OTHER	0.105	0.072	0.062	-0.153	-0.048	0.008	0.035
SET#2 REGION		**	**			**	**
NORTHEAST	-0.047	-0.040	-0.030	-0.096	-0.144	-0.101	-0.065
NORTH CENTRAL	-0.015	-0.012	-0.013	0.038	0.023	0.023	0.005
SOUTH	0.010	0.002	-0.006	0.140	0.151	0.108	0.051
WEST	0.072	0.069	0.075	-0.195	-0.123	-0.102	-0.014
HIGH SCHOOL GRADES/D=1 (Cov.)[a]		-0.015 **	-0.012 *			0.049 **	0.019 **
R WILL ATTEND 4YR COLLEGE (Cov.)[a]		-0.056 **	-0.044 **			0.035 **	-0.004
URBANICITY (Cov.)[a]		0.004	0.010			-0.074 **	-0.032 **
SET#3 FOLLOW-UP NUMBER		**	**			**	**
FU #1	0.146	0.147	0.186	-0.050	0.096	0.074	0.130
FU #2	0.014	0.015	0.054	-0.028	-0.014	0.002	0.027
FU #3	-0.048	-0.048	-0.035	-0.013	-0.061	-0.032	-0.034
FU #4	-0.073	-0.073	-0.085	0.016	-0.057	-0.031	-0.058
FU #5	-0.078	-0.079	-0.118	0.037	-0.041	-0.040	-0.079
FU #6	-0.057	-0.059	-0.123	0.057	0.000	-0.031	-0.077
FU #7	-0.037	-0.040	-0.122	0.090	0.054	0.005	-0.058
SET#4 ADMINISTRATION OF FIRST FOLLOW-UP							
ONE YEAR AFTER HIGH SCHOOL	0.002	0.003	0.006	0.012	0.015	0.012	0.009
TWO YEARS AFTER HIGH SCHOOL	-0.003	-0.003	-0.007	-0.013	-0.016	-0.013	-0.010
SET#5 STUDENT STATUS AT FOLLOW-UP						**	*
FULL-TIME STUDENT	0.006		0.005	0.092	0.098	0.090	0.048
PART-TIME STUDENT	0.008		0.020	-0.006	0.002	0.026	0.023
NOT A STUDENT	-0.004		-0.005	-0.041	-0.045	-0.044	-0.025
SET#6 WORK STATUS AT FOLLOW-UP							
FULL-TIME CIVILIAN JOB	-0.014		-0.006	-0.002	-0.016	0.015	0.005
MILITARY SERVICE	0.002		-0.020	-0.093	-0.091	-0.067	-0.044
PART-TIME JOB	0.013		-0.005	0.050	0.062	0.000	-0.003
HOMEMAKER	0.278		0.192	-0.154	0.123	0.066	0.129
NONSTUDENT, NOT EMPLOYED	0.079		0.052	-0.202	-0.123	-0.024	0.014
OTHER	0.014		0.019	0.046	0.060	-0.036	-0.009
SET#7 LIVING ARRANGEMENT AT FOLLOW-UP			**			**	**
MARRIED	0.077		0.121	0.102	0.178	0.195	0.159
PARTNER	-0.131		-0.146	-0.332	-0.462	-0.465	-0.306
PARENT(S)	0.078		0.019	-0.064	0.014	0.029	0.024
DORM	0.026		-0.047	0.166	0.192	0.022	-0.012
LIVE ALONE	-0.129		-0.046	-0.022	-0.151	-0.117	-0.081
OTHER	-0.136		-0.118	0.007	-0.129	-0.124	-0.121
SET#8 ENGAGEMENT STATUS AT FOLLOW-UP			**			**	**
ENGAGED	0.058		0.137	-0.042	0.017	0.252	0.195
NOT ENGAGED	-0.004		-0.010	0.003	-0.001	-0.019	-0.015
SET#9 IS R'S SPS PREGNANT AT FOLLOW-UP?						**	*
YES	0.082		0.024	0.121	0.203	0.068	0.047
NO	-0.013		0.003	-0.017	-0.030	-0.023	-0.010
DATA N.A. (1977-1983)	0.046		-0.023	0.061	0.106	0.099	0.038
SET#10 PARENTHOOD STATUS AT FOLLOW-UP			**			**	**
MARRIED PARENT	0.124		0.087	0.088	0.212	0.090	0.088
SINGLE PARENT	-0.016		0.037	-0.247	-0.262	-0.075	-0.020
NOT A PARENT	-0.025		-0.020	-0.006	-0.031	-0.015	-0.017
RELIGIOUS ATTENDANCE AT BASE YEAR (Cov.)[a]							0.497 **
Multiple R		0.128	0.169			0.274	0.585
R Sqr.		0.016	0.029			0.075	0.342

Notes: * indicates statistical significance at .05 level. ** indicates statistical significance at .01 level. Statistical significance is not indicated for bivariate coefficients or constants. Ns used for significance testing were weighted to approximate the number of individuals (not the number of observations) since each individual could contribute up to seven observations. Sets #5-#10 were measured at follow-up. Sets #3 and #4 were determined by timing of follow-up. All others were measured at Base Year (BY).

[a]Means for covariates: HIGH SCHOOL GRADES 5.794   URBANICITY 3.747
RELIGIOUS ATTENDANCE AT BASE YEAR 2.782   R WILL ATTEND 4YR COLLEGE 2.901

Table A.4.2a
Regression Analyses Linking Post-High School Experiences to Changes in Religious Importance
Females, Senior Years 1976-1997, Follow-ups 1977-1998

Regression Analyses Based on Full Set of Observations from Follow-Ups 1-7
(Wtd. N of Obs: 69,131)
Unstandardized Regression Coefficients

VARIABLE	BIVARIATE COEFF.	Multivariate Coefficients BKGD.	ALL SETS	Bivariate Coeff. With Dependent Variable at BY	at FU	Multivariate Prediction of Dep. Var. at FU: Covarying BY Dep. Var? No	Yes
CONSTANT	0.069	0.069	0.069	2.883	2.951	2.951	2.951
SET#1 RACE		**	**			**	**
WHITE	0.000	0.001	0.001	-0.054	-0.054	-0.057	-0.024
BLACK	0.063	0.047	0.046	0.431	0.494	0.455	0.220
OTHER	-0.060	-0.056	-0.058	0.087	0.027	0.096	0.007
SET#2 REGION			*			**	**
NORTHEAST	-0.002	-0.002	0.005	-0.220	-0.222	-0.172	-0.070
NORTH CENTRAL	0.029	0.022	0.023	-0.032	-0.003	0.017	0.020
SOUTH	0.003	0.002	-0.003	0.239	0.242	0.171	0.071
WEST	-0.057	-0.043	-0.044	-0.084	-0.141	-0.114	-0.074
HIGH SCHOOL GRADES/D=1 (Cov.)[a]		-0.028 **	-0.026 **			0.026 **	-0.004
R WILL ATTEND 4YR COLLEGE (Cov.)[a]		-0.037 **	-0.026 **			0.003	-0.014 *
URBANICITY (Cov.)[a]		0.000	0.003			-0.064 **	-0.026 **
SET#3 FOLLOW-UP NUMBER							
FU #1	-0.018	-0.012	0.013	-0.016	-0.034	-0.045	-0.011
FU #2	-0.015	-0.011	0.007	-0.018	-0.033	-0.016	-0.003
FU #3	-0.010	-0.010	-0.004	-0.007	-0.017	0.002	-0.002
FU #4	-0.005	-0.007	-0.016	0.001	-0.004	0.008	-0.005
FU #5	0.014	0.009	-0.012	0.013	0.026	0.023	0.003
FU #6	0.040	0.033	-0.001	0.030	0.069	0.045	0.018
FU #7	0.052	0.044	0.000	0.050	0.102	0.064	0.027
SET#4 ADMINISTRATION OF FIRST FOLLOW-UP							
ONE YEAR AFTER HIGH SCHOOL	0.005	0.006	0.008	0.005	0.009	0.009	0.008
TWO YEARS AFTER HIGH SCHOOL	-0.005	-0.006	-0.009	-0.005	-0.010	-0.009	-0.009
SET#5 STUDENT STATUS AT FOLLOW-UP							
FULL-TIME STUDENT	-0.063		-0.027	0.012	-0.051	-0.026	-0.027
PART-TIME STUDENT	-0.035		-0.016	0.001	-0.034	-0.001	-0.010
NOT A STUDENT	0.032		0.014	-0.005	0.027	0.011	0.013
SET#6 WORK STATUS AT FOLLOW-UP			*			**	**
FULL-TIME CIVILIAN JOB	-0.013		-0.019	-0.019	-0.032	-0.027	-0.022
MILITARY SERVICE	0.001		-0.006	-0.054	-0.053	-0.085	-0.039
PART-TIME JOB	-0.017		0.009	0.010	-0.007	0.020	0.014
HOMEMAKER	0.159		0.070	0.087	0.246	0.130	0.096
NONSTUDENT, NOT EMPLOYED	0.072		0.010	0.000	0.072	0.010	0.010
OTHER	-0.034		0.019	0.015	-0.019	0.005	0.013
SET#7 LIVING ARRANGEMENT AT FOLLOW-UP			**			**	**
MARRIED	0.067		0.036	0.077	0.144	0.097	0.062
PARTNER	-0.064		-0.088	-0.319	-0.383	-0.390	-0.217
PARENT(S)	-0.005		-0.001	0.018	0.013	0.047	0.019
DORM	-0.053		0.008	0.063	0.010	0.060	0.030
LIVE ALONE	-0.080		-0.032	-0.052	-0.132	-0.116	-0.068
OTHER	-0.053		-0.026	-0.047	-0.099	-0.074	-0.046
SET#8 ENGAGEMENT STATUS AT FOLLOW-UP			**			**	**
ENGAGED	0.022		0.069	-0.043	-0.021	0.158	0.107
NOT ENGAGED	-0.002		-0.007	0.004	0.002	-0.015	-0.010
SET#9 IS R PREGNANT AT FOLLOW-UP?						**	*
YES	0.084		0.030	0.089	0.173	0.071	0.048
NO	-0.006		-0.001	-0.011	-0.017	-0.016	-0.008
DATA N.A. (1977-1983)	0.007		-0.002	0.034	0.042	0.068	0.028
SET#10 PARENTHOOD STATUS AT FOLLOW-UP			**			**	**
MARRIED PARENT	0.114		0.049	0.086	0.200	0.060	0.053
SINGLE PARENT	0.077		0.060	-0.048	0.030	0.007	0.038
NOT A PARENT	-0.040		-0.019	-0.021	-0.060	-0.018	-0.019
RELIGIOUS IMPORTANCE AT BASE YEAR (Cov.)[a]							0.575 **
Multiple R		0.102	0.127			0.299	0.627
R Sqr.		0.010	0.016			0.089	0.393

Notes: * indicates statistical significance at .05 level. ** indicates statistical significance at .01 level. Statistical significance is not indicated for bivariate coefficients or constants. Ns used for significance testing were weighted to approximate the number of individuals (not the number of observations) since each individual could contribute up to seven observations. Sets #5-#10 were measured at follow-up. Sets #3 and #4 were determined by timing of follow-up. All others were measured at Base Year (BY).

[a]Means for covariates: HIGH SCHOOL GRADES 6.332   URBANICITY 3.765
RELIGIOUS IMPORTANCE AT BASE YEAR 2.883   R WILL ATTEND 4YR COLLEGE 2.893

246

Table A.4.2b
Regression Analyses Linking Post-High School Experiences to Changes in Religious Importance
Males, Senior Years 1976-1997, Follow-ups 1977-1998

Regression Analyses Based on Full Set of Observations from Follow-Ups 1-7
(Wtd. N of Obs: 55,100)
Unstandardized Regression Coefficients

VARIABLE	Predicting to Change Scores — BIVARIATE COEFF.	Multivariate Coefficients — BKGD.	ALL SETS	Bivariate Coeff. With Dependent Variable — at BY	at FU	Multivariate Prediction of Dep. Var. at FU: Covarying BY Dep. Var? — No	Yes
CONSTANT	0.030	0.030	0.030	2.622	2.652	2.652	2.652
SET#1 RACE						**	**
WHITE	-0.004	-0.003	-0.004	-0.042	-0.047	-0.049	-0.022
BLACK	0.056	0.050	0.054	0.513	0.569	0.531	0.245
OTHER	0.002	-0.001	-0.002	0.051	0.053	0.105	0.041
SET#2 REGION						**	**
NORTHEAST	-0.019	-0.012	-0.004	-0.196	-0.215	-0.158	-0.065
NORTH CENTRAL	0.018	0.013	0.011	-0.045	-0.027	-0.016	0.000
SOUTH	-0.010	-0.017	-0.023	0.259	0.249	0.183	0.060
WEST	0.010	0.021	0.025	-0.119	-0.109	-0.086	-0.020
HIGH SCHOOL GRADES/D=1 (Cov.)*		-0.023 **	-0.023 **			0.024 **	-0.004
R WILL ATTEND 4YR COLLEGE (Cov.)*		-0.036 **	-0.029 **			0.018	-0.011
URBANICITY (Cov.)*		-0.007	-0.001			-0.079 **	-0.032 **
SET#3 FOLLOW-UP NUMBER							
FU #1	0.007	0.011	0.044	-0.009	-0.002	0.008	0.030
FU #2	-0.006	-0.004	0.024	-0.005	-0.011	0.012	0.019
FU #3	-0.019	-0.019	-0.010	-0.005	-0.024	-0.003	-0.007
FU #4	-0.017	-0.018	-0.029	0.000	-0.017	-0.009	-0.021
FU #5	0.003	0.001	-0.030	0.005	0.008	-0.009	-0.022
FU #6	0.025	0.021	-0.028	0.015	0.039	-0.007	-0.020
FU #7	0.031	0.025	-0.036	0.026	0.057	-0.007	-0.025
SET#4 ADMINISTRATION OF FIRST FOLLOW-UP							
ONE YEAR AFTER HIGH SCHOOL	-0.001	-0.001	0.002	0.018	0.017	0.016	0.007
TWO YEARS AFTER HIGH SCHOOL	0.001	0.001	-0.002	-0.020	-0.018	-0.017	-0.008
SET#5 STUDENT STATUS AT FOLLOW-UP							
FULL-TIME STUDENT	-0.049		-0.012	0.054	0.005	0.048	0.012
PART-TIME STUDENT	0.021		0.033	-0.033	-0.012	0.007	0.023
NOT A STUDENT	0.019		0.001	-0.019	0.000	-0.023	-0.009
SET#6 WORK STATUS AT FOLLOW-UP							
FULL-TIME CIVILIAN JOB	0.006		-0.011	-0.004	0.002	0.004	-0.005
MILITARY SERVICE	0.080		0.044	-0.054	0.026	-0.012	0.022
PART-TIME JOB	-0.037		0.001	0.038	0.001	0.008	0.004
HOMEMAKER	0.147		0.098	0.057	0.204	0.103	0.100
NONSTUDENT, NOT EMPLOYED	0.061		0.045	-0.081	-0.020	0.015	0.033
OTHER	-0.032		0.016	0.016	-0.015	-0.027	-0.001
SET#7 LIVING ARRANGEMENT AT FOLLOW-UP			**			**	**
MARRIED	0.106		0.104	0.083	0.189	0.180	0.134
PARTNER	-0.096		-0.123	-0.238	-0.334	-0.366	-0.220
PARENT(S)	-0.012		-0.031	-0.010	-0.022	-0.006	-0.021
DORM	-0.025		0.002	0.061	0.036	-0.015	-0.005
LIVE ALONE	-0.057		-0.025	-0.042	-0.099	-0.086	-0.050
OTHER	-0.070		-0.054	-0.029	-0.099	-0.082	-0.065
SET#8 ENGAGEMENT STATUS AT FOLLOW-UP			**			**	**
ENGAGED	0.028		0.096	-0.004	0.024	0.203	0.139
NOT ENGAGED	-0.002		-0.007	0.000	-0.002	-0.015	-0.010
SET#9 IS R'S SPS PREGNANT AT FOLLOW-UP?						*	
YES	0.081		-0.005	0.144	0.225	0.072	0.026
NO	-0.005		0.001	-0.011	-0.016	-0.012	-0.005
DATA N.A. (1977-1983)	0.006		-0.002	0.025	0.031	0.047	0.017
SET#10 PARENTHOOD STATUS AT FOLLOW-UP						*	
MARRIED PARENT	0.138		0.048	0.092	0.231	0.070	0.057
SINGLE PARENT	-0.008		0.012	-0.014	-0.022	0.012	0.012
NOT A PARENT	-0.028		-0.011	-0.018	-0.047	-0.015	-0.012
RELIGIOUS IMPORTANCE AT BASE YEAR (Cov.)*							0.599 **
Multiple R		0.087	0.122			0.273	0.629
R Sqr.		0.007	0.015			0.075	0.395

Notes: * indicates statistical significance at .05 level. ** indicates statistical significance at .01 level. Statistical significance is not indicated for bivariate coefficients or constants. Ns used for significance testing approximate the number of individuals (not the number of observations) since each individual could contribute up to seven observations. Sets #5-#10 were measured at follow-up. Sets #3 and #4 were determined by timing of follow-up. All others were measured at Base Year (BY).

*Means for covariates: HIGH SCHOOL GRADES 5.795 URBANICITY 3.747 RELIGIOUS IMPORTANCE AT BASE YEAR 2.622 R WILL ATTEND 4YR COLLEGE 2.902

Table A.5.1a
Regression Analyses Linking Post-High School Experiences to
Changes in Frequency of Evenings Out
Females, Senior Years 1976-1997, Follow-ups 1977-1998

Regression Analyses Based on Full Set of Observations from Follow-Ups 1-7 (Wtd. N of Obs: 68,803)

Unstandardized Regression Coefficients

VARIABLE	Predicting to Change Scores			Bivariate Coeff. With Dependent Variable		Multivariate Prediction of Dep. Var. at FU: Covarying BY Dep. Var?	
	BIVARIATE COEFF.	Multivariate Coefficients BKGD.	ALL SETS	at BY	at FU	No	Yes
CONSTANT	-0.692	-0.692	-0.692	3.403	2.711	2.711	2.711
SET#1 RACE		**	**			**	**
WHITE	-0.064	-0.052	-0.053	0.092	0.029	0.044	0.026
BLACK	0.272	0.250	0.247	-0.485	-0.213	-0.279	-0.181
OTHER	0.340	0.255	0.268	-0.407	-0.068	-0.148	-0.071
SET#2 REGION		**	**				*
NORTHEAST	-0.043	-0.028	-0.086	0.105	0.062	-0.019	-0.032
NORTH CENTRAL	-0.102	-0.050	-0.051	0.093	-0.010	-0.005	-0.014
SOUTH	0.061	0.020	0.050	-0.088	-0.027	0.030	0.034
WEST	0.140	0.097	0.122	-0.156	-0.016	-0.019	0.007
HIGH SCHOOL GRADES/D=1 (Cov.)[a]		0.044 **	0.033 **			-0.017 **	-0.008
R WILL ATTEND 4YR COLLEGE (Cov.)[a]		0.135 **	0.070 **			0.022 **	0.031 **
URBANICITY (Cov.)[a]		0.011	-0.019			0.059 **	0.045 **
SET#3 FOLLOW-UP NUMBER		**	**			**	**
FU #1	0.596	0.568	0.282	-0.018	0.577	0.379	0.361
FU #2	0.233	0.219	0.089	-0.005	0.229	0.125	0.119
FU #3	-0.032	-0.033	-0.050	-0.006	-0.038	-0.072	-0.068
FU #4	-0.214	-0.205	-0.106	0.003	-0.211	-0.148	-0.141
FU #5	-0.385	-0.366	-0.167	0.019	-0.365	-0.217	-0.208
FU #6	-0.532	-0.501	-0.207	0.017	-0.515	-0.282	-0.268
FU #7	-0.644	-0.605	-0.242	0.024	-0.619	-0.328	-0.312
SET#4 ADMINISTRATION OF FIRST FOLLOW-UP		**	**			**	**
ONE YEAR AFTER HIGH SCHOOL	0.071	0.068	0.038	-0.010	0.061	0.041	0.041
TWO YEARS AFTER HIGH SCHOOL	-0.077	-0.073	-0.041	0.010	-0.066	-0.044	-0.044
SET#5 STUDENT STATUS AT FOLLOW-UP			**			**	**
FULL-TIME STUDENT	0.453		-0.128	-0.114	0.339	-0.158	-0.153
PART-TIME STUDENT	0.080		0.001	-0.026	0.054	-0.012	-0.010
NOT A STUDENT	-0.206		0.055	0.053	-0.153	0.069	0.067
SET#6 WORK STATUS AT FOLLOW-UP			**			**	**
FULL-TIME CIVILIAN JOB	-0.054		0.005	0.035	-0.019	0.024	0.021
MILITARY SERVICE	0.545		0.472	-0.351	0.194	0.146	0.207
PART-TIME JOB	0.135		-0.048	-0.031	0.104	-0.042	-0.043
HOMEMAKER	-0.731		-0.019	0.068	-0.663	-0.088	-0.075
NONSTUDENT, NOT EMPLOYED	-0.257		-0.042	0.007	-0.250	-0.105	-0.093
OTHER	0.456		0.059	-0.110	0.346	0.049	0.051
SET#7 LIVING ARRANGEMENT AT FOLLOW-UP			**			**	**
MARRIED	-0.596		-0.330	0.077	-0.518	-0.268	-0.280
PARTNER	-0.297		-0.242	0.211	-0.085	-0.075	-0.106
PARENT(S)	0.450		0.252	-0.047	0.403	0.189	0.201
DORM	0.787		0.419	-0.204	0.583	0.260	0.290
LIVE ALONE	0.255		0.122	-0.159	0.097	0.036	0.052
OTHER	0.297		0.221	-0.045	0.253	0.210	0.212
SET#8 ENGAGEMENT STATUS AT FOLLOW-UP			**			**	**
ENGAGED	0.029		-0.152	0.108	0.137	-0.086	-0.098
NOT ENGAGED	-0.003		0.014	-0.010	-0.013	0.008	0.009
SET#9 IS R PREGNANT AT FOLLOW-UP?							*
YES	-0.511		-0.063	0.004	-0.508	-0.126	-0.114
NO	-0.016		0.008	-0.012	-0.028	0.004	0.004
DATA N.A. (1977-1983)	0.272		-0.025	0.069	0.342	0.022	0.014
SET#10 PARENTHOOD STATUS AT FOLLOW-UP			**			**	**
MARRIED PARENT	-0.888		-0.431	0.111	-0.776	-0.353	-0.368
SINGLE PARENT	-0.584		-0.649	0.083	-0.501	-0.483	-0.514
NOT A PARENT	0.306		0.180	-0.039	0.267	0.143	0.150
EVENINGS OUT AT BASE YEAR (Cov.)[a]							0.186 **
Multiple R		0.298	0.388			0.437	0.476
R Sqr.		0.089	0.150			0.191	0.226

Notes: * indicates statistical significance at .05 level. ** indicates statistical significance at .01 level. Statistical significance is not indicated for bivariate coefficients or constants. Ns used for significance testing were weighted to approximate the number of individuals (not the number of observations) since each individual could contribute up to seven observations. Sets #5-#10 were measured at follow-up. Sets #3 and #4 were determined by timing of follow-up. All others were measured at Base Year (BY).

[a] Means for covariates: HIGH SCHOOL GRADES 6.337 — URBANICITY 3.784 — FREQUENCY OF EVENINGS OUT AT BASE YEAR 3.403 — R WILL ATTEND 4YR COLLEGE 2.895

Table A.5.1b
Regression Analyses Linking Post-High School Experiences to Changes in Frequency of Evenings Out
Males, Senior Years 1976-1997, Follow-ups 1977-1998

Regression Analyses Based on Full Set of Observations from Follow-Ups 1-7 (Wtd. N of Obs: 54,802)
Unstandardized Regression Coefficients

VARIABLE	BIVARIATE COEFF.	Predicting to Change Scores Multivariate Coefficients BKGD.	ALL SETS	Bivariate Coeff. With Dependent Variable at BY	at FU	Multivariate Prediction of Dep. Var. at FU: Covarying BY Dep. Var? No	Yes
CONSTANT	-0.540	-0.540	-0.540	3.595	3.055	3.055	3.055
SET#1 RACE		*	*				**
WHITE	-0.030	-0.016	-0.016	0.027	-0.003	0.013	0.007
BLACK	0.112	0.087	0.084	-0.063	0.049	-0.038	-0.011
OTHER	0.206	0.091	0.098	-0.210	-0.004	-0.097	-0.054
SET#2 REGION		*	*				*
NORTHEAST	0.009	0.004	-0.043	0.069	0.078	0.019	0.005
NORTH CENTRAL	-0.085	-0.048	-0.035	0.064	-0.021	0.010	0.000
SOUTH	0.011	0.006	0.029	-0.029	-0.018	0.012	0.016
WEST	0.130	0.074	0.071	-0.160	-0.031	-0.065	-0.035
HIGH SCHOOL GRADES/D=1 (Cov.)[a]		0.030 **	0.027 **			-0.026 **	-0.014 *
R WILL ATTEND 4YR COLLEGE (Cov.)[a]		0.099 **	0.064 **			0.023 *	0.032 **
URBANICITY (Cov.)[a]		0.034 *	0.002			0.050 **	0.039 **
SET#3 FOLLOW-UP NUMBER		**	**			**	**
FU #1	0.586	0.573	0.342	0.004	0.591	0.440	0.418
FU #2	0.271	0.264	0.122	0.005	0.276	0.166	0.156
FU #3	0.019	0.017	-0.026	-0.007	0.012	-0.040	-0.037
FU #4	-0.239	-0.234	-0.159	0.005	-0.234	-0.194	-0.187
FU #5	-0.421	-0.411	-0.224	-0.001	-0.422	-0.287	-0.273
FU #6	-0.557	-0.542	-0.255	-0.003	-0.560	-0.336	-0.318
FU #7	-0.698	-0.680	-0.316	-0.014	-0.713	-0.426	-0.402
SET#4 ADMINISTRATION OF FIRST FOLLOW-UP		**	**			**	**
ONE YEAR AFTER HIGH SCHOOL	0.067	0.071	0.049	-0.024	0.043	0.036	0.039
TWO YEARS AFTER HIGH SCHOOL	-0.074	-0.077	-0.053	0.026	-0.047	-0.040	-0.043
SET#5 STUDENT STATUS AT FOLLOW-UP			**			**	**
FULL-TIME STUDENT	0.387		-0.118	-0.103	0.285	-0.155	-0.147
PART-TIME STUDENT	0.039		0.020	-0.053	-0.014	-0.021	-0.012
NOT A STUDENT	-0.181		0.051	0.054	-0.127	0.073	0.068
SET#6 WORK STATUS AT FOLLOW-UP							
FULL-TIME CIVILIAN JOB	-0.198		-0.020	0.039	-0.159	-0.011	-0.013
MILITARY SERVICE	0.107		0.150	-0.043	0.065	0.052	0.074
PART-TIME JOB	0.357		0.029	-0.089	0.268	0.002	0.008
HOMEMAKER	-0.272		-0.114	-0.020	-0.291	-0.164	-0.153
NONSTUDENT, NOT EMPLOYED	0.027		-0.049	0.105	0.131	-0.019	-0.026
OTHER	0.392		0.021	-0.080	0.313	0.034	0.031
SET#7 LIVING ARRANGEMENT AT FOLLOW-UP			**			**	**
MARRIED	-0.750		-0.412	0.044	-0.705	-0.367	-0.377
PARTNER	-0.303		-0.201	0.238	-0.066	-0.004	-0.048
PARENT(S)	0.387		0.206	0.002	0.389	0.166	0.175
DORM	0.633		0.291	-0.184	0.449	0.156	0.186
LIVE ALONE	0.113		0.119	-0.126	-0.013	0.034	0.053
OTHER	0.335		0.203	-0.018	0.317	0.223	0.218
SET#8 ENGAGEMENT STATUS AT FOLLOW-UP			**			**	**
ENGAGED	-0.101		-0.210	0.110	0.010	-0.179	-0.186
NOT ENGAGED	0.008		0.016	-0.008	-0.001	0.013	0.014
SET#9 IS R'S SPS PREGNANT AT FOLLOW-UP?							
YES	-0.608		0.026	0.027	-0.581	0.006	0.011
NO	-0.032		0.005	-0.005	-0.037	0.005	0.005
DATA N.A. (1977-1983)	0.299		-0.029	0.021	0.320	-0.029	-0.029
SET#10 PARENTHOOD STATUS AT FOLLOW-UP			**			**	**
MARRIED PARENT	-1.000		-0.415	0.081	-0.919	-0.360	-0.372
SINGLE PARENT	-0.342		-0.265	0.269	-0.072	-0.060	-0.105
NOT A PARENT	0.223		0.098	-0.030	0.194	0.077	0.082
EVENINGS OUT AT BASE YEAR (Cov.)[a]							0.221 **
Multiple R		0.290	0.364			0.422	0.473
R Sqr.		0.084	0.132			0.178	0.224

Notes: * indicates statistical significance at .05 level. ** indicates statistical significance at .01 level. Statistical significance is not indicated for bivariate coefficients or constants. Ns used for significance testing were weighted to approximate the number of individuals (not the number of observations) since each individual could contribute up to seven observations. Sets #5-#10 were measured at follow-up. Sets #3 and #4 were determined by timing of follow-up. All others were measured at Base Year (BY).
[a]Means for covariates: HIGH SCHOOL GRADES 5.802   URBANICITY 3.746
FREQUENCY OF EVENINGS OUT AT BASE YEAR 3.595   R WILL ATTEND 4YR COLLEGE 2.905

Table A.5.2a
Regression Analyses Linking Post-High School Experiences to Changes in Frequency of Dating
Females, Senior Years 1976-1997, Follow-ups 1977-1998

VARIABLE	BIVARIATE COEFF.	BKGD.	ALL SETS	at BY	at FU	No	Yes
		Predicting to Change Scores (Multivariate Coefficients)		Bivariate Coeff. With Dependent Variable		Multivariate Prediction of Dep. Var. at FU: Covarying BY Dep. Var?	
CONSTANT	-0.229	-0.229	-0.229	3.534	3.304	3.304	3.304
SET#1 RACE		**	**			**	**
WHITE	-0.033	-0.028	-0.038	0.093	0.060	0.058	0.039
BLACK	0.043	0.052	0.112	-0.522	-0.479	-0.420	-0.314
OTHER	0.275	0.220	0.251	-0.383	-0.108	-0.145	-0.066
SET#2 REGION		*	*			**	*
NORTHEAST	0.048	0.041	-0.032	0.028	0.076	0.018	0.008
NORTH CENTRAL	-0.051	-0.005	-0.002	0.031	-0.020	-0.029	-0.023
SOUTH	-0.046	-0.057	-0.023	0.037	-0.010	0.053	0.038
WEST	0.118	0.061	0.088	-0.164	-0.046	-0.067	-0.036
HIGH SCHOOL GRADES/D=1 (Cov.)*		0.034 **	0.020 *			-0.002	0.002
R WILL ATTEND 4YR COLLEGE (Cov.)*		0.196 **	0.135 **			0.026 **	0.048 **
URBANICITY (Cov.)*		0.037 *	0.002			0.071 **	0.057 **
SET#3 FOLLOW-UP NUMBER		**				**	**
FU #1	0.278	0.247	-0.101	-0.008	0.269	0.270	0.197
FU #2	0.207	0.190	-0.011	0.008	0.215	0.157	0.124
FU #3	0.083	0.080	0.017	0.007	0.091	0.006	0.008
FU #4	-0.073	-0.063	0.049	0.006	-0.067	-0.106	-0.075
FU #5	-0.230	-0.208	0.058	0.001	-0.228	-0.194	-0.144
FU #6	-0.398	-0.363	0.057	-0.007	-0.406	-0.281	-0.214
FU #7	-0.542	-0.498	0.038	-0.016	-0.559	-0.365	-0.285
SET#4 ADMINISTRATION OF FIRST FOLLOW-UP		*				**	*
ONE YEAR AFTER HIGH SCHOOL	0.039	0.035	-0.003	-0.009	0.030	0.027	0.021
TWO YEARS AFTER HIGH SCHOOL	-0.042	-0.037	0.003	0.010	-0.032	-0.029	-0.022
SET#5 STUDENT STATUS AT FOLLOW-UP						**	**
FULL-TIME STUDENT	0.321		-0.066	-0.198	0.123	-0.023	-0.031
PART-TIME STUDENT	0.132		-0.032	-0.008	0.124	0.013	0.004
NOT A STUDENT	-0.156		0.033	0.086	-0.071	0.008	0.013
SET#6 WORK STATUS AT FOLLOW-UP			*			**	**
FULL-TIME CIVILIAN JOB	0.052		0.014	0.033	0.085	0.067	0.057
MILITARY SERVICE	0.572		0.567	-0.418	0.154	0.129	0.216
PART-TIME JOB	0.049		-0.049	-0.023	0.026	-0.042	-0.043
HOMEMAKER	-0.881		-0.053	0.336	-0.545	-0.126	-0.111
NONSTUDENT, NOT EMPLOYED	-0.302		-0.021	-0.022	-0.324	-0.185	-0.152
OTHER	0.274		0.032	-0.250	0.024	-0.072	-0.051
SET#7 LIVING ARRANGEMENT AT FOLLOW-UP			**			**	**
MARRIED	-0.529		-0.113	0.350	-0.179	0.322	0.236
PARTNER	0.161		-0.013	0.265	0.426	0.101	0.079
PARENT(S)	0.374		0.149	-0.193	0.181	-0.158	-0.097
DORM	0.386		0.070	-0.426	-0.040	-0.450	-0.347
LIVE ALONE	0.331		-0.055	-0.421	-0.090	-0.265	-0.223
OTHER	0.204		0.016	-0.255	-0.051	-0.211	-0.166
SET#8 ENGAGEMENT STATUS AT FOLLOW-UP			**			**	**
ENGAGED	0.499		0.271	0.307	0.805	0.655	0.578
NOT ENGAGED	-0.048		-0.026	-0.029	-0.077	-0.062	-0.055
SET#9 IS R PREGNANT AT FOLLOW-UP?			**			**	**
YES	-0.395		-0.038	0.233	-0.163	-0.076	-0.068
NO	-0.031		-0.034	-0.010	-0.041	-0.014	-0.018
DATA N.A. (1977-1983)	0.324		0.214	-0.025	0.299	0.111	0.132
SET#10 PARENTHOOD STATUS AT FOLLOW-UP			**			**	**
MARRIED PARENT	-1.060		-0.884	0.416	-0.644	-0.693	-0.731
SINGLE PARENT	-0.747		-0.803	0.167	-0.581	-0.336	-0.429
NOT A PARENT	0.373		0.326	-0.135	0.237	0.231	0.250
DATING AT BASE YEAR (Cov.)*							0.198 **
Multiple R		0.201	0.340			0.371	0.433
R Sqr.		0.040	0.116			0.138	0.187

Regression Analyses Based on Full Set of Observations from Follow-Ups 1-7 (Wtd. N of Obs: 68,098) Unstandardized Regression Coefficients

Notes: * indicates statistical significance at .05 level. ** indicates statistical significance at .01 level. Statistical significance is not indicated for bivariate coefficients or constants. Ns used for significance testing were weighted to approximate the number of individuals (not the number of observations) since each individual could contribute up to seven observations. Sets #5-#10 were measured at follow-up. Sets #3 and #4 were determined by timing of follow-up. All others were measured at Base Year (BY).

*Means for covariates:

HIGH SCHOOL GRADES	6.337	URBANICITY	3.762
FREQUENCY OF DATING AT BASE YEAR	3.534	R WILL ATTEND 4YR COLLEGE	2.894

Table A.5.2b
Regression Analyses Linking Post-High School Experiences to Changes in Frequency of Dating
Males, Senior Years 1976-1997, Follow-ups 1977-1998

Regression Analyses Based on Full Set of Observations from Follow-Ups 1-7
(Wtd. N of Obs: 53,952)
Unstandardized Regression Coefficients

VARIABLE	Predicting to Change Scores BIVARIATE COEFF.	Multivariate Coefficients BKGD.	ALL SETS	Bivariate Coeff. With Dependent Variable at BY	at FU	Multivariate Prediction of Dep. Var. at FU: Covarying BY Dep. Var? No	Yes
CONSTANT	0.013	0.013	0.013	3.307	3.319	3.319	3.319
SET#1 RACE		**	**				**
WHITE	-0.029	-0.026	-0.032	0.055	0.026	0.024	0.011
BLACK	0.153	0.183	0.251	-0.312	-0.159	-0.136	-0.045
OTHER	0.172	0.127	0.138	-0.308	-0.137	-0.133	-0.069
SET#2 REGION						**	**
NORTHEAST	0.036	0.030	-0.020	0.054	0.090	0.064	0.045
NORTH CENTRAL	-0.037	-0.010	0.004	0.013	-0.024	-0.025	-0.019
SOUTH	-0.043	-0.049	-0.030	0.067	0.024	0.043	0.026
WEST	0.099	0.066	0.072	-0.213	-0.114	-0.112	-0.069
HIGH SCHOOL GRADES/D=1 (Cov.)[a]		0.029 **	0.027 **			-0.008	0.000
R WILL ATTEND 4YR COLLEGE (Cov.)[a]		0.037 *	0.012			0.038 **	0.032 **
URBANICITY (Cov.)[a]		0.032 *	0.004			0.043 **	0.034 **
SET#3 FOLLOW-UP NUMBER		**				**	**
FU #1	0.090	0.080	-0.083	-0.019	0.072	0.207	0.139
FU #2	0.125	0.120	0.001	-0.003	0.122	0.153	0.118
FU #3	0.078	0.077	0.005	0.009	0.087	0.023	0.019
FU #4	0.004	0.008	0.029	0.027	0.032	-0.075	-0.051
FU #5	-0.091	-0.084	0.055	0.015	-0.076	-0.159	-0.109
FU #6	-0.233	-0.223	0.038	-0.001	-0.234	-0.267	-0.195
FU #7	-0.336	-0.324	0.045	-0.028	-0.365	-0.341	-0.250
SET#4 ADMINISTRATION OF FIRST FOLLOW-UP							
ONE YEAR AFTER HIGH SCHOOL	0.003	0.002	-0.016	0.002	0.004	0.016	0.008
TWO YEARS AFTER HIGH SCHOOL	-0.003	-0.002	0.018	-0.002	-0.005	-0.017	-0.009
SET#5 STUDENT STATUS AT FOLLOW-UP							
FULL-TIME STUDENT	0.089		-0.059	-0.091	-0.002	-0.011	-0.022
PART-TIME STUDENT	0.094		0.031	-0.031	0.063	0.015	0.018
NOT A STUDENT	-0.054		0.022	0.046	-0.009	0.003	0.007
SET#6 WORK STATUS AT FOLLOW-UP						**	**
FULL-TIME CIVILIAN JOB	-0.028		0.018	0.076	0.048	0.077	0.063
MILITARY SERVICE	-0.148		-0.048	-0.004	-0.151	-0.173	-0.144
PART-TIME JOB	0.151		0.028	-0.123	0.027	-0.050	-0.032
HOMEMAKER	-0.255		-0.056	-0.332	-0.587	-0.498	-0.395
NONSTUDENT, NOT EMPLOYED	-0.097		-0.149	-0.156	-0.253	-0.231	-0.211
OTHER	0.036		-0.044	-0.127	-0.091	-0.131	-0.110
SET#7 LIVING ARRANGEMENT AT FOLLOW-UP			**			**	**
MARRIED	-0.405		0.009	0.333	-0.072	0.452	0.348
PARTNER	0.344		0.113	0.289	0.633	0.285	0.245
PARENT(S)	0.231		0.069	-0.192	0.039	-0.209	-0.144
DORM	0.076		-0.015	-0.206	-0.129	-0.366	-0.283
LIVE ALONE	0.095		-0.113	-0.249	-0.154	-0.256	-0.223
OTHER	0.064		-0.098	-0.114	-0.049	-0.198	-0.175
SET#8 ENGAGEMENT STATUS AT FOLLOW-UP			**			**	**
ENGAGED	0.543		0.378	0.332	0.874	0.739	0.654
NOT ENGAGED	-0.041		-0.028	-0.025	-0.066	-0.056	-0.049
SET#9 IS R'S SPS PREGNANT AT FOLLOW-UP?							
YES	-0.273		0.027	0.243	-0.030	-0.030	-0.016
NO	-0.014		-0.012	0.000	-0.013	0.001	-0.002
DATA N.A. (1977-1983)	0.132		0.054	-0.057	0.075	0.003	0.015
SET#10 PARENTHOOD STATUS AT FOLLOW-UP			**			**	**
MARRIED PARENT	-0.859		-0.878	0.376	-0.483	-0.728	-0.763
SINGLE PARENT	-0.288		-0.416	0.271	-0.017	0.000	-0.097
NOT A PARENT	0.193		0.203	-0.092	0.102	0.152	0.164
DATING AT BASE YEAR (Cov.)[a]							0.234 **
Multiple R		0.107	0.247			0.301	0.394
R Sqr.		0.011	0.061			0.091	0.155

Notes: * indicates statistical significance at .05 level. ** indicates statistical significance at .01 level. Statistical significance is not indicated for bivariate coefficients or constants. Ns used for significance testing were weighted to approximate the number of individuals (not the number of observations) since each individual could contribute up to seven observations. Sets #5-#10 were measured at follow-up. Sets #3 and #4 were determined by timing of follow-up. All others were measured at Base Year (BY).

[a]Means for covariates:	HIGH SCHOOL GRADES	5.812		URBANICITY	3.743
	FREQUENCY OF DATING AT BASE YEAR	3.307		R WILL ATTEND 4YR COLLEGE	2.906

Table A.5.3a
Regression Analyses Linking Post-High School Experiences to Changes in Frequency of Attending Parties or Other Social Affairs
Females, Senior Years 1976-1997, Follow-ups 1977-1998

Regression Analyses Based on Full Set of Observations from Follow-Ups 1-7
(Wtd. N of Obs: 13,417)
Unstandardized Regression Coefficients

VARIABLE	BIVARIATE COEFF.	Predicting to Change Scores — Multivariate Coefficients BKGD.	Predicting to Change Scores — Multivariate Coefficients ALL SETS	Bivariate Coeff. With Dependent Variable at BY	Bivariate Coeff. With Dependent Variable at FU	Multivariate Prediction of Dep. Var. at FU: Covarying BY Dep. Var? No	Multivariate Prediction of Dep. Var. at FU: Covarying BY Dep. Var? Yes
CONSTANT	-0.481	-0.481	-0.481	3.009	2.528	2.528	2.528
SET#1 RACE			**			**	*
WHITE	-0.014	-0.018	-0.019	0.040	0.026	0.028	0.016
BLACK	0.015	0.071	0.056	-0.170	-0.156	-0.152	-0.097
OTHER	0.112	0.091	0.108	-0.187	-0.076	-0.095	-0.041
SET#2 REGION			**			**	**
NORTHEAST	0.007	0.012	-0.014	0.085	0.091	0.036	0.023
NORTH CENTRAL	-0.034	-0.020	-0.024	0.093	0.059	0.055	0.034
SOUTH	-0.004	-0.017	0.001	-0.123	-0.127	-0.087	-0.064
WEST	0.062	0.053	0.064	-0.066	-0.005	0.007	0.022
HIGH SCHOOL GRADES/D=1 (Cov.)[a]		0.073 **	0.062 **			-0.019 *	0.003
R WILL ATTEND 4YR COLLEGE (Cov.)[a]		0.055 **	0.009			0.069 **	0.053 **
URBANICITY (Cov.)[a]		0.002	-0.014			0.046 **	0.030 *
SET#3 FOLLOW-UP NUMBER		**	**			**	**
FU #1	0.362	0.353	0.143	-0.004	0.358	0.196	0.182
FU #2	0.171	0.166	0.076	0.000	0.170	0.082	0.080
FU #3	-0.046	-0.045	-0.017	0.012	-0.033	-0.021	-0.020
FU #4	-0.155	-0.153	-0.065	0.009	-0.147	-0.082	-0.078
FU #5	-0.215	-0.208	-0.081	-0.005	-0.220	-0.117	-0.107
FU #6	-0.287	-0.281	-0.122	0.006	-0.281	-0.139	-0.134
FU #7	-0.331	-0.322	-0.141	-0.029	-0.360	-0.186	-0.174
SET#4 ADMINISTRATION OF FIRST FOLLOW-UP		*					
ONE YEAR AFTER HIGH SCHOOL	0.037	0.033	0.015	0.002	0.039	0.020	0.018
TWO YEARS AFTER HIGH SCHOOL	-0.040	-0.035	-0.016	-0.002	-0.042	-0.021	-0.020
SET#5 STUDENT STATUS AT FOLLOW-UP							
FULL-TIME STUDENT	0.400		0.080	-0.009	0.390	0.061	0.066
PART-TIME STUDENT	-0.045		-0.035	-0.006	-0.051	-0.068	-0.059
NOT A STUDENT	-0.160		-0.028	0.005	-0.156	-0.015	-0.019
SET#6 WORK STATUS AT FOLLOW-UP							
FULL-TIME CIVILIAN JOB	-0.099		-0.012	0.028	-0.072	0.011	0.005
MILITARY SERVICE	0.381		0.337	-0.245	0.135	0.045	0.123
PART-TIME JOB	0.141		-0.005	-0.017	0.123	-0.014	-0.012
HOMEMAKER	-0.390		-0.080	0.005	-0.385	-0.062	-0.067
NONSTUDENT, NOT EMPLOYED	-0.102		0.066	-0.173	-0.275	-0.117	-0.068
OTHER	0.402		0.061	-0.011	0.391	0.053	0.055
SET#7 LIVING ARRANGEMENT AT FOLLOW-UP			**			**	**
MARRIED	-0.281		-0.145	-0.034	-0.314	-0.154	-0.152
PARTNER	-0.264		-0.186	0.217	-0.048	0.014	-0.039
PARENT(S)	0.151		0.070	-0.065	0.086	-0.022	0.002
DORM	0.692		0.354	-0.020	0.672	0.316	0.326
LIVE ALONE	0.061		0.045	-0.022	0.039	0.039	0.040
OTHER	0.184		0.130	0.106	0.290	0.233	0.206
SET#8 ENGAGEMENT STATUS AT FOLLOW-UP			*			**	**
ENGAGED	-0.091		-0.134	0.050	-0.041	-0.140	-0.138
NOT ENGAGED	0.008		0.011	-0.004	0.004	0.012	0.012
SET#9 IS R PREGNANT AT FOLLOW-UP?							
YES	-0.314		-0.072	0.028	-0.286	-0.048	-0.054
NO	-0.018		0.002	0.002	-0.016	0.001	0.001
DATA N.A. (1977-1983)	0.200		0.014	-0.019	0.181	0.010	0.011
SET#10 PARENTHOOD STATUS AT FOLLOW-UP			**			**	**
MARRIED PARENT	-0.384		-0.116	-0.040	-0.424	-0.110	-0.111
SINGLE PARENT	-0.284		-0.208	0.022	-0.262	-0.202	-0.203
NOT A PARENT	0.134		0.050	0.010	0.144	0.048	0.048
ATTENDING PARTIES AT BASE YEAR (Cov.)[a]							0.265 **
Multiple R		0.302	0.361			0.459	0.539
R Sqr.		0.091	0.130			0.211	0.291

Notes: * indicates statistical significance at .05 level. ** indicates statistical significance at .01 level. Statistical significance is not indicated for bivariate coefficients or constants. Ns used for significance testing were weighted to approximate the number of individuals (not the number of observations) since each individual could contribute up to seven observations. Sets #5-#10 were measured at follow-up. Sets #3 and #4 were determined by timing of follow-up. All others were measured at Base Year (BY).

[a]Means for covariates: HIGH SCHOOL GRADES 6.329   URBANICITY 3.764
                          FREQUENCY OF ATTENDING PARTIES AT BASE YEAR 3.009   R WILL ATTEND 4YR COLLEGE 2.897

Table A.5.3b
Regression Analyses Linking Post-High School Experiences to
Changes in Frequency of Attending Parties or Other Social Affairs
Males, Senior Years 1976-1997, Follow-ups 1977-1998

VARIABLE	BIVARIATE COEFF.	Predicting to Change Scores — Multivariate Coefficients — BKGD.	ALL SETS	Bivariate Coeff. With Dependent Variable at BY	at FU	Multivariate Prediction of Dep. Var. at FU: Covarying BY Dep. Var? No	Yes
CONSTANT	-0.477	-0.477	-0.477	3.114	2.638	2.638	2.638
SET#1 RACE							
WHITE	-0.008	-0.005	-0.005	0.009	0.001	0.005	0.003
BLACK	0.032	0.024	0.013	-0.020	0.011	-0.010	-0.004
OTHER	0.053	0.032	0.034	-0.068	-0.015	-0.039	-0.021
SET#2 REGION							**
NORTHEAST	-0.032	-0.025	-0.050	0.137	0.104	0.066	0.037
NORTH CENTRAL	-0.066	-0.049	-0.046	0.079	0.013	0.035	0.014
SOUTH	0.054	0.049	0.064	-0.149	-0.095	-0.072	-0.038
WEST	0.071	0.037	0.039	-0.060	0.010	-0.023	-0.008
HIGH SCHOOL GRADES/D=1 (Cov.)*		0.058 **	0.049 **			-0.017	-0.001
R WILL ATTEND 4YR COLLEGE (Cov.)*		0.053 **	0.013			0.072 **	0.057 **
URBANICITY (Cov.)*		-0.006	-0.017			0.048 **	0.032 *
SET#3 FOLLOW-UP NUMBER			**	**		**	**
FU #1	0.352	0.342	0.159	0.005	0.357	0.222	0.206
FU #2	0.215	0.211	0.109	0.006	0.221	0.127	0.122
FU #3	-0.039	-0.041	-0.030	0.020	-0.018	-0.019	-0.022
FU #4	-0.162	-0.159	-0.079	0.006	-0.156	-0.093	-0.090
FU #5	-0.261	-0.254	-0.125	0.008	-0.253	-0.157	-0.149
FU #6	-0.323	-0.312	-0.146	-0.035	-0.358	-0.211	-0.195
FU #7	-0.324	-0.313	-0.127	-0.051	-0.375	-0.212	-0.191
SET#4 ADMINISTRATION OF FIRST FOLLOW-UP							
ONE YEAR AFTER HIGH SCHOOL	0.012	0.014	-0.003	0.013	0.025	0.021	0.015
TWO YEARS AFTER HIGH SCHOOL	-0.013	-0.015	0.003	-0.014	-0.027	-0.023	-0.016
SET#5 STUDENT STATUS AT FOLLOW-UP							
FULL-TIME STUDENT	0.368		0.027	0.004	0.371	0.051	0.045
PART-TIME STUDENT	-0.060		-0.058	0.042	-0.018	-0.022	-0.031
NOT A STUDENT	-0.147		-0.003	-0.007	-0.154	-0.018	-0.015
SET#6 WORK STATUS AT FOLLOW-UP							
FULL-TIME CIVILIAN JOB	-0.165		-0.045	0.019	-0.146	-0.007	-0.016
MILITARY SERVICE	0.138		0.156	-0.105	0.033	0.022	0.055
PART-TIME JOB	0.241		0.034	-0.040	0.201	-0.031	-0.015
HOMEMAKER	-0.119		0.008	0.178	0.059	0.159	0.122
NONSTUDENT, NOT EMPLOYED	-0.081		-0.067	-0.053	-0.133	-0.110	-0.099
OTHER	0.420		0.123	0.009	0.428	0.082	0.092
SET#7 LIVING ARRANGEMENT AT FOLLOW-UP			**			**	**
MARRIED	-0.352		-0.182	-0.048	-0.400	-0.189	-0.187
PARTNER	-0.207		-0.079	0.148	-0.060	0.033	0.006
PARENT(S)	0.114		0.049	-0.029	0.085	-0.018	-0.002
DORM	0.612		0.272	-0.040	0.572	0.222	0.235
LIVE ALONE	0.002		0.036	-0.038	-0.036	0.014	0.019
OTHER	0.205		0.111	0.099	0.304	0.215	0.189
SET#8 ENGAGEMENT STATUS AT FOLLOW-UP			*			**	**
ENGAGED	-0.157		-0.176	0.045	-0.112	-0.183	-0.182
NOT ENGAGED	0.012		0.013	-0.003	0.008	0.014	0.014
SET#9 IS R'S SPS PREGNANT AT FOLLOW-UP?							
YES	-0.276		-0.005	-0.076	-0.353	-0.048	-0.037
NO	-0.034		-0.009	0.007	-0.028	-0.002	-0.004
DATA N.A. (1977-1983)	0.234		0.045	-0.015	0.219	0.023	0.029
SET#10 PARENTHOOD STATUS AT FOLLOW-UP							*
MARRIED PARENT	-0.435		-0.116	-0.053	-0.488	-0.107	-0.109
SINGLE PARENT	-0.241		-0.128	0.174	-0.067	0.034	-0.006
NOT A PARENT	0.108		0.032	0.003	0.110	0.022	0.024
ATTENDING PARTIES AT BASE YEAR (Cov.)*							0.248 **
Multiple R		0.286	0.332			0.439	0.517
R Sqr.		0.082	0.110			0.192	0.268

Notes: * indicates statistical significance at .05 level. ** indicates statistical significance at .01 level. Statistical significance is not indicated for bivariate coefficients or constants. Ns used for significance testing were weighted to approximate the number of individuals (not the number of observations) since each individual could contribute up to seven observations. Sets #5–#10 were measured at follow-up. Sets #3 and #4 were determined by timing of follow-up. All others were measured at Base Year (BY).

[a]Means for covariates: HIGH SCHOOL GRADES 5.808   URBANICITY 3.750
FREQUENCY OF ATTENDING PARTIES AT BASE YEAR 3.114   R WILL ATTEND 4YR COLLEGE 2.883

Table A.5.4a
Regression Analyses Linking Post-High School Experiences to Changes in Frequency of Getting Together With Friends Informally
Females, Senior Years 1976-1997, Follow-ups 1977-1998

VARIABLE	BIVARIATE COEFF.	Predicting to Change Scores — Multivariate Coefficients BKGD.	Predicting to Change Scores — Multivariate Coefficients ALL SETS	Bivariate Coeff. With Dependent Variable at BY	Bivariate Coeff. With Dependent Variable at FU	Multivariate Prediction of Dep. Var. at FU: Covarying BY Dep. Var? No	Multivariate Prediction of Dep. Var. at FU: Covarying BY Dep. Var? Yes
CONSTANT	-0.587	-0.587	-0.587	4.259	3.672	3.672	3.672
SET#1 RACE						**	**
WHITE	-0.010	-0.009	-0.011	0.041	0.030	0.039	0.029
BLACK	-0.002	0.022	0.003	-0.117	-0.119	-0.168	-0.131
OTHER	0.095	0.062	0.091	-0.245	-0.151	-0.182	-0.123
SET#2 REGION							
NORTHEAST	0.046	0.052	0.027	0.024	0.070	0.022	0.023
NORTH CENTRAL	-0.031	-0.019	-0.025	0.038	0.008	-0.003	-0.008
SOUTH	-0.011	-0.022	-0.002	-0.043	-0.054	-0.022	-0.017
WEST	0.014	0.005	0.013	-0.026	-0.012	0.016	0.015
HIGH SCHOOL GRADES/D=1 (Cov.)[a]		0.040 **	0.027 *			-0.037 **	-0.023 **
R WILL ATTEND 4YR COLLEGE (Cov.)[a]		0.043 **	-0.014			0.031 *	0.021
URBANICITY (Cov.)[a]		0.002	-0.014			0.017	0.010
SET#3 FOLLOW-UP NUMBER		**	**			**	**
FU #1	0.461	0.455	0.219	-0.004	0.458	0.248	0.242
FU #2	0.196	0.193	0.094	0.003	0.199	0.105	0.102
FU #3	-0.051	-0.050	-0.014	0.007	-0.044	-0.019	-0.018
FU #4	-0.169	-0.167	-0.069	0.005	-0.164	-0.080	-0.077
FU #5	-0.273	-0.268	-0.128	-0.013	-0.286	-0.158	-0.152
FU #6	-0.381	-0.377	-0.204	0.011	-0.370	-0.207	-0.206
FU #7	-0.415	-0.409	-0.214	-0.013	-0.428	-0.238	-0.233
SET#4 ADMINISTRATION OF FIRST FOLLOW-UP							
ONE YEAR AFTER HIGH SCHOOL	0.021	0.018	-0.001	0.024	0.046	0.025	0.020
TWO YEARS AFTER HIGH SCHOOL	-0.023	-0.020	0.001	-0.026	-0.049	-0.027	-0.021
SET#5 STUDENT STATUS AT FOLLOW-UP							
FULL-TIME STUDENT	0.449		0.049	-0.026	0.423	0.025	0.031
PART-TIME STUDENT	-0.031		0.008	-0.012	-0.043	-0.029	-0.021
NOT A STUDENT	-0.183		-0.022	0.013	-0.170	-0.006	-0.010
SET#6 WORK STATUS AT FOLLOW-UP							
FULL-TIME CIVILIAN JOB	-0.146		-0.049	0.030	-0.117	-0.021	-0.027
MILITARY SERVICE	0.477		0.408	-0.304	0.173	0.078	0.149
PART-TIME JOB	0.179		0.029	-0.023	0.156	0.013	0.017
HOMEMAKER	-0.278		0.078	-0.002	-0.279	0.073	0.074
NONSTUDENT, NOT EMPLOYED	-0.095		0.074	-0.101	-0.196	-0.049	-0.023
OTHER	0.461		0.064	-0.031	0.430	0.040	0.045
SET#7 LIVING ARRANGEMENT AT FOLLOW-UP			**			**	**
MARRIED	-0.345		-0.205	-0.022	-0.367	-0.226	-0.222
PARTNER	-0.176		-0.094	0.134	-0.042	0.016	-0.007
PARENT(S)	0.130		0.018	-0.011	0.119	0.000	0.004
DORM	0.885		0.548	-0.022	0.863	0.548	0.548
LIVE ALONE	0.048		0.088	-0.012	0.036	0.087	0.087
OTHER	0.238		0.201	0.023	0.261	0.230	0.224
SET#8 ENGAGEMENT STATUS AT FOLLOW-UP			*			*	**
ENGAGED	-0.070		-0.154	0.060	-0.009	-0.133	-0.138
NOT ENGAGED	0.006		0.013	-0.005	0.001	0.011	0.012
SET#9 IS R PREGNANT AT FOLLOW-UP?							
YES	-0.347		-0.067	0.015	-0.332	-0.059	-0.061
NO	-0.023		0.006	-0.004	-0.026	0.001	0.002
DATA N.A. (1977-1983)	0.238		-0.010	0.015	0.253	0.015	0.009
SET#10 PARENTHOOD STATUS AT FOLLOW-UP			**			**	**
MARRIED PARENT	-0.434		-0.126	-0.014	-0.448	-0.098	-0.104
SINGLE PARENT	-0.237		-0.214	0.024	-0.213	-0.195	-0.199
NOT A PARENT	0.145		0.053	0.002	0.147	0.044	0.046
GETTING TOGETHER W/ FRIENDS AT BASE YEAR (Cov.)[a]							0.215 **
Multiple R		0.305	0.376			0.457	0.495
R Sqr.		0.093	0.141			0.209	0.245

Regression Analyses Based on Full Set of Observations from Follow-Ups 1-7 (Wtd. N of Obs: 13,381). Unstandardized Regression Coefficients.

Notes: * indicates statistical significance at .05 level. ** indicates statistical significance at .01 level. Statistical significance is not indicated for bivariate coefficients or constants. Ns used for significance testing were weighted to approximate the number of individuals (not the number of observations) since each individual could contribute up to seven observations. Sets #5-#10 were measured at follow-up. Sets #3 and #4 were determined by timing of follow-up. All others were measured at Base Year (BY).

[a] Means for covariates: HIGH SCHOOL GRADES 6.331   URBANICITY 3.763
FREQUENCY OF GETTING TOGETHER W/FRIENDS AT BASE YEAR 4.259   R WILL ATTEND 4YR COLLEGE 2.898

Table A.5.4b
Regression Analyses Linking Post-High School Experiences to Changes in Frequency of Getting Together With Friends Informally
Males, Senior Years 1976-1997, Follow-ups 1977-1998

	Regression Analyses Based on Full Set of Observations from Follow-Ups 1-7 (Wtd. N of Obs: 10,705) Unstandardized Regression Coefficients						
	Predicting to Change Scores			Bivariate Coeff. With Dependent Variable		Multivariate Prediction of Dep. Var. at FU: Covarying BY Dep. Var?	
	BIVARIATE	Multivariate Coefficients					
VARIABLE	COEFF.	BKGD.	ALL SETS	at BY	at FU	No	Yes
CONSTANT	-0.545	-0.545	-0.545	4.372	3.827	3.827	3.827
SET#1 RACE							*
WHITE	-0.004	-0.004	-0.002	0.011	0.007	0.015	0.011
BLACK	-0.029	-0.023	-0.033	0.075	0.046	-0.008	-0.013
OTHER	0.060	0.052	0.046	-0.155	-0.095	-0.135	-0.099
SET#2 REGION							
NORTHEAST	0.038	0.037	0.006	0.036	0.075	0.033	0.027
NORTH CENTRAL	0.007	0.028	0.031	-0.029	-0.022	-0.005	0.002
SOUTH	-0.021	-0.019	0.000	-0.001	-0.021	0.000	0.000
WEST	-0.025	-0.066	-0.065	0.011	-0.015	-0.032	-0.039
HIGH SCHOOL GRADES/D=1 (Cov.)[a]		0.043 **	0.034 **			-0.015	-0.005
R WILL ATTEND 4YR COLLEGE (Cov.)[a]		0.036	-0.012			0.023	0.016
URBANICITY (Cov.)[a]		0.024	0.008			0.037 *	0.031 *
SET#3 FOLLOW-UP NUMBER		**	**			**	**
FU #1	0.438	0.435	0.237	0.004	0.443	0.254	0.250
FU #2	0.275	0.273	0.162	-0.001	0.275	0.158	0.159
FU #3	0.007	0.005	0.003	0.016	0.023	0.017	0.015
FU #4	-0.197	-0.196	-0.117	0.010	-0.187	-0.108	-0.110
FU #5	-0.304	-0.301	-0.159	-0.003	-0.307	-0.169	-0.167
FU #6	-0.449	-0.443	-0.247	-0.017	-0.465	-0.268	-0.264
FU #7	-0.521	-0.515	-0.296	-0.039	-0.559	-0.339	-0.331
SET#4 ADMINISTRATION OF FIRST FOLLOW-UP							
ONE YEAR AFTER HIGH SCHOOL	0.024	0.030	0.013	-0.011	0.013	0.007	0.008
TWO YEARS AFTER HIGH SCHOOL	-0.026	-0.033	-0.014	0.012	-0.015	-0.008	-0.009
SET#5 STUDENT STATUS AT FOLLOW-UP							
FULL-TIME STUDENT	0.399		-0.010	0.004	0.403	0.037	0.028
PART-TIME STUDENT	-0.024		-0.017	0.006	-0.018	-0.016	-0.016
NOT A STUDENT	-0.165		0.006	-0.003	-0.167	-0.013	-0.009
SET#6 WORK STATUS AT FOLLOW-UP							
FULL-TIME CIVILIAN JOB	-0.183		-0.040	0.002	-0.181	-0.026	-0.029
MILITARY SERVICE	-0.039		-0.025	0.083	0.045	0.039	0.027
PART-TIME JOB	0.331		0.083	-0.043	0.288	0.024	0.036
HOMEMAKER	-0.073		0.086	0.021	-0.052	0.075	0.078
NONSTUDENT, NOT EMPLOYED	0.089		0.062	-0.022	0.067	0.044	0.048
OTHER	0.413		0.070	0.012	0.426	0.056	0.058
SET#7 LIVING ARRANGEMENT AT FOLLOW-UP			**			**	**
MARRIED	-0.505		-0.293	-0.010	-0.515	-0.288	-0.289
PARTNER	-0.195		-0.081	0.099	-0.096	0.010	-0.008
PARENT(S)	0.210		0.084	-0.022	0.188	0.052	0.058
DORM	0.694		0.373	-0.045	0.649	0.319	0.330
LIVE ALONE	0.024		0.085	-0.034	-0.009	0.061	0.066
OTHER	0.248		0.168	0.049	0.296	0.209	0.201
SET#8 ENGAGEMENT STATUS AT FOLLOW-UP			*			**	**
ENGAGED	-0.095		-0.164	0.020	-0.075	-0.179	-0.176
NOT ENGAGED	0.007		0.012	-0.001	0.006	0.013	0.013
SET#9 IS R'S SPS PREGNANT AT FOLLOW-UP?							
YES	-0.453		-0.051	0.006	-0.447	-0.050	-0.050
NO	-0.026		0.009	-0.006	-0.033	0.003	0.004
DATA N.A. (1977-1983)	0.236		-0.034	0.029	0.266	-0.003	-0.009
SET#10 PARENTHOOD STATUS AT FOLLOW-UP			*			*	*
MARRIED PARENT	-0.603		-0.131	-0.006	-0.609	-0.118	-0.120
SINGLE PARENT	-0.244		-0.160	0.131	-0.112	-0.052	-0.073
NOT A PARENT	0.144		0.037	-0.005	0.139	0.028	0.030
GETTING TOGETHER W/ FRIENDS AT BASE YEAR (Cov.)[a]							0.197 **
Multiple R		0.340	0.401			0.483	0.511
R Sqr.		0.115	0.161			0.233	0.261

Notes: * indicates statistical significance at .05 level. ** indicates statistical significance at .01 level. Statistical significance is not indicated for bivariate coefficients or constants. Ns used for significance testing were weighted to approximate the number of individuals (not the number of observations) since each individual could contribute up to seven observations. Sets #5-#10 were measured at follow-up. Sets #3 and #4 were determined by timing of follow-up. All others were measured at Base Year (BY).

[a]Means for covariates:
HIGH SCHOOL GRADES 5.810   URBANICITY 3.752
FREQUENCY OF GETTING TOGETHER W/FRIENDS AT BASE YEAR 4.372   R WILL ATTEND 4YR COLLEGE 2.884

Table A.5.5a
Regression Analyses Linking Post-High School Experiences to Changes in Frequency of Going to Bars, Taverns, or Nightclubs
Females, Senior Years 1976-1997, Follow-ups 1977-1998

Regression Analyses Based on Full Set of Observations from Follow-Ups 1-7 (Wtd. N of Obs: 13,389)
Unstandardized Regression Coefficients

VARIABLE	BIVARIATE COEFF.	Predicting to Change Scores — Multivariate Coefficients BKGD.	ALL SETS	Bivariate Coeff. With Dependent Variable at BY	at FU	Multivariate Prediction of Dep. Var. at FU: Covarying BY Dep. Var? No	Yes
CONSTANT	0.418	0.418	0.418	1.926	2.345	2.345	2.345
SET#1 RACE		**	**			**	**
WHITE	0.041	0.034	0.037	0.014	0.055	0.056	0.051
BLACK	-0.225	-0.131	-0.187	-0.058	-0.284	-0.334	-0.294
OTHER	-0.137	-0.173	-0.145	-0.067	-0.204	-0.163	-0.158
SET#2 REGION		**	**			**	**
NORTHEAST	-0.047	-0.073	-0.119	0.255	0.208	0.118	0.053
NORTH CENTRAL	0.159	0.154	0.150	-0.023	0.135	0.122	0.130
SOUTH	-0.175	-0.160	-0.125	-0.027	-0.202	-0.123	-0.123
WEST	0.092	0.112	0.116	-0.266	-0.173	-0.170	-0.092
HIGH SCHOOL GRADES/D=1 (Cov.)*		0.039 **	0.032 *			-0.045 **	-0.024 *
R WILL ATTEND 4YR COLLEGE (Cov.)*		0.109 **	0.048 *			0.037 *	0.040 *
URBANICITY (Cov.)*		0.041	0.010			0.057 **	0.044 **
SET#3 FOLLOW-UP NUMBER		**	**			**	**
FU #1	-0.027	-0.031	-0.274	-0.020	-0.047	-0.232	-0.243
FU #2	0.270	0.266	0.134	-0.009	0.260	0.123	0.126
FU #3	0.215	0.216	0.208	-0.004	0.211	0.174	0.183
FU #4	0.031	0.029	0.120	0.004	0.035	0.102	0.107
FU #5	-0.146	-0.145	0.024	0.009	-0.138	0.010	0.014
FU #6	-0.321	-0.316	-0.084	0.026	-0.295	-0.072	-0.075
FU #7	-0.440	-0.427	-0.150	0.032	-0.408	-0.127	-0.133
SET#4 ADMINISTRATION OF FIRST FOLLOW-UP							
ONE YEAR AFTER HIGH SCHOOL	0.019	0.008	-0.016	-0.010	0.008	-0.019	-0.018
TWO YEARS AFTER HIGH SCHOOL	-0.020	-0.009	0.017	0.011	-0.009	0.020	0.020
SET#5 STUDENT STATUS AT FOLLOW-UP							
FULL-TIME STUDENT	0.270		-0.003	-0.081	0.190	0.001	0.000
PART-TIME STUDENT	0.043		-0.027	0.030	0.073	-0.014	-0.017
NOT A STUDENT	-0.119		0.005	0.029	-0.090	0.001	0.002
SET#6 WORK STATUS AT FOLLOW-UP						**	*
FULL-TIME CIVILIAN JOB	0.008		0.009	0.060	0.068	0.052	0.040
MILITARY SERVICE	0.327		0.215	-0.013	0.314	0.254	0.244
PART-TIME JOB	0.106		0.034	-0.096	0.010	-0.032	-0.014
HOMEMAKER	-0.593		-0.146	-0.039	-0.632	-0.192	-0.179
NONSTUDENT, NOT EMPLOYED	-0.260		-0.068	-0.060	-0.319	-0.169	-0.141
OTHER	0.199		0.005	-0.043	0.157	-0.001	0.001
SET#7 LIVING ARRANGEMENT AT FOLLOW-UP			**			**	**
MARRIED	-0.407		-0.351	-0.027	-0.434	-0.345	-0.346
PARTNER	0.016		0.044	0.309	0.325	0.348	0.265
PARENT(S)	0.133		0.155	-0.043	0.090	0.053	0.081
DORM	0.371		0.370	-0.165	0.206	0.209	0.253
LIVE ALONE	0.348		0.175	0.021	0.369	0.218	0.206
OTHER	0.423		0.309	0.061	0.483	0.381	0.361
SET#8 ENGAGEMENT STATUS AT FOLLOW-UP			**			**	**
ENGAGED	-0.086		-0.289	0.068	-0.018	-0.323	-0.313
NOT ENGAGED	0.007		0.025	-0.006	0.002	0.028	0.027
SET#9 IS R PREGNANT AT FOLLOW-UP?						**	*
YES	-0.434		-0.110	-0.045	-0.479	-0.167	-0.152
NO	0.015		0.009	-0.017	-0.002	-0.010	-0.005
DATA N.A. (1977-1983)	0.061		-0.012	0.106	0.168	0.112	0.078
SET#10 PARENTHOOD STATUS AT FOLLOW-UP			**			**	**
MARRIED PARENT	-0.576		-0.208	-0.038	-0.614	-0.220	-0.216
SINGLE PARENT	-0.180		-0.253	0.127	-0.054	-0.207	-0.220
NOT A PARENT	0.182		0.080	0.002	0.184	0.080	0.080
GOING TO BARS AT BASE YEAR (Cov.)*							0.273 **
Multiple R		0.256	0.359			0.456	0.531
R Sqr.		0.065	0.129			0.208	0.282

Notes: * indicates statistical significance at .05 level. ** indicates statistical significance at .01 level. Statistical significance is not indicated for bivariate coefficients or constants. Ns used for significance testing were weighted to approximate the number of individuals (not the number of observations) since each individual could contribute up to seven observations. Sets #5-#10 were measured at follow-up. Sets #3 and #4 were determined by timing of follow-up. All others were measured at Base Year (BY).

*Means for covariates: HIGH SCHOOL GRADES 6.330 URBANICITY 3.765 FREQUENCY OF GOING TO BARS AT BASE YEAR 1.926 R WILL ATTEND 4YR COLLEGE 2.898

Table A.5.5b
Regression Analyses Linking Post-High School Experiences to Changes in Frequency of Going to Bars, Taverns, or Nightclubs
Males, Senior Years 1976-1997, Follow-ups 1977-1998

Regression Analyses Based on Full Set of Observations from Follow-Ups 1-7
(Wtd. N of Obs: 10,723)
Unstandardized Regression Coefficients

VARIABLE	BIVARIATE COEFF.	Predicting to Change Scores — Multivariate Coefficients BKGD.	ALL SETS	Bivariate Coeff. With Dependent Variable at BY	at FU	Multivariate Prediction of Dep. Var. at FU: Covarying BY Dep. Var? No	Yes
CONSTANT	0.462	0.462	0.462	2.158	2.620	2.620	2.620
SET#1 RACE							*
WHITE	0.013	0.008	0.011	0.013	0.026	0.022	0.020
BLACK	-0.004	0.115	0.079	-0.141	-0.145	-0.174	-0.113
OTHER	-0.124	-0.162	-0.165	-0.023	-0.147	-0.091	-0.109
SET#2 REGION		**	**			**	**
NORTHEAST	0.077	0.054	0.003	0.202	0.278	0.198	0.151
NORTH CENTRAL	0.066	0.082	0.095	0.044	0.110	0.131	0.122
SOUTH	-0.251	-0.244	-0.216	0.059	-0.192	-0.138	-0.157
WEST	0.216	0.203	0.193	-0.439	-0.223	-0.253	-0.145
HIGH SCHOOL GRADES/D=1 (Cov.)[a]		0.032 *	0.022			-0.050 **	-0.033 **
R WILL ATTEND 4YR COLLEGE (Cov.)[a]		0.141 **	0.083 **			0.065 **	0.069 **
URBANICITY (Cov.)[a]		0.043	0.017			0.062 **	0.051 **
SET#3 FOLLOW-UP NUMBER		**	**			**	**
FU #1	-0.124	-0.135	-0.354	-0.050	-0.175	-0.342	-0.345
FU #2	0.259	0.252	0.105	-0.040	0.219	0.079	0.085
FU #3	0.253	0.245	0.218	-0.010	0.243	0.195	0.201
FU #4	0.042	0.047	0.127	0.037	0.079	0.150	0.144
FU #5	-0.092	-0.090	0.082	0.038	-0.054	0.088	0.086
FU #6	-0.311	-0.288	-0.025	0.059	-0.252	-0.012	-0.015
FU #7	-0.378	-0.358	-0.063	0.061	-0.317	-0.051	-0.054
SET#4 ADMINISTRATION OF FIRST FOLLOW-UP		*				*	*
ONE YEAR AFTER HIGH SCHOOL	-0.049	-0.045	-0.064	0.014	-0.035	-0.040	-0.046
TWO YEARS AFTER HIGH SCHOOL	0.053	0.049	0.069	-0.015	0.039	0.043	0.050
SET#5 STUDENT STATUS AT FOLLOW-UP							
FULL-TIME STUDENT	0.227		0.025	-0.156	0.071	-0.025	-0.013
PART-TIME STUDENT	0.032		-0.054	-0.023	0.009	-0.035	-0.040
NOT A STUDENT	-0.100		-0.003	0.069	-0.031	0.015	0.011
SET#6 WORK STATUS AT FOLLOW-UP						*	*
FULL-TIME CIVILIAN JOB	-0.102		-0.005	0.063	-0.038	0.009	0.005
MILITARY SERVICE	0.295		0.362	-0.028	0.267	0.285	0.303
PART-TIME JOB	0.158		-0.021	-0.151	0.007	-0.058	-0.049
HOMEMAKER	-0.350		-0.126	0.168	-0.182	-0.014	-0.041
NONSTUDENT, NOT EMPLOYED	-0.117		-0.139	0.023	-0.094	-0.180	-0.170
OTHER	0.206		-0.032	-0.110	0.096	-0.016	-0.020
SET#7 LIVING ARRANGEMENT AT FOLLOW-UP			**			**	**
MARRIED	-0.547		-0.488	0.064	-0.482	-0.467	-0.472
PARTNER	-0.021		0.007	0.263	0.242	0.258	0.198
PARENT(S)	0.066		0.126	-0.040	0.026	0.053	0.070
DORM	0.272		0.345	-0.255	0.017	0.178	0.218
LIVE ALONE	0.405		0.262	-0.064	0.341	0.235	0.242
OTHER	0.448		0.294	-0.003	0.445	0.362	0.345
SET#8 ENGAGEMENT STATUS AT FOLLOW-UP			**			**	**
ENGAGED	-0.166		-0.347	0.093	-0.072	-0.341	-0.343
NOT ENGAGED	0.012		0.026	-0.007	0.005	0.025	0.026
SET#9 IS R'S SPS PREGNANT AT FOLLOW-UP?							**
YES	-0.488		-0.067	0.027	-0.461	-0.098	-0.091
NO	0.029		0.017	-0.039	-0.010	-0.030	-0.018
DATA N.A. (1977-1983)	-0.027		-0.067	0.185	0.158	0.168	0.111
SET#10 PARENTHOOD STATUS AT FOLLOW-UP			*			*	*
MARRIED PARENT	-0.692		-0.226	0.102	-0.590	-0.169	-0.183
SINGLE PARENT	-0.032		-0.091	0.264	0.232	0.089	0.046
NOT A PARENT	0.153		0.054	-0.036	0.117	0.033	0.038
GOING TO BARS AT BASE YEAR (Cov.)[a]							0.242 **
Multiple R		0.255	0.360			0.427	0.496
R Sqr.		0.065	0.129			0.182	0.246

Notes: * indicates statistical significance at .05 level. ** indicates statistical significance at .01 level. Statistical significance is not indicated for bivariate coefficients or constants. Ns used for significance testing were weighted to approximate the number of individuals (not the number of observations) since each individual could contribute up to seven observations. Sets #5-#10 were measured at follow-up. Sets #3 and #4 were determined by timing of follow-up. All others were measured at Base Year (BY).

[a]Means for covariates: HIGH SCHOOL GRADES 5.812   URBANICITY 3.750   FREQUENCY OF GOING TO BARS AT BASE YEAR 2.158   R WILL ATTEND 4YR COLLEGE 2.883

Table A.6.1a
Regression Analyses Linking Post-High School Experiences to
Changes Perceived Risk of Smoking 1+ Packs of Cigarettes Per Day
Females, Senior Years 1976-1997, Follow-ups 1977-1998

Regression Analyses Based on Full Set of Observations from Follow-Ups 1-7 (Wtd. N of Obs: 12,915)
Unstandardized Regression Coefficients

VARIABLE	BIVARIATE COEFF.	Multivariate Coefficients BKGD.	Multivariate Coefficients ALL SETS	Bivariate Coeff. With Dependent Variable at BY	Bivariate Coeff. With Dependent Variable at FU	Multivariate Prediction of Dep. Var. at FU: Covarying BY Dep. Var? No	Multivariate Prediction of Dep. Var. at FU: Covarying BY Dep. Var? Yes
CONSTANT	0.127	0.127	0.127	3.603	3.730	3.730	3.730
SET#1 RACE							
WHITE	-0.005	-0.006	-0.006	0.008	0.003	-0.001	-0.002
BLACK	0.028	0.026	0.028	-0.051	-0.024	0.019	0.021
OTHER	0.021	0.031	0.031	-0.024	-0.003	-0.008	0.001
SET#2 REGION							**
NORTHEAST	-0.020	-0.016	-0.016	0.012	-0.008	-0.008	-0.009
NORTH CENTRAL	0.013	0.012	0.012	-0.037	-0.024	-0.019	-0.012
SOUTH	0.011	0.007	0.007	-0.027	-0.016	-0.017	-0.011
WEST	-0.017	-0.013	-0.014	0.103	0.086	0.078	0.056
HIGH SCHOOL GRADES/D=1 (Cov.)*		-0.010	-0.011			0.017 **	0.011
R WILL ATTEND 4YR COLLEGE (Cov.)*		-0.010	-0.011			0.041 **	0.029 **
URBANICITY (Cov.)*		-0.016	-0.016			-0.001	-0.005
SET#3 FOLLOW-UP NUMBER		**					*
FU #1	-0.073	-0.072	-0.076	0.022	-0.050	-0.059	-0.063
FU #2	-0.042	-0.041	-0.043	0.009	-0.032	-0.035	-0.037
FU #3	-0.003	-0.003	0.000	0.001	-0.002	0.007	0.005
FU #4	0.037	0.037	0.041	-0.010	0.027	0.031	0.034
FU #5	0.033	0.033	0.035	-0.006	0.027	0.027	0.029
FU #6	0.073	0.073	0.073	-0.029	0.044	0.046	0.052
FU #7	0.104	0.104	0.101	-0.024	0.080	0.084	0.088
SET#4 ADMINISTRATION OF FIRST FOLLOW-UP							
ONE YEAR AFTER HIGH SCHOOL	-0.008	-0.009	-0.009	0.004	-0.004	-0.007	-0.007
TWO YEARS AFTER HIGH SCHOOL	0.009	0.010	0.010	-0.005	0.005	0.008	0.008
SET#5 STUDENT STATUS AT FOLLOW-UP			*			*	*
FULL-TIME STUDENT	-0.045		0.026	0.089	0.045	0.057	0.050
PART-TIME STUDENT	-0.004		-0.005	0.050	0.046	0.038	0.028
NOT A STUDENT	0.019		-0.010	-0.044	-0.025	-0.029	-0.024
SET#6 WORK STATUS AT FOLLOW-UP							
FULL-TIME CIVILIAN JOB	0.015		0.006	-0.019	-0.004	0.001	0.002
MILITARY SERVICE	-0.107		-0.087	-0.078	-0.184	-0.156	-0.139
PART-TIME JOB	-0.016		0.005	0.043	0.027	0.012	0.011
HOMEMAKER	0.027		-0.021	-0.015	0.012	0.014	0.006
NONSTUDENT, NOT EMPLOYED	0.000		-0.017	-0.089	-0.089	-0.021	-0.020
OTHER	-0.046		-0.008	0.056	0.010	-0.017	-0.015
SET#7 LIVING ARRANGEMENT AT FOLLOW-UP							
MARRIED	0.041		0.001	-0.008	0.033	0.032	0.025
PARTNER	0.002		0.000	-0.055	-0.054	-0.039	-0.030
PARENT(S)	-0.032		0.001	-0.026	-0.057	-0.028	-0.021
DORM	-0.078		-0.009	0.118	0.040	-0.006	-0.007
LIVE ALONE	0.017		0.005	0.026	0.042	0.006	0.006
OTHER	-0.016		-0.003	0.023	0.006	-0.008	-0.007
SET#8 ENGAGEMENT STATUS AT FOLLOW-UP							
ENGAGED	-0.018		0.002	-0.023	-0.041	0.008	0.007
NOT ENGAGED	0.002		0.000	0.002	0.004	-0.001	-0.001
SET#9 IS R PREGNANT AT FOLLOW-UP?							*
YES	0.015		-0.013	0.001	0.016	0.006	0.001
NO	0.006		0.000	0.013	0.019	0.011	0.009
DATA N.A. (1977-1983)	-0.040		0.007	-0.073	-0.113	-0.066	-0.049
SET#10 PARENTHOOD STATUS AT FOLLOW-UP							
MARRIED PARENT	0.067		0.025	-0.038	0.029	-0.004	0.003
SINGLE PARENT	0.029		-0.004	-0.148	-0.120	-0.078	-0.061
NOT A PARENT	-0.023		-0.007	0.025	0.002	0.008	0.005
RISK OF CIGARETTES AT BASE YEAR (Cov.)*							0.235 **
Multiple R		0.098	0.102			0.217	0.349
R Sqr.		0.010	0.010			0.047	0.122

Notes: * indicates statistical significance at .05 level. ** indicates statistical significance at .01 level. Statistical significance is not indicated for bivariate coefficients or constants. Ns used for significance testing were weighted to approximate the number of individuals (not the number of observations) since each individual could contribute up to seven observations. Sets #5-#10 were measured at follow-up. Sets #3 and #4 were determined by timing of follow-up. All others were measured at Base Year (BY).

*Means for covariates: HIGH SCHOOL GRADES 5.333 URBANICITY 3.778
PERCEIVED RISK OF SMOKING 1+ PACKS OF CIGS AT BASE YEAR 3.603 R WILL ATTEND 4YR COLLEGE 2.884

Table A.6.1b
Regression Analyses Linking Post-High School Experiences to Changes in Perceived Risk of Smoking One or More Packs of Cigarettes Per Day Males, Senior Years 1976-1997, Follow-ups 1977-1998

Regression Analyses Based on Full Set of Observations from Follow-Ups 1-7 (Wtd. N of Obs: 10,723) Unstandardized Regression Coefficients

VARIABLE	BIVARIATE COEFF.	BKGD.	ALL SETS	at BY	at FU	No	Yes
		Predicting to Change Scores / Multivariate Coefficients		Bivariate Coeff. With Dependent Variable		Multivariate Prediction of Dep. Var. at FU: Covarying BY Dep. Var?	
CONSTANT	0.111	0.111	0.111	3.561	3.672	3.672	3.672
SET#1 RACE							
WHITE	0.000	0.000	-0.001	-0.001	-0.001	-0.002	-0.002
BLACK	-0.029	-0.053	-0.037	0.011	-0.018	0.033	0.016
OTHER	0.020	0.039	0.037	-0.001	0.019	-0.003	0.006
SET#2 REGION							**
NORTHEAST	-0.037	-0.037	-0.034	0.039	0.002	-0.010	-0.016
NORTH CENTRAL	0.034	0.029	0.028	-0.064	-0.030	-0.022	-0.010
SOUTH	0.024	0.031	0.030	-0.051	-0.027	-0.021	-0.009
WEST	-0.053	-0.055	-0.055	0.152	0.099	0.090	0.056
HIGH SCHOOL GRADES/D=1 (Cov.)[a]		-0.014	-0.014			0.015 *	0.008
R WILL ATTEND 4YR COLLEGE (Cov.)[a]		-0.041 **	-0.043 **			0.044 **	0.024 *
URBANICITY (Cov.)[a]		0.012	0.014			0.024 *	0.021 *
SET#3 FOLLOW-UP NUMBER							
FU #1	-0.065	-0.063	-0.052	0.014	-0.051	-0.065	-0.062
FU #2	-0.017	-0.017	-0.007	0.006	-0.011	-0.017	-0.014
FU #3	-0.011	-0.010	-0.004	0.011	0.000	0.006	0.003
FU #4	0.045	0.044	0.039	-0.005	0.041	0.046	0.045
FU #5	0.038	0.037	0.026	-0.008	0.030	0.035	0.033
FU #6	0.042	0.041	0.026	-0.022	0.020	0.028	0.028
FU #7	0.057	0.053	0.031	-0.028	0.029	0.042	0.039
SET#4 ADMINISTRATION OF FIRST FOLLOW-UP							
ONE YEAR AFTER HIGH SCHOOL	-0.015	-0.013	-0.012	0.001	-0.014	-0.018	-0.016
TWO YEARS AFTER HIGH SCHOOL	0.017	0.015	0.013	-0.001	0.015	0.020	0.018
SET#5 STUDENT STATUS AT FOLLOW-UP							
FULL-TIME STUDENT	-0.049		0.018	0.115	0.065	0.059	0.050
PART-TIME STUDENT	-0.033		-0.029	0.053	0.020	0.006	-0.002
NOT A STUDENT	0.028		-0.004	-0.060	-0.033	-0.028	-0.022
SET#6 WORK STATUS AT FOLLOW-UP							
FULL-TIME CIVILIAN JOB	0.030		0.008	-0.042	-0.012	0.003	0.004
MILITARY SERVICE	-0.092		-0.090	0.037	-0.055	-0.030	-0.044
PART-TIME JOB	-0.043		-0.002	0.087	0.044	0.004	0.003
HOMEMAKER	-0.038		-0.060	-0.142	-0.181	-0.160	-0.137
NONSTUDENT, NOT EMPLOYED	0.013		0.003	-0.069	-0.057	0.019	0.015
OTHER	-0.050		-0.001	0.093	0.043	-0.009	-0.007
SET#7 LIVING ARRANGEMENT AT FOLLOW-UP							
MARRIED	0.064		0.019	-0.043	0.020	0.027	0.025
PARTNER	0.013		0.001	-0.055	-0.042	-0.045	-0.034
PARENT(S)	-0.017		-0.009	-0.023	-0.040	-0.013	-0.012
DORM	-0.074		0.008	0.133	0.059	0.012	0.011
LIVE ALONE	-0.020		-0.020	0.031	0.010	-0.006	-0.010
OTHER	-0.036		-0.009	0.051	0.015	-0.009	-0.009
SET#8 ENGAGEMENT STATUS AT FOLLOW-UP							
ENGAGED	0.009		0.022	-0.026	-0.017	0.024	0.023
NOT ENGAGED	-0.001		-0.002	0.002	0.001	-0.002	-0.002
SET#9 IS R'S SPS PREGNANT AT FOLLOW-UP?							
YES	0.046		0.001	-0.048	-0.003	-0.016	-0.012
NO	0.010		0.008	0.008	0.018	0.012	0.011
DATA N.A. (1977-1983)	-0.059		-0.036	-0.027	-0.085	-0.054	-0.050
SET#10 PARENTHOOD STATUS AT FOLLOW-UP							
MARRIED PARENT	0.088		0.028	-0.081	0.006	-0.006	0.002
SINGLE PARENT	-0.037		-0.072	-0.098	-0.135	-0.090	-0.086
NOT A PARENT	-0.016		-0.002	0.021	0.004	0.005	0.003
PERCEIVED RISK OF CIGARETTES AT BASE YEAR (Cov.)[a]							0.234 **
Multiple R		0.118	0.129			0.209	0.333
R Sqr.		0.014	0.017			0.044	0.111

Notes: * indicates statistical significance at .05 level. ** indicates statistical significance at .01 level. Statistical significance is not indicated for bivariate coefficients or constants. Ns used for significance testing were weighted to approximate the number of individuals (not the number of observations) since each individual could contribute up to seven observations. Sets #5-#10 were measured at follow-up. Sets #3 and #4 were determined by timing of follow-up. All others were measured at Base Year (BY).

[a] Means for covariates:

HIGH SCHOOL GRADES	5.784	URBANICITY	3.749
PERCEIVED RISK OF SMOKING 1+ PACKS OF CIGS AT BASE YEAR	3.561	R WILL ATTEND 4YR COLLEGE	2.930

Table A.6.2a
Regression Analyses Linking Post-High School Experiences to
Changes in Disapproval of Smoking One or More Packs of Cigarettes Per Day
Females, Senior Years 1976-1997, Follow-ups 1977-1998

VARIABLE	BIVARIATE COEFF.	Multivariate Coefficients BKGD.	ALL SETS	Bivariate Coeff. With Dependent Variable at BY	at FU	Multivariate Prediction of Dep. Var. at FU: Covarying BY Dep. Var? No	Yes
CONSTANT	0.010	0.010	0.010	2.113	2.124	2.124	2.124
SET#1 RACE						**	**
WHITE	-0.001	-0.001	-0.002	-0.030	-0.031	-0.036	-0.022
BLACK	0.006	0.003	0.018	0.146	0.153	0.239	0.144
OTHER	0.002	0.008	0.006	0.151	0.154	0.118	0.070
SET#2 REGION						**	
NORTHEAST	0.025	0.018	0.025	-0.048	-0.023	-0.005	0.008
NORTH CENTRAL	0.009	0.008	0.008	-0.073	-0.064	-0.038	-0.018
SOUTH	-0.016	-0.010	-0.013	0.020	0.004	-0.028	-0.021
WEST	-0.020	-0.023	-0.025	0.165	0.145	0.129	0.063
HIGH SCHOOL GRADES/D=1 (Cov.)a		-0.014	-0.015			0.058 **	0.027 **
R WILL ATTEND 4YR COLLEGE (Cov.)a		-0.001	-0.001			0.043 **	0.024
URBANICITY (Cov.)a		0.013	0.015			0.005	0.009
SET#3 FOLLOW-UP NUMBER							
FU #1	-0.021	-0.021	-0.008	0.006	-0.014	-0.051	-0.032
FU #2	-0.050	-0.051	-0.044	0.009	-0.041	-0.054	-0.050
FU #3	-0.011	-0.011	-0.001	0.008	-0.003	0.012	0.006
FU #4	-0.013	-0.013	-0.015	-0.001	-0.013	0.006	-0.003
FU #5	0.042	0.042	0.030	-0.008	0.033	0.049	0.041
FU #6	0.063	0.063	0.041	-0.005	0.058	0.074	0.060
FU #7	0.089	0.089	0.063	-0.039	0.050	0.072	0.068
SET#4 ADMINISTRATION OF FIRST FOLLOW-UP							
ONE YEAR AFTER HIGH SCHOOL	-0.001	-0.002	-0.001	0.011	0.010	0.010	0.005
TWO YEARS AFTER HIGH SCHOOL	0.001	0.002	0.001	-0.011	-0.010	-0.010	-0.005
SET#5 STUDENT STATUS AT FOLLOW-UP							
FULL-TIME STUDENT	-0.010		0.043	0.096	0.086	0.064	0.055
PART-TIME STUDENT	0.003		0.006	-0.005	-0.002	-0.006	0.000
NOT A STUDENT	0.004		-0.019	-0.039	-0.035	-0.025	-0.023
SET#6 WORK STATUS AT FOLLOW-UP							
FULL-TIME CIVILIAN JOB	-0.015		-0.010	-0.021	-0.035	-0.018	-0.015
MILITARY SERVICE	0.052		0.058	0.026	0.077	0.105	0.084
PART-TIME JOB	0.021		0.023	0.038	0.059	0.021	0.022
HOMEMAKER	0.110		0.045	-0.026	0.083	0.103	0.078
NONSTUDENT, NOT EMPLOYED	-0.013		-0.016	-0.074	-0.087	-0.005	-0.010
OTHER	-0.029		-0.016	0.066	0.037	-0.017	-0.016
SET#7 LIVING ARRANGEMENT AT FOLLOW-UP						**	**
MARRIED	0.073		0.065	-0.020	0.053	0.084	0.076
PARTNER	-0.088		-0.092	-0.156	-0.244	-0.235	-0.173
PARENT(S)	-0.026		-0.021	0.019	-0.007	0.006	-0.006
DORM	-0.025		-0.030	0.132	0.106	-0.004	-0.015
LIVE ALONE	-0.072		-0.060	0.011	-0.061	-0.105	-0.086
OTHER	-0.035		-0.025	0.034	0.000	-0.027	-0.026
SET#8 ENGAGEMENT STATUS AT FOLLOW-UP							
ENGAGED	-0.032		0.033	-0.027	-0.058	0.052	0.044
NOT ENGAGED	0.003		-0.004	0.003	0.006	-0.006	-0.005
SET#9 IS R PREGNANT AT FOLLOW-UP?							
YES	0.089		0.041	-0.023	0.066	0.051	0.047
NO	0.005		0.005	0.008	0.014	0.007	0.006
DATA N.A. (1977-1983)	-0.063		-0.041	-0.040	-0.103	-0.061	-0.052
SET#10 PARENTHOOD STATUS AT FOLLOW-UP							
MARRIED PARENT	0.094		0.013	-0.060	0.034	-0.043	-0.019
SINGLE PARENT	-0.019		0.006	-0.163	-0.182	-0.104	-0.057
NOT A PARENT	-0.027		-0.005	0.033	0.006	0.022	0.011
DISAPPROVAL OF CIGARETTES AT BASE YEAR (Cov.)a							0.432 **
Multiple R		0.065	0.100			0.253	0.483
R Sqr.		0.004	0.010			0.064	0.233

Regression Analyses Based on Full Set of Observations from Follow-Ups 1-7 (Wtd. N of Obs: 13,247). Unstandardized Regression Coefficients.

Notes: * Indicates statistical significance at .05 level. ** Indicates statistical significance at .01 level. Statistical significance is not indicated for bivariate coefficients or constants. Ns used for significance testing were weighted to approximate the number of individuals (not the number of observations) since each individual could contribute up to seven observations. Sets #5-#10 were measured at follow-up. Sets #3 and #4 were determined by timing of follow-up. All others were measured at Base Year (BY).

aMeans for covariates: HIGH SCHOOL GRADES 6.260 URBANICITY 3.754 DISAPPROVAL OF SMOKING 1+ PACKS OF CIGS AT BASE YEAR 2.113 R WILL ATTEND 4YR COLLEGE 2.848

Table A.6.2b
Regression Analyses Linking Post-High School Experiences to
Changes in Disapproval of Smoking One or More Packs of Cigarettes Per Day
Males, Senior Years 1976-1997, Follow-ups 1977-1998

Regression Analyses Based on Full Set of Observations from Follow-Ups 1-7
(Wtd. N of Obs: 10,673)
Unstandardized Regression Coefficients

VARIABLE	BIVARIATE COEFF.	Predicting to Change Scores Multivariate Coefficients		Bivariate Coeff. With Dependent Variable		Multivariate Prediction of Dep. Var. at FU: Covarying BY Dep. Var?	
		BKGD.	ALL SETS	at BY	at FU	No	Yes
CONSTANT	-0.029	-0.029	-0.029	2.093	2.064	2.064	2.064
SET#1 RACE						**	*
WHITE	-0.006	-0.006	-0.007	-0.011	-0.017	-0.019	-0.015
BLACK	0.073	0.057	0.071	0.081	0.154	0.225	0.168
OTHER	0.014	0.016	0.019	0.047	0.062	0.035	0.029
SET#2 REGION							
NORTHEAST	-0.034	-0.037	-0.038	0.049	0.015	0.018	-0.003
NORTH CENTRAL	-0.011	-0.010	-0.008	-0.057	-0.068	-0.046	-0.032
SOUTH	0.039	0.038	0.038	-0.021	0.018	0.003	0.016
WEST	-0.007	-0.003	-0.003	0.079	0.072	0.055	0.034
HIGH SCHOOL GRADES/D=1 (Cov.)[a]		-0.001	-0.002			0.049 **	0.030 **
R WILL ATTEND 4YR COLLEGE (Cov.)[a]		-0.024	-0.028			0.056 **	0.025
URBANICITY (Cov.)[a]		0.010	0.009			0.015	0.013
SET#3 FOLLOW-UP NUMBER							
FU #1	0.016	0.017	-0.005	0.001	0.017	-0.023	-0.016
FU #2	-0.021	-0.021	-0.037	0.010	-0.011	-0.034	-0.035
FU #3	-0.037	-0.038	-0.042	0.003	-0.034	-0.031	-0.035
FU #4	0.017	0.017	0.026	0.011	0.027	0.042	0.036
FU #5	0.015	0.015	0.032	-0.007	0.008	0.032	0.032
FU #6	0.000	-0.001	0.022	-0.011	-0.011	0.023	0.023
FU #7	0.031	0.031	0.066	-0.027	0.005	0.055	0.059
SET#4 ADMINISTRATION OF FIRST FOLLOW-UP							
ONE YEAR AFTER HIGH SCHOOL	-0.013	-0.014	-0.017	0.019	0.006	0.000	-0.007
TWO YEARS AFTER HIGH SCHOOL	0.015	0.016	0.019	-0.021	-0.006	0.000	0.007
SET#5 STUDENT STATUS AT FOLLOW-UP							
FULL-TIME STUDENT	-0.002		0.019	0.110	0.108	0.039	0.031
PART-TIME STUDENT	-0.009		-0.010	0.047	0.038	0.034	0.018
NOT A STUDENT	0.002		-0.007	-0.056	-0.053	-0.022	-0.017
SET#6 WORK STATUS AT FOLLOW-UP							
FULL-TIME CIVILIAN JOB	-0.001		-0.006	-0.026	-0.027	-0.003	-0.004
MILITARY SERVICE	0.001		-0.008	-0.088	-0.086	-0.029	-0.021
PART-TIME JOB	-0.006		0.004	0.083	0.077	0.017	0.012
HOMEMAKER	0.231		0.227	-0.125	0.106	0.216	0.220
NONSTUDENT, NOT EMPLOYED	-0.001		-0.005	-0.136	-0.137	-0.054	-0.037
OTHER	0.007		0.019	0.090	0.098	0.014	0.016
SET#7 LIVING ARRANGEMENT AT FOLLOW-UP							
MARRIED	0.024		0.041	-0.015	0.009	0.072	0.061
PARTNER	-0.030		-0.020	-0.059	-0.089	-0.091	-0.065
PARENT(S)	0.003		-0.009	-0.020	-0.017	-0.009	-0.009
DORM	-0.028		-0.044	0.178	0.150	0.014	-0.007
LIVE ALONE	-0.045		-0.057	-0.028	-0.072	-0.096	-0.082
OTHER	0.003		0.002	0.017	0.020	-0.023	-0.014
SET#8 ENGAGEMENT STATUS AT FOLLOW-UP							
ENGAGED	-0.031		-0.012	0.016	-0.015	0.067	0.038
NOT ENGAGED	-0.003		0.001	-0.001	0.001	-0.006	-0.003
SET#9 IS R'S SPS PREGNANT AT FOLLOW-UP?							
YES	0.110		0.098	0.018	0.128	0.136	0.122
NO	-0.012		-0.013	0.012	0.000	-0.005	-0.008
DATA N.A. (1977-1983)	0.033		0.038	-0.060	-0.026	-0.003	0.012
SET#10 PARENTHOOD STATUS AT FOLLOW-UP						*	*
MARRIED PARENT	-0.010		-0.081	-0.040	-0.049	-0.078	-0.079
SINGLE PARENT	-0.075		-0.081	-0.143	-0.218	-0.162	-0.132
NOT A PARENT	0.006		0.022	0.016	0.022	0.026	0.024
DISAPPROVAL OF CIGARETTES AT BASE YEAR (Cov.)[a]						0.366 **	
Multiple R		0.056	0.079			0.218	0.414
R Sqr.		0.003	0.006			0.047	0.171

Notes: * indicates statistical significance at .05 level. ** indicates statistical significance at .01 level. Statistical significance is not indicated for bivariate coefficients or constants. Ns used for significance testing were weighted to approximate the number of individuals (not the number of observations) since each individual could contribute up to seven observations. Sets #5-#10 were measured at follow-up. Sets #3 and #4 were determined by timing of follow-up. All others were measured at Base Year (BY).
[a]Means for covariates: HIGH SCHOOL GRADES   5.784   URBANICITY   3.725
DISAPPROVAL OF SMOKING 1+ PACKS OF CIGS AT BASE YEAR   2.093   R WILL ATTEND 4YR COLLEGE   2.881

261

Table A.6.3a
Regression Analyses Linking Post-High School Experiences to
Changes in Perceived Risk of Having 5+ Drinks Once or Twice Each Weekend
Females, Senior Years 1976-1997, Follow-ups 1977-1998

Regression Analyses Based on Full Set of Observations from Follow-Ups 1-7
(Wtd. N of Obs: 12,871)
Unstandardized Regression Coefficients

VARIABLE	Predicting to Change Scores BIVARIATE COEFF.	Multivariate Coefficients BKGD.	ALL SETS	Bivariate Coeff. With Dependent Variable at BY	at FU	Multivariate Prediction of Dep. Var. at FU: Covarying BY Dep. Var? No	Yes
CONSTANT	0.037	0.037	0.037	3.175	3.213	3.213	3.213
SET#1 RACE						**	**
WHITE	0.011	0.011	0.010	-0.046	-0.036	-0.036	-0.024
BLACK	-0.073	-0.079	-0.064	0.315	0.242	0.264	0.176
OTHER	-0.030	-0.026	-0.032	0.139	0.109	0.093	0.059
SET#2 REGION						**	**
NORTHEAST	0.040	0.039	0.045	-0.159	-0.119	-0.088	-0.052
NORTH CENTRAL	-0.013	-0.026	-0.021	-0.063	-0.076	-0.058	-0.048
SOUTH	-0.009	0.002	-0.002	0.109	0.100	0.057	0.041
WEST	-0.016	-0.008	-0.017	0.141	0.126	0.126	0.088
HIGH SCHOOL GRADES/D=1 (Cov.)[a]		-0.024 *	-0.023 *			0.033 **	0.018 *
R WILL ATTEND 4YR COLLEGE (Cov.)[a]		-0.034 *	-0.025			0.026	0.012
URBANICITY (Cov.)[a]		-0.011	-0.008			-0.041 **	-0.032 *
SET#3 FOLLOW-UP NUMBER		**	**			*	**
FU #1	-0.099	-0.093	-0.059	0.050	-0.050	-0.006	-0.020
FU #2	-0.094	-0.092	-0.080	0.018	-0.076	-0.041	-0.052
FU #3	-0.057	-0.058	-0.057	-0.003	-0.060	-0.052	-0.054
FU #4	-0.004	-0.006	-0.016	-0.015	-0.019	-0.039	-0.033
FU #5	0.099	0.097	0.078	-0.027	0.072	0.035	0.046
FU #6	0.180	0.174	0.142	-0.045	0.135	0.079	0.096
FU #7	0.261	0.255	0.214	-0.054	0.208	0.146	0.164
SET#4 ADMINISTRATION OF FIRST FOLLOW-UP							
ONE YEAR AFTER HIGH SCHOOL	-0.001	0.001	0.005	-0.011	-0.012	-0.012	-0.008
TWO YEARS AFTER HIGH SCHOOL	0.001	-0.001	-0.006	0.013	0.013	0.014	0.009
SET#5 STUDENT STATUS AT FOLLOW-UP							
FULL-TIME STUDENT	-0.111		0.029	0.072	-0.038	0.026	0.026
PART-TIME STUDENT	0.017		0.026	0.003	0.021	0.028	0.028
NOT A STUDENT	0.042		-0.015	-0.030	0.012	-0.015	-0.015
SET#6 WORK STATUS AT FOLLOW-UP							
FULL-TIME CIVILIAN JOB	0.010		-0.012	-0.028	-0.018	-0.017	-0.016
MILITARY SERVICE	-0.235		-0.200	0.166	-0.069	-0.026	-0.073
PART-TIME JOB	-0.040		0.005	0.052	0.012	0.018	0.014
HOMEMAKER	0.174		0.046	0.016	0.190	0.085	0.075
NONSTUDENT, NOT EMPLOYED	0.063		0.025	-0.040	0.024	0.018	0.020
OTHER	-0.087		0.013	0.027	-0.060	-0.014	-0.007
SET#7 LIVING ARRANGEMENT AT FOLLOW-UP						**	**
MARRIED	0.133		0.063	0.000	0.133	0.106	0.094
PARTNER	-0.020		-0.012	-0.124	-0.144	-0.166	-0.125
PARENT(S)	-0.057		-0.013	0.026	-0.031	0.016	0.008
DORM	-0.229		-0.149	0.135	-0.094	-0.099	-0.112
LIVE ALONE	-0.057		-0.044	0.026	-0.031	-0.021	-0.027
OTHER	-0.078		-0.031	-0.052	-0.129	-0.130	-0.103
SET#8 ENGAGEMENT STATUS AT FOLLOW-UP						*	
ENGAGED	-0.032		0.034	0.024	-0.008	0.110	0.090
NOT ENGAGED	0.003		-0.003	-0.002	0.001	-0.010	-0.008
SET#9 IS R PREGNANT AT FOLLOW-UP?						**	
YES	0.142		0.055	0.028	0.170	0.082	0.074
NO	0.003		-0.005	0.019	0.021	0.016	0.011
DATA N.A. (1977-1983)	-0.061		0.008	-0.115	-0.176	-0.118	-0.084
SET#10 PARENTHOOD STATUS AT FOLLOW-UP							
MARRIED PARENT	0.189		0.046	-0.012	0.178	0.035	0.038
SINGLE PARENT	-0.025		-0.034	0.047	0.022	0.051	0.028
NOT A PARENT	-0.055		-0.011	-0.001	-0.056	-0.015	-0.014
RISK OF BINGE DRINKING AT BASE YEAR (Cov.)[a]							0.268 **
Multiple R		0.138	0.155			0.251	0.378
R Sqr.		0.019	0.024			0.063	0.143

Notes: * indicates statistical significance at .05 level. ** indicates statistical significance at .01 level. Statistical significance is not indicated for bivariate coefficients or constants. Ns used for significance testing were weighted to approximate the number of individuals (not the number of observations) since each individual could contribute up to seven observations. Sets #5-#10 were measured at follow-up. Sets #3 and #4 were determined by timing of follow-up. All others were measured at Base Year (BY).
[a]Means for covariates: HIGH SCHOOL GRADES 6.325   URBANICITY 3.777
PERCEIVED RISK OF BINGE DRINKING AT BASE YEAR 3.175   R WILL ATTEND 4YR COLLEGE 2.881

Table A.6.3b
Regression Analyses Linking Post-High School Experiences to Changes in Perceived Risk of Having 5+ Drinks Once or Twice Each Weekend
Males, Senior Years 1976-1997, Follow-ups 1977-1998

Regression Analyses Based on Full Set of Observations from Follow-Ups 1-7
(Wtd. N of Obs: 10,313)
Unstandardized Regression Coefficients

VARIABLE	Predicting to Change Scores BIVARIATE COEFF.	Multivariate Coefficients BKGD.	ALL SETS	Bivariate Coeff. With Dependent Variable at BY	at FU	Multivariate Prediction of Dep. Var. at FU: Covarying BY Dep. Var? No	Yes
CONSTANT	0.041	0.041	0.041	2.908	2.949	2.949	2.949
SET#1 RACE						**	**
WHITE	-0.008	-0.009	-0.009	-0.029	-0.036	-0.033	-0.026
BLACK	0.038	0.014	0.023	0.295	0.333	0.343	0.249
OTHER	0.052	0.079	0.078	0.094	0.146	0.102	0.095
SET#2 REGION						**	**
NORTHEAST	-0.027	-0.019	-0.017	-0.140	-0.167	-0.144	-0.107
NORTH CENTRAL	0.021	0.013	0.012	-0.099	-0.078	-0.066	-0.043
SOUTH	0.023	0.023	0.022	0.094	0.117	0.086	0.067
WEST	-0.041	-0.038	-0.036	0.210	0.169	0.170	0.109
HIGH SCHOOL GRADES/D=1 (Cov.)*		-0.022	-0.021			0.029 **	0.014
R WILL ATTEND 4YR COLLEGE (Cov.)*		-0.077 **	-0.036 **			0.005	-0.017
URBANICITY (Cov.)*		-0.006	-0.002			-0.006	-0.005
SET#3 FOLLOW-UP NUMBER			**				
FU #1	-0.070	-0.068	-0.058	0.041	-0.029	0.000	-0.017
FU #2	-0.123	-0.122	-0.118	0.027	-0.096	-0.064	-0.080
FU #3	-0.034	-0.032	-0.033	0.013	-0.021	-0.009	-0.016
FU #4	0.039	0.037	0.037	-0.009	0.030	0.020	0.025
FU #5	0.069	0.068	0.063	-0.034	0.035	0.001	0.019
FU #6	0.158	0.156	0.145	-0.057	0.101	0.055	0.081
FU #7	0.202	0.197	0.185	-0.069	0.133	0.074	0.107
SET#4 ADMINISTRATION OF FIRST FOLLOW-UP							
ONE YEAR AFTER HIGH SCHOOL	0.009	0.011	0.012	-0.014	-0.005	-0.002	0.002
TWO YEARS AFTER HIGH SCHOOL	-0.010	-0.012	-0.013	0.015	0.005	0.003	-0.002
SET#5 STUDENT STATUS AT FOLLOW-UP							
FULL-TIME STUDENT	-0.133		0.009	0.107	-0.026	0.029	0.023
PART-TIME STUDENT	-0.041		-0.035	0.058	0.017	0.008	-0.004
NOT A STUDENT	0.067		0.001	-0.058	0.009	-0.015	-0.010
SET#6 WORK STATUS AT FOLLOW-UP							
FULL-TIME CIVILIAN JOB	0.043		-0.009	-0.036	0.007	-0.011	-0.010
MILITARY SERVICE	0.025		0.023	-0.048	-0.023	-0.027	-0.013
PART-TIME JOB	-0.073		0.028	0.100	0.027	0.048	0.043
HOMEMAKER	-0.097		-0.138	0.195	0.098	0.040	-0.012
NONSTUDENT, NOT EMPLOYED	0.149		0.107	-0.106	0.043	0.088	0.093
OTHER	-0.151		-0.029	0.086	-0.065	-0.024	-0.025
SET#7 LIVING ARRANGEMENT AT FOLLOW-UP						**	**
MARRIED	0.151		0.091	0.022	0.173	0.161	0.140
PARTNER	0.025		-0.022	-0.127	-0.103	-0.144	-0.108
PARENT(S)	-0.017		-0.008	0.002	-0.015	0.004	0.000
DORM	-0.214		-0.077	0.133	-0.081	-0.079	-0.079
LIVE ALONE	-0.060		-0.076	-0.009	-0.069	-0.070	-0.072
OTHER	-0.097		-0.050	-0.044	-0.141	-0.137	-0.111
SET#8 ENGAGEMENT STATUS AT FOLLOW-UP						*	*
ENGAGED	0.064		0.109	0.011	0.075	0.188	0.164
NOT ENGAGED	-0.005		-0.008	-0.001	-0.005	-0.013	-0.012
SET#9 IS R'S SPS PREGNANT AT FOLLOW-UP?							
YES	0.221		0.100	-0.057	0.164	0.020	0.044
NO	-0.010		-0.019	0.027	0.017	0.012	0.003
DATA N.A. (1977-1983)	0.002		0.068	-0.115	-0.113	-0.060	-0.022
SET#10 PARENTHOOD STATUS AT FOLLOW-UP							
MARRIED PARENT	0.171		-0.019	0.030	0.201	0.035	0.019
SINGLE PARENT	0.008		-0.060	-0.043	-0.035	-0.042	-0.047
NOT A PARENT	-0.035		0.006	-0.004	-0.039	-0.005	-0.002
RISK OF BINGE DRINKING AT BASE YEAR (Cov.)*							0.295 **
Multiple R		0.141	0.157			0.232	0.385
R Sqr.		0.020	0.025			0.054	0.148

Notes: * indicates statistical significance at .05 level. ** indicates statistical significance at .01 level. Statistical significance is not indicated for bivariate coefficients or constants. Ns used for significance testing were weighted to approximate the number of individuals (not the number of observations) since each individual could contribute up to seven observations. Sets #5-#10 were measured at follow-up. Sets #3 and #4 were determined by timing of follow-up. All others were measured at Base Year (BY).

*Means for covariates:

HIGH SCHOOL GRADES	5.784	URBANICITY	3.749
PERCEIVED RISK OF BINGE DRINKING AT BASE YEAR	2.908	R WILL ATTEND 4YR COLLEGE	2.930

Table A.6.4a
Regression Analyses Linking Post-High School Experiences to
Changes in Disapproval of Having Five or More Drinks Once or Twice Each Weekend
Females, Senior Years 1976-1997, Follow-ups 1977-1998

VARIABLE	BIVARIATE COEFF.	Predicting to Change Scores Multivariate Coefficients BKGD.	ALL SETS	Bivariate Coeff. With Dependent Variable at BY	at FU	Multivariate Prediction of Dep. Var. at FU: Covarying BY Dep. Var? No	Yes
CONSTANT	0.049	0.049	0.049	2.095	2.145	2.145	2.145
SET#1 RACE						**	**
WHITE	0.007	0.006	0.004	-0.055	-0.047	-0.050	-0.032
BLACK	-0.083	-0.089	-0.068	0.384	0.302	0.347	0.206
OTHER	0.015	0.042	0.039	0.151	0.166	0.145	0.109
SET#2 REGION						**	
NORTHEAST	0.047	0.042	0.056	-0.133	-0.086	-0.042	-0.008
NORTH CENTRAL	0.025	0.011	0.012	-0.103	-0.078	-0.058	-0.034
SOUTH	-0.042	-0.023	-0.030	0.119	0.077	0.026	0.007
WEST	-0.035	-0.036	-0.042	0.157	0.122	0.120	0.065
HIGH SCHOOL GRADES/D=1 (Cov.)[a]		-0.049 **	-0.046 **			0.030 **	0.004
R WILL ATTEND 4YR COLLEGE (Cov.)[a]		-0.030 *	-0.010			0.016	0.007
URBANICITY (Cov.)[a]		-0.016	-0.012			-0.032 *	-0.025
SET#3 FOLLOW-UP NUMBER		**	**				**
FU #1	-0.119	-0.113	-0.041	0.048	-0.071	-0.012	-0.022
FU #2	-0.127	-0.125	-0.096	0.022	-0.106	-0.066	-0.076
FU #3	-0.041	-0.039	-0.039	0.005	-0.037	-0.028	-0.032
FU #4	0.032	0.029	0.003	-0.013	0.019	-0.004	-0.002
FU #5	0.108	0.105	0.060	-0.042	0.066	0.017	0.032
FU #6	0.211	0.204	0.139	-0.043	0.168	0.097	0.111
FU #7	0.252	0.243	0.165	-0.058	0.195	0.118	0.134
SET#4 ADMINISTRATION OF FIRST FOLLOW-UP							
ONE YEAR AFTER HIGH SCHOOL	-0.009	-0.012	-0.004	0.001	-0.008	-0.001	-0.002
TWO YEARS AFTER HIGH SCHOOL	0.009	0.012	0.004	-0.001	0.008	0.001	0.002
SET#5 STUDENT STATUS AT FOLLOW-UP							
FULL-TIME STUDENT	-0.172		0.009	0.087	-0.085	0.015	0.013
PART-TIME STUDENT	0.046		0.054	-0.031	0.014	0.029	0.038
NOT A STUDENT	0.063		-0.012	-0.031	0.033	-0.011	-0.011
SET#6 WORK STATUS AT FOLLOW-UP							
FULL-TIME CIVILIAN JOB	0.025		0.003	-0.034	-0.009	-0.011	-0.006
MILITARY SERVICE	0.041		0.008	0.120	0.160	0.113	0.077
PART-TIME JOB	-0.056		0.002	0.043	-0.014	0.002	0.002
HOMEMAKER	0.190		-0.009	0.044	0.233	0.107	0.068
NONSTUDENT, NOT EMPLOYED	0.112		0.035	-0.011	0.101	0.071	0.059
OTHER	-0.160		-0.025	0.047	-0.113	-0.048	-0.040
SET#7 LIVING ARRANGEMENT AT FOLLOW-UP						**	**
MARRIED	0.175		0.089	-0.004	0.172	0.146	0.126
PARTNER	-0.019		-0.048	-0.188	-0.207	-0.242	-0.176
PARENT(S)	-0.071		-0.026	0.052	-0.019	0.010	-0.002
DORM	-0.280		-0.136	0.154	-0.126	-0.092	-0.107
LIVE ALONE	-0.068		-0.045	-0.030	-0.098	-0.095	-0.078
OTHER	-0.115		-0.052	-0.035	-0.150	-0.137	-0.108
SET#8 ENGAGEMENT STATUS AT FOLLOW-UP			*			**	**
ENGAGED	0.031		0.129	-0.016	0.014	0.162	0.151
NOT ENGAGED	-0.003		-0.014	0.002	-0.002	-0.018	-0.017
SET#9 IS R PREGNANT AT FOLLOW-UP?						*	
YES	0.239		0.108	-0.029	0.210	0.094	0.099
NO	-0.001		-0.008	0.015	0.014	0.010	0.004
DATA N.A. (1977-1983)	-0.077		0.007	-0.076	-0.152	-0.089	-0.057
SET#10 PARENTHOOD STATUS AT FOLLOW-UP							
MARRIED PARENT	0.255		0.104	-0.035	0.220	0.043	0.064
SINGLE PARENT	0.023		0.008	-0.029	-0.005	0.018	0.015
NOT A PARENT	-0.079		-0.032	0.013	-0.066	-0.015	-0.021
DISAPPROVAL OF BINGE DRINKING AT BASE YEAR (Cov.)[a]							0.338 **
Multiple R		0.188	0.219			0.285	0.440
R Sqr.		0.035	0.048			0.081	0.194

Regression Analyses Based on Full Set of Observations from Follow-Ups 1-7
(Wtd. N of Obs: 13,162)
Unstandardized Regression Coefficients

Notes: * indicates statistical significance at .05 level. ** indicates statistical significance at .01 level. Statistical significance is not
indicated for bivariate coefficients or constants. Ns used for significance testing were weighted to approximate the number of
individuals (not the number of observations) since each individual could contribute up to seven observations. Sets #5-#10
were measured at follow-up. Sets #3 and #4 were determined by timing of follow-up. All others were measured at Base Year (BY).
[a] Means for covariates: HIGH SCHOOL GRADES 6.258 URBANICITY 3.753
DISAPPROVAL OF BINGE DRINKING AT BASE YEAR 2.095 R WILL ATTEND 4YR COLLEGE 2.848

Table A.6.4b
Regression Analyses Linking Post-High School Experiences to
Changes in Disapproval of Having Five or More Drinks Once or Twice Each Weekend
Males, Senior Years 1976-1997, Follow-ups 1977-1998

	Predicting to Change Scores			Bivariate Coeff. With Dependent Variable		Multivariate Prediction of Dep. Var. at FU: Covarying BY Dep. Var?	
	BIVARIATE COEFF.	Multivariate Coefficients BKGD.	ALL SETS	at BY	at FU	No	Yes
VARIABLE							
CONSTANT	0.050	0.050	0.050	1.828	1.877	1.877	1.877
SET#1 RACE						**	**
WHITE	0.013	0.011	0.011	-0.050	-0.038	-0.037	-0.019
BLACK	-0.115	-0.145	-0.135	0.436	0.321	0.366	0.183
OTHER	-0.048	-0.011	-0.020	0.195	0.147	0.111	0.063
SET#2 REGION						**	*
NORTHEAST	-0.051	-0.054	-0.047	-0.059	-0.110	-0.086	-0.072
NORTH CENTRAL	0.047	0.030	0.028	-0.112	-0.064	-0.051	-0.022
SOUTH	0.014	0.022	0.018	0.059	0.073	0.041	0.033
WEST	-0.045	-0.025	-0.022	0.175	0.130	0.132	0.076
HIGH SCHOOL GRADES/D=1 (Cov.)ᵃ		-0.034 **	-0.030 **			0.049 **	0.020 *
R WILL ATTEND 4YR COLLEGE (Cov.)ᵃ		-0.058 **	-0.038 *			-0.017	-0.025
URBANICITY (Cov.)ᵃ		-0.013	-0.007			0.001	-0.002
SET#3 FOLLOW-UP NUMBER			**				
FU #1	-0.090	-0.082	-0.001	0.042	-0.049	-0.024	-0.015
FU #2	-0.104	-0.099	-0.047	0.032	-0.072	-0.040	-0.043
FU #3	-0.050	-0.051	-0.046	0.002	-0.049	-0.038	-0.041
FU #4	0.026	0.025	-0.006	0.001	0.027	0.019	0.010
FU #5	0.087	0.081	0.019	-0.038	0.049	0.016	0.017
FU #6	0.159	0.148	0.066	-0.055	0.105	0.059	0.061
FU #7	0.218	0.206	0.109	-0.068	0.150	0.104	0.105
SET#4 ADMINISTRATION OF FIRST FOLLOW-UP							
ONE YEAR AFTER HIGH SCHOOL	-0.010	-0.010	-0.003	0.021	0.011	0.007	0.003
TWO YEARS AFTER HIGH SCHOOL	0.011	0.011	0.003	-0.023	-0.012	-0.008	-0.004
SET#5 STUDENT STATUS AT FOLLOW-UP							
FULL-TIME STUDENT	-0.168		-0.037	0.132	-0.036	0.013	-0.005
PART-TIME STUDENT	-0.030		-0.025	0.087	0.057	0.060	0.029
NOT A STUDENT	0.079		0.020	-0.072	0.007	-0.015	-0.002
SET#6 WORK STATUS AT FOLLOW-UP							
FULL-TIME CIVILIAN JOB	0.072		0.006	-0.059	0.013	-0.013	-0.006
MILITARY SERVICE	-0.167		-0.200	0.056	-0.111	-0.064	-0.114
PART-TIME JOB	-0.140		-0.014	0.129	-0.011	0.021	0.008
HOMEMAKER	0.301		0.167	0.045	0.346	0.311	0.258
NONSTUDENT, NOT EMPLOYED	0.076		0.031	0.000	0.076	0.101	0.075
OTHER	-0.133		0.040	0.096	-0.038	0.017	0.026
SET#7 LIVING ARRANGEMENT AT FOLLOW-UP						**	**
MARRIED	0.186		0.109	-0.035	0.151	0.152	0.136
PARTNER	0.060		0.020	-0.113	-0.053	-0.099	-0.056
PARENT(S)	-0.032		-0.015	0.034	0.001	0.018	0.006
DORM	-0.260		-0.148	0.224	-0.035	-0.052	-0.087
LIVE ALONE	-0.007		-0.006	-0.035	-0.043	-0.053	-0.036
OTHER	-0.158		-0.095	-0.023	-0.182	-0.178	-0.147
SET#8 ENGAGEMENT STATUS AT FOLLOW-UP						*	*
ENGAGED	0.050		0.068	0.003	0.053	0.147	0.118
NOT ENGAGED	-0.004		-0.006	0.000	-0.005	-0.013	-0.010
SET#9 IS R'S SPS PREGNANT AT FOLLOW-UP?							
YES	0.191		0.044	0.016	0.208	0.096	0.077
NO	0.005		0.000	0.010	0.015	0.010	0.006
DATA N.A. (1977-1983)	-0.066		-0.008	-0.051	-0.118	-0.066	-0.045
SET#10 PARENTHOOD STATUS AT FOLLOW-UP							
MARRIED PARENT	0.233		0.043	-0.077	0.156	0.002	0.017
SINGLE PARENT	0.075		0.050	-0.113	-0.037	-0.047	-0.011
NOT A PARENT	-0.055		-0.012	0.023	-0.033	0.002	-0.003
DISAPPROVAL OF BINGE DRINKING AT BASE YEAR (Cov.)ᵃ							0.366 **
Multiple R		0.175	0.204			0.251	0.437
R Sqr.		0.031	0.042			0.063	0.191

Notes: * indicates statistical significance at .05 level. ** indicates statistical significance at .01 level. Statistical significance is not indicated for bivariate coefficients or constants. Ns used for significance testing were weighted to approximate the number of individuals (not the number of observations) since each individual could contribute up to seven observations. Sets #5-#10 were measured at follow-up. Sets #3 and #4 were determined by timing of follow-up. All others were measured at Base Year (BY).
ᵃMeans for covariates: HIGH SCHOOL GRADES 5.789 — URBANICITY 3.727 — DISAPPROVAL OF BINGE DRINKING AT BASE YEAR 1.828 — R WILL ATTEND 4YR COLLEGE 2.881

Table A.6.5a
Regression Analyses Linking Post-High School Experiences to Changes in Perceived Risk of Using Marijuana Index
Females, Senior Years 1976-1997, Follow-ups 1977-1998

Regression Analyses Based on Full Set of Observations from Follow-Ups 1-7 (Wtd. N of Obs: 12,483) Unstandardized Regression Coefficients

VARIABLE	BIVARIATE COEFF.	BKGD.	ALL SETS	at BY	at FU	No	Yes
		Predicting to Change Scores / Multivariate Coefficients		Bivariate Coeff. With Dependent Variable		Multivariate Prediction of Dep. Var. at FU: Covarying BY Dep. Var?	
CONSTANT	0.085	0.085	0.085	3.378	3.463	3.463	3.463
SET#1 RACE						**	*
WHITE	0.007	0.004	0.006	-0.052	-0.045	-0.046	-0.024
BLACK	-0.014	0.002	-0.010	0.273	0.260	0.267	0.150
OTHER	-0.056	-0.047	-0.046	0.248	0.192	0.197	0.094
SET#2 REGION						**	
NORTHEAST	0.045	0.032	0.043	-0.261	-0.216	-0.158	-0.074
NORTH CENTRAL	0.060	0.042	0.047	-0.064	-0.004	0.018	0.030
SOUTH	-0.085	-0.066	-0.074	0.271	0.185	0.119	0.037
WEST	-0.024	-0.007	-0.017	-0.002	-0.027	-0.028	-0.023
HIGH SCHOOL GRADES/D=1 (Cov.)[a]		-0.036 **	-0.033 *			0.044 **	0.012
R WILL ATTEND 4YR COLLEGE (Cov.)[a]		-0.098 **	-0.068 **			-0.004	-0.031
URBANICITY (Cov.)[a]		0.029	0.034			-0.087 **	-0.036
SET#3 FOLLOW-UP NUMBER		**	**				
FU #1	-0.202	-0.188	-0.131	0.139	-0.062	0.068	-0.016
FU #2	-0.155	-0.148	-0.113	0.083	-0.072	0.031	-0.030
FU #3	-0.113	-0.114	-0.109	0.048	-0.064	-0.044	-0.071
FU #4	0.024	0.017	0.006	-0.012	0.012	-0.058	-0.031
FU #5	0.174	0.168	0.133	-0.089	0.085	-0.028	0.040
FU #6	0.349	0.337	0.266	-0.192	0.157	0.003	0.114
FU #7	0.431	0.414	0.321	-0.296	0.135	-0.032	0.117
SET#4 ADMINISTRATION OF FIRST FOLLOW-UP							
ONE YEAR AFTER HIGH SCHOOL	0.006	0.009	0.016	0.013	0.019	0.028	0.023
TWO YEARS AFTER HIGH SCHOOL	-0.006	-0.010	-0.018	-0.015	-0.021	-0.031	-0.026
SET#5 STUDENT STATUS AT FOLLOW-UP							
FULL-TIME STUDENT	-0.254		0.003	0.161	-0.093	-0.024	-0.013
PART-TIME STUDENT	0.038		0.062	-0.048	-0.010	0.010	0.032
NOT A STUDENT	0.099		-0.011	-0.060	0.040	0.009	0.001
SET#6 WORK STATUS AT FOLLOW-UP							
FULL-TIME CIVILIAN JOB	0.046		0.012	-0.060	-0.014	-0.016	-0.004
MILITARY SERVICE	-0.053		0.012	0.177	0.124	0.214	0.129
PART-TIME JOB	-0.114		-0.019	0.116	0.002	0.009	-0.003
HOMEMAKER	0.258		-0.018	0.004	0.263	0.078	0.037
NONSTUDENT, NOT EMPLOYED	0.156		0.040	-0.137	0.019	-0.021	0.005
OTHER	-0.208		-0.026	0.098	-0.110	0.003	-0.009
SET#7 LIVING ARRANGEMENT AT FOLLOW-UP						**	**
MARRIED	0.247		0.107	-0.042	0.205	0.153	0.134
PARTNER	-0.165		-0.192	-0.199	-0.365	-0.422	-0.325
PARENT(S)	-0.080		-0.002	0.116	0.036	0.106	0.060
DORM	-0.334		-0.072	0.205	-0.129	-0.085	-0.080
LIVE ALONE	-0.044		-0.009	-0.078	-0.122	-0.092	-0.057
OTHER	-0.180		-0.105	-0.045	-0.225	-0.218	-0.170
SET#8 ENGAGEMENT STATUS AT FOLLOW-UP						*	*
ENGAGED	-0.084		0.070	0.075	-0.009	0.183	0.136
NOT ENGAGED	0.008		-0.006	-0.007	0.001	-0.017	-0.012
SET#9 IS R PREGNANT AT FOLLOW-UP?			*			**	**
YES	0.206		0.035	0.027	0.233	0.104	0.075
NO	-0.014		-0.027	0.082	0.068	0.077	0.033
DATA N.A. (1977-1983)	0.012		0.146	-0.482	-0.470	-0.475	-0.213
SET#10 PARENTHOOD STATUS AT FOLLOW-UP			**				**
MARRIED PARENT	0.370		0.140	-0.086	0.284	0.099	0.116
SINGLE PARENT	0.158		0.186	-0.118	0.040	0.108	0.141
NOT A PARENT	-0.126		-0.059	0.037	-0.089	-0.040	-0.048
RISK OF MARIJUANA AT BASE YEAR (Cov.)[a]						0.422 **	
Multiple R		0.214	0.245			0.297	0.513
R Sqr.		0.046	0.060			0.088	0.263

Notes: * indicates statistical significance at .05 level. ** indicates statistical significance at .01 level. Statistical significance is not indicated for bivariate coefficients or constants. Ns used for significance testing were weighted to approximate the number of individuals (not the number of observations) since each individual could contribute up to seven observations. Sets #5-#10 were measured at follow-up. Sets #3 and #4 were determined by timing of follow-up. All others were measured at Base Year (BY).

[a]Means for covariates: HIGH SCHOOL GRADES 6.347   URBANICITY 3.784   PERCEIVED RISK OF MARIJUANA USE (INDEX) AT BASE YEAR 3.378   R WILL ATTEND 4YR COLLEGE 2.896

Table A.6.5b
Regression Analyses Linking Post-High School Experiences to Changes in Perceived Risk of Using Marijuana Index
Males, Senior Years 1976-1997, Follow-ups 1977-1998

Regression Analyses Based on Full Set of Observations from Follow-Ups 1-7
(Wtd. N of Obs: 9,965)
Unstandardized Regression Coefficients

VARIABLE	Predicting to Change Scores			Bivariate Coeff. With Dependent Variable		Multivariate Prediction of Dep. Var. at FU: Covarying BY Dep. Var?	
	BIVARIATE COEFF.	Multivariate Coefficients BKGD.	ALL SETS	at BY	at FU	No	Yes
CONSTANT	0.024	0.024	0.024	3.246	3.270	3.270	3.270
SET#1 RACE						**	**
WHITE	-0.004	-0.004	-0.003	-0.045	-0.049	-0.052	-0.031
BLACK	0.190	0.181	0.162	0.114	0.304	0.348	0.266
OTHER	-0.091	-0.078	-0.076	0.395	0.303	0.312	0.141
SET#2 REGION					**		
NORTHEAST	-0.047	-0.050	-0.041	-0.196	-0.243	-0.166	-0.111
NORTH CENTRAL	0.060	0.050	0.045	-0.051	0.009	0.015	0.029
SOUTH	-0.035	-0.035	-0.045	0.196	0.161	0.092	0.032
WEST	0.013	0.036	0.049	0.030	0.043	0.043	0.046
HIGH SCHOOL GRADES/D=1 (Cov.)[a]		-0.046 **	-0.040 **			0.036 *	0.002
R WILL ATTEND 4YR COLLEGE (Cov.)[a]		-0.071 **	-0.047 **			0.004	-0.018
URBANICITY (Cov.)[a]		0.032	0.045			-0.108 **	-0.041
SET#3 FOLLOW-UP NUMBER		**	*				
FU #1	-0.127	-0.124	-0.082	0.108	-0.020	0.083	0.011
FU #2	-0.163	-0.164	-0.128	0.094	-0.069	0.024	-0.043
FU #3	-0.091	-0.090	-0.083	0.066	-0.025	0.003	-0.035
FU #4	0.017	0.017	0.014	-0.012	0.005	-0.047	-0.020
FU #5	0.137	0.134	0.101	-0.106	0.031	-0.071	0.005
FU #6	0.296	0.294	0.230	-0.181	0.116	-0.022	0.089
FU #7	0.346	0.342	0.258	-0.267	0.079	-0.081	0.068
SET#4 ADMINISTRATION OF FIRST FOLLOW-UP							
ONE YEAR AFTER HIGH SCHOOL	-0.013	-0.009	-0.005	0.006	-0.007	0.001	-0.002
TWO YEARS AFTER HIGH SCHOOL	0.014	0.010	0.006	-0.006	0.008	-0.001	0.002
SET#5 STUDENT STATUS AT FOLLOW-UP							
FULL-TIME STUDENT	-0.221		-0.015	0.155	-0.066	0.005	-0.004
PART-TIME STUDENT	-0.043		-0.049	0.023	-0.020	-0.020	-0.033
NOT A STUDENT	0.108		0.015	-0.075	0.033	0.001	0.007
SET#6 WORK STATUS AT FOLLOW-UP							
FULL-TIME CIVILIAN JOB	0.081		0.004	-0.061	0.020	-0.005	-0.001
MILITARY SERVICE	0.125		0.106	0.059	0.184	0.175	0.145
PART-TIME JOB	-0.186		-0.029	0.151	-0.035	-0.010	-0.019
HOMEMAKER	-0.024		-0.079	0.293	0.269	0.172	0.061
NONSTUDENT, NOT EMPLOYED	0.104		0.042	-0.153	-0.049	0.002	0.020
OTHER	-0.214		-0.034	0.112	-0.102	-0.036	-0.035
SET#7 LIVING ARRANGEMENT AT FOLLOW-UP						**	**
MARRIED	0.279		0.157	-0.021	0.258	0.181	0.171
PARTNER	-0.044		-0.131	-0.386	-0.430	-0.451	-0.310
PARENT(S)	-0.062		-0.014	0.091	0.030	0.078	0.038
DORM	-0.276		-0.062	0.180	-0.096	-0.042	-0.051
LIVE ALONE	-0.045		-0.068	-0.050	-0.095	-0.072	-0.071
OTHER	-0.183		-0.114	-0.023	-0.205	-0.188	-0.156
SET#8 ENGAGEMENT STATUS AT FOLLOW-UP							*
ENGAGED	0.055		0.158	-0.070	-0.015	0.185	0.173
NOT ENGAGED	-0.004		-0.011	0.005	0.001	-0.013	-0.012
SET#9 IS R'S SPS PREGNANT AT FOLLOW-UP?			**			**	*
YES	0.375		0.122	-0.069	0.305	0.130	0.126
NO	-0.030		-0.045	0.102	0.072	0.079	0.024
DATA N.A. (1977-1983)	0.062		0.188	-0.465	-0.402	-0.402	-0.142
SET#10 PARENTHOOD STATUS AT FOLLOW-UP							
MARRIED PARENT	0.367		0.082	-0.039	0.328	0.104	0.095
SINGLE PARENT	0.222		0.167	-0.355	-0.133	-0.081	0.028
NOT A PARENT	-0.083		-0.023	0.023	-0.060	-0.018	-0.020
RISK OF MARIJUANA AT BASE YEAR (Cov.)[a]							0.440 **
Multiple R		0.182	0.220			0.286	0.523
R Sqr.		0.033	0.049			0.082	0.274

Notes: * indicates statistical significance at .05 level. ** indicates statistical significance at .01 level. Statistical significance is not indicated for bivariate coefficients or constants. Ns used for significance testing were weighted to approximate the number of individuals (not the number of observations) since each individual could contribute up to seven observations. Sets #5-#10 were measured at follow-up. Sets #3 and #4 were determined by timing of follow-up. All others were measured at Base Year (BY).
[a]Means for covariates:

HIGH SCHOOL GRADES	5.794	URBANICITY	3.768
PERCEIVED RISK OF MARIJUANA USE (INDEX) AT BASE YEAR	3.246	R WILL ATTEND 4YR COLLEGE	2.944

Table A.6.6a
Regression Analyses Linking Post-High School Experiences to Changes in Disapproval Index of Using Marijuana
Females, Senior Years 1976-1997, Follow-ups 1977-1998

Regression Analyses Based on Full Set of Observations from Follow-Ups 1-7
(Wtd. N of Obs: 13,169)
Unstandardized Regression Coefficients

VARIABLE	BIVARIATE COEFF.	Multivariate Coefficients BKGD.	ALL SETS	Bivariate Coeff. With Dependent Variable at BY	at FU	Multivariate Prediction of Dep. Var. at FU: Covarying BY Dep. Var? No	Yes
CONSTANT	0.144	0.144	0.144	6.387	6.531	6.531	6.531
SET#1 RACE						**	**
WHITE	-0.007	-0.009	-0.009	-0.084	-0.091	-0.100	-0.053
BLACK	0.045	0.047	0.052	0.368	0.413	0.445	0.244
OTHER	0.024	0.040	0.040	0.483	0.508	0.560	0.294
SET#2 REGION						**	
NORTHEAST	0.145	0.135	0.168	-0.589	-0.443	-0.295	-0.058
NORTH CENTRAL	-0.033	-0.067	-0.065	0.003	-0.031	0.008	-0.029
SOUTH	-0.062	-0.035	-0.058	0.390	0.327	0.195	0.066
WEST	-0.015	0.014	0.009	0.063	0.048	0.017	0.013
HIGH SCHOOL GRADES/D=1 (Cov.)[a]		-0.081 **	-0.073 **			0.125 **	0.024
R WILL ATTEND 4YR COLLEGE (Cov.)[a]		-0.177 **	-0.115 **			0.021	-0.049
URBANICITY (Cov.)[a]		-0.002	0.007			-0.220 **	-0.104 **
SET#3 FOLLOW-UP NUMBER		**	**				**
FU #1	-0.214	-0.193	-0.023	0.157	-0.057	0.140	0.057
FU #2	-0.275	-0.265	-0.171	0.143	-0.132	0.042	-0.067
FU #3	-0.212	-0.205	-0.196	0.085	-0.126	-0.083	-0.141
FU #4	-0.054	-0.062	-0.122	-0.014	-0.068	-0.169	-0.145
FU #5	0.272	0.262	0.139	-0.150	0.122	-0.070	0.037
FU #6	0.569	0.545	0.369	-0.259	0.310	0.056	0.216
FU #7	0.709	0.672	0.466	-0.401	0.308	0.030	0.253
SET#4 ADMINISTRATION OF FIRST FOLLOW-UP							
ONE YEAR AFTER HIGH SCHOOL	0.016	0.015	0.031	0.025	0.042	0.067	0.048
TWO YEARS AFTER HIGH SCHOOL	-0.017	-0.016	-0.031	-0.026	-0.042	-0.068	-0.049
SET#5 STUDENT STATUS AT FOLLOW-UP							
FULL-TIME STUDENT	-0.428		-0.088	0.323	-0.105	-0.019	-0.054
PART-TIME STUDENT	-0.035		-0.002	-0.071	-0.106	-0.044	-0.023
NOT A STUDENT	0.181		0.036	-0.122	0.059	0.014	0.026
SET#6 WORK STATUS AT FOLLOW-UP							
FULL-TIME CIVILIAN JOB	0.028		-0.034	-0.072	-0.044	-0.018	-0.026
MILITARY SERVICE	0.576		0.483	0.053	0.629	0.628	0.554
PART-TIME JOB	-0.108		0.071	0.146	0.038	0.010	0.041
HOMEMAKER	0.657		0.134	-0.123	0.534	0.246	0.188
NONSTUDENT, NOT EMPLOYED	0.099		-0.168	-0.072	0.027	-0.046	-0.108
OTHER	-0.356		-0.001	0.152	-0.205	-0.081	-0.040
SET#7 LIVING ARRANGEMENT AT FOLLOW-UP			**			**	**
MARRIED	0.442		0.263	-0.048	0.394	0.301	0.282
PARTNER	-0.287		-0.372	-0.651	-0.938	-1.019	-0.688
PARENT(S)	-0.105		-0.031	0.259	0.154	0.274	0.118
DORM	-0.553		-0.197	0.438	-0.115	-0.092	-0.146
LIVE ALONE	-0.237		-0.135	-0.073	-0.310	-0.276	-0.204
OTHER	-0.323		-0.200	-0.141	-0.463	-0.426	-0.310
SET#8 ENGAGEMENT STATUS AT FOLLOW-UP						**	**
ENGAGED	-0.057		0.224	0.009	-0.047	0.376	0.299
NOT ENGAGED	0.006		-0.025	-0.001	0.005	-0.042	-0.033
SET#9 IS R PREGNANT AT FOLLOW-UP?						**	**
YES	0.447		0.097	0.009	0.455	0.260	0.177
NO	-0.008		-0.011	0.114	0.106	0.122	0.054
DATA N.A. (1977-1983)	-0.111		0.029	-0.663	-0.774	-0.796	-0.374
SET#10 PARENTHOOD STATUS AT FOLLOW-UP			**				*
MARRIED PARENT	0.635		0.158	-0.106	0.529	0.168	0.163
SINGLE PARENT	0.351		0.346	-0.446	-0.095	0.150	0.250
NOT A PARENT	-0.221		-0.079	0.072	-0.150	-0.064	-0.071
DISAPPROVAL OF MARIJUANA AT BASE YEAR (Cov.)[a]							0.512 **
Multiple R		0.219	0.257			0.337	0.607
R Sqr.		0.048	0.066			0.114	0.368

Notes: * indicates statistical significance at .05 level. ** indicates statistical significance at .01 level. Statistical significance is not indicated for bivariate coefficients or constants. Ns used for significance testing were weighted to approximate the number of individuals (not the number of observations) since each individual could contribute up to seven observations. Sets #5-#10 were measured at follow-up. Sets #3 and #4 were determined by timing of follow-up. All others were measured at Base Year (BY).

[a]Means for covariates: HIGH SCHOOL GRADES 6.264   URBANICITY 3.751
   DISAPPROVAL OF MARIJUANA USE (INDEX) AT BASE YEAR 6.387   R WILL ATTEND 4YR COLLEGE 2.852

Table A.6.6b
Regression Analyses Linking Post-High School Experiences to
Changes in Disapproval Index of Using Marijuana
Males, Senior Years 1976-1997, Follow-ups 1977-1998

		Regression Analyses Based on Full Set of Observations from Follow-Ups 1-7 (Wtd. N of Obs: 10,578) Unstandardized Regression Coefficients					
	Predicting to Change Scores			Bivariate Coeff. With Dependent Variable		Multivariate Prediction of Dep. Var. at FU: Covarying BY Dep. Var?	
	BIVARIATE	Multivariate Coefficients					
VARIABLE	COEFF.	BKGD.	ALL SETS	at BY	at FU	No	Yes
CONSTANT	0.174	0.174	0.174	6.025	6.200	6.200	6.200
SET#1 RACE						**	**
WHITE	-0.015	-0.018	-0.018	-0.061	-0.076	-0.083	-0.050
BLACK	0.019	-0.076	-0.035	0.484	0.503	0.622	0.286
OTHER	0.130	0.214	0.190	0.261	0.391	0.385	0.285
SET#2 REGION							*
NORTHEAST	0.063	0.038	0.061	-0.382	-0.319	-0.193	-0.063
NORTH CENTRAL	0.003	-0.011	-0.016	-0.032	-0.028	-0.018	-0.017
SOUTH	0.070	0.092	0.077	0.226	0.297	0.197	0.136
WEST	-0.218	-0.199	-0.193	0.147	-0.072	-0.075	-0.135
HIGH SCHOOL GRADES/D=1 (Cov.)[a]		-0.063 *	-0.053 *			0.127 **	0.035
R WILL ATTEND 4YR COLLEGE (Cov.)[a]		-0.202 **	-0.165 **			-0.087	-0.127 **
URBANICITY (Cov.)[a]		0.057	0.066			-0.148 **	-0.039
SET#3 FOLLOW-UP NUMBER			**	*			
FU #1	-0.179	-0.163	-0.054	0.181	0.002	0.164	0.053
FU #2	-0.222	-0.211	-0.130	0.160	-0.062	0.096	-0.019
FU #3	-0.192	-0.196	-0.179	0.076	-0.115	-0.056	-0.119
FU #4	-0.013	-0.013	-0.043	0.024	0.011	-0.064	-0.053
FU #5	0.197	0.189	0.093	-0.171	0.026	-0.159	-0.030
FU #6	0.407	0.388	0.250	-0.303	0.103	-0.133	0.063
FU #7	0.618	0.597	0.440	-0.428	0.189	-0.042	0.204
SET#4 ADMINISTRATION OF FIRST FOLLOW-UP							
ONE YEAR AFTER HIGH SCHOOL	-0.006	-0.004	0.009	0.074	0.069	0.072	0.040
TWO YEARS AFTER HIGH SCHOOL	0.006	0.004	-0.010	-0.082	-0.076	-0.079	-0.044
SET#5 STUDENT STATUS AT FOLLOW-UP							
FULL-TIME STUDENT	-0.384		-0.049	0.339	-0.045	0.094	0.021
PART-TIME STUDENT	0.101		0.122	0.039	0.140	0.165	0.143
NOT A STUDENT	0.155		0.003	-0.156	-0.001	-0.067	-0.031
SET#6 WORK STATUS AT FOLLOW-UP							
FULL-TIME CIVILIAN JOB	0.135		-0.006	-0.092	0.043	0.025	0.009
MILITARY SERVICE	0.049		-0.006	-0.013	0.037	0.155	0.073
PART-TIME JOB	-0.322		-0.050	0.272	-0.050	-0.063	-0.056
HOMEMAKER	0.675		0.315	0.534	1.209	1.007	0.653
NONSTUDENT, NOT EMPLOYED	0.122		0.025	-0.303	-0.181	-0.075	-0.024
OTHER	-0.296		0.066	0.183	-0.113	-0.085	-0.008
SET#7 LIVING ARRANGEMENT AT FOLLOW-UP						**	**
MARRIED	0.451		0.229	-0.041	0.410	0.338	0.282
PARTNER	-0.152		-0.209	-0.345	-0.498	-0.637	-0.418
PARENT(S)	-0.016		0.032	0.114	0.098	0.175	0.102
DORM	-0.504		-0.212	0.567	0.063	0.023	-0.097
LIVE ALONE	-0.107		-0.093	-0.155	-0.262	-0.199	-0.145
OTHER	-0.361		-0.190	-0.122	-0.483	-0.444	-0.314
SET#8 ENGAGEMENT STATUS AT FOLLOW-UP						**	**
ENGAGED	0.030		0.192	0.152	0.182	0.531	0.358
NOT ENGAGED	-0.003		-0.017	-0.013	-0.016	-0.046	-0.031
SET#9 IS R'S SPS PREGNANT AT FOLLOW-UP?						**	**
YES	0.520		0.187	0.211	0.731	0.535	0.357
NO	-0.002		-0.013	0.119	0.117	0.138	0.061
DATA N.A. (1977-1983)	-0.100		0.023	-0.612	-0.712	-0.770	-0.365
SET#10 PARENTHOOD STATUS AT FOLLOW-UP							
MARRIED PARENT	0.598		0.154	-0.132	0.466	0.117	0.136
SINGLE PARENT	-0.005		-0.060	-0.428	-0.433	-0.349	-0.202
NOT A PARENT	-0.131		-0.031	0.051	-0.079	-0.007	-0.019
DISAPPROVAL OF MARIJUANA AT BASE YEAR (Cov.)[a]							0.511 **
Multiple R		0.190	0.213			0.288	0.578
R Sqr.		0.036	0.046			0.083	0.334

Notes: * indicates statistical significance at .05 level. ** indicates statistical significance at .01 level. Statistical significance is not indicated for bivariate coefficients or constants. Ns used for significance testing were weighted to approximate the number of individuals (not the number of observations) since each individual could contribute to seven observations. Sets #5-#10 were measured at follow-up. Sets #3 and #4 were determined by timing of follow-up. All others were measured at Base Year (BY).
[a]Means for covariates: HIGH SCHOOL GRADES 5.791   URBANICITY 3.727
DISAPPROVAL OF MARIJUANA USE (INDEX) AT BASE YEAR 6.025   R WILL ATTEND 4YR COLLEGE 2.882

Table A.6.7a
Regression Analyses Linking Post-High School Experiences to Changes in Perceived Risk of Using Cocaine Index
Females, Senior Years 1976-1997, Follow-ups 1977-1998

	Regression Analyses Based on Full Set of Observations from Follow-Ups 1-7 (Wtd. N of Obs: 11,816) Unstandardized Regression Coefficients						
	Predicting to Change Scores			Bivariate Coeff. With Dependent Variable		Multivariate Prediction of Dep. Var. at FU: Covarying BY Dep. Var?	
		Multivariate Coefficients					
VARIABLE	BIVARIATE COEFF.	BKGD.	ALL SETS	at BY	at FU	No	Yes
CONSTANT	0.221	0.221	0.221	6.904	7.124	7.124	7.124
SET#1 RACE							
WHITE	-0.012	-0.009	-0.009	-0.008	-0.020	-0.021	-0.017
BLACK	0.057	0.038	0.059	0.075	0.132	0.115	0.097
OTHER	0.062	0.058	0.035	0.011	0.074	0.099	0.078
SET#2 REGION						**	**
NORTHEAST	0.042	0.030	0.040	-0.238	-0.197	-0.161	-0.095
NORTH CENTRAL	-0.029	-0.030	-0.027	0.072	0.043	0.060	0.031
SOUTH	-0.009	0.003	-0.007	0.180	0.172	0.134	0.087
WEST	0.011	0.010	0.008	-0.121	-0.110	-0.124	-0.081
HIGH SCHOOL GRADES/D=1 (Cov.)[a]		-0.052 **	-0.051 **			0.038 **	0.009
R WILL ATTEND 4YR COLLEGE (Cov.)[a]		-0.003	-0.008			0.056 **	0.035
URBANICITY (Cov.)[a]		0.009	0.010			-0.037	-0.021
SET#3 FOLLOW-UP NUMBER		**	**				
FU #1	-0.206	-0.208	-0.148	0.121	-0.085	0.042	-0.020
FU #2	-0.161	-0.161	-0.123	0.071	-0.090	-0.008	-0.046
FU #3	-0.080	-0.082	-0.071	0.022	-0.058	-0.042	-0.051
FU #4	0.025	0.024	-0.007	-0.022	0.002	-0.064	-0.045
FU #5	0.224	0.227	0.177	-0.073	0.151	0.040	0.085
FU #6	0.331	0.335	0.266	-0.180	0.151	0.014	0.097
FU #7	0.356	0.360	0.285	-0.190	0.166	0.023	0.109
SET#4 ADMINISTRATION OF FIRST FOLLOW-UP							
ONE YEAR AFTER HIGH SCHOOL	-0.005	-0.006	0.003	0.026	0.020	0.030	0.021
TWO YEARS AFTER HIGH SCHOOL	0.006	0.006	-0.003	-0.029	-0.023	-0.034	-0.023
SET#5 STUDENT STATUS AT FOLLOW-UP							
FULL-TIME STUDENT	-0.162		0.073	0.139	-0.023	0.064	0.067
PART-TIME STUDENT	0.070		0.060	-0.071	-0.001	0.004	0.023
NOT A STUDENT	0.058		-0.040	-0.048	0.010	-0.027	-0.032
SET#6 WORK STATUS AT FOLLOW-UP							
FULL-TIME CIVILIAN JOB	0.042		0.018	-0.036	0.006	0.017	0.017
MILITARY SERVICE	-0.118		-0.031	0.062	-0.056	0.062	0.031
PART-TIME JOB	-0.070		-0.019	0.087	0.017	0.000	-0.007
HOMEMAKER	0.172		0.002	-0.019	0.153	0.037	0.025
NONSTUDENT, NOT EMPLOYED	0.102		0.080	-0.162	-0.060	-0.003	0.025
OTHER	-0.189		-0.072	0.077	-0.112	-0.092	-0.085
SET#7 LIVING ARRANGEMENT AT FOLLOW-UP						**	**
MARRIED	0.187		0.088	-0.024	0.163	0.139	0.122
PARTNER	-0.129		-0.176	-0.089	-0.218	-0.248	-0.224
PARENT(S)	-0.063		0.014	-0.001	-0.065	0.003	0.006
DORM	-0.259		-0.055	0.223	-0.036	-0.072	-0.067
LIVE ALONE	-0.038		-0.068	0.030	-0.008	-0.029	-0.042
OTHER	-0.120		-0.076	-0.017	-0.138	-0.149	-0.125
SET#8 ENGAGEMENT STATUS AT FOLLOW-UP							
ENGAGED	-0.027		0.107	0.008	-0.019	0.127	0.120
NOT ENGAGED	0.002		-0.010	-0.001	0.002	-0.012	-0.011
SET#9 IS R PREGNANT AT FOLLOW-UP?		**				**	**
YES	0.062		-0.049	0.044	0.106	0.008	-0.011
NO	0.060		0.045	0.024	0.083	0.081	0.070
DATA N.A. (1977-1983)	-0.380		-0.257	-0.159	-0.538	-0.493	-0.415
SET#10 PARENTHOOD STATUS AT FOLLOW-UP							
MARRIED PARENT	0.266		0.057	-0.052	0.214	0.079	0.071
SINGLE PARENT	0.025		-0.022	-0.026	0.000	0.093	0.055
NOT A PARENT	-0.081		-0.015	0.018	-0.063	-0.032	-0.026
RISK OF COCAINE AT BASE YEAR (Cov.)[a]							0.331 **
Multiple R		0.168	0.195			0.270	0.451
R Sqr.		0.028	0.038			0.073	0.203

Notes: * indicates statistical significance at .05 level. ** indicates statistical significance at .01 level. Statistical significance is not indicated for bivariate coefficients or constants. Ns used for significance testing were weighted to approximate the number of individuals (not the number of observations) since each individual could contribute up to seven observations. Sets #5-#10 were measured at follow-up. Sets #3 and #4 were determined by timing of follow-up. All others were measured at Base Year (BY).

[a] Means for covariates: HIGH SCHOOL GRADES 6.365   URBANICITY 3.797
PERCEIVED RISK OF COCAINE USE (INDEX) AT BASE YEAR 6.904   R WILL ATTEND 4YR COLLEGE 2.919

Table A.6.7b

**Regression Analyses Linking Post-High School Experiences to
Changes in Perceived Risk of Using Cocaine Index
Males, Senior Years 1976-1997, Follow-ups 1977-1998**

Regression Analyses Based on Full Set of Observations from Follow-Ups 1-7
(Wtd. N of Obs: 9,450)
Unstandardized Regression Coefficients

| VARIABLE | Predicting to Change Scores | | | Bivariate Coeff. With Dependent Variable | | Multivariate Prediction of Dep. Var. at FU: Covarying BY Dep. Var? | |
| | BIVARIATE COEFF. | Multivariate Coefficients | | | | | |
		BKGD.	ALL SETS	at BY	at FU	No	Yes
CONSTANT	0.165	0.165	0.165	6.759	6.924	6.924	6.924
SET#1 RACE						**	*
WHITE	-0.012	-0.013	-0.007	-0.021	-0.033	-0.038	-0.028
BLACK	0.021	0.020	-0.029	0.260	0.280	0.300	0.193
OTHER	0.114	0.120	0.086	0.052	0.166	0.197	0.161
SET#2 REGION						**	**
NORTHEAST	-0.112	-0.107	-0.094	-0.152	-0.264	-0.189	-0.158
NORTH CENTRAL	0.020	0.011	0.002	0.021	0.042	0.039	0.027
SOUTH	-0.005	-0.003	-0.004	0.210	0.205	0.142	0.094
WEST	0.122	0.128	0.128	-0.178	-0.056	-0.049	0.009
HIGH SCHOOL GRADES/D=1 (Cov.)*		-0.029	-0.022			0.027	0.011
R WILL ATTEND 4YR COLLEGE (Cov.)*		-0.083 *	-0.071 *			0.056 *	0.014
URBANICITY (Cov.)*		-0.005	0.008			-0.117 **	-0.076 **
SET#3 FOLLOW-UP NUMBER			**				
FU #1	-0.176	-0.177	-0.052	0.117	-0.059	0.100	0.050
FU #2	-0.165	-0.168	-0.086	0.082	-0.083	0.032	-0.006
FU #3	-0.094	-0.092	-0.088	0.047	-0.047	-0.016	-0.040
FU #4	0.046	0.046	-0.021	-0.029	0.017	-0.068	-0.053
FU #5	0.166	0.167	0.061	-0.097	0.069	-0.077	-0.032
FU #6	0.329	0.331	0.212	-0.166	0.163	-0.015	0.059
FU #7	0.365	0.366	0.232	-0.228	0.137	-0.068	0.030
SET#4 ADMINISTRATION OF FIRST FOLLOW-UP							
ONE YEAR AFTER HIGH SCHOOL	0.006	0.009	0.019	-0.004	0.002	0.014	0.016
TWO YEARS AFTER HIGH SCHOOL	-0.007	-0.010	-0.021	0.004	-0.003	-0.016	-0.017
SET#5 STUDENT STATUS AT FOLLOW-UP							
FULL-TIME STUDENT	-0.247		-0.050	0.205	-0.042	0.063	0.026
PART-TIME STUDENT	-0.067		-0.054	0.001	-0.067	-0.078	-0.070
NOT A STUDENT	0.126		0.032	-0.095	0.030	-0.017	-0.001
SET#6 WORK STATUS AT FOLLOW-UP							
FULL-TIME CIVILIAN JOB	0.084		-0.005	-0.046	0.038	0.030	0.018
MILITARY SERVICE	-0.004		0.006	0.182	0.179	0.190	0.130
PART-TIME JOB	-0.192		-0.035	0.135	-0.057	-0.067	-0.057
HOMEMAKER	0.145		0.078	-0.242	-0.097	-0.191	-0.103
NONSTUDENT, NOT EMPLOYED	0.347		0.281	-0.520	-0.173	-0.058	0.052
OTHER	-0.239		-0.024	0.131	-0.109	-0.095	-0.072
SET#7 LIVING ARRANGEMENT AT FOLLOW-UP						**	**
MARRIED	0.203		0.041	0.050	0.252	0.152	0.116
PARTNER	0.041		-0.120	-0.358	-0.316	-0.359	-0.281
PARENT(S)	-0.019		0.052	0.000	-0.019	0.064	0.060
DORM	-0.326		-0.010	0.282	-0.045	0.003	-0.001
LIVE ALONE	0.020		-0.019	-0.101	-0.081	-0.071	-0.054
OTHER	-0.166		-0.085	-0.021	-0.187	-0.170	-0.143
SET#8 ENGAGEMENT STATUS AT FOLLOW-UP						*	
ENGAGED	0.120		0.156	-0.064	0.056	0.221	0.200
NOT ENGAGED	-0.008		-0.011	0.004	-0.004	-0.015	-0.014
SET#9 IS R'S SPS PREGNANT AT FOLLOW-UP?			**			**	**
YES	0.352		0.205	-0.095	0.257	0.112	0.142
NO	0.077		0.068	0.051	0.128	0.134	0.112
DATA N.A. (1977-1983)	-0.453		-0.375	-0.228	-0.680	-0.678	-0.579
SET#10 PARENTHOOD STATUS AT FOLLOW-UP							
MARRIED PARENT	0.293		0.052	0.030	0.323	0.104	0.087
SINGLE PARENT	0.493		0.373	-0.529	-0.036	-0.011	0.115
NOT A PARENT	-0.076		-0.025	0.015	-0.061	-0.020	-0.021
RISK OF COCAINE AT BASE YEAR (Cov.)*							0.326 **
Multiple R		0.159	0.205			0.317	0.480
R Sqr.		0.025	0.042			0.100	0.230

Notes: * indicates statistical significance at .05 level. ** indicates statistical significance at .01 level. Statistical significance is not indicated for bivariate coefficients or constants. Ns used for significance testing were weighted to approximate the number of individuals (not the number of observations) since each individual could contribute up to seven observations. Sets #5-#10 were measured at follow-up. Sets #3 and #4 were determined by timing of follow-up. All others were measured at Base Year (BY).

*Means for covariates: HIGH SCHOOL GRADES   5.829   URBANICITY   3.771
PERCEIVED RISK OF COCAINE USE (INDEX) AT BASE YEAR   6.759   R WILL ATTEND 4YR COLLEGE   2.967

271

Table A.6.8a
Regression Analyses Linking Post-High School Experiences to Changes in Disapproval Index of Using Cocaine
Females, Senior Years 1976-1997, Follow-ups 1977-1998

Regression Analyses Based on Full Set of Observations from Follow-Ups 1-7 (Wtd. N of Obs: 13,048)

Unstandardized Regression Coefficients

VARIABLE	BIVARIATE COEFF.	Multivariate Coefficients BKGD.	Multivariate Coefficients ALL SETS	Bivariate Coeff. With Dependent Variable at BY	at FU	Multivariate Prediction of Dep. Var. at FU: Covarying BY Dep. Var? No	Yes
CONSTANT	0.100	0.100	0.100	5.360	5.460	5.460	5.460
SET#1 RACE		*	*				
WHITE	0.014	0.017	0.017	-0.025	-0.010	-0.015	-0.004
BLACK	-0.154	-0.187	-0.189	0.179	0.025	0.024	-0.050
OTHER	0.021	0.031	0.025	0.061	0.083	0.130	0.093
SET#2 REGION						**	*
NORTHEAST	0.026	0.014	0.023	-0.174	-0.148	-0.097	-0.055
NORTH CENTRAL	0.018	-0.002	-0.002	0.033	0.051	0.056	0.035
SOUTH	-0.027	0.006	-0.001	0.121	0.094	0.060	0.039
WEST	-0.019	-0.026	-0.024	-0.056	-0.075	-0.088	-0.066
HIGH SCHOOL GRADES/D=1 (Cov.)[a]		-0.065 **	-0.063 **			0.027 *	-0.005
R WILL ATTEND 4YR COLLEGE (Cov.)[a]		-0.036	-0.027			0.030	0.010
URBANICITY (Cov.)[a]		-0.006	-0.003			-0.074 **	-0.049 **
SET#3 FOLLOW-UP NUMBER		**					
FU #1	-0.089	-0.081	-0.034	0.071	-0.018	0.089	0.046
FU #2	-0.099	-0.097	-0.062	0.047	-0.052	0.022	-0.008
FU #3	-0.077	-0.074	-0.062	0.028	-0.049	-0.031	-0.042
FU #4	0.021	0.017	-0.003	-0.006	0.015	-0.035	-0.024
FU #5	0.087	0.084	0.042	-0.048	0.038	-0.054	-0.021
FU #6	0.217	0.209	0.151	-0.112	0.105	-0.015	0.043
FU #7	0.215	0.206	0.134	-0.152	0.064	-0.071	0.001
SET#4 ADMINISTRATION OF FIRST FOLLOW-UP						*	
ONE YEAR AFTER HIGH SCHOOL	0.013	0.010	0.014	0.014	0.027	0.038	0.029
TWO YEARS AFTER HIGH SCHOOL	-0.014	-0.010	-0.014	-0.014	-0.028	-0.038	-0.030
SET#5 STUDENT STATUS AT FOLLOW-UP							
FULL-TIME STUDENT	-0.134		-0.005	0.112	-0.022	0.019	0.011
PART-TIME STUDENT	-0.017		-0.010	-0.021	-0.038	-0.011	-0.011
NOT A STUDENT	0.058		0.004	-0.043	0.015	-0.006	-0.003
SET#6 WORK STATUS AT FOLLOW-UP							
FULL-TIME CIVILIAN JOB	0.010		-0.010	-0.027	-0.016	0.005	0.000
MILITARY SERVICE	0.135		0.155	-0.010	0.125	0.139	0.144
PART-TIME JOB	-0.017		0.042	0.045	0.028	0.007	0.019
HOMEMAKER	0.150		-0.043	0.039	0.189	0.059	0.023
NONSTUDENT, NOT EMPLOYED	0.049		-0.042	-0.068	-0.020	-0.037	-0.038
OTHER	-0.120		0.007	0.044	-0.076	-0.057	-0.035
SET#7 LIVING ARRANGEMENT AT FOLLOW-UP						**	**
MARRIED	0.146		0.072	0.010	0.156	0.129	0.109
PARTNER	-0.060		-0.096	-0.246	-0.305	-0.343	-0.257
PARENT(S)	-0.038		-0.002	0.041	0.003	0.043	0.027
DORM	-0.160		-0.011	0.156	-0.003	-0.024	-0.019
LIVE ALONE	-0.028		0.005	-0.077	-0.105	-0.076	-0.047
OTHER	-0.156		-0.110	0.003	-0.152	-0.137	-0.127
SET#8 ENGAGEMENT STATUS AT FOLLOW-UP						**	*
ENGAGED	-0.011		0.077	0.009	-0.003	0.158	0.130
NOT ENGAGED	0.001		-0.009	-0.001	0.000	-0.017	-0.014
SET#9 IS R PREGNANT AT FOLLOW-UP?						**	**
YES	0.142		0.029	0.046	0.188	0.106	0.079
NO	0.015		0.012	0.028	0.042	0.048	0.036
DATA N.A. (1977-1983)	-0.136		-0.083	-0.178	-0.314	-0.321	-0.238
SET#10 PARENTHOOD STATUS AT FOLLOW-UP						*	*
MARRIED PARENT	0.219		0.074	-0.006	0.213	0.102	0.092
SINGLE PARENT	0.084		0.108	-0.104	-0.021	0.117	0.114
NOT A PARENT	-0.073		-0.032	0.011	-0.062	-0.041	-0.039
DISAPPROVAL OF COCAINE AT BASE YEAR (Cov.)[a]							0.349 **
Multiple R		0.162	0.180			0.251	0.449
R Sqr.		0.026	0.032			0.063	0.202

Notes: * indicates statistical significance at .05 level. ** indicates statistical significance at .01 level. Statistical significance is not indicated for bivariate coefficients or constants. Statistical significance testing were weighted to approximate the number of individuals (not the number of observations) since each individual could contribute up to seven observations. Sets #5-#10 were measured at follow-up. Sets #3 and #4 were determined by timing of follow-up. All others were measured at Base Year (BY).

[a]Means for covariates:
HIGH SCHOOL GRADES 6.272   URBANICITY 3.759
DISAPPROVAL OF COCAINE USE (INDEX) AT BASE YEAR 5.360   R WILL ATTEND 4YR COLLEGE 2.855

Table A.6.8b
Regression Analyses Linking Post-High School Experiences to Changes in Disapproval Index of Using Cocaine
Males, Senior Years 1976-1997, Follow-ups 1977-1998

Regression Analyses Based on Full Set of Observations from Follow-Ups 1-7
(Wtd. N of Obs: 10,562)
Unstandardized Regression Coefficients

VARIABLE	BIVARIATE COEFF.	Predicting to Change Scores — Multivariate Coefficients BKGD.	ALL SETS	Bivariate Coeff. With Dependent Variable at BY	at FU	Multivariate Prediction of Dep. Var. at FU: Covarying BY Dep. Var? No	Yes
CONSTANT	0.054	0.054	0.054	5.188	5.242	5.242	5.242
SET#1 RACE							
WHITE	-0.008	-0.010	-0.007	-0.005	-0.013	-0.020	-0.015
BLACK	-0.071	-0.108	-0.110	0.201	0.129	0.195	0.082
OTHER	0.121	0.159	0.133	-0.079	0.042	0.067	0.091
SET#2 REGION							*
NORTHEAST	0.040	0.027	0.032	-0.166	-0.126	-0.075	-0.036
NORTH CENTRAL	0.001	-0.005	-0.008	0.069	0.070	0.067	0.039
SOUTH	0.016	0.030	0.028	0.072	0.088	0.051	0.042
WEST	-0.084	-0.082	-0.080	-0.041	-0.125	-0.117	-0.103
HIGH SCHOOL GRADES/D=1 (Cov.)*						0.048	**
R WILL ATTEND 4YR COLLEGE (Cov.)*		-0.109 **	-0.106 **			-0.031	-0.059 **
URBANICITY (Cov.)*		0.024	0.024			-0.063 **	-0.031
SET#3 FOLLOW-UP NUMBER			**				
FU #1	-0.068	-0.061	-0.006	0.079	0.011	0.095	0.058
FU #2	-0.144	-0.139	-0.100	0.063	-0.081	-0.008	-0.042
FU #3	-0.077	-0.079	-0.072	-0.011	-0.088	-0.055	-0.061
FU #4	0.007	0.007	-0.026	0.004	0.011	-0.031	-0.029
FU #5	0.122	0.118	0.069	-0.067	0.055	-0.036	0.003
FU #6	0.187	0.178	0.127	-0.094	0.093	-0.021	0.033
FU #7	0.250	0.241	0.181	-0.126	0.124	0.009	0.072
SET#4 ADMINISTRATION OF FIRST FOLLOW-UP						*	
ONE YEAR AFTER HIGH SCHOOL	-0.011	-0.011	-0.005	0.055	0.044	0.049	0.029
TWO YEARS AFTER HIGH SCHOOL	0.012	0.012	0.006	-0.061	-0.048	-0.054	-0.032
SET#5 STUDENT STATUS AT FOLLOW-UP							
FULL-TIME STUDENT	-0.151		0.069	0.152	0.001	0.109	0.094
PART-TIME STUDENT	-0.055		-0.062	0.060	0.005	0.010	-0.016
NOT A STUDENT	0.075		-0.021	-0.077	-0.001	-0.050	-0.039
SET#6 WORK STATUS AT FOLLOW-UP							
FULL-TIME CIVILIAN JOB	0.067		0.020	-0.035	0.032	0.031	0.027
MILITARY SERVICE	-0.018		0.015	0.021	0.003	0.095	0.066
PART-TIME JOB	-0.119		-0.037	0.118	-0.001	-0.028	-0.031
HOMEMAKER	0.648		0.492	-0.114	0.534	0.427	0.451
NONSTUDENT, NOT EMPLOYED	0.120		0.086	-0.338	-0.218	-0.137	-0.055
OTHER	-0.198		-0.085	0.114	-0.084	-0.100	-0.095
SET#7 LIVING ARRANGEMENT AT FOLLOW-UP						**	**
MARRIED	0.150		0.065	0.053	0.203	0.176	0.135
PARTNER	0.019		-0.080	-0.182	-0.163	-0.267	-0.198
PARENT(S)	0.018		0.038	0.006	0.024	0.074	0.061
DORM	-0.213		-0.042	0.269	0.056	0.018	-0.004
LIVE ALONE	-0.007		-0.019	-0.128	-0.135	-0.121	-0.083
OTHER	-0.178		-0.100	-0.066	-0.244	-0.226	-0.179
SET#8 ENGAGEMENT STATUS AT FOLLOW-UP						**	**
ENGAGED	0.104		0.139	0.043	0.147	0.310	0.246
NOT ENGAGED	-0.009		-0.012	-0.004	-0.013	-0.027	-0.021
SET#9 IS R'S SPS PREGNANT AT FOLLOW-UP?			**		**	**	**
YES	0.122		0.017	0.115	0.236	0.130	0.089
NO	0.049		0.047	0.027	0.076	0.086	0.071
DATA N.A. (1977-1983)	-0.261		-0.229	-0.156	-0.417	-0.439	-0.361
SET#10 PARENTHOOD STATUS AT FOLLOW-UP							
MARRIED PARENT	0.194		-0.007	0.028	0.222	0.030	0.017
SINGLE PARENT	0.151		0.083	-0.348	-0.197	-0.158	-0.069
NOT A PARENT	-0.051		-0.003	0.012	-0.039	0.001	0.000
DISAPPROVAL OF COCAINE AT BASE YEAR (Cov.)*						0.370	**
Multiple R		0.157	0.184			0.265	0.465
R Sqr.		0.025	0.034			0.070	0.217

Notes: * indicates statistical significance at .05 level. ** indicates statistical significance at .01 level. Statistical significance is not indicated for bivariate coefficients or constants. Ns used for significance testing were weighted to approximate the number of individuals (not the number of observations) since each individual could contribute up to seven observations. Sets #5-#10 were measured at follow-up. Sets #3 and #4 were determined by timing of follow-up. All others were measured at Base Year (BY).

*Means for covariates: HIGH SCHOOL GRADES 5.788   URBANICITY 3.728
DISAPPROVAL OF COCAINE USE (INDEX) AT BASE YEAR 5.188   R WILL ATTEND 4YR COLLEGE 2.884

Table A.7.1a
Regression Analyses Linking Post-High School Experiences to
Changes in Friends' Use of Cigarettes
Females, Senior Years 1976-1997, Follow-ups 1977-1998

Regression Analyses Based on Full Set of Observations from Follow-Ups 1-7
(Wtd. N of Obs: 12,712)
Unstandardized Regression Coefficients

VARIABLE	Predicting to Change Scores			Bivariate Coeff. With Dependent Variable		Multivariate Prediction of Dep. Var. at FU: Covarying BY Dep. Var?	
	BIVARIATE COEFF.	Multivariate Coefficients BKGD.	ALL SETS=	at BY	at FU	No	Yes
CONSTANT	-0.166	-0.166	-0.166	2.668	2.502	2.502	2.502
SET#1 RACE						**	**
WHITE	-0.008	-0.004	-0.002	0.040	0.032	0.043	0.028
BLACK	-0.039	-0.028	-0.049	-0.213	-0.252	-0.379	-0.268
OTHER	0.112	0.063	0.070	-0.164	-0.052	-0.039	-0.002
SET#2 REGION			**	**			**
NORTHEAST	-0.161	-0.139	-0.147	0.217	0.056	0.064	-0.006
NORTH CENTRAL	0.007	0.006	0.004	0.046	0.053	0.033	0.023
SOUTH	0.036	0.025	0.031	-0.034	0.002	0.029	0.030
WEST	0.137	0.129	0.132	-0.321	-0.184	-0.205	-0.092
HIGH SCHOOL GRADES/D=1 (Cov.)ᵃ		0.012	0.012			-0.079 **	-0.049 **
R WILL ATTEND 4YR COLLEGE (Cov.)ᵃ		-0.021	-0.026			-0.107 **	-0.080 **
URBANICITY (Cov.)ᵃ		-0.042 *	-0.046 *			-0.024	-0.032 *
SET#3 FOLLOW-UP NUMBER			**	**			**
FU #1	0.212	0.213	0.176	0.001	0.212	0.260	0.232
FU #2	0.143	0.145	0.128	-0.003	0.140	0.142	0.137
FU #3	0.058	0.057	0.052	-0.019	0.039	0.006	0.022
FU #4	-0.064	-0.066	-0.056	-0.010	-0.074	-0.090	-0.078
FU #5	-0.177	-0.178	-0.153	0.005	-0.173	-0.183	-0.173
FU #6	-0.268	-0.268	-0.230	0.017	-0.251	-0.257	-0.248
FU #7	-0.305	-0.308	-0.260	0.034	-0.271	-0.283	-0.276
SET#4 ADMINISTRATION OF FIRST FOLLOW-UP							
ONE YEAR AFTER HIGH SCHOOL	0.034	0.034	0.030	-0.023	0.011	0.018	0.022
TWO YEARS AFTER HIGH SCHOOL	-0.037	-0.037	-0.033	0.025	-0.011	-0.019	-0.024
SET#5 STUDENT STATUS AT FOLLOW-UP						*	
FULL-TIME STUDENT	0.123		-0.034	-0.156	-0.033	-0.087	-0.069
PART-TIME STUDENT	-0.047		-0.035	-0.036	-0.082	-0.051	-0.045
NOT A STUDENT	-0.045		0.020	0.071	0.026	0.044	0.036
SET#6 WORK STATUS AT FOLLOW-UP							
FULL-TIME CIVILIAN JOB	-0.026		0.014	0.034	0.009	0.019	0.017
MILITARY SERVICE	0.286		0.164	-0.026	0.260	0.181	0.175
PART-TIME JOB	0.037		-0.015	-0.076	-0.038	-0.033	-0.027
HOMEMAKER	-0.165		-0.050	0.101	-0.065	-0.044	-0.046
NONSTUDENT, NOT EMPLOYED	-0.007		-0.002	0.143	0.136	0.021	0.013
OTHER	0.120		-0.012	-0.118	0.002	-0.014	-0.013
SET#7 LIVING ARRANGEMENT AT FOLLOW-UP						**	**
MARRIED	-0.143		-0.062	0.010	-0.132	-0.089	-0.080
PARTNER	0.079		0.065	0.277	0.356	0.339	0.248
PARENT(S)	0.084		0.006	-0.007	0.076	-0.033	-0.020
DORM	0.245		0.150	-0.247	-0.002	0.001	0.051
LIVE ALONE	-0.101		-0.059	-0.038	-0.139	0.006	-0.016
OTHER	0.088		0.058	-0.009	0.079	0.101	0.086
SET#8 ENGAGEMENT STATUS AT FOLLOW-UP							
ENGAGED	0.075		-0.029	0.069	0.144	-0.061	-0.051
NOT ENGAGED	-0.006		0.002	-0.006	-0.012	0.005	0.004
SET#9 IS R PREGNANT AT FOLLOW-UP?						**	*
YES	-0.082		0.020	-0.018	-0.100	-0.047	-0.025
NO	-0.025		-0.003	-0.031	-0.057	-0.027	-0.019
DATA N.A. (1977-1983)	0.165		0.012	0.176	0.341	0.164	0.113
SET#10 PARENTHOOD STATUS AT FOLLOW-UP						*	
MARRIED PARENT	-0.203		-0.055	0.069	-0.134	0.012	-0.010
SINGLE PARENT	0.036		0.046	0.248	0.284	0.213	0.157
NOT A PARENT	0.057		0.013	-0.038	0.018	-0.019	-0.008
FRIENDS' USE OF CIGARETTES AT BASE YEAR (Cov.)ᵃ							0.334 **
Multiple R		0.202	0.214			0.377	0.508
R Sqr.		0.041	0.046			0.142	0.258

Notes: * indicates statistical significance at .05 level. ** indicates statistical significance at .01 level. Statistical significance is not indicated for bivariate coefficients or constants. Ns used for significance testing were weighted to approximate the number of individuals (not the number of observations) since each individual could contribute up to seven observations. Sets #5-#10 were measured at follow-up. Sets #3 and #4 were determined by timing of follow-up. All others were measured at Base Year (BY).

ᵃMeans for covariates:　　HIGH SCHOOL GRADES 6.362　　　　　URBANICITY 3.753
　　　　FRIENDS' USE OF CIGARETTES AT BASE YEAR 2.668　　　R WILL ATTEND 4YR COLLEGE 2.914

Table A.7.1b
Regression Analyses Linking Post-High School Experiences to Changes in Friends' Use of Cigarettes
Males, Senior Years 1976-1997, Follow-ups 1977-1998

Regression Analyses Based on Full Set of Observations from Follow-Ups 1-7 (Wtd. N of Obs: 10,005)

Unstandardized Regression Coefficients

VARIABLE	BIVARIATE COEFF.	Multivariate Coefficients Predicting to Change Scores — BKGD.	ALL SETS	Bivariate Coeff. With Dependent Variable at BY	at FU	Multivariate Prediction of Dep. Var. at FU: Covarying BY Dep. Var? No	Yes
CONSTANT	-0.019	-0.019	-0.019	2.621	2.602	2.602	2.602
SET#1 RACE							
WHITE	-0.009	-0.008	-0.005	0.012	0.003	0.005	0.002
BLACK	0.138	0.149	0.108	-0.042	0.096	0.000	0.033
OTHER	-0.007	-0.021	-0.027	-0.088	-0.096	-0.050	-0.043
SET#2 REGION						**	**
NORTHEAST	-0.036	-0.035	-0.040	0.091	0.055	0.064	0.032
NORTH CENTRAL	0.055	0.064	0.070	-0.003	0.052	0.042	0.051
SOUTH	-0.056	-0.066	-0.065	0.126	0.070	0.058	0.021
WEST	0.036	0.035	0.027	-0.327	-0.290	-0.262	-0.174
HIGH SCHOOL GRADES/D=1 (Cov.)*		-0.017	-0.013			-0.056 **	-0.043 **
R WILL ATTEND 4YR COLLEGE (Cov.)*		0.022	0.029			-0.095 **	-0.057 **
URBANICITY (Cov.)*		0.008	0.006			0.002	0.003
SET#3 FOLLOW-UP NUMBER			**		**	**	**
FU #1	0.101	0.101	0.121	-0.015	0.086	0.159	0.147
FU #2	0.110	0.110	0.111	-0.024	0.086	0.118	0.115
FU #3	0.042	0.041	0.022	-0.012	0.030	0.011	0.014
FU #4	-0.022	-0.021	-0.038	0.007	-0.015	-0.046	-0.043
FU #5	-0.065	-0.066	-0.072	0.020	-0.045	-0.084	-0.080
FU #6	-0.202	-0.200	-0.190	0.030	-0.172	-0.222	-0.212
FU #7	-0.251	-0.250	-0.238	0.047	-0.204	-0.266	-0.258
SET#4 ADMINISTRATION OF FIRST FOLLOW-UP							
ONE YEAR AFTER HIGH SCHOOL	0.015	0.017	0.021	-0.026	-0.012	-0.001	0.005
TWO YEARS AFTER HIGH SCHOOL	-0.016	-0.019	-0.022	0.028	0.012	0.001	-0.006
SET#5 STUDENT STATUS AT FOLLOW-UP						**	**
FULL-TIME STUDENT	0.027		-0.106	-0.181	-0.154	-0.148	-0.135
PART-TIME STUDENT	0.011		-0.011	-0.051	-0.040	-0.012	-0.012
NOT A STUDENT	-0.013		0.048	0.086	0.072	0.066	0.060
SET#6 WORK STATUS AT FOLLOW-UP							
FULL-TIME CIVILIAN JOB	-0.048		-0.028	0.066	0.018	-0.007	-0.014
MILITARY SERVICE	0.262		0.221	0.011	0.273	0.176	0.190
PART-TIME JOB	0.078		0.050	-0.124	-0.046	0.030	0.036
HOMEMAKER	0.065		0.048	0.251	0.317	0.225	0.171
NONSTUDENT, NOT EMPLOYED	0.019		-0.067	0.136	0.155	-0.023	-0.037
OTHER	0.025		0.013	-0.193	-0.169	-0.055	-0.034
SET#7 LIVING ARRANGEMENT AT FOLLOW-UP						**	*
MARRIED	-0.173		-0.078	0.096	-0.077	-0.130	-0.114
PARTNER	0.074		0.033	0.131	0.205	0.222	0.164
PARENT(S)	0.079		0.032	0.002	0.081	0.022	0.025
DORM	0.007		-0.027	-0.197	-0.190	-0.028	-0.028
LIVE ALONE	0.055		0.058	-0.079	-0.025	0.055	0.056
OTHER	0.092		0.043	-0.082	0.010	0.069	0.061
SET#8 ENGAGEMENT STATUS AT FOLLOW-UP							
ENGAGED	0.070		-0.013	-0.023	0.047	-0.098	-0.072
NOT ENGAGED	-0.005		0.001	0.002	-0.004	0.007	0.005
SET#9 IS R'S SPS PREGNANT AT FOLLOW-UP?						**	**
YES	-0.092		0.028	0.069	-0.023	0.031	0.030
NO	-0.004		0.009	-0.030	-0.033	-0.018	-0.010
DATA N.A. (1977-1983)	0.039		-0.048	0.129	0.168	0.081	0.042
SET#10 PARENTHOOD STATUS AT FOLLOW-UP			*				
MARRIED PARENT	-0.218		-0.061	0.201	-0.016	0.104	0.053
SINGLE PARENT	0.306		0.295	0.067	0.372	0.230	0.250
NOT A PARENT	0.032		-0.001	-0.047	-0.015	-0.034	-0.024
FRIENDS' USE OF CIGARETTES AT BASE YEAR (Cov.)*							0.305 **
Multiple R		0.138	0.180			0.345	0.459
R Sqr.		0.019	0.032			0.119	0.211

Notes: * indicates statistical significance at .05 level. ** indicates statistical significance at .01 level. Statistical significance is not indicated for bivariate coefficients or constants. Ns used for significance testing were weighted to approximate the number of individuals (not the number of observations) since each individual could contribute up to seven observations. Sets #5-#10 were measured at follow-up. Sets #3 and #4 were determined by timing of follow-up. All others were measured at Base Year (BY).

Means for covariates:
HIGH SCHOOL GRADES 5.863
FRIENDS' USE OF CIGARETTES AT BASE YEAR 2.621
URBANICITY 3.744
R WILL ATTEND 4YR COLLEGE 2.909

Table A.7.2a
Regression Analyses Linking Post-High School Experiences to Changes in Friends Getting Drunk
Females, Senior Years 1976-1997, Follow-ups 1977-1998

Regression Analyses Based on Full Set of Observations from Follow-Ups 1-7
(Wtd. N of Obs: 12,608)
Unstandardized Regression Coefficients

VARIABLE	Predicting to Change Scores			Bivariate Coeff. With Dependent Variable		Multivariate Prediction of Dep. Var. at FU: Covarying BY Dep. Var?	
	BIVARIATE COEFF.	Multivariate Coefficients					
		BKGD.	ALL SETS	at BY	at FU	No	Yes
CONSTANT	-0.510	-0.510	-0.510	2.661	2.152	2.152	2.152
SET#1 RACE						**	**
WHITE	-0.014	-0.020	-0.018	0.064	0.050	0.061	0.039
BLACK	0.076	0.158	0.128	-0.500	-0.423	-0.516	-0.334
OTHER	0.061	0.033	0.049	-0.118	-0.057	-0.078	-0.042
SET#2 REGION			*			**	*
NORTHEAST	0.009	0.014	-0.009	0.059	0.068	0.032	0.020
NORTH CENTRAL	0.033	0.051	0.049	0.058	0.091	0.074	0.067
SOUTH	-0.071	-0.096	-0.079	-0.028	-0.098	-0.046	-0.055
WEST	0.056	0.064	0.066	-0.138	-0.082	-0.100	-0.054
HIGH SCHOOL GRADES/D=1 (Cov.)[a]		0.067 **	0.062 **			-0.059 **	-0.025 *
R WILL ATTEND 4YR COLLEGE (Cov.)[a]		0.100 **	0.065 **			0.004	0.021
URBANICITY (Cov.)[a]		-0.002	-0.016			0.007	0.001
SET#3 FOLLOW-UP NUMBER		**	**			**	**
FU #1	0.401	0.389	0.223	0.015	0.415	0.345	0.311
FU #2	0.238	0.233	0.156	0.015	0.254	0.201	0.188
FU #3	-0.004	-0.002	0.011	0.011	0.008	0.003	0.005
FU #4	-0.162	-0.160	-0.090	-0.003	-0.165	-0.139	-0.125
FU #5	-0.320	-0.312	-0.208	0.004	-0.316	-0.264	-0.248
FU #6	-0.370	-0.362	-0.230	-0.038	-0.408	-0.330	-0.301
FU #7	-0.393	-0.379	-0.226	-0.052	-0.445	-0.346	-0.312
SET#4 ADMINISTRATION OF FIRST FOLLOW-UP							
ONE YEAR AFTER HIGH SCHOOL	0.024	0.017	0.002	-0.017	0.007	-0.004	-0.002
TWO YEARS AFTER HIGH SCHOOL	-0.026	-0.018	-0.002	0.018	-0.008	0.004	0.002
SET#5 STUDENT STATUS AT FOLLOW-UP							
FULL-TIME STUDENT	0.415		0.050	-0.094	0.321	0.028	0.034
PART-TIME STUDENT	0.004		0.015	-0.053	-0.049	-0.038	-0.023
NOT A STUDENT	-0.176		-0.023	0.047	-0.128	-0.006	-0.011
SET#6 WORK STATUS AT FOLLOW-UP							
FULL-TIME CIVILIAN JOB	-0.097		0.003	0.027	-0.070	0.017	0.013
MILITARY SERVICE	0.349		0.247	0.054	0.403	0.254	0.252
PART-TIME JOB	0.151		-0.015	-0.044	0.107	-0.026	-0.023
HOMEMAKER	-0.385		-0.035	0.046	-0.339	-0.068	-0.059
NONSTUDENT, NOT EMPLOYED	-0.147		0.028	0.063	-0.084	-0.006	0.003
OTHER	0.384		0.012	-0.084	0.300	0.001	0.004
SET#7 LIVING ARRANGEMENT AT FOLLOW-UP			**			**	**
MARRIED	-0.330		-0.171	-0.015	-0.345	-0.217	-0.204
PARTNER	-0.018		0.089	0.271	0.253	0.325	0.259
PARENT(S)	0.167		0.064	-0.052	0.115	-0.011	0.010
DORM	0.680		0.288	-0.159	0.521	0.237	0.251
LIVE ALONE	-0.040		-0.025	-0.034	-0.074	0.045	0.025
OTHER	0.210		0.132	0.085	0.295	0.248	0.215
SET#8 ENGAGEMENT STATUS AT FOLLOW-UP			**			**	**
ENGAGED	-0.091		-0.246	0.092	0.001	-0.245	-0.245
NOT ENGAGED	0.008		0.021	-0.008	0.000	0.021	0.021
SET#9 IS R PREGNANT AT FOLLOW-UP?							
YES	-0.263		0.000	0.018	-0.246	0.000	0.000
NO	-0.029		-0.007	0.010	-0.019	0.014	0.008
DATA N.A. (1977-1983)	0.241		0.038	-0.059	0.182	-0.077	-0.044
SET#10 PARENTHOOD STATUS AT FOLLOW-UP							
MARRIED PARENT	-0.436		-0.087	0.031	-0.405	-0.026	-0.044
SINGLE PARENT	-0.166		-0.103	0.187	0.021	0.035	-0.004
NOT A PARENT	0.139		0.033	-0.022	0.117	0.005	0.013
FRIENDS GET DRUNK AT BASE YEAR (Cov.)[a]							0.282 **
Multiple R		0.275	0.302			0.391	0.494
R Sqr.		0.076	0.091			0.153	0.244

Notes: * indicates statistical significance at .05 level. ** indicates statistical significance at .01 level. Statistical significance is not indicated for bivariate coefficients or constants. Ns used for significance testing were weighted to approximate the number of individuals (not the number of observations) since each individual could contribute up to seven observations. Sets #5-#10 were measured at follow-up. Sets #3 and #4 were measured by timing of follow-up. All others were measured at Base Year (BY).

[a]Means for covariates:

HIGH SCHOOL GRADES	6.368	URBANICITY	3.748
FRIENDS GET DRUNK AT BASE YEAR	2.661	R WILL ATTEND 4YR COLLEGE	2.912

Table A.7.2b
Regression Analyses Linking Post-High School Experiences to
Changes in Friends Getting Drunk
Males, Senior Years 1976-1997, Follow-ups 1977-1998

Regression Analyses Based on Full Set of Observations from Follow-Ups 1-7
(Wtd. N of Obs: 9,922)
Unstandardized Regression Coefficients

VARIABLE	BIVARIATE COEFF.	Predicting to Change Scores Multivariate Coefficients BKGD.	ALL SETS	Bivariate Coeff. With Dependent Variable at BY	at FU	Multivariate Prediction of Dep. Var. at FU: Covarying BY Dep. Var? No	Yes
CONSTANT	-0.312	-0.312	-0.312	2.817	2.505	2.505	2.505
SET#1 RACE						**	*
WHITE	-0.006	-0.007	-0.002	0.038	0.032	0.036	0.024
BLACK	0.125	0.175	0.113	-0.361	-0.236	-0.314	-0.182
OTHER	-0.022	-0.045	-0.053	-0.136	-0.158	-0.147	-0.118
SET#2 REGION			*			**	**
NORTHEAST	-0.015	-0.005	-0.027	0.175	0.161	0.128	0.081
NORTH CENTRAL	0.029	0.051	0.057	0.050	0.079	0.075	0.070
SOUTH	-0.092	-0.107	-0.089	0.004	-0.088	-0.055	-0.065
WEST	0.123	0.095	0.078	-0.321	-0.199	-0.209	-0.121
HIGH SCHOOL GRADES/D=1 (Cov.)*		0.052 **	0.049 **			-0.061 **	-0.027 *
R WILL ATTEND 4YR COLLEGE (Cov.)*		0.076 **	0.048 **			0.007	0.019
URBANICITY (Cov.)*		-0.003	-0.012			0.042 *	0.025
SET#3 FOLLOW-UP NUMBER		**	**			**	**
FU #1	0.302	0.294	0.156	-0.032	0.271	0.218	0.199
FU #2	0.279	0.276	0.184	-0.016	0.262	0.202	0.197
FU #3	0.075	0.072	0.069	-0.012	0.063	0.056	0.060
FU #4	-0.125	-0.121	-0.058	0.024	-0.102	-0.075	-0.069
FU #5	-0.293	-0.290	-0.183	0.039	-0.254	-0.205	-0.198
FU #6	-0.424	-0.413	-0.270	0.024	-0.401	-0.322	-0.306
FU #7	-0.475	-0.464	-0.309	0.019	-0.456	-0.369	-0.350
SET#4 ADMINISTRATION OF FIRST FOLLOW-UP							
ONE YEAR AFTER HIGH SCHOOL	0.032	0.037	0.026	-0.019	0.013	0.021	0.023
TWO YEARS AFTER HIGH SCHOOL	-0.034	-0.039	-0.028	0.020	-0.014	-0.023	-0.025
SET#5 STUDENT STATUS AT FOLLOW-UP							
FULL-TIME STUDENT	0.345		-0.007	-0.132	0.212	-0.045	-0.033
PART-TIME STUDENT	0.007		-0.015	-0.092	-0.085	-0.066	-0.050
NOT A STUDENT	-0.151		0.005	0.070	-0.080	0.029	0.021
SET#6 WORK STATUS AT FOLLOW-UP			*				*
FULL-TIME CIVILIAN JOB	-0.189		-0.062	0.066	-0.123	-0.040	-0.046
MILITARY SERVICE	0.391		0.400	-0.139	0.252	0.200	0.262
PART-TIME JOB	0.260		0.039	-0.129	0.130	0.014	0.022
HOMEMAKER	0.071		0.149	0.111	0.182	0.204	0.187
NONSTUDENT, NOT EMPLOYED	0.008		-0.018	0.027	0.034	-0.051	-0.041
OTHER	0.374		0.085	-0.101	0.273	0.093	0.090
SET#7 LIVING ARRANGEMENT AT FOLLOW-UP			**			**	**
MARRIED	-0.456		-0.343	0.072	-0.385	-0.299	-0.312
PARTNER	-0.040		0.089	0.180	0.140	0.248	0.199
PARENT(S)	0.143		0.119	-0.050	0.094	0.006	0.041
DORM	0.453		0.175	-0.147	0.306	0.155	0.161
LIVE ALONE	0.043		0.102	-0.064	-0.020	0.091	0.095
OTHER	0.303		0.199	-0.014	0.290	0.252	0.236
SET#8 ENGAGEMENT STATUS AT FOLLOW-UP			*			*	**
ENGAGED	-0.102		-0.218	0.064	-0.038	-0.211	-0.213
NOT ENGAGED	0.008		0.016	-0.005	0.003	0.016	0.016
SET#9 IS R'S SPS PREGNANT AT FOLLOW-UP?							
YES	-0.270		0.083	-0.023	-0.294	0.017	0.038
NO	-0.022		0.004	0.000	-0.022	0.006	0.005
DATA N.A. (1977-1983)	0.172		-0.039	0.006	0.178	-0.033	-0.035
SET#10 PARENTHOOD STATUS AT FOLLOW-UP							
MARRIED PARENT	-0.467		0.067	0.086	-0.381	0.075	0.072
SINGLE PARENT	0.060		0.099	0.070	0.131	0.114	0.110
NOT A PARENT	0.098		-0.019	-0.022	0.076	-0.022	-0.021
FRIENDS GET DRUNK AT BASE YEAR (Cov.)*						0.309 **	
Multiple R		0.262	0.308			0.351	0.478
R Sqr.		0.069	0.095			0.123	0.228

Notes: * indicates statistical significance at .05 level. ** indicates statistical significance at .01 level. Statistical significance is not indicated for bivariate coefficients or constants. Ns used for significance testing were weighted to approximate the number of individuals (not the number of observations) since each individual could contribute up to seven observations. Sets #5-#10 were measured at follow-up. Sets #3 and #4 were determined by timing of follow-up. All others were measured at Base Year (BY).

*Means for covariates: HIGH SCHOOL GRADES 5.863   URBANICITY 3.743
FRIENDS GET DRUNK AT BASE YEAR 2.817   R WILL ATTEND 4YR COLLEGE 2.908

Table A.7.3a
Regression Analyses Linking Post-High School Experiences to Changes in Friends' Use of Marijuana
Females, Senior Years 1976-1997, Follow-ups 1977-1998

Regression Analyses Based on Full Set of Observations from Follow-Ups 1-7
(Wtd. N of Obs: 12,685)
Unstandardized Regression Coefficients

VARIABLE	BIVARIATE COEFF.	Predicting to Change Scores — Multivariate Coefficients BKGD.	ALL SETS	Bivariate Coeff. With Dependent Variable at BY	at FU	Multivariate Prediction of Dep. Var. at FU: Covarying BY Dep. Var? No	Yes
CONSTANT	-0.394	-0.394	-0.394	2.410	2.016	2.016	2.016
SET#1 RACE							*
WHITE	-0.007	-0.007	-0.007	0.014	0.007	0.020	0.011
BLACK	-0.026	0.001	-0.022	0.012	-0.014	-0.087	-0.065
OTHER	0.091	0.066	0.081	-0.142	-0.051	-0.098	-0.037
SET#2 REGION		**	**				**
NORTHEAST	-0.153	-0.132	-0.149	0.323	0.169	0.140	0.041
NORTH CENTRAL	0.032	0.038	0.035	-0.040	-0.008	-0.009	0.006
SOUTH	0.043	0.021	0.035	-0.157	-0.114	-0.092	-0.049
WEST	0.065	0.065	0.068	-0.065	0.000	0.000	0.024
HIGH SCHOOL GRADES/D=1 (Cov.)[a]		0.048 **	0.043 **			-0.071 **	-0.032 **
R WILL ATTEND 4YR COLLEGE (Cov.)[a]		0.058 **	0.038			-0.024	-0.003
URBANICITY (Cov.)[a]		-0.049 *	-0.058 **			0.036 *	0.004
SET#3 FOLLOW-UP NUMBER		**	**			**	**
FU #1	0.360	0.353	0.227	-0.039	0.321	0.252	0.244
FU #2	0.242	0.239	0.170	-0.049	0.192	0.125	0.141
FU #3	0.059	0.060	0.068	-0.033	0.026	0.002	0.025
FU #4	-0.123	-0.123	-0.065	-0.004	-0.127	-0.083	-0.077
FU #5	-0.290	-0.285	-0.199	0.052	-0.239	-0.168	-0.179
FU #6	-0.396	-0.390	-0.284	0.074	-0.322	-0.232	-0.250
FU #7	-0.503	-0.496	-0.377	0.126	-0.377	-0.282	-0.314
SET#4 ADMINISTRATION OF FIRST FOLLOW-UP							
ONE YEAR AFTER HIGH SCHOOL	0.026	0.021	0.011	-0.008	0.017	0.013	0.012
TWO YEARS AFTER HIGH SCHOOL	-0.028	-0.023	-0.012	0.009	-0.019	-0.014	-0.014
SET#5 STUDENT STATUS AT FOLLOW-UP							
FULL-TIME STUDENT	0.344		0.035	-0.175	0.168	-0.021	-0.002
PART-TIME STUDENT	-0.070		-0.048	0.026	-0.045	-0.029	-0.035
NOT A STUDENT	-0.135		-0.008	0.070	-0.065	0.013	0.006
SET#6 WORK STATUS AT FOLLOW-UP							
FULL-TIME CIVILIAN JOB	-0.093		-0.006	0.053	-0.040	0.010	0.004
MILITARY SERVICE	0.026		-0.139	-0.358	-0.332	-0.397	-0.309
PART-TIME JOB	0.135		0.004	-0.095	0.041	-0.019	-0.011
HOMEMAKER	-0.253		0.020	0.059	-0.194	-0.015	-0.003
NONSTUDENT, NOT EMPLOYED	-0.060		0.051	0.090	0.030	0.020	0.030
OTHER	0.306		-0.006	-0.109	0.197	0.007	0.003
SET#7 LIVING ARRANGEMENT AT FOLLOW-UP			*			**	**
MARRIED	-0.262		-0.118	-0.008	-0.270	-0.142	-0.134
PARTNER	-0.041		0.025	0.388	0.347	0.385	0.262
PARENT(S)	0.126		0.022	-0.031	0.094	-0.069	-0.038
DORM	0.532		0.205	-0.246	0.286	0.087	0.127
LIVE ALONE	-0.078		-0.029	0.005	-0.073	0.053	0.025
OTHER	0.212		0.147	0.003	0.215	0.203	0.184
SET#8 ENGAGEMENT STATUS AT FOLLOW-UP						**	**
ENGAGED	-0.014		-0.137	0.063	0.050	-0.180	-0.165
NOT ENGAGED	0.001		0.012	-0.005	-0.004	0.015	0.014
SET#9 IS R PREGNANT AT FOLLOW-UP?						**	**
YES	-0.237		-0.036	-0.011	-0.248	-0.108	-0.083
NO	-0.042		-0.017	-0.039	-0.081	-0.058	-0.044
DATA N.A. (1977-1983)	0.305		0.102	0.214	0.519	0.351	0.266
SET#10 PARENTHOOD STATUS AT FOLLOW-UP						*	*
MARRIED PARENT	-0.359		-0.076	0.048	-0.310	-0.022	-0.040
SINGLE PARENT	-0.124		-0.053	0.302	0.178	0.104	0.051
NOT A PARENT	0.113		0.026	-0.036	0.077	-0.001	0.008
FRIENDS USE MARIJUANA AT BASE YEAR (Cov.)[a]							0.341 **
Multiple R		0.294	0.315			0.384	0.536
R Sqr.		0.087	0.099			0.148	0.287

Notes: * indicates statistical significance at .05 level. ** indicates statistical significance at .01 level. Statistical significance is not indicated for bivariate coefficients or constants. Ns used for significance testing were weighted to approximate the number of individuals (not the number of observations) since each individual could contribute up to seven observations. Sets #5-#10 were measured at follow-up. Sets #3 and #4 were determined by timing of follow-up. All others were measured at Base Year (BY).

[a] Means for covariates: HIGH SCHOOL GRADES 6.366   URBANICITY 3.752
   FRIENDS' USE OF MARIJUANA AT BASE YEAR 2.410   R WILL ATTEND 4YR COLLEGE 2.913

278

Table A.7.3b
Regression Analyses Linking Post-High School Experiences to
Changes in Friends' Use of Marijuana
Males, Senior Years 1976-1997, Follow-ups 1977-1998

Regression Analyses Based on Full Set of Observations from Follow-Ups 1-7
(Wtd. N of Obs: 9,998)
Unstandardized Regression Coefficients

VARIABLE	BIVARIATE COEFF.	Predicting to Change Scores — Multivariate Coefficients BKGD.	ALL SETS	Bivariate Coeff. With Dependent Variable at BY	at FU	Multivariate Prediction of Dep. Var. at FU: Covarying BY Dep. Var? No	Yes
CONSTANT	-0.303	-0.303	-0.303	2.531	2.228	2.228	2.228
SET#1 RACE							*
WHITE	0.003	0.002	0.004	-0.017	-0.014	-0.007	-0.003
BLACK	0.042	0.066	0.057	0.244	0.286	0.216	0.158
OTHER	-0.060	-0.062	-0.073	0.010	-0.050	-0.075	-0.075
SET#2 REGION		*				**	
NORTHEAST	-0.078	-0.062	-0.080	0.255	0.177	0.149	0.065
NORTH CENTRAL	0.078	0.090	0.091	-0.088	-0.010	-0.001	0.033
SOUTH	-0.062	-0.078	-0.062	0.012	-0.050	-0.040	-0.048
WEST	0.054	0.039	0.033	-0.169	-0.114	-0.115	-0.061
HIGH SCHOOL GRADES/D=1 (Cov.)[a]		0.025	0.023			-0.068 **	-0.034 **
R WILL ATTEND 4YR COLLEGE (Cov.)[a]		0.075 **	0.056 *			0.001	0.022
URBANICITY (Cov.)[a]		-0.030	-0.039			0.071 **	0.030
SET#3 FOLLOW-UP NUMBER		**	**			**	**
FU #1	0.290	0.284	0.200	-0.068	0.221	0.149	0.168
FU #2	0.233	0.231	0.168	-0.068	0.165	0.104	0.128
FU #3	0.098	0.096	0.079	-0.042	0.056	0.030	0.048
FU #4	-0.106	-0.102	-0.068	0.024	-0.082	-0.037	-0.048
FU #5	-0.247	-0.244	-0.171	0.075	-0.171	-0.103	-0.128
FU #6	-0.422	-0.416	-0.309	0.105	-0.317	-0.220	-0.252
FU #7	-0.483	-0.476	-0.361	0.155	-0.328	-0.231	-0.279
SET#4 ADMINISTRATION OF FIRST FOLLOW-UP		*	*				
ONE YEAR AFTER HIGH SCHOOL	0.047	0.052	0.044	-0.027	0.020	0.021	0.030
TWO YEARS AFTER HIGH SCHOOL	-0.050	-0.056	-0.048	0.029	-0.021	-0.023	-0.032
SET#5 STUDENT STATUS AT FOLLOW-UP							
FULL-TIME STUDENT	0.279		-0.021	-0.194	0.085	-0.117	-0.082
PART-TIME STUDENT	-0.048		-0.063	0.005	-0.043	-0.018	-0.034
NOT A STUDENT	-0.114		0.018	0.083	-0.031	0.053	0.040
SET#6 WORK STATUS AT FOLLOW-UP						**	*
FULL-TIME CIVILIAN JOB	-0.118		-0.003	0.069	-0.049	0.004	0.002
MILITARY SERVICE	-0.160		-0.169	-0.106	-0.266	-0.363	-0.292
PART-TIME JOB	0.246		0.049	-0.167	0.078	0.036	0.041
HOMEMAKER	0.001		0.083	0.155	0.156	0.175	0.141
NONSTUDENT, NOT EMPLOYED	0.071		0.019	0.133	0.205	0.071	0.052
OTHER	0.264		0.010	-0.120	0.144	0.039	0.028
SET#7 LIVING ARRANGEMENT AT FOLLOW-UP			**			**	**
MARRIED	-0.405		-0.228	0.074	-0.330	-0.238	-0.234
PARTNER	0.056		0.139	0.284	0.340	0.418	0.315
PARENT(S)	0.156		0.055	-0.066	0.090	-0.054	-0.014
DORM	0.337		0.066	-0.160	0.177	0.104	0.090
LIVE ALONE	0.047		0.097	-0.068	-0.020	0.067	0.078
OTHER	0.213		0.144	-0.025	0.188	0.218	0.191
SET#8 ENGAGEMENT STATUS AT FOLLOW-UP						**	**
ENGAGED	-0.015		-0.150	0.000	-0.016	-0.232	-0.202
NOT ENGAGED	0.001		0.011	0.000	0.001	0.017	0.015
SET#9 IS R'S SPS PREGNANT AT FOLLOW-UP?						**	**
YES	-0.393		-0.092	0.095	-0.298	-0.079	-0.084
NO	-0.030		-0.006	-0.059	-0.090	-0.077	-0.051
DATA N.A. (1977-1983)	0.243		0.049	0.270	0.513	0.397	0.269
SET#10 PARENTHOOD STATUS AT FOLLOW-UP							
MARRIED PARENT	-0.466		-0.045	0.134	-0.332	0.026	0.000
SINGLE PARENT	-0.029		-0.005	0.244	0.215	0.066	0.040
NOT A PARENT	0.103		0.010	-0.041	0.062	-0.009	-0.002
FRIENDS USE MARIJUANA AT BASE YEAR (Cov.)[a]							0.368 **
Multiple R		0.274	0.307			0.376	0.533
R Sqr.		0.075	0.094			0.142	0.284

Notes: * indicates statistical significance at .05 level. ** indicates statistical significance at .01 level. Statistical significance is not indicated for bivariate coefficients or constants. Ns used for significance testing were weighted to approximate the number of individuals (not the number of observations) since each individual could contribute up to seven observations. Sets #5-#10 were measured at follow-up. Sets #3 and #4 were determined by timing of follow-up. All others were measured at Base Year (BY).
[a]Means for covariates: HIGH SCHOOL GRADES 5.859 URBANICITY 3.745
FRIENDS' USE OF MARIJUANA AT BASE YEAR 2.531 R WILL ATTEND 4YR COLLEGE 2.907

Table A.7.4a
Regression Analyses Linking Post-High School Experiences to Changes in Friends' Use of Cocaine
Females, Senior Years 1976-1997, Follow-ups 1977-1998

Regression Analyses Based on Full Set of Observations from Follow-Ups 1-7
(Wtd. N of Obs: 12,500)
Unstandardized Regression Coefficients

VARIABLE	BIVARIATE COEFF.	Predicting to Change Scores — Multivariate Coefficients BKGD.	Predicting to Change Scores — Multivariate Coefficients ALL SETS	Bivariate Coeff. With Dependent Variable at BY	at FU	Multivariate Prediction of Dep. Var. at FU: Covarying BY Dep. Var? No	Yes
CONSTANT	-0.066	-0.066	-0.066	1.488	1.422	1.422	1.422
SET#1 RACE						*	
WHITE	0.007	0.002	0.001	0.001	0.008	0.018	0.013
BLACK	0.018	0.058	0.050	-0.087	-0.069	-0.108	-0.067
OTHER	-0.087	-0.072	-0.055	0.075	-0.012	-0.064	-0.062
SET#2 REGION		**	*			**	**
NORTHEAST	-0.038	-0.036	-0.047	0.144	0.107	0.083	0.050
NORTH CENTRAL	0.083	0.083	0.081	-0.137	-0.054	-0.057	-0.021
SOUTH	-0.030	-0.041	-0.030	-0.044	-0.075	-0.051	-0.046
WEST	-0.053	-0.037	-0.036	0.153	0.101	0.093	0.059
HIGH SCHOOL GRADES/D=1 (Cov.)[a]		0.028 **	0.027 **			-0.043 **	-0.025 **
R WILL ATTEND 4YR COLLEGE (Cov.)[a]		0.015	0.021			-0.018	-0.008
URBANICITY (Cov.)[a]		-0.005	-0.006			0.036 **	0.025 *
SET#3 FOLLOW-UP NUMBER			**				
FU #1	0.063	0.063	-0.007	-0.013	0.050	0.041	0.028
FU #2	0.088	0.089	0.043	0.004	0.093	0.065	0.059
FU #3	0.036	0.038	0.028	0.004	0.040	0.016	0.019
FU #4	-0.034	-0.034	0.003	0.018	-0.016	-0.008	-0.005
FU #5	-0.081	-0.082	-0.025	0.016	-0.065	-0.042	-0.037
FU #6	-0.121	-0.124	-0.055	-0.003	-0.124	-0.087	-0.078
FU #7	-0.117	-0.118	-0.041	-0.036	-0.153	-0.109	-0.091
SET#4 ADMINISTRATION OF FIRST FOLLOW-UP							
ONE YEAR AFTER HIGH SCHOOL	0.004	0.002	-0.005	-0.007	-0.003	-0.005	-0.005
TWO YEARS AFTER HIGH SCHOOL	-0.004	-0.002	0.005	0.007	0.003	0.006	0.005
SET#5 STUDENT STATUS AT FOLLOW-UP							
FULL-TIME STUDENT	0.070		-0.034	-0.063	0.007	-0.049	-0.045
PART-TIME STUDENT	-0.018		-0.004	0.024	0.006	0.000	-0.001
NOT A STUDENT	-0.027		0.015	0.023	-0.004	0.021	0.019
SET#6 WORK STATUS AT FOLLOW-UP							
FULL-TIME CIVILIAN JOB	-0.012		0.000	0.020	0.008	0.007	0.006
MILITARY SERVICE	0.030		-0.036	-0.194	-0.164	-0.197	-0.156
PART-TIME JOB	0.004		-0.016	-0.030	-0.026	-0.024	-0.022
HOMEMAKER	-0.068		0.050	-0.009	-0.077	0.002	0.014
NONSTUDENT, NOT EMPLOYED	0.023		0.071	0.041	0.065	0.045	0.051
OTHER	0.065		-0.026	-0.034	0.031	-0.001	-0.007
SET#7 LIVING ARRANGEMENT AT FOLLOW-UP			*			**	**
MARRIED	-0.091		-0.073	-0.037	-0.128	-0.110	-0.100
PARTNER	-0.021		0.030	0.295	0.275	0.295	0.227
PARENT(S)	0.005		-0.007	0.006	0.011	-0.041	-0.032
DORM	0.160		0.106	-0.147	0.013	0.033	0.052
LIVE ALONE	0.018		0.000	0.016	0.033	0.071	0.053
OTHER	0.135		0.122	0.002	0.137	0.143	0.138
SET#8 ENGAGEMENT STATUS AT FOLLOW-UP			*			**	**
ENGAGED	-0.068		-0.117	0.064	-0.004	-0.148	-0.140
NOT ENGAGED	0.006		0.010	-0.005	0.000	0.013	0.012
SET#9 IS R PREGNANT AT FOLLOW-UP?			**			**	**
YES	-0.120		-0.058	-0.001	-0.120	-0.061	-0.061
NO	-0.041		-0.041	0.012	-0.030	-0.025	-0.029
DATA N.A. (1977-1983)	0.265		0.241	-0.064	0.201	0.159	0.180
SET#10 PARENTHOOD STATUS AT FOLLOW-UP							
MARRIED PARENT	-0.132		-0.042	-0.008	-0.139	-0.007	-0.016
SINGLE PARENT	-0.067		-0.078	0.156	0.090	-0.007	-0.025
NOT A PARENT	0.043		0.018	-0.009	0.034	0.003	0.007
FRIENDS USE COCAINE AT BASE YEAR (Cov.)[a]							0.257 **
Multiple R		0.130	0.187			0.281	0.395
R Sqr.		0.017	0.035			0.079	0.156

Notes: * indicates statistical significance at .05 level. ** indicates statistical significance at .01 level. Statistical significance is not indicated for bivariate coefficients or constants. Ns used for significance testing were weighted to approximate the number of individuals (not the number of observations) since each individual could contribute up to seven observations. Sets #5-#10 were measured at follow-up. Sets #3 and #4 were determined by timing of follow-up. All others were measured at Base Year (BY).

[a]Means for covariates: HIGH SCHOOL GRADES 6.366   URBANICITY 3.750
       FRIENDS' USE OF COCAINE AT BASE YEAR 1.488   R WILL ATTEND 4YR COLLEGE 2.911

Table A.7.4b
Regression Analyses Linking Post-High School Experiences to Changes in Friends' Use of Cocaine
Males, Senior Years 1976-1997, Follow-ups 1977-1998

Regression Analyses Based on Full Set of Observations from Follow-Ups 1-7
(Wtd. N of Obs: 9,859)
Unstandardized Regression Coefficients

VARIABLE	BIVARIATE COEFF.	Predicting to Change Scores Multivariate Coefficients BKGD.	ALL SETS	Bivariate Coeff. With Dependent Variable at BY	at FU	Multivariate Prediction of Dep. Var. at FU: Covarying BY Dep. Var? No	Yes
CONSTANT	0.073	0.073	0.073	1.502	1.575	1.575	1.575
SET#1 RACE		**	*				
WHITE	-0.012	-0.017	-0.016	0.002	-0.010	-0.004	-0.008
BLACK	0.205	0.246	0.225	-0.108	0.098	0.061	0.117
OTHER	-0.017	0.009	0.007	0.051	0.034	-0.006	-0.001
SET#2 REGION		*	*			**	*
NORTHEAST	0.010	0.014	0.001	0.167	0.177	0.150	0.099
NORTH CENTRAL	0.067	0.082	0.086	-0.132	-0.064	-0.058	-0.009
SOUTH	-0.054	-0.069	-0.060	0.002	-0.053	-0.036	-0.044
WEST	-0.047	-0.055	-0.060	0.042	-0.005	-0.012	-0.029
HIGH SCHOOL GRADES/D=1 (Cov.)[a]		0.022	0.023 *			-0.047 **	-0.023 *
R WILL ATTEND 4YR COLLEGE (Cov.)[a]		0.020	0.021			-0.005	0.004
URBANICITY (Cov.)[a]		0.003	-0.004			0.052 **	0.033 *
SET#3 FOLLOW-UP NUMBER		**					
FU #1	-0.007	-0.010	-0.100	-0.032	-0.039	-0.083	-0.089
FU #2	0.078	0.079	0.018	-0.020	0.059	0.015	0.016
FU #3	0.085	0.085	0.067	-0.012	0.073	0.046	0.053
FU #4	0.020	0.020	0.064	0.027	0.046	0.071	0.069
FU #5	-0.039	-0.039	0.040	0.035	-0.003	0.043	0.042
FU #6	-0.129	-0.125	-0.022	0.027	-0.101	-0.028	-0.026
FU #7	-0.172	-0.170	-0.059	0.027	-0.145	-0.066	-0.064
SET#4 ADMINISTRATION OF FIRST FOLLOW-UP							
ONE YEAR AFTER HIGH SCHOOL	0.007	0.008	0.000	0.002	0.009	0.008	0.005
TWO YEARS AFTER HIGH SCHOOL	-0.007	-0.009	0.000	-0.002	-0.010	-0.008	-0.005
SET#5 STUDENT STATUS AT FOLLOW-UP							
FULL-TIME STUDENT	0.033		-0.101	-0.088	-0.055	-0.100	-0.101
PART-TIME STUDENT	-0.023		-0.035	0.046	0.023	0.020	0.001
NOT A STUDENT	-0.011		0.049	0.032	0.021	0.041	0.044
SET#6 WORK STATUS AT FOLLOW-UP							
FULL-TIME CIVILIAN JOB	-0.031		-0.025	0.038	0.007	-0.005	-0.012
MILITARY SERVICE	-0.016		-0.022	-0.102	-0.118	-0.172	-0.121
PART-TIME JOB	0.068		0.071	-0.088	-0.019	0.028	0.042
HOMEMAKER	0.360		0.413	0.113	0.473	0.491	0.464
NONSTUDENT, NOT EMPLOYED	0.004		-0.080	0.111	0.116	0.019	-0.015
OTHER	0.055		0.051	-0.068	-0.013	0.033	0.039
SET#7 LIVING ARRANGEMENT AT FOLLOW-UP			*			**	**
MARRIED	-0.174		-0.148	0.009	-0.165	-0.153	-0.151
PARTNER	0.097		0.090	0.175	0.272	0.276	0.213
PARENT(S)	0.047		0.046	-0.017	0.029	-0.023	0.000
DORM	0.046		0.048	-0.142	-0.096	0.006	0.020
LIVE ALONE	0.045		0.009	0.007	0.052	0.052	0.037
OTHER	0.121		0.101	0.001	0.121	0.139	0.126
SET#8 ENGAGEMENT STATUS AT FOLLOW-UP						*	
ENGAGED	0.030		-0.052	-0.026	0.005	-0.149	-0.116
NOT ENGAGED	-0.002		0.004	0.002	0.000	0.011	0.009
SET#9 IS R'S SPS PREGNANT AT FOLLOW-UP?		**				**	**
YES	-0.112		-0.003	0.006	-0.106	-0.008	-0.006
NO	-0.044		-0.049	-0.003	-0.047	-0.054	-0.053
DATA N.A. (1977-1983)	0.245		0.245	0.013	0.259	0.271	0.263
SET#10 PARENTHOOD STATUS AT FOLLOW-UP							
MARRIED PARENT	-0.207		-0.049	0.021	-0.185	-0.034	-0.039
SINGLE PARENT	0.102		0.033	0.092	0.194	0.058	0.049
NOT A PARENT	0.040		0.009	-0.009	0.031	0.005	0.006
FRIENDS USE COCAINE AT BASE YEAR (Cov.)[a]							0.342 **
Multiple R		0.136	0.208			0.289	0.429
R Sqr.		0.018	0.043			0.084	0.184

Notes: * indicates statistical significance at .05 level. ** indicates statistical significance at .01 level. Statistical significance is not indicated for bivariate coefficients or constants. Ns used for significance testing were weighted to approximate the number of individuals (not the number of observations) since each individual could contribute up to seven observations. Sets #5-#10 were measured at follow-up. Sets #3 and #4 were determined by timing of follow-up. All others were measured at Base Year (BY).

[a] Means for covariates: HIGH SCHOOL GRADES 5.865   URBANICITY 3.745
FRIENDS' USE OF COCAINE AT BASE YEAR 1.502   R WILL ATTEND 4YR COLLEGE 2.911

Table A.7.5a
Regression Analyses Linking Post-High School Experiences to
Changes in Availability of Marijuana
Females, Senior Years 1976-1997, Follow-ups 1977-1998

Regression Analyses Based on Full Set of Observations from Follow-Ups 1-7
(Wtd. N of Obs: 13,117)
Unstandardized Regression Coefficients

VARIABLE	BIVARIATE COEFF.	Multivariate Coefficients BKGD.	Multivariate Coefficients ALL SETS	Bivariate Coeff. With Dependent Variable at BY	Bivariate Coeff. With Dependent Variable at FU	Multivariate Prediction of Dep. Var. at FU: Covarying BY Dep. Var? No	Multivariate Prediction of Dep. Var. at FU: Covarying BY Dep. Var? Yes
		Predicting to Change Scores					
CONSTANT	0.001	0.001	0.001	4.263	4.264	4.264	4.264
SET#1 RACE		**	**			**	*
WHITE	-0.048	-0.051	-0.048	0.082	0.033	0.035	0.004
BLACK	0.370	0.371	0.338	-0.399	-0.028	-0.042	0.099
OTHER	0.060	0.085	0.092	-0.328	-0.268	-0.266	-0.133
SET#2 REGION						**	
NORTHEAST	-0.077	-0.027	-0.044	0.183	0.106	0.091	0.041
NORTH CENTRAL	-0.008	0.008	0.008	0.065	0.057	0.044	0.030
SOUTH	0.101	0.041	0.052	-0.209	-0.108	-0.105	-0.047
WEST	-0.065	-0.055	-0.050	0.007	-0.058	-0.016	-0.029
HIGH SCHOOL GRADES/D=1 (Cov.)[a]		0.003	0.002			-0.031 **	-0.019
R WILL ATTEND 4YR COLLEGE (Cov.)[a]		-0.014	-0.028			0.026	0.006
URBANICITY (Cov.)[a]		-0.088 **	-0.098 **			-0.006	-0.040 *
SET#3 FOLLOW-UP NUMBER		**	*			*	**
FU #1	0.096	0.093	-0.017	-0.008	0.088	0.051	0.025
FU #2	0.130	0.130	0.081	-0.020	0.110	0.077	0.079
FU #3	0.059	0.060	0.074	-0.011	0.047	0.047	0.057
FU #4	0.015	0.017	0.069	-0.015	0.000	0.028	0.044
FU #5	-0.136	-0.132	-0.059	0.028	-0.108	-0.073	-0.068
FU #6	-0.206	-0.206	-0.126	0.026	-0.179	-0.145	-0.138
FU #7	-0.254	-0.260	-0.175	0.045	-0.209	-0.176	-0.176
SET#4 ADMINISTRATION OF FIRST FOLLOW-UP		*					
ONE YEAR AFTER HIGH SCHOOL	0.036	0.040	0.031	-0.014	0.022	0.018	0.023
TWO YEARS AFTER HIGH SCHOOL	-0.038	-0.042	-0.033	0.015	-0.024	-0.019	-0.024
SET#5 STUDENT STATUS AT FOLLOW-UP							
FULL-TIME STUDENT	0.124		0.023	-0.005	0.119	0.039	0.033
PART-TIME STUDENT	-0.041		-0.024	-0.014	-0.054	-0.046	-0.038
NOT A STUDENT	-0.046		-0.006	0.004	-0.042	-0.010	-0.008
SET#6 WORK STATUS AT FOLLOW-UP							
FULL-TIME CIVILIAN JOB	-0.034		-0.002	0.024	-0.010	0.029	0.017
MILITARY SERVICE	-0.204		-0.237	-0.268	-0.472	-0.524	-0.417
PART-TIME JOB	0.051		0.013	-0.005	0.046	0.000	0.005
HOMEMAKER	-0.096		0.008	-0.018	-0.114	-0.022	-0.011
NONSTUDENT, NOT EMPLOYED	-0.046		-0.049	-0.029	-0.075	-0.051	-0.050
OTHER	0.133		0.010	-0.058	0.075	-0.065	-0.037
SET#7 LIVING ARRANGEMENT AT FOLLOW-UP			*			**	**
MARRIED	-0.150		-0.133	0.005	-0.145	-0.104	-0.115
PARTNER	-0.026		-0.002	0.259	0.233	0.244	0.152
PARENT(S)	0.110		0.084	-0.116	-0.006	-0.043	0.004
DORM	0.217		0.199	0.014	0.231	0.151	0.169
LIVE ALONE	-0.055		-0.029	0.027	-0.028	0.020	0.002
OTHER	0.103		0.093	0.039	0.142	0.121	0.111
SET#8 ENGAGEMENT STATUS AT FOLLOW-UP							
ENGAGED	-0.005		-0.089	0.053	0.048	-0.077	-0.082
NOT ENGAGED	0.000		0.008	-0.005	-0.004	0.007	0.007
SET#9 IS R PREGNANT AT FOLLOW-UP?						**	*
YES	-0.141		-0.032	0.021	-0.120	-0.044	-0.040
NO	-0.020		-0.008	-0.013	-0.032	-0.026	-0.020
DATA N.A. (1977-1983)	0.155		0.057	0.063	0.218	0.161	0.122
SET#10 PARENTHOOD STATUS AT FOLLOW-UP							
MARRIED PARENT	-0.150		0.013	0.007	-0.142	0.055	0.040
SINGLE PARENT	0.146		0.010	0.002	0.147	0.129	0.085
NOT A PARENT	0.033		-0.005	-0.002	0.030	-0.026	-0.018
AVAILABILITY OF MARIJUANA AT BASE YEAR (Cov.)[a]							0.372 **
Multiple R		0.180	0.199			0.212	0.436
R Sqr.		0.032	0.040			0.045	0.190

Notes: * indicates statistical significance at .05 level. ** indicates statistical significance at .01 level. Statistical significance is not indicated for bivariate coefficients or constants. Ns used for significance testing were weighted to approximate the number of individuals (not the number of observations) since each individual could contribute up to seven observations. Sets #5-#10 were measured at follow-up. Sets #3 and #4 were determined by timing of follow-up. All others were measured at Base Year (BY).

[a]Means for covariates: HIGH SCHOOL GRADES   6.325   URBANICITY   3.764
         AVAILABILITY OF MARIJUANA AT BASE YEAR   4.263   R WILL ATTEND 4YR COLLEGE   2.898

Table A.7.5b
Regression Analyses Linking Post-High School Experiences to
Changes in Availability of Marijuana
Males, Senior Years 1976-1997, Follow-ups 1977-1998

Regression Analyses Based on Full Set of Observations from Follow-Ups 1-7
(Wtd. N of Obs: 10,558)
Unstandardized Regression Coefficients

| VARIABLE | Predicting to Change Scores | | | Bivariate Coeff. With Dependent Variable | | Multivariate Prediction of Dep. Var. at FU: Covarying BY Dep. Var? | |
| | BIVARIATE COEFF. | Multivariate Coefficients | | | | | |
		BKGD.	ALL SETS	at BY	at FU	No	Yes
CONSTANT	-0.031	-0.031	-0.031	4.427	4.396	4.396	4.396
SET#1 RACE		**	**			**	*
WHITE	-0.027	-0.029	-0.028	0.039	0.012	0.014	-0.001
BLACK	0.314	0.317	0.310	-0.230	0.084	0.062	0.148
OTHER	0.041	0.059	0.056	-0.215	-0.174	-0.175	-0.095
SET#2 REGION							
NORTHEAST	-0.091	-0.067	-0.074	0.174	0.083	0.066	0.018
NORTH CENTRAL	0.038	0.050	0.049	-0.031	0.007	0.002	0.018
SOUTH	0.036	0.003	0.010	-0.062	-0.026	-0.018	-0.008
WEST	-0.019	-0.015	-0.016	-0.052	-0.072	-0.056	-0.043
HIGH SCHOOL GRADES/D=1 (Cov.)[a]		0.003	0.001			-0.023 *	-0.015
R WILL ATTEND 4YR COLLEGE (Cov.)[a]		-0.004	-0.018			0.001	-0.006
URBANICITY (Cov.)[a]		-0.043 *	-0.049 *			0.051 **	0.017
SET#3 FOLLOW-UP NUMBER			**				
FU #1	0.087	0.083	0.013	-0.017	0.070	0.055	0.041
FU #2	0.101	0.101	0.062	-0.027	0.074	0.055	0.058
FU #3	0.036	0.038	0.040	-0.011	0.025	0.022	0.028
FU #4	-0.017	-0.017	0.018	-0.002	-0.020	-0.006	0.002
FU #5	-0.098	-0.095	-0.042	0.041	-0.057	-0.042	-0.042
FU #6	-0.158	-0.157	-0.093	0.027	-0.130	-0.107	-0.102
FU #7	-0.188	-0.190	-0.129	0.045	-0.143	-0.127	-0.128
SET#4 ADMINISTRATION OF FIRST FOLLOW-UP							
ONE YEAR AFTER HIGH SCHOOL	0.003	0.000	-0.007	0.004	0.006	0.009	0.004
TWO YEARS AFTER HIGH SCHOOL	-0.003	0.000	0.007	-0.004	-0.007	-0.010	-0.004
SET#5 STUDENT STATUS AT FOLLOW-UP							
FULL-TIME STUDENT	0.100		0.011	-0.021	0.080	0.034	0.026
PART-TIME STUDENT	-0.012		-0.011	0.024	0.012	0.025	0.013
NOT A STUDENT	-0.041		-0.003	0.005	-0.035	-0.018	-0.013
SET#6 WORK STATUS AT FOLLOW-UP							
FULL-TIME CIVILIAN JOB	-0.044		-0.005	0.032	-0.012	0.030	0.018
MILITARY SERVICE	-0.130		-0.141	0.017	-0.113	-0.154	-0.150
PART-TIME JOB	0.125		0.062	-0.110	0.014	-0.037	-0.003
HOMEMAKER	0.345		0.313	-0.337	0.009	0.022	0.123
NONSTUDENT, NOT EMPLOYED	0.036		-0.017	-0.097	-0.062	-0.046	-0.036
OTHER	0.080		0.003	0.008	0.088	-0.024	-0.015
SET#7 LIVING ARRANGEMENT AT FOLLOW-UP			*			**	**
MARRIED	-0.165		-0.186	0.046	-0.119	-0.082	-0.118
PARTNER	0.020		0.069	0.103	0.124	0.142	0.117
PARENT(S)	0.067		0.056	-0.095	-0.028	-0.073	-0.028
DORM	0.149		0.118	-0.007	0.142	0.079	0.093
LIVE ALONE	0.055		0.104	-0.011	0.044	0.083	0.091
OTHER	0.057		0.077	0.045	0.102	0.112	0.100
SET#8 ENGAGEMENT STATUS AT FOLLOW-UP							
ENGAGED	0.007		-0.048	0.057	0.064	0.003	-0.015
NOT ENGAGED	-0.001		0.004	-0.004	-0.005	0.000	0.001
SET#9 IS R'S SPS PREGNANT AT FOLLOW-UP?						**	*
YES	-0.172		-0.041	0.016	-0.156	-0.082	-0.068
NO	-0.013		-0.005	-0.014	-0.027	-0.023	-0.016
DATA N.A. (1977-1983)	0.105		0.033	0.066	0.172	0.131	0.097
SET#10 PARENTHOOD STATUS AT FOLLOW-UP							
MARRIED PARENT	-0.113		0.106	0.012	-0.102	0.060	0.076
SINGLE PARENT	0.008		-0.102	0.033	0.041	-0.003	-0.037
NOT A PARENT	0.024		-0.018	-0.004	0.020	-0.013	-0.015
AVAILABILITY OF MARIJUANA AT BASE YEAR (Cov.)[a]							0.347 **
Multiple R		0.144	0.175			0.187	0.395
R Sqr.		0.021	0.031			0.035	0.156

Notes: * indicates statistical significance at .05 level. ** indicates statistical significance at .01 level. Statistical significance is not indicated for bivariate coefficients or constants. Ns used for significance testing were weighted to approximate the number of individuals (not the number of observations) since each individual could contribute up to seven observations. Sets #5-#10 were measured at follow-up. Sets #3 and #4 were determined by timing of follow-up. All others were measured at Base Year (BY).

[a]Means for covariates: HIGH SCHOOL GRADES 5.805   URBANICITY 3.755
    AVAILABILITY OF MARIJUANA AT BASE YEAR 4.427   R WILL ATTEND 4YR COLLEGE 2.880

Table A.7.6a
Regression Analyses Linking Post-High School Experiences to Changes in Availability of Cocaine
Females, Senior Years 1976-1997, Follow-ups 1977-1998

		Regression Analyses Based on Full Set of Observations from Follow-Ups 1-7 (Wtd. N of Obs: 12,858) Unstandardized Regression Coefficients					
		Predicting to Change Scores		Bivariate Coeff. With Dependent Variable Covarying		Multivariate Prediction of Dep. Var. at FU: BY Dep. Var?	
	BIVARIATE	Multivariate Coefficients	ALL				
VARIABLE	COEFF.	BKGD.	SETS	at BY	at FU	No	Yes
CONSTANT	0.273	0.273	0.273	3.131	3.404	3.404	3.404
SET#1 RACE		**	**			**	**
WHITE	-0.049	-0.062	-0.060	0.047	-0.003	0.004	-0.017
BLACK	0.519	0.551	0.517	-0.277	0.242	0.222	0.316
OTHER	-0.077	0.003	0.023	-0.140	-0.216	-0.251	-0.163
SET#2 REGION						**	*
NORTHEAST	-0.037	0.013	-0.007	0.242	0.205	0.187	0.125
NORTH CENTRAL	0.053	0.069	0.065	-0.108	-0.055	-0.050	-0.013
SOUTH	0.070	0.001	0.017	-0.185	-0.115	-0.129	-0.082
WEST	-0.180	-0.152	-0.146	0.212	0.031	0.071	0.002
HIGH SCHOOL GRADES/D=1 (Cov.)[a]		0.009	0.006			-0.032 *	-0.020
R WILL ATTEND 4YR COLLEGE (Cov.)[a]		-0.072 **	-0.083 **			0.010	-0.020
URBANICITY (Cov.)[a]		-0.078 **	-0.085 **			0.032	-0.006
SET#3 FOLLOW-UP NUMBER			*				
FU #1	-0.135	-0.130	-0.250	0.058	-0.077	-0.069	-0.127
FU #2	0.000	0.005	-0.062	0.049	0.049	0.038	0.006
FU #3	0.027	0.030	0.032	0.038	0.065	0.057	0.049
FU #4	0.068	0.070	0.128	-0.017	0.051	0.051	0.076
FU #5	0.071	0.068	0.155	-0.061	0.010	0.013	0.059
FU #6	0.043	0.033	0.134	-0.079	-0.036	-0.032	0.021
FU #7	0.028	0.010	0.127	-0.132	-0.103	-0.094	-0.023
SET#4 ADMINISTRATION OF FIRST FOLLOW-UP							
ONE YEAR AFTER HIGH SCHOOL	0.029	0.035	0.025	-0.036	-0.007	-0.007	0.003
TWO YEARS AFTER HIGH SCHOOL	-0.031	-0.038	-0.027	0.039	0.007	0.008	-0.003
SET#5 STUDENT STATUS AT FOLLOW-UP							
FULL-TIME STUDENT	-0.051		0.022	0.059	0.008	0.017	0.019
PART-TIME STUDENT	-0.068		-0.051	0.039	-0.030	-0.045	-0.047
NOT A STUDENT	0.031		-0.002	-0.030	0.001	0.000	-0.001
SET#6 WORK STATUS AT FOLLOW-UP							
FULL-TIME CIVILIAN JOB	0.041		0.019	-0.007	0.033	0.035	0.030
MILITARY SERVICE	-0.121		-0.080	-0.081	-0.202	-0.185	-0.152
PART-TIME JOB	-0.058		-0.009	0.031	-0.027	-0.026	-0.021
HOMEMAKER	-0.056		-0.025	-0.082	-0.138	-0.083	-0.064
NONSTUDENT, NOT EMPLOYED	-0.023		-0.053	0.012	-0.011	-0.021	-0.031
OTHER	-0.027		-0.024	0.022	-0.005	-0.039	-0.034
SET#7 LIVING ARRANGEMENT AT FOLLOW-UP						**	**
MARRIED	-0.065		-0.147	-0.067	-0.132	-0.148	-0.147
PARTNER	0.027		0.041	0.306	0.334	0.324	0.234
PARENT(S)	-0.015		0.041	-0.004	-0.018	-0.017	0.001
DORM	0.005		0.213	0.019	0.024	0.111	0.144
LIVE ALONE	0.101		0.040	-0.030	0.071	0.076	0.065
OTHER	0.123		0.144	0.020	0.143	0.138	0.140
SET#8 ENGAGEMENT STATUS AT FOLLOW-UP							
ENGAGED	-0.056		-0.111	0.095	0.039	-0.105	-0.107
NOT ENGAGED	0.005		0.010	-0.008	-0.003	0.009	0.009
SET#9 IS R PREGNANT AT FOLLOW-UP?			*				
YES	-0.012		0.036	0.020	0.007	0.074	0.062
NO	-0.026		-0.035	0.033	0.007	0.002	-0.010
DATA N.A. (1977-1983)	0.147		0.185	-0.191	-0.044	-0.034	0.036
SET#10 PARENTHOOD STATUS AT FOLLOW-UP							
MARRIED PARENT	-0.054		-0.028	-0.046	-0.099	0.078	0.044
SINGLE PARENT	0.271		0.004	0.022	0.293	0.116	0.080
NOT A PARENT	-0.005		0.008	0.012	0.007	-0.032	-0.019
AVAILABILITY OF COCAINE AT BASE YEAR (Cov.)[a]							0.319 **
Multiple R		0.151	0.174			0.176	0.355
R Sqr.		0.023	0.030			0.031	0.126

Notes: * indicates statistical significance at .05 level. ** indicates statistical significance at .01 level. Statistical significance is not indicated for bivariate coefficients or constants. Ns used for significance testing were weighted to approximate the number of individuals (not the number of observations) since each individual could contribute up to seven observations. Sets #5-#10 were measured at follow-up. Sets #3 and #4 were determined by timing of follow-up. All others were measured at Base Year (BY).

[a]Means for covariates: HIGH SCHOOL GRADES 6.315 | URBANICITY 3.763
AVAILABILITY OF COCAINE AT BASE YEAR 3.131 | R WILL ATTEND 4YR COLLEGE 2.896

284

Table A.7.6b
Regression Analyses Linking Post-High School Experiences to Changes in Availability of Cocaine
Males, Senior Years 1976-1997, Follow-ups 1977-1998

Regression Analyses Based on Full Set of Observations from Follow-Ups 1-7
(Wtd. N of Obs: 10,419)
Unstandardized Regression Coefficients

VARIABLE	BIVARIATE COEFF.	Multivariate Coefficients BKGD.	ALL SETS	Bivariate Coeff. With Dependent Variable at BY	at FU	Multivariate Prediction of Dep. Var. at FU: Covarying BY Dep. Var? No	Yes
CONSTANT	0.418	0.418	0.418	3.181	3.598	3.598	3.598
SET#1 RACE		**	**			*	**
WHITE	-0.011	-0.021	-0.021	0.005	-0.007	-0.001	-0.007
BLACK	0.371	0.407	0.400	-0.120	0.251	0.233	0.287
OTHER	-0.146	-0.074	-0.069	0.036	-0.110	-0.153	-0.126
SET#2 REGION							**
NORTHEAST	-0.043	-0.027	-0.036	0.276	0.233	0.191	0.118
NORTH CENTRAL	0.078	0.081	0.083	-0.172	-0.093	-0.080	-0.027
SOUTH	0.039	0.008	0.013	-0.101	-0.061	-0.050	-0.029
WEST	-0.162	-0.134	-0.136	0.149	-0.013	-0.007	-0.049
HIGH SCHOOL GRADES/D=1 (Cov.)*		0.033 *	0.033			-0.042 **	-0.017
R WILL ATTEND 4YR COLLEGE (Cov.)*		-0.034	-0.036			0.019	0.001
URBANICITY (Cov.)*		-0.026	-0.031			0.095 **	0.054 *
SET#3 FOLLOW-UP NUMBER		**	**			*	**
FU #1	-0.224	-0.225	-0.297	0.021	-0.203	-0.202	-0.233
FU #2	-0.023	-0.020	-0.059	0.012	-0.011	-0.026	-0.037
FU #3	0.034	0.038	0.030	0.016	0.050	0.029	0.029
FU #4	0.131	0.128	0.165	0.006	0.137	0.136	0.146
FU #5	0.116	0.117	0.175	0.008	0.125	0.129	0.144
FU #6	0.097	0.096	0.166	-0.068	0.029	0.062	0.096
FU #7	0.071	0.065	0.132	-0.063	0.008	0.041	0.070
SET#4 ADMINISTRATION OF FIRST FOLLOW-UP							
ONE YEAR AFTER HIGH SCHOOL	-0.017	-0.021	-0.028	-0.009	-0.026	-0.024	-0.025
TWO YEARS AFTER HIGH SCHOOL	0.019	0.023	0.030	0.010	0.028	0.026	0.027
SET#5 STUDENT STATUS AT FOLLOW-UP							
FULL-TIME STUDENT	-0.103		-0.043	0.006	-0.097	-0.003	-0.016
PART-TIME STUDENT	0.001		0.006	0.124	0.125	0.104	0.073
NOT A STUDENT	0.043		0.017	-0.020	0.024	-0.013	-0.004
SET#6 WORK STATUS AT FOLLOW-UP							
FULL-TIME CIVILIAN JOB	0.034		-0.009	0.011	0.044	0.023	0.013
MILITARY SERVICE	-0.024		-0.016	-0.016	-0.039	-0.059	-0.045
PART-TIME JOB	0.008		0.096	-0.066	-0.059	-0.015	0.021
HOMEMAKER	0.335		0.338	-0.102	0.233	0.257	0.283
NONSTUDENT, NOT EMPLOYED	0.014		-0.026	-0.013	0.002	0.003	-0.007
OTHER	-0.150		-0.056	0.035	-0.116	-0.065	-0.062
SET#7 LIVING ARRANGEMENT AT FOLLOW-UP						*	*
MARRIED	-0.004		-0.174	-0.073	-0.077	-0.148	-0.157
PARTNER	0.051		0.066	0.210	0.261	0.234	0.179
PARENT(S)	-0.052		0.046	0.012	-0.040	-0.012	0.007
DORM	-0.106		0.113	-0.084	-0.189	0.001	0.037
LIVE ALONE	0.175		0.113	-0.026	0.150	0.106	0.108
OTHER	0.025		0.072	0.060	0.085	0.107	0.096
SET#8 ENGAGEMENT STATUS AT FOLLOW-UP							
ENGAGED	-0.038		-0.075	0.070	0.032	-0.090	-0.085
NOT ENGAGED	0.003		0.006	-0.005	-0.002	0.007	0.006
SET#9 IS R'S SPS PREGNANT AT FOLLOW-UP?							
YES	-0.112		-0.107	0.086	-0.026	0.020	-0.021
NO	-0.003		-0.026	0.015	0.012	-0.007	-0.013
DATA N.A. (1977-1983)	0.042		0.156	-0.096	-0.054	0.032	0.072
SET#10 PARENTHOOD STATUS AT FOLLOW-UP							
MARRIED PARENT	0.060		0.093	-0.123	-0.064	0.035	0.053
SINGLE PARENT	0.019		-0.177	0.147	0.166	-0.013	-0.066
NOT A PARENT	-0.014		-0.011	0.019	0.006	-0.007	-0.008
AVAILABILITY OF COCAINE AT BASE YEAR (Cov.)*							0.324 **
Multiple R		0.134	0.157			0.204	0.383
R Sqr.		0.018	0.025			0.041	0.147

Notes: * indicates statistical significance at .05 level. ** indicates statistical significance at .01 level. Statistical significance is not indicated for bivariate coefficients or constants. Ns used for significance testing were weighted to approximate the number of individuals (not the number of observations) since each individual could contribute up to seven observations. Sets #5-#10 were measured at follow-up. Sets #3 and #4 were determined by timing of follow-up. All others were measured at Base Year (BY).

*Means for covariates:
HIGH SCHOOL GRADES 5.802 URBANICITY 3.754
AVAILABILITY OF COCAINE AT BASE YEAR 3.181 R WILL ATTEND 4YR COLLEGE 2.881

References

Andrews, F. M., Morgan, J. N., & Sonquist, J. A. (1967). *Multiple classification analysis, a report on a computer program for multiple regression using categorical predictors.* Ann Arbor: The University of Michigan.

Arnett, J. J. (1998). Risk behavior and family role transitions during the twenties. *Journal of Youth and Adolescence, 27,* 301–320.

Arnett, J. J. (2000). Emerging adulthood: A theory of development from the late teens through the twenties. *American Psychologist, 55,* 469–480.

Aseltine, R. H., & Gore, S. (1993). Mental health and social adaptation following the transition from high school. *Journal of Research on Adolescence, 3,* 247–270.

Bachman, J. G. (1987, July). *Changes in deviant behavior during late adolescence and early adulthood.* Paper presented at the ninth biennial meeting of the International Society for the Study of Behavioral Development, Tokyo, Japan. (ERIC Document ED No. 309 365).

Bachman, J. G. (1994). Incorporating trend data to aid in the causal interpretation of individual-level correlations among variables: Examples focusing on the recent decline in marijuana use. In L. Collins & L. Seitz (Eds.), *Advances in data analysis for prevention intervention research* (NIDA Research Monograph No. 142; pp. 112–139).

Bachman, J. G., Freedman-Doan, P., O'Malley, P. M., Johnston, L. D., & Segal, D. R. (1999). Changing patterns of drug use among U.S. military recruits before and after enlistment. *American Journal of Public Health, 89,* 672–677.

Bachman, J. G., Johnston, L. D., & O'Malley, P. M. (1981). Smoking, drinking, and drug use among American high school students: Correlates and trends, 1975–1979. *American Journal of Public Health, 71,* 59–69.

Bachman, J. G., Johnston, L. D., & O'Malley, P. M. (1990). Explaining the recent decline in cocaine use among young adults: Further evidence that perceived risks and disapproval lead to reduced drug use. *Journal of Health and Social Behavior, 31,* 173–184.

Bachman, J. G., Johnston, L. D., & O'Malley, P. M. (1991). How changes in drug use are linked to perceived risks and disapproval: Evidence from national studies that youth and young adults respond to information about the consequences of drug use. In R. L. Donohew, H. Sypher, & W. Bukoski (Eds.), *Persuasive communication and drug abuse prevention* (pp. 133–156). Hillsdale, NJ: Lawrence Erlbaum Associates.

Bachman, J. G., Johnston, L. D., & O'Malley, P. M. (1996). *The Monitoring the Future project after twenty-two years: Design and procedures* (Monitoring the Future Occasional Paper No. 38). Ann Arbor, MI: Institute for Social Research.

Bachman, J. G., Johnston, L. D., & O'Malley, P. M. (1998). Explaining the recent increases in students' marijuana use: The impacts of perceived risks and disapproval from 1976 through 1996. *American Journal of Public Health, 88,* 887–892.

Bachman, J. G., Johnston, L. D., O'Malley, P. M., & Humphrey, R. H. (1988). Explaining the recent decline in marijuana use: Differentiating the effects of perceived risks, disapproval, and general lifestyle factors. *Journal of Health and Social Behavior, 29,* 92–112.

Bachman, J. G., Johnston, L. D., O'Malley, P. M., & Schulenberg, J. E. (1996). Transitions in alcohol and other drug use and abuse during late adolescence and young adulthood. In J. A. Graber, J. Brooks-Gunn, & A. C. Petersen (Eds.), *Transitions through adolescence: Interpersonal domains and contexts.* Hillsdale, NJ: Lawrence Erlbaum Associates.

Bachman, J. G., & O'Malley, P. M. (1989). When four months equal a year: Inconsistencies in students' reports of drug use. In E. Singer & S. Presser (Eds.), *Survey research methods* (pp. 173–185). Chicago: University of Chicago Press. (Reprinted from *Public Opinion Quarterly, 45,* 536–548, 1981.)

Bachman, J. G., O'Malley, P. M., & Johnston, L. D. (1981). *Changes in drug use after high school as a function of role status and social environment* (Monitoring the Future Occasional Paper No. 11). Ann Arbor, MI: Institute for Social Research.

Bachman, J. G., O'Malley, P. M., & Johnston, L. D. (1984). Drug use among young adults: The impacts of role status and social environments. *Journal of Personality and Social Psychology, 47,* 629–645.

Bachman, J. G., O'Malley, P. M., Johnston, L. D., Rodgers, W. L., & Schulenberg, J. (1992). *Changes in drug use during the post-high school years* (Monitoring the Future Occasional Paper No. 35). Ann Arbor: MI, Institute for Social Research.

Bachman, J. G., O'Malley, P. M., Schulenberg, J. E., Johnston, L. D., Bryant, A. L., Merline, A. C., Freedman-Doan, P., Ridenour, N. J., & Hart, T. C. (2001). *Analyses showing how religiosity, social activities, and drug-related beliefs mediate relationships between post-high-school experiences and substance use* (Monitoring the Future Occasional Paper No. 50). Ann Arbor, MI: Institute for Social Research.

Bachman, J. G., O'Malley, P. M., Johnston, L. D., Rodgers, W. L., Schulenberg, J. E., Lim, J., & Wadsworth, K. N. (1996). *Changes in drug use during ages 18–32* (Monitoring the Future Occasional Paper No. 39). Ann Arbor, MI: Institute for Social Research.

Bachman, J. G., Safron, D. J., & Schulenberg, J. (under review). *Wishing to work: New findings on why adolescents' part-time work intensity correlates with educational disengagement, drug use, and problem behavior.*

Bachman, J. G., Schulenberg, J., O'Malley, P. M., & Johnston, L. D. (1990, March). *Short-term and longer-term effects of educational commitment and success on the use of cigarettes, alcohol, and illicit drugs.* Paper presented at the third biennial meeting of the Society for Research on Adolescence, Atlanta, GA.

Bachman, J. G., Wadsworth, K. N., O'Malley, P. M., Johnston, L. D., & Schulenberg, J. (1997). *Smoking, drinking and drug use in young adulthood: The impacts of new freedoms and new responsibilities.* Mahwah, NJ: Lawrence Erlbaum Associates.

Bahr, S. J., Maughan, S. L., Marcos, A. C., & Li, B. (1998). Family, religiosity, and the risk of adolescent drug use. *Journal of Marriage and the Family, 60,* 979–992.

Belsky, J., & Pensky, E. (1988). Marital change across the transition to parenthood. *Marriage & Family Review, 12,* 133–156.

Bentler, P. M. (1995). *EQS structural equations program manual.* Encino, CA: Multivariate Software, Inc.

Bray, R. M., Marsden, M. E., & Peterson, M. R. (1991). Standardized comparisons of the use of alcohol, drugs, and cigarettes among military personnel and civilians. *American Journal of Public Health, 81*(7), 865–869.

Brennan, A. F., Walfish, S., & AuBuchon, P. (1986). Alcohol use and abuse in college students: II. Social/environmental correlates, methodological issues, and implications for intervention. *International Journal of the Addictions, 21*(4–5), 475–493.

Brook, J. S., Richter, L., Whiteman, M., & Cohen, P. (1999). Consequences of adolescent marijuana use: Incompatibility with the assumption of adult roles. *Genetic, Social, & General Psychology Monographs, 125*(2), 193–207.

Brown, J. W., Glaser, D., Waxer, E., & Geis, G. (1974). Turning off: Cessation of marijuana use after college. *Social Problems, 21,* 527–538.

Brown, T. N., Schulenberg, J., Bachman, J. G., O'Malley, P. M., & Johnston, L. D. (2001). Are risk and protective factors for substance use consistent across historical time?: National data from the high school classes of 1976 through 1997. *Prevention Science, 2*(1), 29–43.

Browne, M. W., & Cudeck, R. (1993). Alternative ways of assessing model fit. In K. A. Bollen & J. S. Long (Eds.), *Testing structural equation models* (pp. 136–161). Newbury Park, CA: Sage.

Brunswick, A. F., Messeri, P. A., & Titus, S. P. (1992). Predictive factors in adult substance abuse: A prospective study of African American adolescents. In M. Glantz & R. Pickens (Eds.), *Vulnerability to drug abuse* (pp. 419–472). Washington, DC: American Psychological Association.

Burton, R. P. D., Johnson, R. J., Ritter, C., & Clayton, R. R. (1996). The effects of role socialization on the initiation of cocaine use: An event history analysis from adolescence into middle adulthood. *Journal of Health and Social Behavior, 37,* 75–90.

Chassin, L., Presson, C., Sherman, S. J., & Edwards, D. A. (1992). The natural history of cigarette smoking and young adult social roles. *Journal of Health and Social Behavior, 33,* 328–347.

Clayton, R. R. (1992). Transitions in drug use: Risk and protective factors. In M. D. Glantz & R. Pickens (Eds.), *Vulnerability to drug abuse* (pp. 15–51). Washington, DC: American Psychological Association.

Cornwall, M. (1989). Faith development of men and women over the life span. In S. J. Bahr & E. T. Peterson (Eds.), *Aging and the family* (pp. 115–139). Lexington, KY: Lexington Books.

Crawford, D. W., & Huston, T. L. (1993). The impact of the transition to parenthood on marital leisure. *Personality and Social Psychology Bulletin, 19,* 39–46.

Cronbach, L., & Furby, L. (1969). How to measure change—or should we? *Psychological Bulletin, 74,* 68–80.

DeMaris, A., & MacDonald, W. (1993). Premarital cohabitation and marital instability: A test of the unconventionality hypothesis. *Journal of Marriage and the Family, 55,* 399–407.

Donahue, M. J. (1995). Religion and the well-being of adolescents. *Journal of Social Issues [Special Issue: Religious influences on personal and societal well-being], 51,* 145–160.

Donovan, J. E., Jessor, R., & Costa, F. M. (1991). Adolescent health behavior and conventionality–unconventionality: An extension of problem-behavior therapy. *Health Psychology, 10,* 52–61.

Donovan, J. E., Jessor, R., & Jessor, L. (1983). Problem drinking in adolescence and young adulthood: A follow-up study. *Journal of Studies on Alcohol, 44,* 109–137.

Ennett, S. T., & Bauman, K. E. (1994). The contribution of influence and selection to adolescent peer group homogeneity: The case of adolescent cigarette smoking. *Journal of Personality & Social Psychology, 67,* 653–63.

Francis, L. J. (1997). The impact of personality and religion on attitudes towards substance use among 13–15 year olds. *Drug and Alcohol Dependence, 44,* 95–103.

Galambos, N. L., & Leadbeater, B. J. (2000). Trends in adolescent research for the new millennium. *International Journal of Behavioral Development, 24,* 289–294.

Gotham, H. J., Sher, K. J., & Wood, P. K. (1997). Predicting stability and change in frequency of intoxication from the college years to beyond: Individual-difference and role transition variables, *Journal of Abnormal Psychology, 106,* 619–629.

Hawking, S. (1993). *Black holes and baby universes and other essays.* New York: Bantam Books.

Hawkins, J. D., Catalano, R. F., & Miller, J. Y. (1992). Risk and protective factors for alcohol and other drug problems in adolescence and early adulthood: Implications for substance abuse prevention. *Psychological Bulletin, 112,* 64–105.

Horwitz, A. V., & White, H. R. (1991). Becoming married, depression, and alcohol problems among young adults. *Journal of Health and Social Behavior, 32,* 221–237.

Hu, L., & Bentler, P. M. (1999). Cutoff criteria for fit indexes in covariance structure analysis: Conventional criteria versus new alternatives. *Structural Equation Modeling, 6,* 1–55.

Hundelby, J. D. (1987). Adolescent drug use in a behavioral matrix: A confirmation and comparison of the sexes. *Addictive Behaviors, 12,* 103–112.

Jaccard, J., & Wan, C. K. (1996). *Lisrel approaches to interaction effects in multiple regression.* Thousand Oaks, CA: Sage.

Jessor, R., Donovan, J. E., & Costa, F. M. (1991). *Beyond adolescence: Problem behavior and young adult development.* New York: Cambridge University Press.

Johnson, J. G., Cohen, P., Pine, D. S., Klein, D. F., Kasen, S., & Brook, J. (2000). Association between cigarette smoking and anxiety disorders during adolescence and early adulthood. *Journal of American Medical Association, 284,* 2348–2351.

Johnson, V., & Pandina, R. J. (2000). Alcohol problems among a community sample: longitudinal influences of stress, coping, and gender. *Substance Use & Misuse, 35*(5), 669–86.

Johnston, L. D. (1973). *Drugs and American youth.* Ann Arbor, MI: Institute for Social Research.

Johnston, L. D. (1982). A review and analysis of recent changes in marijuana use by American young people. In *Marijuana: The national impact on education* (pp. 8–13). New York: American Council on Marijuana.

Johnston, L. D., Bachman, J. G., & O'Malley, P. M. (1997). *Monitoring the Future: Questionnaire responses from the nation's high school seniors, 1995.* Ann Arbor, MI: Institute for Social Research.

Johnston, L. D., & O'Malley, P. M. (1985). Issues of validity and population coverage in student surveys of drug use. In B. A. Rouse, N. J. Kozel, & L. G. Richards (Eds.), *Self-report methods of estimating drug use: Meeting current challenges to validity* (National Institute on Drug Abuse Research Monograph No. 57, [ADM] 85-1402, pp. 31–54). Washington, DC: U.S. Government Printing Office.

Johnston, L. D., O'Malley, P. M., & Bachman, J. G. (2000a). *Monitoring the Future national survey results on drug use, 1975–1999. Volume I: Secondary school students* (NIH Publication No. 00-4802). Rockville, MD: National Institute on Drug Abuse.

Johnston, L. D., O'Malley, P. M., & Bachman, J. G. (2000b). *Monitoring the Future national survey results on drug use, 1975–1999. Volume II: College students and young adults* (NIH Publication No. 00-4803). Rockville, MD: National Institute on Drug Abuse.

Jöreskog, K., & Sörbom, D. (1996). *LISREL 8: User's reference guide.* Chicago, IL: Scientific Software International.

Kandel, D. B., & Davies, M. (1991). Cocaine use in a national sample of U.S. youth (NLSY): Ethnic patterns, progression, and predictors. In S. Schrober & C. Schade (Eds.), *The epidemiology of cocaine use and abuse* (DHHS Publication No. [ADM] 91-1787, pp. 151–188). Rockville, MD: National Institute on Drug Abuse.

Kandel, D. B., & Raveis, V. H. (1989). Cessation of illicit drug use in young adulthood. *Archives of General Psychiatry, 46,* 109–116.

Kessler, R. C., & Greenberg, D. F. (1981). *Linear panel analysis: Models of quantitative change.* New York: Academic Press.

Kroutil, L. A., Bray, R. M., & Marsden, M. E. (1994). Cigarette smoking in the United States military: Findings from the 1992 worldwide survey. *Preventive Medicine, 23*(4), 521–528.

Labouvie, E. W. (1976). Longitudinal designs. In P. M. Bentler, D. J. Lettieri, & G. A. Austin (Eds.), *Data analysis strategies and designs for substance abuse research* (National Institute on Drug Abuse Research Issues No. 13, pp. 45–60). Rockville, MD: National Institute on Drug Abuse.

Leonard, K. E., & Rothbard, J. C. (1999). Alcohol and the marriage effect. *Journal of Studies on Alcohol, 13,* 139–146.

Liker, J. K., Augustyniak, S., & Duncan, G. J. (1985). Panel data and models of change: A comparison of first differences and conventional two-wave models. *Social Science Research, 14,* 80–101.

MacCallum, R. C., & Austin, J. T. (2000). Applications of structural equation modeling in psychological research. *Annual Review of Psychology, 51,* 201–226.

Maggs, J. L., Frome, P. M., Eccles, J. S., & Barber, B. L. (1997). Psychological resources, adolescent risk behavior and young adult adjustment: Is risk taking more dangerous for some than others? *Journal of Adolescence, 20,* 103–119.

McGee, R., Williams, S., Poulton, R., & Moffitt, R. (2000). A longitudinal study of cannabis use and mental health from adolescence to early adulthood. *Addiction, 95,* 491–503.

Miller-Tutzauer, C., Leonard, K. E., & Windle, M. (1991). Marriage and alcohol use: A longitudinal study of "maturing out." *Journal of Studies on Alcohol, 52,* 434–440.

Newcomb, M. D. (1987). Cohabitation and marriage: A quest for independence and relatedness. *Applied Social Psychology Annual, 7,* 128–156.

Newcomb, M. D., & Bentler, P. M. (1985). The impact of high school substance use on choice of young adult living environment and career direction. *Journal of Drug Education, 15*(3), 253–261.

Newcomb, M. D., & Bentler, P. M. (1987). Changes in drug use from high school to young adulthood: Effects of living arrangement and current life pursuit. *Journal of Applied Developmental Psychology, 8,* 221–246.

Newcomb, M. D., & Felix-Oritz, M. (1992). Multiple protective and risk factors for drug use and abuse: Cross-sectional and prospective findings. *Journal of Personality and Social Psychology, 63,* 280–296.

Nock, S. (1995). A comparison of marriages and cohabiting relationships. *Journal of Family Issues, 16*(1), 53–76.

Oetting, E. R., & Donnermeyer, J. G. (1998). Primary socialization theory: The etiology of drug use and deviance. I. *Substance Use & Misuse, 33,* 995–1026.

O'Malley, P. M., Bachman, J. G., & Johnston, L. D. (1983). Reliability and consistency of self-reports of drug use. *International Journal of the Addictions, 18,* 805–824.

O'Malley, P. M., Bachman, J. G., & Johnston, L. D. (1984). Period, age, and cohort effects on substance use among American youth. *American Journal of Public Health, 74,* 682–688.

O'Malley, P. M., Bachman, J. G., & Johnston, L. D. (1988a). Period, age, and cohort effects on substance use among young Americans: A decade of change, 1976–1986. *American Journal of Public Health, 78,* 1315–1321.

O'Malley, P. M., Bachman, J. G., & Johnston, L. D. (1988b). *Differentiation of period, age, and cohort effects on drug use 1976–1986* (Monitoring the Future Occasional Paper No. 22). Ann Arbor, MI: Institute for Social Research.

O'Malley, P. M., & Wagenaar, A. C. (1991). Effects of minimum drinking age laws on alcohol use, related behaviors, and traffic crash involvement among American youth: 1976–1987. *Journal Studies on Alcohol, 52,* 478–491.

Osgood, D. W., Johnston, L. D., O'Malley, P. M., & Bachman, J. G. (1988). The generality of deviance in late adolescence and early adulthood. *American Sociological Review, 53,* 81–93.

Osgood, D. W., Wilson, J. K., O'Malley, P. M., Bachman, J. G., & Johnston, L. D. (1996). Routine activities and individual deviant behaviors. *American Sociological Review, 61,* 635–674.

Resnicow, K., Smith, M., Harrison, L., & Drucker, E. (1999). Correlates of occasional cigarette and marijuana use: Are teens harm reducing? *Addictive Behaviors, 24,* 251–266.

Robbins, C. A. (1991). Social roles and alcohol abuse among older men and women. *Family and Community Health, 13,* 126–139.

Robins, L. N. (1974). *The Vietnam drug user returns* (Special Action Office Monograph, Series A, No. 2). Washington, DC: Executive Office of the President, Special Action Office for Drug Abuse Prevention.

Rodgers, W. L. (1989, September). *Reliability and validity in measures of subjective well-being.* Paper presented at the International Conference on Social Reporting, Wissenschaftszentrum Berlin fur Sozialforschung.

Rodgers, W. L., & Bachman, J. G. (1988). *The subjective well-being of young adults.* Ann Arbor, MI: Institute for Social Research.

Roof, W. C. (1993). *A generation of seekers: The spiritual journeys of the baby boom generation.* San Francisco: Harper.

Rose, J. S., Chassin, L., Presson, C. C., & Sherman, S. J. (1999). Peer influences on adolescent cigarette smoking: A prospective sibling analysis. *Merrill-Palmer Quarterly: Special Issue: Peer influences in childhood and adolescence, 45,* 62–84.

Schaie, K. W. (1965). A general model for the study of developmental problems. *Psychological Bulletin, 64,* 92–107.

Schulenberg, J. E., Bachman, J. G., O'Malley, P. M., & Johnston, L. D. (1994). High school educational success and subsequent substance use: A panel analysis following adolescents into young adulthood. *Journal of Health and Social Behavior, 35*(1), 45–62.

Schulenberg, J., & Maggs, J. L. (in press). A developmental perspective on alcohol use and heavy drinking during adolescence and the transition to young adulthood. *Journal of Studies on Alcohol.*

Schulenberg, J., Maggs, J. L., Dielman, T. E., Leech, S. L., Kloska, D. D., Shope, J. T., & Laetz, V. B. (1999). On peer influences to get drunk: A panel study of young adolescents. *Merrill-Palmer Quarterly, 45,* 108–142.

Schulenberg, J., O'Malley, P. M., Bachman, J. G., & Johnston, L. D. (2000). "Spread your wings and fly": The course of well-being and substance use during the transition to young adulthood. In L. J. Crockett & R. K. Silbereisen (Eds.), *Negotiating adolescence in times of social change* (pp. 224–255). New York: Cambridge University Press.

Schulenberg, J. E., O'Malley, P. M., Bachman, J. G., Wadsworth, K. N., & Johnston, L. D. (1996). Getting drunk and growing up: Trajectories of frequent binge drinking during the transition to young adulthood. *Journal of Studies on Alcohol, 57,* 289–304.

Schulenberg, J. E., Wadsworth, K. N., O'Malley, P. M., Bachman, J. G., & Johnston, L. D. (1996). Adolescent risk factors for binge drinking during the transition to young adulthood: Variable- and pattern-centered approaches to change. *Developmental Psychology, 32*(4), 659–674.

Segal, D. R. (1977). Illicit drug use in the U.S. Army. *Sociological Symposium, 18,* 66–83.

Stolzenberg, R. M., Blair-Loy, M., & Waite, L. (1995). Religious participation in early adulthood: Age and family life cycle effects on church membership. *American Sociological Review, 60,* 84–103.

Thornton, A., Axinn, W. G., & Hill, D. H. (1992). Reciprocal effects of religiosity, cohabitation, and marriage. *American Journal of Sociology, 98*(3), 628–651.

Thun, M. J., Peto, R., Lopez, A. D., Monaco, J. H., Henley, S. J., Heath, C. W., Jr., & Doll, R. (1997). Alcohol consumption and mortality among middle-aged and elderly U.S. adults. *New England Journal of Medicine, 337,* 1705–1714.

Urberg, K. A., Degirmencioglu, S. M., & Pilgrim, C. (1997). Close friend and group influence on adolescent cigarette smoking and alcohol use. *Developmental Psychology, 33,* 834–844.

Urberg, K. A., Degirmencioglu, S. M., & Tolson, J. M (1998). Adolescent friendship selection and termination: The role of similarity. *Journal of Social and Personal Relationships, 15,* 703–710.

Wallace, J. M., Jr., & Bachman, J. G. (1991). Explaining racial/ethnic differences in adolescent drug use: The impact of background and lifestyle. *Social Problems, 38*(3), 333–357.

Wallace, J. M., Jr., & Bachman, J. G. (1993). Validity of self-reports in student-based studies on minority populations: Issues and concerns. In M. de LaRosa & J. L. Andrados (Eds.), *Drug abuse among minority youth: Advances in research and methodology* (National Institute on Drug Abuse Research Monograph, No. 130, pp. 167–200). Rockville, MD: National Institute on Drug Abuse.

Wallace, J. M., Jr., & Forman, T. A. (1998). Religion's role in promoting health and reducing risk among American youth. *Health Education & Behavior, 25*(6), 721–741.

Wechsler, H., Dowdall, G., Davenport, A., & Castillo, S. (1995). Correlates of college students' binge drinking. *American Journal of Public Health, 85*(7), 921–926.

Wilsnack, R. W., & Wilsnack, S. C. (1992). Women, work, and alcohol: Failures of simple theories. *Alcoholism: Clinical and Experimental Research, 16,* 172–179.

Yamaguchi, K., & Kandel, D. B. (1985a). Dynamic relationships between premarital cohabitation and illicit drug use: An event-history analysis of role selection and role socialization. *American Sociological Review, 50*(4), 530–546.

Yamaguchi, K., & Kandel, D. B. (1985b). On the resolution of role incompatibility: Life event history analysis of family roles and marijuana use. *American Journal of Sociology, 90,* 1284–1325.

Author Index

A

Andrews, F. M., 236, 287
Arnett, J. J., 2, 9, 10, 14, 16, 18, 19, 287
Aseltine, R. H., 9, 287
AuBuchon, P., 14, 289
Augustyniak, S., 38, 291
Austin, J. T., 190, 291
Axinn, W. G., 15, 212, 293

B

Bachman, J. G., xiii, 1, 2, 3, 4, 5, 6, 10, 11, 12,
        13, 14, 15, 16, 17, 18, 19, 20, 21, 22,
        25, 27, 31, 32, 33, 35, 38, 39, 43, 46,
        49, 52, 53, 54, 56, 57, 60, 65, 67, 69,
        72, 76, 81, 82, 86, 88, 91, 94, 98, 99,
        104, 105, 107, 114, 119, 122, 124,
        126, 127, 128, 129, 130, 131, 133,
        136, 140, 143, 145, 146, 147, 148,
        151, 152, 153, 154, 158, 161, 162,
        163, 165, 167, 168, 169, 170, 172,
        173, 175, 176, 177, 178, 179, 181,
        188, 205, 206, 209, 210, 211, 212,
        214, 216, 221, 223, 224, 239, 241,
        287, 288, 289, 290, 291, 292, 293
Bahr, S. J., 2, 17, 288
Barber, B. L., 9, 291
Bauman, K. E., 21, 290
Belsky, J., 20, 289

Bentler, P. M., 14, 189, 190, 289, 290, 291
Blair-Loy, M., 18, 19, 293
Bray, R. M., 13, 210, 289, 291
Brennan, A. F., 14, 289
Brook, J. S., 9, 12, 14, 289, 290
Brown, J. W., 14, 289
Brown, T. N., 17, 289
Browne, M. W., 190, 289
Brunswick, A. F., 14, 289
Bryant, A. L., xiii, 38, 43, 46, 49, 52, 54, 57, 60,
        67, 69, 72, 76, 82, 91, 94, 98, 104,
        107, 114, 124, 128, 131, 133, 140,
        143, 148, 151, 152, 153, 154, 168,
        170, 173, 175, 176, 177, 178, 205,
        288
Burton, R. P. D., 14, 16, 289

C

Castillo, S., 11, 14, 293
Catalano, R. F., 2, 9, 17, 21, 136, 290
Chassin, L., 2, 12, 21, 289, 292
Clayton, R. R., 14, 16, 136, 289
Cohen, P., 9, 12, 14, 289, 290
Cornwall, M., 18, 289
Costa, F. M., 21, 81, 289, 290
Crawford, D. W., 20, 289
Cronbach, L., 38, 289
Cudeck, R., 190, 289

D

Davenport, A., 11, 14, 293
Davies, M., 14, 291
Degirmencioglu, S. M., 2, 21, 293
DeMaris, A., 212, 289
Dielman, T. E., 21, 292
Doll, R., 50, 293
Donahue, M. J., 2, 17 , 289
Donnermeyer, J. G., 19, 291
Donovan, J. E., 14, 21, 81, 289, 290
Dowdall, G., 11, 14, 293
Drucker, E., 2, 20, 292
Duncan, G. J., 38, 291

E

Eccles, J. S., 9, 291
Edwards, D. A., 12, 289
Ennett, S. T., 21, 290

F

Felix-Oritz, M., 18, 291
Forman, T. A., 18, 293
Francis, L. J., 17, 290
Freedman-Doan, P., xiii, 13, 38, 43, 46, 49, 52,
        54, 57, 60, 67, 69, 72, 76, 82, 91, 94,
        98, 99, 104, 107, 114, 124, 128, 131,
        133, 140, 143, 148, 151, 152, 153,
        154, 168, 170, 173, 175, 176, 177,
        178, 205, 210, 287, 288
Frome, P. M., 9, 291
Furby, L., 38, 289

G

Galambos, N. L., 9, 290
Geis, G., 14, 289
Glaser, D., 14, 289
Gore, S., 9, 287
Gotham, H. J., 13, 14, 16, 290
Greenberg, D. F., 38, 291

H

Harrison, L., 2, 20, 292
Hart, T. C., xiii, 38, 43, 46, 49, 52, 54, 57, 60,
        67, 69, 72, 76, 82, 91, 94, 98, 104,
        107, 114, 124, 128, 131, 133, 140,
        143, 148, 151, 152, 153, 154, 168,
        170, 173, 175, 176, 177, 178, 205,
        288

Hawking, S., 32, 290
Hawkins, J. D., 2, 9, 17, 21, 136, 290
Heath, C. W., Jr., 50, 293
Henley, S. J., 50, 293
Hill, D. H., 15, 212, 293
Horwitz, A. V., 14, 290
Hu, L., 190, 290
Humphrey, R. H., 56, 86, 122, 288
Hundelby, J. D., 2, 19, 290
Huston, T. L., 20, 289

J

Jaccard, J., 190, 290
Jessor, L., 14, 289
Jessor, R., 14, 21, 81, 289, 290
Johnson, J. G., 9, 290
Johnson, R. J., 14, 16, 289
Johnson, V., 9, 290
Johnston, L. D., xiii, 1, 2, 3, 4, 5, 6, 10, 11, 12,
        13, 14, 15, 16, 17, 18, 19, 20, 21, 25,
        27, 31, 32, 33, 35, 38, 39, 43, 46, 49,
        52, 53, 54, 56, 57, 60, 65, 67, 69, 72,
        76, 81, 82, 86, 88, 91, 94, 98, 99,
        104, 105, 107, 114, 119, 122, 124,
        126, 127, 128, 129, 130, 131, 133,
        136, 140, 143, 145, 146, 147, 148,
        151, 152, 153, 154, 158, 161, 162,
        163, 165, 167, 168, 169, 170, 172,
        173, 175, 176, 177, 178, 179, 181,
        188, 205, 206, 209, 210, 211, 212,
        214, 216, 221, 223, 224, 239, 241,
        287, 288, 289, 290, 291, 292
Jöreskog, K., 190, 290

K

Kandel, D. B., 9, 14, 15, 16, 17, 212, 291, 293
Kasen, S., 9, 290
Kessler, R. C., 38, 291
Klein, D. F., 9, 290
Kloska, D. D., 21, 292
Kroutil, L. A., 13, 210, 291

L

Labouvie, E. W., 222, 291
Laetz, V. B., 21, 292
Leadbeater, B. J., 9, 290
Leech, S. L., 21, 292
Leonard, K. E., 10, 14, 291
Li, B., 2, 17, 288
Liker, J. K., 38, 291

Lim, J., 5, 27, 224, 288
Lopez, A. D., 50, 293

M

MacCallum, R. C., 190, 291
MacDonald, W., 212, 289
Maggs, J. L., 9, 21, 206, 210, 291, 292
Marcos, A. C., 2, 17, 288
Marsden, M. E., 13, 210, 289, 291
Maughan, S. L., 2, 17, 288
McGee, R., 9, 291
Merline, A. C., xiii, 38, 43, 46, 49, 52, 54, 57,
    60, 67, 69, 72, 76, 82, 91, 94, 98,
    104, 107, 114, 124, 128, 131, 133,
    140, 143, 148, 151, 152, 153, 154,
    168, 170, 173, 175, 176, 177, 178,
    205, 288
Messeri, P. A., 14, 289
Miller, J. Y., 2, 9, 17, 21, 136, 290
Miller-Tutzauer, C., 14, 291
Moffitt, R., 9, 291
Monaco, J. H., 50, 293
Morgan, J. N., 236, 287

N

Newcomb, M. D., 14, 15, 18, 212, 291
Nock, S., 212, 291

O

Oetting, E. R., 19, 291
O'Malley, P. M., xiii, 1, 2, 3, 4, 5, 6, 10, 11, 12,
    13, 14, 15, 16, 17, 18, 19, 20, 21, 25,
    27, 31, 32, 33, 35, 38, 39, 43, 46, 49,
    52, 53, 54, 56, 57, 60, 65, 67, 69, 72,
    76, 81, 82, 86, 88, 91, 94, 98, 99,
    104, 105, 107, 114, 119, 122, 124,
    126, 127, 128, 129, 130, 131, 133,
    136, 140, 143, 145, 146, 147, 148,
    151, 152, 153, 154, 158, 161, 162,
    163, 165, 167, 168, 169, 170, 172,
    173, 175, 176, 177, 178, 179, 181,
    188, 205, 206, 209, 210, 211, 212,
    214, 216, 221, 223, 224, 239, 241,
    287, 288, 289, 290, 291, 292
Osgood, D. W., 2, 19, 32, 292

P

Pandina, R. J., 9, 290
Pensky, E., 20, 289
Peterson, M. R., 13, 210, 289
Peto, R., 50, 293

Pilgrim, C., 2, 21, 293
Pine, D. S., 9, 290
Poulton, R., 9, 291
Presson, C., 2, 12, 21, 289, 292

R

Raveis, V. H., 16, 17, 291
Resnicow, K., 2, 20, 292
Richter, L., 12, 14, 289
Ridenour, N. J., xiii, 38, 43, 46, 49, 52, 54, 57,
    60, 67, 69, 72, 76, 82, 91, 94, 98,
    104, 107, 114, 124, 128, 131, 133,
    140, 148, 151, 152, 153, 154, 168,
    170, 173, 175, 176, 177, 178, 205,
    288
Ritter, C., 14, 16, 289
Robbins, C. A., 14, 292
Robins, L. N., 13, 292
Rodgers, W. L., 5, 27, 38, 224, 241, 288, 292
Roof, W. C., 18, 292
Rose, J. S., 2, 21, 292
Rothbard, J. C., 10, 14, 291

S

Safron, D. J., 81, 88, 288
Schaie, K. W., 222, 292
Schulenberg, J. E., xiii, 1, 2, 3, 4, 5, 6, 9, 10, 11,
    12, 13, 14, 15, 16, 17, 18, 19, 21, 25,
    27, 31, 32, 33, 35, 38, 39, 43, 46, 49,
    52, 54, 57, 60, 65, 67, 69, 72, 76, 81,
    82, 86, 88, 91, 94, 98, 99, 104, 105,
    107, 114, 119, 124, 128, 131, 133,
    140, 143, 146, 147, 148, 151, 152,
    153, 154, 158, 161, 162, 165, 167,
    168, 170, 172, 173, 175, 176, 177,
    178, 179, 181, 188, 205, 206, 209,
    210, 211, 212, 214, 216, 224, 241,
    288, 289, 292
Segal, D. R., 13, 99, 148, 173, 210, 287, 293
Sher, K. J., 13, 14, 16, 290
Sherman, S. J., 2, 12, 21, 289, 292
Shope, J. T., 21, 292
Smith, M., 2, 20, 292
Sonquist, J. A., 236, 287
Sörbom, D., 190, 290
Stolzenberg, R. M., 18, 19, 293

T

Thornton, A., 15, 212, 293
Thun, M. J., 50, 293
Titus, S. P., 14, 289
Tolson, J. M., 21, 293

U

Urberg, K. A., 2, 21, 293

W

Wadsworth, K. N., 1, 3, 4, 5, 6, 10, 11, 12, 13,
    14, 15, 16, 25, 27, 31, 33, 35, 39, 54,
    65, 81, 86, 99, 104, 105, 107, 119,
    146, 147, 148, 151, 152, 158, 161,
    162, 165, 167, 172, 173, 177, 178,
    179, 181, 188, 206, 209, 210, 211,
    212, 214, 216, 224, 288, 292
Wagenaar, A. C., 76, 292
Waite, L., 18, 19, 293
Walfish, S., 14, 289

Wallace, J. M., Jr., 2, 6, 18, 20, 293
Wan, C. K., 190, 290
Waxer, E., 14, 289
Wechsler, H., 11, 14, 293
White, H. R., 14, 290
Whiteman, M., 12, 14, 289
Williams, S., 9, 291
Wilsnack, R. W., 13, 293
Wilsnack, S. C., 13, 293
Wilson, J. K., 2, 19, 292
Windle, M., 14, 291
Wood, P. K., 13, 14, 16, 290

Y

Yamaguchi, K., 9, 14, 15, 16, 212, 293

Subject Index

A

Age
    effects, 28–29
    related to
        alcohol, perceived risk and disapproval of,
            126–128, 139–141, 230–235
        alcohol use, 50–54, 57–59, 82–85,
            91–97, 139–141, 167–172,
            230–235
        availability of illicit drugs (perceived),
            165–167, 169–172, 230–235
        bars, taverns, or nightclubs, going to, 19,
            76, 78, 94–97, 230–235
        cigarette use, 46–50, 57–59, 79–82,
            91–97, 136–139, 167–172,
            230–235
        cigarettes, perceived risk and disapproval
            of pack-a-day smoking,
            124–126, 136–139, 230–235
        cocaine, perceived risk and disapproval of,
            131–134, 143–145, 230–235
        cocaine use, 57–59, 88–97,131–134,
            143–145, 167–192, 230–235
        cohabitation, 227
        dating, 19, 74, 91–92, 116, 118, 230–235
        employment status, 226
        engagement, 227
        evenings out, 72–73, 77–91, 116–117,
            230–235
        friends, getting together informally with,
            76, 230–235
        friends' use of substances (perceived),
            158–164, 167–169, 230–235
        living arrangements, 227
        marijuana, perceived risk and disap-
            proval of, 128–131, 140–143,
            230–235
        marijuana use, 53–59, 86–88, 90–97,
            140–143, 167–172, 230–235
        marital status, 227
        military service, 226
        parenthood, 228
        parties, attending, 19, 76–77, 92–96,
            230–235
        religiosity, 18, 40–44, 59, 70, 230–235
        student status, 226
Alcohol, friends' use, see Friends' use of sub-
        stances (perceived)
Alcohol, perceived risk and disapproval of heavy
        use
    causal-conceptual overview, 1–4, 202–209
    correlation matrices including, 230–235
    levels of, 126–128
    MCA results, 146–154, 262–265
    measure of, 126, 228–229
    period effects, 126–127
    related to

age, 126–128, 139–141, 230–235
  alcohol use, 139–141, 195–197, 199–201
  employment status, 148
  engagement, 153
  living arrangements, 148–152
  marital status, 148–150, 153, 195–197,
    199–201
  parenthood, 153
  pregnancy, 152–153
  religiosity, 135, 195–197, 199–201,
    230–235
  student status, 147–148
  structural equation models, 195–197,
    199–201
Alcohol use
  causal-conceptual overview, 1–4, 202–209
  correlation matrices including, 230–235
  measures of, 228
  related to
    age, 50–54, 57–59, 82–85, 91–97,
      139–141, 167–172, 230–235
    alcohol, perceived risk and disapproval
      of heavy use, 139–141,
      195–197, 199–201
    bars, taverns, or nightclubs, going to, 97
    cohabitation, 15
    dating, 91–92
    divorce, 15
    dormitory, living in, 14, 151–152
    employment status, 12–13
    engagement, 14–15
    evenings out, 19, 82–85, 91, 195–197,
      199–201
    friends' use of substances (perceived),
      21, 167–169
    living arrangements, 14–16
    marital status, 14–15, 195–197, 199–201
    military service, 13
    parenthood, 16–17
    parties, attending, 92–94
    pregnancy, 16
    religiosity, 17–18, 50–54, 57–59, 195–197,
      199–201
    student status, 11–12, 151–152
  structural equation models, 195–197,
    199–201
Analysis strategy, xii, 27–39
  see also, Structural equation modeling
Attendance at religious services, see Religiosity
Attitudes toward drug use, see Alcohol, per-
    ceived risk and disapproval of heavy
    use, Cigarettes, perceived risk and
    disapproval of pack-a-day smoking,
    Cocaine, perceived risk and disap-
    proval of use, Marijuana, perceived
    risk and disapproval of use
Attrition from sample, 27, 135, 223–224

Availability of illicit drugs (perceived), 21–22,
  156–180, 184–185
  causal-conceptual considerations, 1–4,
    184–185
  correlation matrices including, 230–235
  MCA results, 178–179, 282–285
  measure of, 228–229
  period effects, 165–167
  related to
    age, 165–167, 169–172, 230–235
    cocaine use, 169–172
    engagement, 178
    living arrangements, 178–179
    marijuana use, 169–172
    marital status, 178
    military service, 178

B

Background factors, 69, 238, 244–285
Bars, taverns, or nightclubs, going to
  causal-conceptual overview, 1–4, 202–209
  correlation matrices including, 230–235
  frequency of, 76, 78
  MCA results, 98–99, 104, 113–115, 256–257
  measure of, 76, 228–229
  period effects, 76, 78
  related to
    age, 19, 76, 78, 94–97, 230–235
    alcohol use, 97
    cigarette use, 94
    cocaine use, 97
    employment status, 99
    engagement, 107–108
    living arrangements, 98–105
    marijuana use, 97
    marital status, 99, 103, 107–109, 111
    parenthood, 107
    pregnancy, 105
    student status, 98
Binge drinking, see Alcohol use

C

Career, see Employment status
Carson's dictum, 27–28, 85
Causal modeling, 6–7, 181–201
  see also Change and stability
Causation, 1–4, 27–32, 71, 84–88, 119–122,
    139, 155–158, 164–165, 170, 176,
    179–180, 206–209
  inferring from panel data, 6–7, 122
Change and stability, 204, 216–218
  evenings out, 79, 81, 84–85, 90–91
  religiosity, 45–46, 57–59, 67–70
Change scores for mediating variables, 38, 241

rationale for using, 30–31
Changes, drug use, *see* Alcohol use, Cigarette use, Cocaine use, Marijuana use
Changes, mediating variables, *see* Alcohol, perceived risk and disapproval of heavy use, Availability of illicit drugs (perceived), Bars, taverns, or nightclubs, going to, Cigarettes, perceived risk and disapproval of pack-a-day smoking, Cocaine, perceived risk and disapproval of use, Dating, Evenings out, Friends, getting together informally with, Friends' use of substances (perceived), Marijuana, perceived risk and disapproval of use, Parties, attending, Religiosity
Childbearing, *see* Parenthood, Pregnancy
Cigarette use
  causal-conceptual overview, 1–4, 202–209
  correlation matrices including, 230–235
  measure of, 228
  related to
    age, 46–50, 57–59, 79–82, 91–97, 136–139, 167–172, 230–235
    bars, taverns, or nightclubs, going to, 94
    cigarettes, perceived risk and disapproval of pack-a-day smoking, 20, 136–139, 197–201
    cohabitation, 15
    dating, 91–92
    divorce, 15
    dormitory, living in, 14
    employment status, 12–13
    engagement, 14–15
    evenings out, 19, 79–82, 91, 197–201
    friends' use of substances (perceived), 21, 167–169
    living arrangements, 14–16
    marital status, 14–15, 197–201
    military service, 12–13
    parenthood, 16
    parties, attending, 92
    pregnancy, 16
    religiosity, 17–18, 46–50, 57–59, 197–201
    student status, 11–12
    unemployment, 12
  structural equation models, 197–201
Cigarettes, friends' use, *see* Friends' use of substances (perceived)
Cigarettes, perceived risk and disapproval of pack-a-day smoking
  causal-conceptual overview, 1–4, 202–209
  correlation matrices including, 230–235
  levels of, 124–126
  MCA results, 146–154, 258–261
  measure of, 124, 228–229

period effects, 124–125
  related to
    age, 124–126, 136–139, 230–235
    cigarette use, 20, 136–139, 197–201
    employment status, 148
    evenings out, 197–201
    living arrangements, 148–152
    marital status, 148–150, 153, 197–201
    parenthood, 153
    pregnancy, 152–153
    religiosity, 135, 197–201, 230–235
    student status, 147–148
  structural equation models, 197–201
Civilian employment, *see* Employment status
Cocaine, availability, *see* Availability of illicit drugs (perceived)
Cocaine, friends' use, *see* Friends' use of substances (perceived)
Cocaine, perceived risk and disapproval of use
  causal-conceptual overview, 1–4, 202–209
  correlation matrices including, 230–235
  levels of, 131–134
  MCA results, 146–154, 270–273
  measure of, 131, 228–229
  period effects, 131–134
  related to
    age, 131–134, 143–145, 230–235
    cocaine use, 20, 143–145, 193–195, 199–201
    employment status, 148
    engagement, 153
    evenings out, 193–195, 199–201
    living arrangements, 148–152
    marital status, 148–150, 153, 193–195, 199–201
    parenthood, 153
    pregnancy, 152–153
    religiosity, 135, 193–195, 199–201, 230–235
    student status, 147–148
  structural equation models, 193–195, 199–201
Cocaine use
  causal-conceptual overview, 1–4, 202–209
  correlation matrices including, 230–235
  measure of, 228
  related to
    age, 57–59, 88–97, 131–134, 143–145, 167–192, 230–235
    availability of illicit drugs (perceived), 169–172
    bars, taverns, or nightclubs, going to, 97
    cocaine, perceived risk and disapproval of, 20, 143–145, 193–195, 199–201
    cohabitation, 15
    dating, 91–92

divorce, 15
evenings out, 88–91, 193–195, 199–201
friends' use of substances (perceived),
    167–169
marital status, 14–15, 193–195, 199–201
military service, 13
parenthood, 16
parties, attending, 92–94
pregnancy, 16
religiosity, 17–18, 57–59, 193–195,
    199–201
student status, 11–12
structural equation models, 193–195,
    199–201
Cohabitation, 212
causal-conceptual overview, 1–4, 202–209
frequency of, 225, 227
related to
    age, 227
    alcohol use, 15
    cigarette use, 15
    cocaine use, 15
    evenings out, 100–103
    marijuana use, 15
    religiosity, 19, 62–64, 70
see also Living arrangements
College attendance, see Student status
College plans, 238, 244–285
Conceptual overview, 1–4, 202–209
Conclusions, 216–219
Correlation versus causation, see Causation

D

Data collection procedures, 221–224
Dating
causal-conceptual overview, 1–4, 202–209
correlation matrices including, 230–235
frequency of, 73–75
MCA results, 113–118, 250–251
measure of, 73–74, 228–229
related to
    age, 19, 74, 91–92, 116–118, 230–235
    alcohol use, 91–92
    cigarette use, 91–92
    cocaine use, 91–92
    living arrangements, 99–105
    marijuana use, 91–92
    marital status, 99–102, 113–114
    parenthood, 107
Demographic factors, see Background factors
Disapproval of substance use, see Alcohol, per-
    ceived risk and disapproval of heavy
    use, Cigarettes, perceived risk and
    disapproval of pack-a-day smoking,
    Cocaine, perceived risk and disap-
    proval of use, Marijuana, perceived
    risk and disapproval of use

Divorce, 216
related to
    alcohol use, 15
    cigarette use, 15
    cocaine use, 15
    evenings out, 107–110
    friends' use of substances (perceived),
        177
    marijuana use, 15
    religiosity, 19, 67
see also Marital status
Dormitory, living in, 213, 227
related to
    alcohol use, 14, 151–152
    availability of illicit drugs (perceived),
        178–179
    cigarette use, 14
    evenings out, 98, 100–104
    friends' use of substances (perceived),
        172–176
    religiosity, 62–64
    social and recreational activities, 98
    substance use, risk and disapproval of,
        151–152
see also Living arrangements
Dropouts, high school, 27
Drug use, 1–4, 29–30, 204–205
causal-conceptual overview, 1–4, 202–209
correlations among substances, 230–235
cross-time correlations, see Change and sta-
    bility
linked to new roles, 10–17
measures, 228
see also Alcohol use, Cigarette use, Cocaine
    use, Marijuana use

E

Education, see Student status
Employment status, 12–13, 210–211, 226,
    244–285
causal-conceptual overview, 1–4, 202–209
related to
    age, 226
    alcohol use, 12–13
    cigarette use, 12–13
    cocaine use, 12–13
    evenings out, 20, 98–99
    friends' use of substances (perceived),
        173
    marijuana use, 12–13
    religiosity, 62
    social and recreational activities, 20,
        98–99
    substance use, perceived risk and disap-
        proval of, 99, 148
Engagement, 215–216, 227
causal-conceptual overview, 1–4, 202–209

related to
  age, 227
  alcohol use, 14–15
  availability of illicit drugs (perceived), 178
  cigarette use, 14–15
  cocaine use, 14–15
  evenings out, 107–108
  friends' use of substances (perceived), 177
  marijuana use, 14–15
  religiosity, 67–68, 70
  social and recreational activities, 107–108
  substance use, risk and disapproval of, 153
EQS, 189
Ethnicity, see Race
Evenings out
  causal-conceptual overview, 1–4, 202–209
  change and stability, 79, 81, 84–85, 90–91
  correlation matrices including, 230–235
  frequency of, 72–73, 79
  MCA results, 98–99, 101, 104–107,
          113–117, 248–249
  measures of, 72, 228–229
  related to
    age, 72–73, 77–91, 116–117, 230–235
    alcohol use, 19, 82–85, 91, 195–197,
          199–201
    cigarette use, 19, 79–82, 91, 197–201
    cocaine use, 88–91, 193–195, 199–201
    cohabitation, 100–103
    divorce, 107–110
    dormitory, living in, 98, 100–104
    employment status, 20, 98–99
    engagement, 107–108
    living arrangements, 98–105
    marijuana use, 86–88, 91, 192–193,
          199–201
    marital status, 20, 99–101, 107–113,
          181–201
    military service, 98–99, 115
    parenthood, 20, 101, 105–107
    pregnancy, 105
    religiosity, 181–201
    student status, 98
    substance use, risk and disapproval of,
          192–201
  structural equation models, 181–201
Explained variance, see Multiple Classification
          Analysis

F

Fatherhood, see Parenthood
Fit indices, 190–191
Freedom, see New freedoms and responsibilities,
          Post-high school roles and experi-
          ences
Friends, getting together informally with

causal-conceptual considerations, 1–4,
          202–209
  correlation matrices including, 230–235
  frequency of, 74–76
  MCA results, 98–99, 113–115, 254–255
  measures of, 74–75, 228–229
  related to
    age, 76, 230–235
    living arrangements, 98
    student status, 98
Friends' use of substances (perceived), 21,
          156–180, 184–185
  causal-conceptual considerations, 1–4,
          156–158, 179–180, 184–185
  correlation matrices including, 230–235
  frequency of, 158–164
  MCA results, 172–178, 274–281
  measures of, 158, 228–229
  period effects, 159, 161–164
  related to
    age, 158–164, 167–169, 230–235
    alcohol use, 21, 167–169
    cigarette use, 21, 167–169
    cocaine use, 167–169
    divorce, 177
    employment status, 173
    engagement, 177
    living arrangements, 172–176
    marijuana use, 167–169
    marital status, 173–175, 177
    parenthood, 177
    pregnancy, 176–177
    student status, 172–173

G

Gender differences and similarities, 13, 14, 15,
          17, 74
  in recreational activities, 105–112
Geographic differences, see Region
Grades during high school, 239, 244–285

H

Heavy drinking, see Alcohol use
Homemakers, see Employment status

I

Illicit drug use, see Cocaine use, Marijuana use
Implications of findings, 216–219
Importance of religion, see Religiosity

L

Living arrangements, 14–16, 211–214, 227
  causal-conceptual overview, 1–4, 202–209

related to
  age, 227
  alcohol, perceived risk and disapproval
    of, 148–152
  alcohol use, 14–16
  availability of illicit drugs (perceived),
    178–179
  bars, taverns, or nightclubs, going to,
    98–105
  cigarette use, 14–16
  cigarettes, perceived risk and disapproval
    of pack-a-day smoking,
    148–152
  cocaine, perceived risk and disapproval
    of, 148–152
  cocaine use, 14–16
  dating, 99–105
  evenings out, 98–105
  friends, getting together informally with, 98
  friends' use of substances (perceived),
    173–176
  marijuana, perceived risk and disap-
    proval of, 148–152
  marijuana use, 14–16
  parties, attending, 98–105
  religiosity, 62–64, 70

M

Marijuana, availability, see Availability of illicit
  drugs (perceived)
Marijuana, (perceived) friends' use, see Friends'
  use of substances (perceived)
Marijuana, perceived risk and disapproval of use
  causal-conceptual overview, 1–4, 202–209
  correlation matrices including, 230–235
  levels of, 128–131
  MCA results, 146–154, 266–269
  measures of, 128, 228–229
  period effects, 129–131
  related to
    age, 128–131, 140–143, 230–235
    employment status, 148
    engagement, 153
    evenings out, 192–193, 199–201
    living arrangements, 148–152
    marijuana use, 20, 140–143, 192–193,
      199–201
    marital status, 148–150, 153, 192–193,
      199–201
    parenthood, 153
    pregnancy, 152–153
    religiosity, 135, 192–193, 199–201,
      230–235
    student status, 147–148
  structural equation models, 192–193,
    199–201

Marijuana use
  causal-conceptual overview, 1–4, 202–209
  correlation matrices including, 230–235
  measures of, 228
  period effects, 86
  related to
    age, 55–59, 86–88, 90–97, 140–143,
      167–172, 230–235
    availability of illicit drugs (perceived),
      169–172
    bars, taverns, or nightclubs, going to, 97
    cohabitation, 15
    college attendance, 11–12
    dating, 91–92
    divorce, 15
    dormitory, living in, 14
    employment status, 12–13
    engagement, 14–15
    evenings out, 86–88, 91, 192–193,
      199–201
    friends' use of substances (perceived),
      167–169
    living arrangements, 14–16
    marijuana, perceived risk and disap-
      proval of, 20, 140–143,
      192–193, 199–201
    marital status, 14–15, 192–193, 199–201
    military service, 13
    parenthood, 16–17
    parties, attending, 92–94
    pregnancy, 16
    religiosity, 17–18, 53–56, 192–193, 199–201
    student status, 11–12
    unemployment, 12
  structural equation models, 192–193,
    199–201
Marital status, 211–212, 227
  causal-conceptual overview, 1–4, 202–209
  related to
    age, 227
    alcohol, perceived risk and disapproval
      of, 148–150, 153, 195–197,
      199–201
    alcohol use, 14–15, 195–197, 199–201
    availability of illicit drugs (perceived),
      178
    bars, taverns, or nightclubs, going to, 99,
      103, 107–109, 111
    cigarette use, 14–15, 197–201
    cigarettes, perceived risk and disapproval
      of pack-a-day smoking,
      148–150, 153, 197–201
    cocaine, perceived risk and disapproval
      of, 148–150, 153, 193–195,
      199–201
    cocaine use, 14–15, 193–195, 199–201
    dating, 99–102, 113–114

evenings out, 20, 99–101, 107–113, 181–201

friends' use of substances (perceived), 173–175, 177

marijuana, perceived risk and disapproval of, 148–150, 153, 192–193, 199–201

marijuana use, 14–15, 33–35, 192–193, 199–201

parties, attending, 99–100, 107–109

religiosity, 19, 62–64, 67–68, 181–201

structural equation models, 181–201

see also Parenthood

Mediating variables, xi–xii, 2–4, 28–32, 37–39, 206–209

see also Alcohol, perceived risk and disapproval of heavy use, Availability of illicit drugs (perceived), Bars, taverns, or nightclubs, going to, Cigarettes, perceived risk and disapproval of pack-a-day smoking, Cocaine, perceived risk and disapproval of use, Dating, Evenings out, Friends, getting together informally with, Friends' use of substances (perceived), Marijuana, perceived risk and disapproval of use, Parties, attending, Religiosity

Methods, 24–39, 221–243

Military service, 12–13, 210–211

causal-conceptual overview, 1–4, 202–209

related to

age, 226

alcohol use, 13

availability of illicit drugs (perceived), 178

cigarette use, 12–13

cocaine use, 13

evenings out, 98–99, 115

marijuana use, 13

religiosity, 62

see also Employment status

Missing data

for pregnancy, 153

Monitoring the Future project, ix, xi, xiv, 4–5, 25, 32–33, 221–224

Motherhood, *see* Parenthood

Multiple Classification Analysis (MCA), 236–242

conventions followed, 37–39, 239–241

guidelines for interpreting, 241–242

mediating variables as dependent variables, 38–39, 237

numbers of cases specified, 239

predictor variables, 238

tables of results for

attending parties, 252–253

availability of cocaine, 284–285

availability of marijuana, 282–283

dating, 250–251

disapproval of cigarettes, 260–261

disapproval of cocaine use, 272–273

disapproval of heavy drinking, 264–265

disapproval of marijuana use, 268–269

evenings out, 248–249

friends' heavy drinking (perceived), 276–277

friends' use of cigarettes (perceived), 274–275

friends' use of cocaine (perceived), 280–281

friends' use of marijuana (perceived), 278–279

getting together with friends informally, 254–255

going to bars, 256–257

perceived risk of cigarettes, 258–259

perceived risk of cocaine use, 270–271

perceived risk of heavy drinking, 262–263

perceived risk of marijuana use, 266–267

religious attendance, 244–245

religious importance, 246–247

see also Research methodology

Multistage samples, *see* Samples

Multivariate analyses, *see* Multiple Classification Analysis, Structural equation modeling

N

National Institute on Drug Abuse, xiv

New freedoms and responsibilities, xi, 1–4, 8–17, 205–206, 209–216

see also Post-high school roles and experiences

Nonparticipation in study, 27, 135, 223–224

Numbers of cases specified for multiple classification analyses, 239

O

Occupation, *see* Employment status

P

Panel analyses, 6–7, 32–39

see also Analysis strategy

Panel attrition, 27, 135, 223–224

Parenthood, 214–215, 228

causal-conceptual overview, 1–4, 202–209

related to

age, 228
alcohol use, 16–17
cigarette use, 16
cocaine use, 16
evenings out, 20, 101, 105–107
friends' use of substances (perceived), 177
marijuana use, 16–17
religiosity, 19, 65–67, 70
social and recreational activities, 107
substance use, perceived risk and disapproval of, 153
Parties, attending
causal-conceptual overview, 1–4, 202–209
correlation matrices including, 230–235
frequency of, 74–77
MCA results, 98–99, 113–115, 252–253
measure of, 74–75, 228–229
related to
age, 19, 76–77, 92–96, 230–235
alcohol use, 92–94
cigarette use, 92
cocaine use, 92
engagement, 107
living arrangements, 98–105
marijuana use, 92–94
marital status, 99–100, 107–109
parenthood, 107
pregnancy, 105
student status, 98
Part-time work, see Employment status
Peers, see Friends' use of substances (perceived)
Perceived availability of illicit substances, see Availability of illicit drugs (perceived)
Perceived friends' substance use, see Friends' use of substances (perceived)
Perceived risks and disapproval of substance use, see Risk and disapproval of substance use
Period effects, 41–44
Pooling data
across multiple cohorts, 37
across multiple follow-ups, 36–37
Population density, 238, 244–285
Post-high-school roles and experiences, 1–4, 206–216, 224–228
causal-conceptual overview, 1–4, 202–209
related to
availability of illicit drugs (perceived), 178–179
friends' use of substances (perceived), 172–178
perceived risks and disapproval of substance use, 146–154
religiosity, 59–70
social and recreational activities, 97–116
see also Cohabitation, Divorce, Employment status, Engagement, Living arrangements, Marital status, New freedoms and responsibilities, Parenthood, Pregnancy, Single parenthood, Student status
Pregnancy, 214
causal-conceptual overview, 1–4, 202–209
missing data about, 153
related to
alcohol use, 16
cigarette use, 16
cocaine use, 16
evenings out, 105
friends' use of substances (perceived), 176–177
marijuana use, 16
religiosity, 65
social and recreational activities, 105
substance use, perceived risk and disapproval of, 152–153

Q

Questionnaires, 224

R

Race, 69, 238, 244–285
Recreational activities, 19–20, 105–112
see also Social and recreational activities
Regression analyses, see Multiple Classification Analysis
Region of country, 238, 244–285
Religiosity, 40–70, 208–209
causal-conceptual overview, 1–4, 202–209
change and stability, 45–46, 57–59, 67–70
correlation matrices including, 230–235
MCA results, 59–70, 244–247
measures of, 228–229
period effects, 41–44
related to
age, 18, 40–44, 59, 70, 230–235
alcohol use, 17–18, 50–54, 57–59, 195–197, 199–201
background factors, 69
cigarette use, 17–18, 46–50, 57–59, 197–201
cocaine use, 17–18, 57–59, 193–195, 199–201
cohabitation, 19, 62–64, 70
college attendance, 62
divorce, 19, 67
dormitory, living in, 62–64
employment status, 62
engagement, 67–68, 70
evenings out, 181–201
living arrangements, 62–64, 70

marijuana use, 17–18, 53–56, 57–59,
192–193, 199–201
marital status, 19, 62–64, 67–68,
181–201
military service, 62
parenthood, 19, 65–67, 70
pregnancy, 65
student status, 60–62
substance use, risk and disapproval of,
135, 192–201, 230–235
unemployment, 62
structural equation models, 181–201
Representativeness of findings, 4–6, 25–27,
223–224
Research methodology, 24–39, 221–243
Responsibilities, *see* New freedoms and responsibilities, Post–high–school roles and
experiences
Risk and disapproval of substance use, 121–155,
207
causal-conceptual overview, 1–4, 202–209
correlation between, 123–124, 230–235
correlations with use, 121–122, 133–146,
230–235
focus on specific substances, 122–123
related to
age, 123–133, 136, 230–235
religiosity, 135, 181–201, 230–235
structural equation models, 181–201
see also Alcohol, perceived risk and disapproval of heavy use, Cigarettes,
perceived risk and disapproval of
pack-a-day smoking, Cocaine,
perceived risk and disapproval of
use, Marijuana, perceived risk
and disapproval of use
Risk taking, 9, 21
Roles, *see* New freedoms and responsibilities,
Post-high-school roles and experiences

S

Samples, 4–5, 25–27, 221–224
used in analyses of age–related changes,
25–26, 28–29
used in MCA analyses, 25–26, 30–31, 223,
239
used in structural equation models, 185–186
Secular trends, *see also* Period effects
SEM, *see* Structural equation modeling
Single parenthood, *see* Parenthood
Smoking, *see* Cigarette use
Social and recreational activities, 19–20,
71–120, 207–208
causal-conceptual overview, 1–4, 202–209
structural equation models, 181–201

see also Bars, taverns, or nightclubs, going to,
Dating, Evenings out, Friends,
getting together informally with,
Parties, attending
Stability, *see* Change and stability
Structural equation modeling, 31–32, 181–201
analytic approach, 31–32, 189–190
fit indices, 190–191
rationale for causal ordering, 186–189
selection of variables, 182–185
structural models
alcohol, 195–197, 199–201
cigarettes, 197–201
cocaine, 193–195, 199–201
marijuana, 192–193, 199–201
Student status, 11–12, 209–210, 226
causal-conceptual overview, 1–4, 201–204
related to
age, 226
alcohol, perceived risk and disapproval
of, 147–148
alcohol use, 11–12, 151–152
bars, taverns, or nightclubs, going to, 98
cigarette use, 11–12
cigarettes, perceived risk and disapproval
of pack-a-day smoking,
147–148
cocaine, perceived risk and disapproval
of, 147–148
cocaine use, 11–12
evenings out, 98
friends, getting together informally with,
98
friends' use of substances (perceived),
172–173
marijuana, perceived risk and disapproval of, 147–148
marijuana use, 11–12
parties, attending, 98
religiosity, 60–62
Substance use, *see* Drug use
Survey methods, 221–224

T

Tobacco, *see* Cigarette use

U

Unemployment, *see* Employment status
Urbanicity, 238, 244–285

W

Weighting of samples, 222
Work, *see* Employment status